TELECOMMUNICATIONS
FOR
MANAGEMENT

McGraw-Hill Series in Management Information Systems

Gordon B. Davis, *Consulting Editor*

Davis: Management Information Systems: Conceptual Foundations, Structure, and Development

Davis and Everest: Readings in Management Information Systems

Dickson and Wetherbe: The Management of Information Systems

Dickson and Wetherbe: The Management of Information Systems Casebook

Everest: Database Management: Objectives, Organization, and System Function

Lucas: The Analysis, Design, and Implementation of Information Systems

Lucas: Information Systems Concepts for Management

Lucas and Gibson: A Casebook for Management Information Systems

Meadow and Tedesco: Telecommunications for Management

Weber: EDP Auditing: Conceptual Foundations and Practice

TELECOMMUNICATIONS FOR MANAGEMENT

Charles T. Meadow

DIALOG Information Services, Inc.

Albert S. Tedesco

WWSG-TV, Philadelphia

McGRAW-HILL BOOK COMPANY
New York   St. Louis   San Francisco   Auckland   Bogotá
Hamburg   Johannesburg   London   Madrid   Mexico   Montreal   New Delhi
Panama   Paris   São Paulo   Singapore   Sydney   Tokyo   Toronto

This book was set in Times Roman by Black Dot, Inc. (ECU).
The editors were Eric M. Munson and Jonathan Palace;
the production supervisor was Diane Renda.
The drawings were done by Burmar.
Halliday Lithograph Corporation was printer and binder.

TELECOMMUNICATIONS FOR MANAGEMENT

1 2 3 4 5 6 7 8 9 0 HALHAL 8 9 8 7 6 5 4

ISBN 0-07-041198-0

Library of Congress Cataloging in Publication Data

Meadow, Charles T.
    Telecommunications for management.

    (McGraw-Hill series in management information systems)
    includes bibliographies and index.
    1. Management—Communication systems.   2. Management information systems.   3. Communication in management.
I. Tedesco, Albert S.   II. Title.   III. Series.
HD30.335.M43   1985   384'.024658   84-4339
ISBN 0-07-041198-0

CONTENTS

PART 4   MANAGEMENT OF TELECOMMUNICATIONS

PREFACE

Communication is far more than just another technology. The way we communicate among ourselves is fundamental to our culture, indeed it may even be defined *as* our culture. Communication involves not just gadgetry, but spoken, written, and symbolic language, art, and music, and how we *use* such technological devices as the telephone, printing press, or television. More specific to the purposes of this book, the technology of communication affects the way we do business. Communication (of which transportation is a form) enables decentralization of organizations and also centralized control over physically dispersed divisions. Because of new methods of internal communication, most employees are better informed about their organization than they were, say, a generation ago. This means the manager is no longer the only one with information, and it means he or she must make managerial decisions more openly than before. This changes the role of the manager and is one of the forces encouraging more participative management. Customers are both better informed and more demanding. They want good information about products and "hotlines" for asking questions. Lawsuits by consumer groups or government regulatory bodies may make a corporation's entire internal communication system open to public scrutiny.

Thus, telecommunications has invaded the domain of just about all managers, not just the corporate telecommunications manager. Today, a marketing manager, for example, has to buy Wide Area Telephone Service (WATS), digital communication service from a data communication network, and perhaps teleconferencing software to keep in touch with field managers. Most such managers will not have had formal training in telecommunications, yet they must make the decisions.

This book should help the nontechnical manager cope with modern telecommunications and its effects. It is not aimed at the telecommunications manager or engineer, who should already know most of this material. Rather, it is aimed at people in marketing, accounting, manufacturing, planning, personnel, purchasing—almost any traditionally nontechnical occupation—who are facing the need to buy telecommunications equipment or services, who must restructure their organizations around new ways of communicating among elements of the company, and whose traditional ideas on how managing is done are being challenged in part by the new technology.

Our primary intended audience is the student of management, probably in a business school, but possibly in a department of engineering administration, industrial engineering, or information science. We were both in academic life when this project started, and we were convinced that there are too few courses on this subject, in any department on a typical campus. One reason for this might have been the lack of appropriate text material. We hope we have filled that gap.

A secondary audience is the practicing manager, out of school, and now facing the kinds of problems we describe herein.

Because the field is so diverse, we have assembled a panel of authors specializing in the various disciplines and technologies. As editors, we have contributed some of the chapters and have attempted to keep all the writing on a reasonably constant level and integrated in usage and coverage.

In each of our chapters on a specific technology, we begin with a background or historical review, to provide a context in which to understand how this technology was developed and nurtured. Understanding technology is *not* merely a matter of understanding physical principles.

The book is organized into six main parts, each with a brief introduction. They are:

Part One, "Elements of Communication," covering the nature of communication, some of the underlying scientific concepts, and how people communicate with machines.

Part Two, "Basic Technology," concerned with how things work. Emphasis is on the technologies used by working telecommunications systems: transmission systems; the telephone system, which is important in itself but also because it is used as a carrier by so many other systems; and digital communication networks, which have enabled the recent rapid growth in remote computer use.

Part Three, "Applications," in which we survey some of the more important uses of telecommunications in today's industry: television and other video techniques, electronic mail, teleconferencing, mobile communication, and videotex, the new combination of computers and video.

Part Four, "Management of Telecommunications," in which we consider the manager's point of view and cover such topics as cost-benefit analysis, particularly as applied to equipment procurement; regulation in the United States and internationally; and the problems of the corporate telecommunications manager.

Part Five, "Case Histories," containing two studies of the use of telecommunications by large, geographically widespread organizations, and how communications has affected them.

Part Six, "The Future," reviewing some of what has gone before and looks forward in time, not to forecast technology, but to consider its effect on managers and the nature of work itself.

A collection of brief biographies of our authors is found following Chapter 19.

We are deeply appreciative of the help of many people in the conception, writing, and production of this book: Giulana Lavendal and Dr. Allen L. Brown of Xerox Corporation; Marilyn Ruell of Hewlett-Packard; Bill Gross of Radio Broadcasting Company; Larry Miller of Schwartz, Woods, and Miller; Harry Jenny and Tony Evasew of WWSG-TV; Joe Roizen of Telegen, Margaret Goya of DIALOG Information Services; and Mary A. Navarro. A special thanks to the staff of the wonderful AT&T photo library, and to Joyce Weiner of E. R. Squibb & Sons, Inc., for her helpful comments and suggestions.

Charles T. Meadow

Albert S. Tedesco

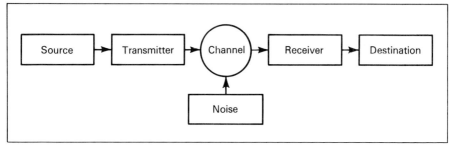

Chapter 1: Introduction

Chapter 2: The Basics of Communication

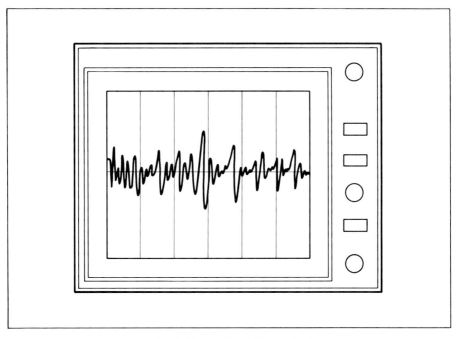

Chapter 3: Communication between People and Machines

PART **ONE**

ELEMENTS OF
COMMUNICATION

The first part of this book has a two-fold purpose: to establish the conceptual framework within which the reader may view current developments in telecommunications and to provide the vocabulary to assist in understanding what follows.

In Chapter 1 the goals and organization of the text are outlined. The reader is introduced to the central role of communication in managing and to some ideas about how telecommunication systems function. Chapter 2 deals with the fundamentals of communication for the nontechnical reader, with emphasis on the "common sense" as well as the technical interpretation of communications phenomena. While no background in physics or mathematics is required of the reader, this chapter includes sections on aspects of the physics of communication, such as wave mechanics and the electromagnetic spectrum, and noise, multiplexing, error detection and correction, and networking. The goal is to present and clarify basic concepts which reappear in subsequent chapters. In Chapter 3 we address the nature of communication between people and machines, with special attention to styles of discourse and the social impact of this form of interaction.

CHAPTER 1

INTRODUCTION

Charles T. Meadow
DIALOG Information Services, Inc.
Palo Alto, CA 94304

1.1 WHAT IS COMMUNICATION?

There are many views of what communication is, but they generally have the common concept that meaning or information is represented by symbols and that as we exchange these symbols, we can convey meaning from one person or organism to another. The more obvious symbols are the letters that make up printed words or the sounds that make up spoken words, but we must also include gestures, pictures, or the sound of a barking dog. To people interested in the humanities, the behavioral sciences, or the more human aspects of communication, the emphasis is on *meaning* or *feelings* and how these may be conveyed from one person to another, as well as on what happens when there is a failure to communicate. We talk of the generation gap as a crisis of communication between older and younger people. We call our advertising and public relations departments *communications* departments because their job is to convey impressions, attitudes, and feelings about an organization to the public.

Engineers are more likely to be concerned with the physical aspects of communication. How do we actually send a message from one point or person to another? How do we make sure it is accurately received or that the cost is low enough? In a formal sense, engineers may go so far as to say they are not concerned with meaning, that the technical goal of communication is to transmit the message, not the meaning.

Data processing people and most managers fall somewhere between these views. They are concerned with communication between computers, for instance, as well as between departments of an organization. They must be concerned with both the physical aspects of cost-effective, reliable transmission and the content of what is being transmitted and received. We tend to follow this approach throughout this book. The ultimate purpose of communication is to convey meaning, but often we must have a great deal of knowledge and understanding of *how* this is done in order to insure that meaning is being effectively transmitted.

Claude E. Shannon (Shannon & Weaver, 1949) of Bell Laboratories, generally regarded as the originator of mathematical communication theory, proposed a model of the communications process that is simple yet elegant in its near-universal applicability. Shannon identified five major elements in the process of communication.

1 The *source* of a message, best typified as a human being intending to send a message to another—say by telephone or post.

2 The *transmitter,* which normally transforms the source's message into the form required for actual delivery. In a telephone system the transmitter is a part of the telephone instrument in the user's hand.

3 The *channel,* which is the physical means of moving the message from one point to another. Channels are rarely simple single elements. The entire telephone system may be viewed as a single channel, but it is actually a complex of transmitters, channels, receivers, and retransmitters, all seen as a single entity to most users.

4 The *receiver,* which receives the message from the channel and converts the message into a form that is useful to or able to be sensed by the person for whom it is intended.

5 The *destination,* which is the recipient or addressee or target of the communication, again typified by the person who answers the telephone or reads the letter.

We generally define *transmission* to include both the sending and receipt of a message. Transmission is said not to occur *unless the destination has received the message sent by the source.* This is an important consideration. It means that the person who utters a statement that is not heard cannot be said to have communicated or even transmitted a message. The business that sends out a letter stating, "Unless we receive payment by . . ." has not communicated unless the destination actually received the letter.

Almost any real communication system involves a series of transmissions and retransmissions: from source's mind to letter form, to mail box, to sorting office, to airline, to another sorting office, and so on. Often, as in the case of television signals, the "message" is recoded and transformed many times from its origin to destination, so that the Shannon model is used over and over again to describe the actual path of a "signal," such as the face of an actor on television. The pictorial image is transmitted to a television camera, transformed and transmitted to a telephone line, transformed and transmitted to a central television transmitter, transformed and sent "over the air," transformed and displayed on the home receiving set. Problems in the form of noise or distortions or complete failures to transmit can occur anywhere in this complex chain, but all have the same effect: the communication from source to destination is blocked or distorted.

The selection of the most appropriate channels of transmission can be one of the most difficult problems of communications management. Figures 1.1 and 1.2 show two forms of communication used today by modern high-technology companies: satellite communication and the carrier pigeon!

1.2 COMMUNICATION IN MANAGEMENT

Like almost all other people, managers view communication in several different ways. Managers must communicate with the following people:

1 Employees. Communication takes the form of explaining orders and policies and inspiring employees to work toward some goal.

2 Colleagues, that is, persons with whom they must bargain and negotiate, cooperate and compete: This is usually a highly personal, subjective form of communication.

3 Higher managers. This is often a more intensely personal action, perhaps involving only one or two people but again concerned with plans, activities, performance, goals.

4 The public or a particular clientele or constituency: customers, suppliers, clients, patients, students, or voters. This is more likely to be mass communication; both the message and the methods may be quite different from those used in person-to-person communication.

FIGURE 1.1
A small satellite receiving antenna and its associated signal conversion equipment. Together, they are priced with typical microcomputers and enable almost anyone who may have the need to use this new communication medium. (Photo courtesy Equitorial Communications Company.)

FIGURE 1.2
Pigeons carrying messages are an ancient form of communication technology. This one is being used today by the high-technology Lockheed Missiles and Space Company to transmit information between its Sunnyvale, California, plant and a difficult-to-reach site in the nearby Santa Cruz Mountains. (Photo courtesy Lockheed Missiles and Space Company.)

5 Other parts of an organization. This is often highly technical. It might involve access to the corporate computer or simply a telephone call involving specific details of inventory levels or personnel actions. Much of the managerial communication covered in this book falls into this category.

The average manager, today, makes use of a wide range of communication technologies and techniques. In an average day, these might well include:

1 A face-to-face, one-on-one conversation with an employee or colleague.

2 A direct-dialled long-distance telephone call, made through one of the new, independent long-distance telephone services.

3 A large number of telephone calls internal to the organization's building.

4 Remote use of a computer.

5 A teleconference—a multiperson telephone conversation or conference mediated by a computer, with the participants not necessarily all being actively involved at the same time.

6 Advertising on television or in newspapers.

7 The mail, including letters, newspapers, and journals, which may be delivered from outside by the post office or originated internally.

All these are valid, ordinary activities of management. The cost of the activities and the potential impact on the organization are such that managers must know not only how to perform them but also how to *decide* how to do them, which communication techniques to use, and how to get others to use them effectively.

1.3 COMMUNICATION TECHNOLOGY

In a sense, almost all communication is technology-based, and we can drop the "almost" if we accept the idea that the languages of writing, speech, and gesture are largely inventions, involving technique if not hardware. That means that there is always some technological aspect of communication, always some difference between knowing what we would like to communicate and doing it effectively through the technological means at hand. While we shall have a great deal to say about hardware, we cannot be permitted to forget that hardware merely conveys messages. It does not usually create them (except for computers programmed by people to create certain messages), and it does not usually understand them (again, with some exception in the computer area).

After language and writing, the major communication developments began to rely more and more on technology. Printing, certainly, was the next major step. It involved not merely the invention of movable type, but the creation of an industry for the construction of presses, the manufacture of paper in large quantities, and the distribution of books. Next, in relatively quick succession, came the electrical methods of communication: telegraph, wireless telegraphy, voice radio, and telephone. Figure 1.3 shows the historical development of communications technologies.

But communication technology includes more than new means of transmis-

Date	Invention
BC 100000	Speech
3000	Writing
2500	Sea-going sailing ships
1000	Alphabet (Phoenician)
AD 100	Book (bound sheets of parchment)
105	Paper
1000	Magnetic compass for ocean navigation
1450	Moveable type printing - Gutenburg
1769	Steam railway used in mine
1801	Jacquard loom (binary card–controlled processing)
1807	Steamship
1833	Babbage's analytical engine
1844	Telegraph
1865	Atlantic cable successful
1873	Typewriter
1876	Telephone
1886	Linotype
1888	Eastman Kodak camera
1891	Gasoline-powered automobile
1898	Wireless telegraphy
1902	Speech by radio
1903	Airplane
1920	Broadcast radio
1925	Television
1946	ENIAC (first electronic computer)
1964	Communications satellite
1969	ARPAnet (computer-computer communication)

FIGURE 1.3
Some of the major inventions in the history of communication.
Included are a few transportation and computer inventions, both of
which are forms of communication. Dates, even of some modern
inventions, are often only approximate because the invention was not
a discrete event in time.

sion and recording of messages. It also involves improving the speed, reliability, and cost of transmission. Other important developments have included undersea cables, terrestrial microwave and communication satellites, teletex, cellular radio, packet switching, statistical multiplexing, and fiber-optic transmission cables. Perhaps most significantly, the list seems to grow daily.

A change fully as great as that wrought by movable type or electrical communication is now coming upon us—the marriage of computers and communication. Called by various names (telecomputing, communication, informatics*) the combination gives us computers that can communicate with each other and with remote users and communication systems that can control themselves in terms of routing of messages and detecting and correcting

*In common use in Europe in the sense used here, in the United States the capitalized word *Informatics* is a trademark of Informatics, Inc.

transmission errors. It gives us faster, more reliable, and less expensive telephone service—to a large extent because of faster computer-operated switching. It enables us to use computers 3000 miles away for a communication cost of about $5 to $10 per hour. It is beginning to provide us electronic journals, i.e., periodicals that never are produced in print form, but are created, distributed, and read only in electronic form.

The computer-communication marriage is changing both the computer and communication industries and will ultimately change those that depend upon them. The American Telephone and Telegraph Company (AT&T) has recently agreed to divest itself of its local subsidiary telephone companies. AT&T will itself engage in long-distance communication and other activities that may include information processing, activities that were previously prohibited by U.S. government regulations. International Business Machine Corp. (IBM), previously strictly a computer company and not permitted in the common-carrier communication business, is a major partner in a new communication company called Satellite Business System. Harry L. Freeman (1981), of the American Express Company, predicted that "the nature of the business enterprise and the nature of communications will be so interrelated that they will be largely the same subject" (p. 163).

1.4 THE SOCIAL EFFECT OF TELECOMMUNICATIONS

In 1939 the French aviation pioneer-writer Antoine de Saint-Exupéry (1967) said, "The central struggle of men has ever been to understand one another, to join together for the common weal. And it is this very thing that the machine helps them to do! It begins by annihilating time and space" (p. 48). In the field of foreign policy, space and time have indeed been annihilated, perhaps with more dramatic impact than in business management.

Think . . . what it was like making foreign policy decisions 200 years ago. Negotiating by exchange of messages between distant heads of state was not practical. Instead, ambassadors were appointed to make decisions, not merely report proposals. The Battle of New Orleans was fought in 1815, after the end of the war in which it occurred, because news simply could not travel fast enough to prevent the battle.

Modern information systems allow heads of state to keep informed, up to the minute, on events and on the likely effect of any decision throughout the world. Speed is essential, particularly in the military sphere, where the capabilities of modern missiles may permit less than 30 minutes' time to decide on questions of war and peace.

An excellent example of the impact of modern communications in international affairs was reflected in the final negotiations for the release by Iran of the American hostages in January 1981. Both countries sent emissaries to Algeria to negotiate through an intermediary, as in olden times. However, both delegations were in constant direct communication with their own governments, so that Teheran and Washington were actively participating in the talks in Algiers. When the Bank of

England was brought in to serve as an additional intermediary, communication links were established from Washington to London to Algiers. As it began to seem likely that the hostages would be released, arrangements for their physical transfer involved Algeria, their destination, but also Greece, where the Algerian aircraft would refuel, and U.S. forces in Germany, who would provide immediate housing and medical care.

In addition to this complex communications network among the various governments, there were the news-communication networks that kept the world informed on a minute-by-minute basis. . . . No doubt, it was a 20th century communications, as well as political, event. (Meadow, 1982, p. 11)

While the technology of communication is important and will continue to be, it is not the only factor of importance. Fundamentally, we are still interested in conveying meaning between people, and this has always and will continue to require *understanding* among people. As more and more business, government, health, and educational agencies routinely use computers and communications, not only for their internal operations but to deal with their constituencies, there is ever greater need for the managers of these organizations to be aware of how the systems affect the people who use them. The users, whether employees, customers, students, or patients may well see the *organization* as the computer-communication system: the *bank* as its remote-teller machine, the *hospital* as its computer-based billing system, the *university* as its telecomputer-based registration system. The organization's effectiveness becomes indistinguishable from the communication system's effectiveness.

1.5 PLAN OF THE BOOK

This book is divided into six parts. While we have an underlying plan and suggest most readers follow the normal reading sequence, those with some prior background may well skip around. Relatively few chapters depend directly on a previous one, although most chapters are dependent in a general way on the introductory text concerning the basics of communication.

In Part One we review the fundamentals of telecommunication. We assume almost no knowledge of physics or engineering and invite those who have substantial background in these subjects to skip this segment.

Part Two begins a review of telecommunication technology. Chapters in this part concentrate on those technologies that underlie most applications of telecommunication, such as transmission systems and the telephone network. Parts of Chapter 4 cover topics introduced in Chapter 2, but at a more advanced level.

Part Three presents a selection of applications of telecommunication. The telephone, of course, is itself an application, as are digital-communication networks, but in these chapters we describe systems that build on the basic ones, such as teleconferencing, electronic mail, and videotex.

In Part Four we turn to the management of telecommunication, discussing in successive chapters how complex decisions involving the acquisition or use of telecommunication are made; the regulation of communication which directly affects both users and the communication services; international telecommunication; and the management of a telecommunication facility.

Part Five presents two case studies. The first discusses the use of telecommunication in a management-information system within a large insurance company, the Insurance Company of North America. The second covers the use of telecommunication in the collection and distribution of news by another large organization, The Washington Post.

Finally, in Part Six we hazard a look at the future impact of telecommunication, with particular emphasis on the role of the manager and the practice of management.

REFERENCES

Freeman, H. L., "The Long-Term Outlook in Communications," in R. W. Haigh, G. Gerbner, & R. B. Byrne (eds.), *Communications in the Twenty-First Century,* New York: Wiley-Interscience, 1981.

Meadow, C. T., "The Information World: An Overview," in J. F. Spivack (ed.), *Carriers in Information,* White Plains, N.Y.: Knowledge Industry, 1982.

Saint-Exupéry, A. de, *Wind, Sand and Stars,* 1939. Reprint New York. Harcourt, Brace Jovanovich, 1967.

Shannon, C. E., & Weaver, W., *The Mathematical Theory of Communication,* Urbana, Ill.: University of Illinois Press, 1949.

RECOMMENDED READINGS

Bagdikian, Ben H., *The Information Machines: Their Impact on Men and the Media,* New York: Harper & Row, 1971. (Although the title is broad, this is a book about information technology and its effect on the news and mass media.)

Cherry, Colin, *On Human Communication: A Review, A Survey, and a Criticism* (3d ed.), Cambridge: MIT Press, 1978. (This is a survey of all aspects of human communication. It includes chapters on semiotics, signal analysis, statistics of communication, and psychology of communication. It is a rather technical but brilliant work, well written, and it will reward any amount of effort invested in reading it.)

Forester, Tom (ed.), *The Microelectronic Revolution,* Cambridge: MIT Press, 1981. (A not-too-technical review of the impact of modern electronics on society.)

Haigh, Robert W., Gerbner, George, and Byrne, Richard B. (eds.), *Communications in the Twenty-First Century,* New York: Wiley-Interscience, 1981. (A projection of the impact of changes in communications patterns and technology, especially as regards management.)

Hiltz, Starr Roxanne, Turoff, Murray, *The Network Nation,* Reading, Mass.: Addison-Wesley, 1978. (A look into the future world of offices and households interconnected by high-speed digital communications networks, written by two pioneers of computer conferencing.)

Johnson, Elmer D., *Communication: An Introduction to the History of Writing, Printing, Books, and Libraries,* Metuchen, N.J.: Scarecrow Press, 1973. (For those who may otherwise forget that the alphabet, printing press, and the book, itself, are technological artifacts and communications media.)

Martin, James, *Future Developments in Telecommunications* (2d ed.), Englewood Cliffs, N.J.: Prentice-Hall, 1977. (A projection of technology of telecommunications by one of the foremost writers in the field. Martin's books are always readable.)

Nora, Simon, and Minc, Alain (eds.), *The Computerization of Society: A Report to the President of France,* Cambridge: MIT Press, 1980. (A view of the impact of computers and communications on society as seen in France, where telecommunications developments lagged those in some other countries, but are now leaping forward.)

Pei, Mario A., *The Story of Language,* Philadelphia: Lippincott, 1949. (A general history of the development of natural language.)

Pool, Ithiel de Sola, *Forecasting the Telephone: A Retrospective Technology Assessment,* Norwood, N.J.: Ablex, 1982. (The telephone is the fundamental telecommunications development of the past century. Pool has been its principal modern interpreter.)

CHAPTER 2

THE BASICS OF COMMUNICATION

Charles T. Meadow
DIALOG Information Services, Inc.
Palo Alto, CA 94304

2.1 THE NATURE OF COMMUNICATION

Perhaps the most important point of all to make about communication is that it involves at least two: people, machines, animals, or whatever. Communication does not take place because one person *sends* a message. That message must also be *received* and *understood*. Some of the most vexing problems of communication, in any of the senses in which that word may be used, arise because the receiver of a message gives it a different meaning than the sender intended. This can happen when some mechanical fault or random occurrence physically distorts a message in transit, perhaps changing an "a" to a "b" or, more dramatically, a STOP signal to a GO signal. In human communication it is well known that a slight inflectional variation can change meaning; a message such as "That is very nice" can have many meanings, including the opposite of the apparent meaning of the words as they appear in print. Failure by a hearer to pick up the inflectional signals, therefore, can change meaning.

Thus, communication is said to be successful when a message has been transmitted and the same message has been received.

What are these messages? What do they convey? The general answer is *information,* but a more mechanical answer is *a set of symbols.* The average person's concept of information is related to the meaning of the symbols and perhaps to whether or not prior knowledge of them existed. But communication engineers go their own way and say they are not concerned with *meaning* but with the *accurate transmission* of symbols. The laymen's definition of information is often approximately that of *news*—something that has meaning but is not already known. The engineers' definition is related to this. They say the measure of information content is a function of the extent to which the symbols were expected. Both would agree, then, that there is no information in a situation where there can be no variation, that the rising of the sun carries no information because it always rises.

On the other hand, a newspaper headline stating "The President Makes an Error" can be news or not, depending as much on the attitude of the reader toward the president involved as on what has transpired.

The separation of physical-symbol conveyance from meaning or information conveyance is not always complete, and it behooves those concerned with communication systems of any sort to be aware of this. For instance,

• A conventional telephone line cannot convey what an opera singer has to "tell" us because the telephone does not carry the full frequency range of the human voice. (There are other ways around this.)

• A black-and-white television portrayal of a football game may not carry as much understanding of the game as a color set because sometimes the viewer cannot follow the ball or distinguish players on one team from another.

• A sloppy typed page with crudely drawn illustrations may not convey as much clear meaning as a professionally typeset and illustrated book, even if the set of symbols is intended to be the same, because the visual noise is distracting.

Hence we may say that the conveyance of *meaning* is the purpose of communication and the conveyance of *symbols* is the means of achieving it.

While it is convenient to illustrate the basic communication concepts in terms of one person sending a message to another, real-world telecommunication systems consist of numbers of people communicating with each other through complex systems that may have many people involved in their operation. Consequently, a large part of practical telecommunications is finding how to send a particular message over a particular path through a network to a selected destination, which may be a group instead of an individual.

Another aspect of practical communication is that not every element of the entire sender-system-recipient domain uses or recognizes the same set of symbols for the encoding of meaning. Therefore, there are frequent changes of symbol sets, or translations, going on all through the system. Common examples are the *sounds* of our voices being translated into electrical signals by the telephone system or the colors of a scene being translated, also into electrical signals, by a television system. A more generic word for signal conversion is *modulation*.

In the remainder of this chapter, we will make an excursion through some of the mechanical fundamentals of telecommunication: symbols and codes; the electromagnetic spectrum; transmission; noise; and switching, multiplexing, and networks.

2.2 SYMBOLS AND CODES

A symbol is something so common and intuitive that it becomes difficult to define formally. A symbol must be perceivable, for example, a printed character or a sound that is distinguishable from others (the letter "a" is different from "b," the sound made by one guitar string is different from that of another string) and imbued with meaning.

Difficulties in perception may lead to ambiguity in identification or inability to distinguish symbols from each other. Ambiguities in meaning arise when there is difficulty in distinguishing among symbols or when assigned meanings are not clear. Communication problems arise when meanings are multiply defined (more than one meaning per symbol or symbol per meaning) or where the meaning of one symbol depends on those it is used with; this is called *context dependency*. The printed symbol "." offers a simple example. This symbol has different meanings in each of the following contexts:

This is a sentence. (Termination of a sentence.)
Dr. Jones (Termination of an abbreviation.)
$16.73 (Decimal point.)
"which has . . . these contexts" (Information omitted.)

Let us now consider, in greater depth, how we represent information with symbols.

2.2.1 Representation of Information

Among humanity's oldest symbols are simple marks or pictures made in clay, carved into sticks, etc. These grew into written languages composed of alphabets or ideographs (see Figure 2.1). Letters of an alphabet tend not to have meaning; the unit of meaning is normally a word, but ideographs may be single symbols denoting a semantic meaning. The alphabet-word system is technologically more flexible. With 26 letters, 10 numerals, and a variable number of punctuation marks, we can make seemingly limitless combinations of printed words. Because we can use strings of words to redefine other words, we are not restricted to a fixed number of different or context-dependent symbols made up from the 26 letters. Because letters serve as the building blocks of words, we can use a limited number of symbols to make keyboards with about 40 to 50 keys. A "keyboard" for the full Chinese language would require thousands of different symbols.

The basic sound symbols are tones of varying frequency. Electrical flows of varying voltage may be considered electrical "symbols." More specifically, because this book is mostly concerned with electronic communication, an electric current flowing at a given voltage level may be taken to represent the symbol "0." The voltage does not have to *be* zero to *stand for* zero. Current at another voltage can stand for "1." With these two basic symbols, we can make up codes for letters, decimal numerals, or punctuation symbols. One frequently

FIGURE 2.1
A fragment of Egyptian pictographic writing, a precursor of hieroglyphics, in which each symbol represents a concept. It is from the time of King Zet, Dynasty I, around 3000 B.C. (Photo courtesy Stanford University Art Department.)

used code that makes use of 0s and 1s to represent the entire alphabet as well as numbers and punctuation is called the American Standard Code for Information Interchange (ASCII). It is used with most computers today, and a portion of it is shown in Figure 2.2.

2.2.2   Basic Wave Mechanics

Both sound and electromagnetic energy travel in waves, and these are among the most common means of sending information across space. Printing or handwriting, which is physically transported from one person to another, probably ranks second to the spoken word, but it is electronic transmission that seems to represent the most urgency and for which we are willing to pay the highest price.

Symbol	ASCII code	Symbol	ASCII code	SYmbol	ASCII code
0	011 000				
1	011 0001	A	100 0001	a	110 0001
2	011 0010	B	100 0010	b	110 0010
3	011 0011	C	100 0011	c	110 0011
4	011 0100	D	100 0100	d	110 0100
5	011 0101	E	100 0101	e	110 0101

FIGURE 2.2
Some examples of ASCII codes. ASCII is a commonly used code to
enable computers, whose internal representations of information may be
mutually incompatible, to communicate successfully with each other. Many
of the chapters of this book were transmitted between authors and editors
in this manner.

The written word, of course, depends on light, which is also a form of
electromagnetic energy.

Figure 2.3 shows a simple wave whose *amplitude* (vertical axis) rises and falls
with *time* (horizontal axis). The amplitude may represent pressure, as in a sound
wave, or voltage, as in an electric current. The *frequency* of a wave is the number
of complete cycles that pass a given point in a given unit of time, usually 1
second. An example of a complete wave cycle is shown in Figure 2.4.

Wave frequency is measured in cycles per second or *hertz* (Hz): 1 Hz is one
cycle per second. The sound of the human voice is made by waves that can vary
from 20 to 20,000 Hz (with best reception from 1000 to 4000 Hz); broadcast
radio uses the range from about 1 million to 100 million Hz, or 1 to 100
megahertz (mHz).

Wavelength (represented by λ, Greek lambda) is the distance from any point
on a wave to the corresponding point on the next wave or cycle, as shown in
Figure 2.4. The speed of a wave is the speed at which any given point on a wave
moves with respect to a stationary point. There is a well-known mathematical
relationship among speed, frequency, and wavelength.

$$x = f \lambda$$

FIGURE 2.3
A sequence of waves. The vertical axis represents amplitude; the
horizontal axis is time.

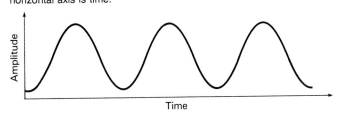

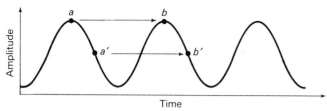

FIGURE 2.4
Wave length and frequency. The wavelength is the linear distance
from any point on one wave to the corresponding point on the next
wave, e.g., *a* to *b* or *a'* to *b'*. The wave's frequency is the number of
complete cycles passing any given point in 1 second.

Electromagnetic waves, of which light is a form, travel at the speed of 300
million meters per second (m/s) in a vacuum. The letter *c* is commonly used to
represent this quantity.

Since it travels at the speed of light, a radio wave of 1 mHz has a wavelength
of 300 meters. Long-wave radio, used for very long distance communication, can
have wavelengths in the range of 1000 to 1 million meters.

Sound travels at a speed that depends on the medium through which it passes,
such as air. Since air has variable density, sound travels faster near the surface of
the earth, where air is dense, than high in the atmosphere, where air is more
rarified. At sea level, sound travels in air at about 300 m/s. Its wavelength in the
human-audible range is of the order of one-tenth to one-half a meter.

Some sounds, such as the ringing of a bell or the hum of a tuning fork, are
fairly pure tones; in other words, all the sound waves are of roughly the same
frequency. Similarly, visible light that is close to monochromatic is made by
waves of nearly the same wavelength, while white light, which is a mixture of all
the colors, contains waves of many different lengths. The human voice is more
like white light; it generates sounds of many different frequencies all at once. In
other words, we "radiate" sounds of many different frequencies, and we can
vary the intensity or power of the sound at the various frequencies, making for a
fairly complex sound pattern. While the sound of a tuning fork may be
represented by a simple wave form, such as shown in Figure 2.3, the sound of the
human voice can only be represented by a graph that shows which frequencies
are being generated at any given time, as well as the intensity at each frequency.
Such a diagram is called a *voice spectrogram,* an example of which is shown in
Figure 2.5. The figure represents the spoken phrase, "What little brass parts are
in the box?" The vertical axis represents frequency; the horizontal, time. The
darkness at any spot represents the intensity of the corresponding frequency at
the time. This is not a very precise graph, but we can perhaps begin to suspect
that the distribution of black and white areas, in any strip of such a diagram (the
set of frequencies being generated at any short time interval), constitute a code
for the recognizable sound being made. We have to be careful, though, because

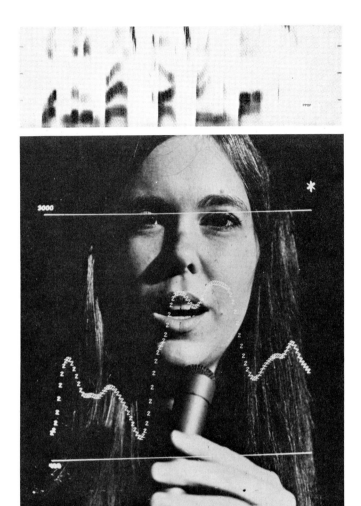

FIGURE 2.5
(a) A voice spectrogram. This shows the intensity (darkness) of
sounds at various frequencies (vertical axis) over time
(horizontal axis). The voice was saying the expression "What
little brass parts are in the box?" (Photo by Dr. D. E. Walker,
SRI International.) (b) A simplified voice spectrogram showing
only variation in the most intense frequency, but also illustrating
the minimum and maximum frequencies (400-3000 Hz) used for
voice telephone transmission. (Reproduced with permission of
AT&T).

a word may be spoken with many different inflections and accents, so the coding
system is complex, indeed.

Practical communication systems transmit more than a single, pure tone over
a transmission channel. The range of frequencies that can be transmitted (that is,

the difference between the highest and lowest frequencies) is called the *bandwidth* of the channel. Bandwidth is a measure of transmission capacity, such as the diameter of a water pipe is a measure of the pipe's water-carrying capacity.

These representations of waves that we have shown here are *analog* representations. An analog measure or representation uses one measure to stand for another: the angle of clock arms to stand for time, the amplitude of a sound wave to stand for pressure, and so forth. Analog measures also tend to be *continuous* rather than *discrete;* there are no gaps between the possible values that can be represented. Earlier we described how a low voltage could be used to represent 0 and a higher voltage to represent 1. This is an analog measure.

2.2.3 Digital or Discrete Signals

It would be possible to transmit a sequence of electrical pulses as shown in Figure 2.6: two high-voltage periods of transmission, followed by three periods of low voltage, each period being of the same duration. This can be taken to represent the binary number 11000. But note that the flow of current is continuous and the values are not *exactly* 0 or 1. It is really only necessary that they be close enough to the target values to be clearly distinguishable from one another.

Digital transmissions, then, are continuous, as are analog, but they are coded to represent discrete values. For an analog signal to pass from 0 to 1, every intervening value must be represented, however briefly, but the digital representations need have no intervening values.

If we are going to send signals of this type there has to be some coordination between sender and receiver. The receiver does not look at these waves from the side, as we do. It measures the voltage level at any moment. If the duration of a pulse is 100 microseconds (μs) and the receiver samples the signal every 10 μs, it may think it has received 10 pulses. Thus, there must be agreement as to pulse length and sampling rate. In *synchronous* transmission, both the transmitter and receiver are effectively on the same clock, while in *asynchronous* transmission

FIGURE 2.6
Representation of binary numbers. Two high-frequency waves followed by three low ones could be used to represent the binary number 11000. It is not necessary that the voltages be exact, but they must be above or below a threshold value.

FIGURE 2.7
The *baud*. A baud is a measure of digital signaling speed, the number of states (zero or one, high or low) of the signal in 1 second. If these six values, representing 100110, took 1 second to be transmitted, the rate would be 6 baud. It is possible to use two consecutive states to represent one bit, so *baud* and *bit* are not necessarily synonyms.

the transmitter must send a special signal that tells the receiver that a message is coming and to get ready to sample the incoming pulses or waves.

A frequently used measure of the speed of signaling, using digital pulses, is the *baud*, which represents the number of distinct pulses a system is capable of transmitting per second. The word *baud* does not mean the same as bits per second, but the meanings are close enough that we shall not bother with the distinction here. The concept is illustrated in Figure 2.7.

Most readers are familiar with a variety of discrete signaling systems. These include:

• Braille. Basically a *printlike* system using a 2 × 3 array of dots or raised bumps on a page to represent letters and numbers.
• Morse code. Basically a sound system using the duration of a sound (actually a light or any other detectable medium, including sounds of varying frequency) to represent a dot or dash and a combination of dots or dashes to represent characters.
• American Standard Code for Information Interchange (ASCII). A computer and communications system for representing letters, numbers, and punctuation symbols using combinations of 0s and 1s (see Figure 2.2). This is a fixed-length code, all characters having the same number of constituent elements (bits), while Morse code uses a variable number of basic elements to make up the character code.

Modern communication systems are tending more and more toward the use of digital representation of information. We now have digital musical recordings,

FIGURE 2.8
A carrier wave. The highest and lowest amplitudes and the wavelength are constant.

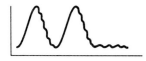

FIGURE 2.9
A hypothetical wave from a musical instrument. Amplitude and wavelength may vary.

in which the frequencies and intensities of sound are represented as discrete measurements, which are then reconverted to analog for output (playing) but are stored and electronically processed in digital form. Many standardized telephone messages are stored in computers in digital form, then retrieved and converted to analog as needed. Many "wrong-number" or telephone time messages are actually digital recordings. Representing a human voice accurately requires very fine grain sampling. But once this is done, the digital recordings can be more reliable because they can be accurately reproduced.

2.2.4 Modulation

We have already shown that many communication systems involve changing the form of a signal. Such transformations are necessary when the transmitter's signals have characteristics different from those the receiver is prepared to interpret. For example, radio and television signals are sent at frequencies much higher than those the human voice can generate or the ear detect. Further, such transmissions must use frequencies such that two or more broadcasts within the same area do not interfere with each other.

Radio transmission, which includes television, is done by sending out a *carrier wave* at a fixed frequency and modifying it with the frequency and amplitude variations of the voice. Here is a simplified example of how that works. Suppose a radio station is assigned a base frequency of 1000 kilohertz (kHz). This wave form is shown in Figure 2.8. Let us simplify a musical instrument's output to an irregular wave, as in Figure 2.9. If we then superimpose the wave of the instrument on that of the carrier, we get the wave shown in Figure 2.10.

The basic frequency of this resultant series of waves is 1000 kHz, but the amplitude varies, as did the amplitude of the instrument. The superimposed signal may cause variations in the resultant frequency from that of the carrier. This is the wave that is transmitted. At the receiver, the carrier must be

FIGURE 2.10
Modulation. The combination of the carrier and signal waves—what is actually transmitted.

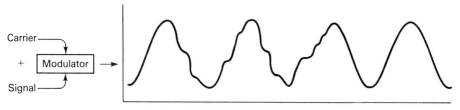

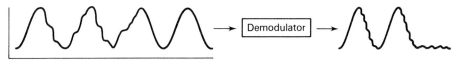

FIGURE 2.11
Demodulation. The demodulator subtracts the carrier waves, resulting in the original signal.

subtracted out, leaving the original instrument wave, as shown in Figure 2.11.

The superimposing of the two waves, in this manner, is called *modulation,* and it is a form of coding. The transformation of the combined wave back into its original form is called *demodulation.* The form of modulation in which the frequency of the carrier remains constant while the amplitude changes is called *amplitude modulation* (AM).

A second common form of modulation of a carrier is done by holding the peak amplitude of the carrier wave constant, but varying its frequency as a function of the amplitude of the signal wave, as shown in Figure 2.12. This is called *frequency modulation* (FM). It has the characteristic of being a more reliable means of representing signals, hence is preferred for musical transmission.

Pulse-code modulation (PCM) transforms analog signals into digital form. This is the form of modulation that converts voice transmission into digital form.

There is no limit to the way signals can be modulated. Computer terminals connected to telephone lines use modulators and demodulators to convert digital signals from a keyboard into analog signals for telephone transmission, and vice versa. A device which performs both functions is called a *mo*dulator-*dem*odulator *(modem).*

2.3 THE ELECTROMAGNETIC SPECTRUM

Much of our communication makes at least some use of electromagnetic waves. The phenomenon of electromagnetic waves has many manifestations, including visible light, radio (hence television), microwaves, and x-rays. The particular form of the waves is a function of wavelength, or frequency. The speed of electromagnetic waves is the same for all forms and is the speed of light: 300 million m/s in a vacuum. The speed varies with the medium through which the

FIGURE 2.12
Frequency modulation. Holding amplitude constant, changes in frequency can be used as a code; the lower frequency can represent 0, the higher frequency 1.

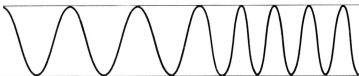

waves pass. Radiation of different wavelengths will be slowed more or less as it passes through some medium other than a vacuum, such as glass. A glass prism will change the speed of the various wavelengths of light that go together to make up white, resulting in a spreading of the constituent waves. This is what makes the familiar rainbow.

The complete spread of frequencies is called the *electromagnetic spectrum.* Figure 2.13 shows the types of electromagnetic waves as a function of wavelength (or, of course, frequency). Recall that a radio transmission does not occur at a single frequency, that of the carrier, but that there are variations around this

FIGURE 2.13
The electromagnetic spectrum. All electromagnetic waves travel at the speed of light ($c = 2.9979 \times 10^8$ meters per second in a vacuum). Wave frequency, in Hz, is wavelength (λ) in meters divided by c: $f = \lambda / c$. Illustrated are the major manifestations of allocation of waves at various lengths.

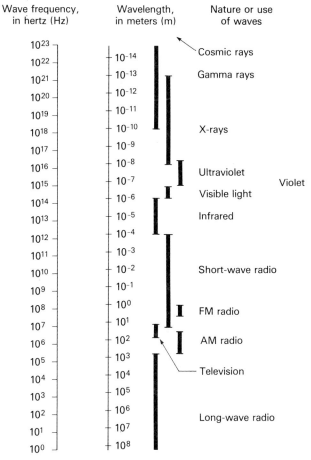

Wave frequency, in hertz (Hz)	Wavelength, in meters (m)	Nature or use of waves
10^{23}		
10^{22}	10^{-14}	Cosmic rays
10^{21}	10^{-13}	Gamma rays
10^{20}	10^{-12}	
10^{19}	10^{-11}	
10^{18}	10^{-10}	X-rays
10^{17}	10^{-9}	
10^{16}	10^{-8}	
10^{15}	10^{-7}	Ultraviolet Violet
10^{14}	10^{-6}	Visible light
10^{13}	10^{-5}	Infrared
10^{12}	10^{-4}	
10^{11}	10^{-3}	
10^{10}	10^{-2}	Short-wave radio
10^{9}	10^{-1}	
10^{8}	10^{0}	FM radio
10^{7}	10^{1}	
10^{6}	10^{2}	AM radio
10^{5}	10^{3}	
10^{4}	10^{4}	Television
10^{3}	10^{5}	
10^{2}	10^{6}	Long-wave radio
10^{1}	10^{7}	
10^{0}	10^{8}	

base frequency, a little to each side of the carrier. Thus, a radio transmitter is not assigned a single frequency but a band or channel on either side of the nominal carrier frequency. Bandwidth, or space in the spectrum, has become a highly valued commodity because there are now so many potential users of the electromagnetic spectrum. Not only must radio stations be protected from interference from other transmitters; they must also be protected from noncommunication transmissions, what to communicators is noise. This form of interference may come from such devices as home computers, many of which come with a printed warning about the possibility of interference with broadcast communications.

The results of the competition for bandwidth are the need to protect transmissions from interference—a technological problem—and the need for an equitable frequency allocation procedure—a political problem. Hence, frequency allocation has moved into the political sphere, both nationally and internationally. More is said about this problem in Chapters 4, 8, 11, 14, and 15.

2.4   TRANSMISSION OF SIGNALS

Let us now begin to look at transmission as a system, that is, as a set of components and procedures linked together in some fashion to accomplish an objective. There are different *modes* in the sense of directionality. There must be *compatibility* of codes and transmission speeds, and there may be some procedure for detecting and correcting errors. Transmissions need not be restricted to sending messages from point A to point B or from point A over a wide area to anyone who is listening; there are other *network configurations* possible.

2.4.1   Transmission Modes

The simplest transmission mode is represented by a stock market ticker or news-dissemination system. For any given link there is a transmitter and one or more receivers. All traffic goes *one way only,* as in Figure 2.14a. This is called *simplex transmission.*

Suppose we have two teletypewriters or telegraph instruments linked together by a single communication line. Either can transmit to the other, but only one can send at any given time, while the other serves as receiver. In order to reverse the flow of traffic, the sender has to stop, to give the other party time to use the transmission line (see Figure 2.14b). This is called *half-duplex* transmission. Traffic can go in either direction, but only one at a time.

The telephone—and some combinations of the telephone with computer terminals and modems—permits both parties to a conversation to send at the same time. Just as in face-to-face communication, two people talking over the telephone may talk at the same time. Neither may hear what the other is saying, but it is possible to converse this way. In computer terminal conversations, there is usually a small *buffer memory,* in which messages can be stored so that both

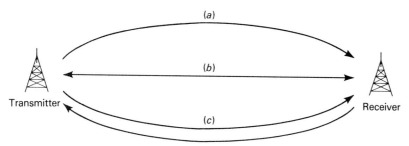

FIGURE 2.14
Three transmission modes. *(a)* Simplex. One-way transmission only. *(b)* Half-duplex.
Two-way communication is possible, but in one direction at a time. *(c)* Duplex.
Two-way communication is possible, in both directions at the same time.

parties can transmit at one time but incoming messages will not be displayed to the sender until the sender has completed his or her own outgoing message. This mode is known as *full-duplex* transmission (see Figure 2.14c). Its advantage lies in the many situations where it is not necessary for the parties to know exactly what is being sent to them in order to send out a meaningful signal. For example, computer users may ask the computer several questions in succession, without waiting for the answers to the earlier questions to appear on a display screen.

2.4.2 Compatibility

This requirement can best be illustrated by considering what would happen if a transmitter and receiver were not compatible. An FM receiver cannot demodulate an AM transmission, even if tuned to the correct carrier frequency. If a transmitter is using a digital character code other than ASCII, but the receiver is ASCII only, the message will not be understood. Perhaps even more simply, two persons in face-to-face conversation will not understand each other if each speaks a different language. Those who have traveled in a foreign country may be aware of what happens when this situation does occur. Usually, there is a joint effort by both parties to try to find some language in common—a third natural language they may both know, a simplified form of one of their own languages, or, if necessary, sign language. It is sometimes amusing to listen when one party, instead of changing languages, merely increases volume. Computers and mechanical communication systems are generally not so versatile, and when an incompatibility occurs, there is simply a failure of communication, without this automatic attempt to adjust to some compatible language.

2.4.3 Introduction to Networks

A *network* is an interconnected set of transmitting and receiving devices (or persons). A more generic term for transmitter or receiver, in this context, is a *node*. Thus, a network is a set of nodes and the communication channels that

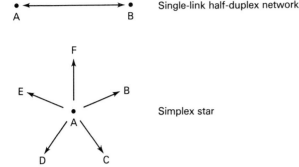

Single-link half-duplex network

Simplex star

FIGURE 2.15
Some network configurations.
(a) A single-line half-duplex
network; two stations able to
talk only to each other. *(b)* A
simplex star has a control
station *(A)* that can talk to all
others but the others cannot
talk back—a typical pay-TV
configuration.

link them. In this brief introductory section, we shall discuss two important attributes of networks: the logical layout, that is, which nodes can communicate with which others, and the various functions required to control operation of a network.

Let us first consider some basic configurations of a communication network.

1 *Single link.* This is the most primitive of networks, consisting of two nodes with a single link between them (see Figure 2.15a). The link may operate in any of the three modes: simplex, half-duplex, or full-duplex.

2 *Star.* Such a network consists of a control station and two or more other nodes that must use the central node in order to communicate, as shown in Figure 2.15b. Commercial radio broadcasting is an example of a star configuration, as is a taxi dispatching system.

Different configurations may be combined with different transmission modes to make for a wide range of possibilities. For example, the broadcast configuration is a simplex star: a star configuration, with simplex (one-way only) transmission. The taxi dispatch system is usually a half-duplex star: either the control or an individual taxi is able to transmit, but only one at a time. A network need not allow for each node to be able to communicate to the central one. We may have a configuration such as shown in Figure 2.16.

Many practical networks are so configured, in particular the digital communication networks to be described in Chapter 6.

The control functions will vary considerably with the type and mission of the network. For example, taxi dispatch networks, which tend to be modeled on military lines, are supposed to maintain discipline among nodes, but one often hears drivers interfering with each other's transmissions and failing to acknowledge messages from the control station, possibly because they do not want to go to the customer pick-up point to which they are being directed. In air traffic control, which uses the same basic type of network, discipline is critical and much better maintained. Digital communication networks must include two functions not necessary to taxi dispatching. One is relay of messages. If the

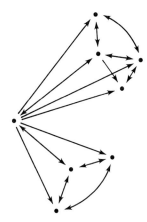

FIGURE 2.16
A complex network in which the control station can transmit to all others, but not all others can transmit directly to control. Typical of military networks in which some outlying stations may lack power to reach the control station.

nodes cannot communicate directly to each other, then a path of relays has to be worked out in order for node A to reach node F (see Figure 2.17).

Also, in a digital network errors must be detected and corrected, often done by retransmission. Other kinds of functions of a network include logging of messages, determining the least expensive route through a network, and deferring or expediting transmission according to a priority that may be assigned to a node, a message, or a destination. We shall meet many more network characteristics in future chapters.

2.5 NOISE

Signals are not always received as they are sent. We are all aware of such phenomena as *static* in a radio transmission or *ghost images* in television. The same effect is generated when printed matter becomes ink-smeared or discolored with age, or when a poorly functioning photocopier is used to make copies from a poor-quality original. In all cases, the signal as received by the

FIGURE 2.17
A complete network. In order to transmit a message from A to F, a path through one or more intermediate nodes must be worked out. Paths A–D–F and A–C–F are the fastest (fewest relays), but busy lines may necessitate a path such as A–B–D–E–F. Typical of modern digital communication networks.

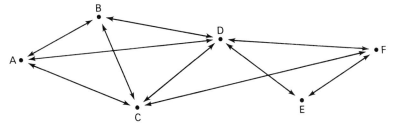

FIGURE 2.18
Noise. An event such as an electrical storm adds electromagnetic energy to a
signal, with the result that the signal received is not the same as the one sent.

destination differs from the signal sent because something unwanted was added
to the signal. In the radio example, some source of radio frequency electromagnetic radiation may have been picked up by the receiver, or perhaps the inner
workings of the receiver itself generated the noise. In the television example,
probably the signals are being reflected off a mountain or high building, resulting
in more than one version of the signal being received by the receiver and then
displayed on the screen. In the printed-page example, some sort of dark material
other than the intentional ink is being added to the page.

The effect of noise is more than just aesthetic degradation. The meaning of
the signal, as received, may appear to differ from the meaning intended to be
sent. A word may be masked by the static or the ink smear. A face may become
unrecognizable in a video display and thereby create an impression the script
writer did not intend.

Any signal which is unintentionally added to a transmission and which
changes the message at the destination is called *noise.* Noise is present in most
communication systems, and a considerable effort is spent to overcome the
effect. Schematically, the addition of noise is shown in Figure 2.18.

Enough random variation, superimposed on the original transmission, can
make the value of a discrete signal ambiguous, as shown here with the third and
fourth pulses. Let us consider how to detect and then correct errors in
transmission caused by noise.

2.5.1 Error Detection

A common error-detection scheme used in digital communication involves
adding one or more bits to a fixed-length binary character code. If, for example,
a 6-bit code is used for numerals and letters, a seventh bit might be added for
error-detection purposes. The extra bit is set by the transmitter to have a value
such as to make the total number of 1s in a code group (now 7 bits) even or odd
(but always consistently one or the other). The extra bit is called a *parity bit.* If it
results in an even number of 1s, the system is said to be using *even parity;* if an

	Basic code		Parity bit	Final code
Even parity	010101	(3 1's)	1	0101011
	011101	(4 1's)	0	0111010
Odd parity	010101	(3 1's)	0	0101010
	111100	(4 1's)	1	1111001

FIGURE 2.19
Use of parity bits. The rightmost bit in the final code makes the
total of 1s in the code either an even or odd number (choice
determined in advance) and this enables transmission errors to be
detected.

odd number, it is using *odd parity*. Many computer terminals have a switch
enabling the user to select either even or odd parity, depending on which
computer system the terminal is linked to. Figure 2.19 shows some examples.

Whenever a code group is received, the number of 1s is counted and the
parity computed by the receiver. If the received parity bit fails to match the
computed bit, an error has been detected. If two errors were made in
transmission, the parity bit would be the same as if no error had been made. If
the parity count is correct, there has been either *no* error or *two* errors, or even
more. Thus, this simple procedure is not infallible. More parity bits can be used
to reduce the probability of an error being undetected, but there is a trade-off
between the cost of protection and the cost of allowing the occasional error to go
through.

2.5.2 Error Correction

A common computer procedure involves both *longitudinal* and *transverse* parity,
most easily illustrated with magnetic-tape recording, shown in Figure 2.20.

Columns 1, 2, and 3 each represent a single encoded character whose
constituent bits are written across the tape transversely. We are using a 4-bit
code for illustration. More conventionally, the code would consist of 6 or 8 bits.
The fifth bit is the *transverse parity bit*. It makes the number of 1s *across* the tape

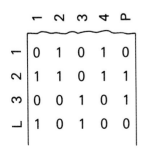

FIGURE 2.20
Longitudinal parity. A transverse parity bit is added to each byte,
or set of bits "across" the message. In addition, an-extra byte of
parity bits is inserted at the end of the message, making the
number of 1s in each row (lengthwise) even or odd, consistently.

1	0	1	0	1	0
2	1	1	0	1	1
3	0	0	1	1	1
L	1	0	1	0	0

FIGURE 2.21
Error correction. If the fourth bit of character 3, originally 0 in Figure 2.20, is changed by error to a 1, both the transverse and longitudinal parity bits will be wrong. Since there is only one bit governed by both these parity bits, it is a simple matter to correct the error from a 1 to a 0.

even. At the end of a record (the record here being illustrated by the three characters at 1, 2, and 3) there is another set of bits, which are *longitudinal parity bits*. Their function is to make an even number of 1s lengthwise in a row.

Now suppose there is a transmission error in sending this small block of data, perhaps bit 4 in character 3, which was 0 in Figure 2.20, is accidentally set as 1 during transmission, after the parity bits have been set by the transmitting unit. As we see in Figure 2.21, the transverse parity bit for character 3 is wrong, because there are now an odd number of 1s in that column. Further, the transverse parity bit for row 4 is wrong—there is also an odd number of 1s in that row. The receiver can detect these errors and, knowing that a bit is in error in column 3, row 4, it knows which bit is in error. Since bits have only two possible values, if the 1 is wrong, it must be a 0. Hence, the correction is easily made.

If there had been two errors, say in bits 3 and 4 of character 3, then the transverse parity bit for that column would be correct (Figure 2.22), but the longitudinal parity bits for rows 3 and 4 would be wrong. However, the receiver would only know there had been two errors but not which column they occurred in. Hence, it could not take corrective action.

Elaborate coding techniques are used in telecommunication systems to arrive at an economic balance between the need to protect against error and the cost of these extra, redundant bits used in error detection and correction.

2.6 SWITCHING, MULTIPLEXING, AND NETWORKS

As we pointed out earlier, practical communication systems usually involve multiple users and stations transmitting among themselves. Often, the source

FIGURE 2.22
A double error. If two bits are in error (see box), then the transverse parity bit shows no error, but two longitudinal bits are wrong. It is not possible to determine the source of the error. Thus, there is detection without correction.

1	0	1	0	1	0
2	1	1	0	1	1
3	0	0	0	1	1
L	1	0	1	0	0

and destination are not in direct communication but must send messages through one or more other intermediary nodes. There are a number of ways of routing messages among the nodes of a network or of temporarily reconfiguring a network to enable two given parties to communicate directly. Routing messages through the network is called *switching*. Another frequent economic necessity is to enable two or more users to share a communication channel at one time. This is called *multiplexing*.

2.6.1 Switching Concepts

The most logical and simplest form of switching is akin to what the railroads do. They physically shift a section of track from one position to another, so that a train passing through a switching point will take the designated path, as in Figure 2.23.

A similar approach is used in some telephone networks. This technique, called *line* or *circuit switching*, involves the physical connection of a user's input line to a selected output line. In older systems, this was done by an operator at a switchboard plugging lines from one source to a given destination (see Figure

FIGURE 2.23
Switching. To change direction of the train, the position of a small portion of track is moved, connecting the branch with the mail track. To restore the line, the branch is disconnected by moving it again.

2.24). This technique is simple in concept and fairly versatile. The outgoing line can lead to another switching center, and that to another, and eventually the caller could be linked to a far-distant receiver. A disadvantage of this method is that the entire line or sequence of lines used to link caller with destination must be dedicated to the one call, which might tie up a considerable amount of expensive capital equipment. Even if the parties are temporarily silent, the lines remain dedicated until one party hangs up.

For some kinds of messages, a more efficient technique is called *message switching.* In this method, a link is established only long enough to transmit a single message. It is commonly used in telegraphy or the more modern version, digital message transmission. While it is possible to use line switching to enable two parties to converse via teletype, the more conventional procedure is for either to send a single message and then terminate the "call." This ties up the channels only for the duration of the message, not for intermessage pauses, and channels are available for highly efficient allocation. Message switching allows a

FIGURE 2.24
A switchboard in operation. This shows the central office switchboard in Richmond, Virginia, in 1882. (Reproduced with permission of AT&T.)

variation not available for voice telephone calls. If an outgoing line is not available when any given node in the network wants one, it can hold the message until a line is available. It can also store the message temporarily until a time of day when traffic is usually low and then transmit it at a lower charge to the sender. This technique is called *store-and-forward switching*.

Today we have communication systems many or all of whose terminal points are computers. This implies large amounts of data going at high speed. We also use computers to control switching, which can also be done at high speed. High switching speed enables the computer to break up a message into small, uniform segments called *packets* and to transmit the packets independently. Each packet, even those containing parts of the same original message, is sent toward its destination as soon as it is received and an outgoing line can be found. It is not necessary to tie up a complete circuit—say from the east coast to west coast—even long enough to send a single complete message. A packet is sent from one node to another, and then it becomes the responsibility of the receiving node to send the packet on to another node, until the final destination is reached. It is entirely possible for two consecutive packets from a given source to travel to their destination by different paths, and even for the second to arrive before the first. One of the functions of the switching control system, in this case, is to reassemble the packets before delivery to the final addressee. This system is called *packet switching*. Dealing in small units enables even more efficient use of communication channels, and this method, or variants of it, has become the standard technique for data communication systems.

2.6.2 Multiplexing

Consider a telegraph system and how long the time interval must be between audible clicks of the apparatus. The electrical system must be timed to suit human perception and reaction times. But if another electrical device, rather than a human operator, is receiving the signals, it could recognize them in much less time. Hence, there would be wasted time on the circuits. If both ends of the transmission are machines, then the signals can be sent and detected much faster than by humans, and if the individual pulses were contracted to the shortest that could reliably be detected, much of the transmission channel would be unused most of the time, as shown in Figure 2.25.

If this channel were being used by machines, it would be possible to use the channel for other purposes during the idle period. This would require rapid line switches, but it would also enable the lines to serve multiple purposes.

Another way to increase the effective use of a channel is to transmit more than one message simultaneously. There are two basic ways to do this: *time-division multiplexing* and *frequency-division multiplexing*. A common abbreviation for the machine that controls multiplexing is MUX.

Time-division multiplexing is, in a sense, very fast line switching—so fast that the switching can be done between individual bits of a message rather than between messages. What is required is rapid switching from one message source

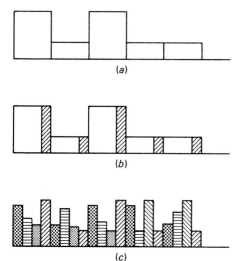

(a)

(b)

(c)

FIGURE 2.25
Time division multiplexing. *(a)* A series of transmitted pulses. *(b)* If the receiver needs only a fraction of the pulse duration to sense its amplitude, the remainder of the duration time could be used to transmit other signals. *(c)* By interleaving other shortened pulses, four sets of signals can be sent in the time originally devoted to just one.

to another, and it results in a transmitted signal that is a mixture of the two input signals.

This form of multiplexing requires a switching mechanism at the transmitting end that can sense incoming signals and combine two or more into an outgoing signal. It also requires a receiver that can take the combined signal and split it back into independent messages again (see Figure 2.26). There is, of course, a requirement for the extra switching, so this is not a benefit gained without cost, but it can save replication of entire channels. Frequency-division multiplexing relies on the ability of a transmitter to send out transmissions that, like the human voice, consist of a band of frequencies, not a single one.

A new form of multiplexing is a variant on time division. It is called *statistical multiplexing.* Under conventional time-division multiplexing, some part of the outgoing composite signal is devoted to each of the input message streams, *whether or not a particular input source is transmitting at the moment.* In other words, each input source ties up a fraction of the output signal, even if not actually transmitting. But statistical multiplexing enables one of the outgoing message components that is otherwise unused to send more fragments from a source that is being used.

Real-life multiplexing systems may be far more complex versions of the basic concepts, but the idea of multiple use of transmission channels is economically critical to modern telecommunications.

2.6.3   Networks Again

Real networks are frequently massively complex combinations of transmitters, receivers, lines (channels), switches, and multiplexers. The human users of these

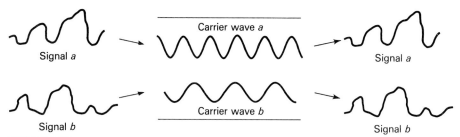

FIGURE 2.26
Frequency division multiplexing. A transmitter able to transmit all frequencies in a bandwidth can use two or more carrier waves at once, each modulated by a different signal.

systems are not normally aware of most of the elements, but sometimes they are forced on the user's attention. In the telephone system in the United States, we receive a different signal if the telephone number we are calling is busy, or engaged, than if there is no free channel through the long-distance system leading to that subscriber telephone. The difference is in the rapidity of the busy signal: a fast signal indicates a busy network; a slow signal indicates a busy individual node.

Another instance in which the user notices the network functioning is when cross talk is heard, that is, when a telephone user can hear another conversation to which he or she is not a party. As we shall see in later chapters, networks solve more problems than they cause. They reduce the cost of communication and increase its reliability. But sometimes the user sees only the problems, such as these, and does not understand their cause or effect. However sophisticated our systems become, they are still used by humans who may make judgments about them from fragmentary evidence. Hence, the human factor in telecommunication system design remains of great importance.

RECOMMENDED READINGS

Cherry, Colin, *On Human Communication: A Review, a Survey, and a Criticism* (3d ed.), Cambridge: MIT Press, 1978. (See the note at the end of Chapter 1. We recommend this technical but remarkable book for all aspects of telecommunications.)

Doll, Dixon R., *Data Communication,* New York: Wiley-Interscience, 1978. (A basic technical book on communication between computers and terminals.)

Martin, James, *Telecommunications and the Computer* (2d ed.), Englewood Cliffs, N.J.: Prentice-Hall, Inc., 1976. (A book for the computer-knowledgable, with clear descriptions of how computers interconnect.)

———, *Future Developments in Telecommunications*, Englewood Cliffs, N.J.: Prentice-Hall, Inc., 1977. (Martin's projection of telecommunications technology.)

———, *Communication Satellite Systems*, Englewood Cliffs, N.J.: Prentice-Hall, Inc., 1978. (One of the more significant telecommunication technologies of our time.)

Nichols, Elizabeth A., Nichols, Joseph C., and Musson, Keith R., *Data Communication for Microcomputers, with Practical Applications,* New York: McGraw-Hill Book Co., 1982. (The linking of personal computers via telephone lines and local area networks is becoming a key to the growing popularity of these small computers.)

Pierce, John, *An Introduction to Information Theory: Symbols, Signals and Noise* (2d rev.), New York: Dover Publications, 1980. (A new edition of a classic introduction to the concepts of communication. Read this first, then Cherry, 1978. Pierce, like Cherry, is a master writer as well as a major contributor to the field.)

Shannon, Claude E., and Weaver, Warren, *The Mathematical Theory of Communication*, Urbana: University of Illinois Press, 1949. (Not for the layman, but a landmark work, probably the most frequently cited book in others' writings on communication.)

Tannenbaum, Andrew S., *Computer Networks*, Englewood Cliffs, N.J.: Prentice-Hall, Inc., 1981. (General review of computer to computer networks.)

Tydeman, John, et al., *Teletext and Videotex in the United States*, Data Communication Book Series, New York: McGraw-Hill Book Co., 1980. (More popular in Europe than in America, teletext and videotex may soon become established in the United States and Canada as major technologies.)

Weaver, Warren, "Recent Contributions to the Mathematical Theory of Communication," in C. E. Shannon and W. Weaver, *The Mathematical Theory of Communication*, Urbana: University of Illinois Press, 1949. (Warren's part of the famous Shannon-Weaver book is more readable by the nontechnical person. It is more concerned with meaning and its communication than with the technical aspects of transmission.)

CHAPTER 3

COMMUNICATION BETWEEN PEOPLE AND MACHINES

Charles T. Meadow
DIALOG Information Services, Inc.
Palo Alto, CA 94304

3.1 THE CONCEPT OF HUMAN-MACHINE COMMUNICATION

While the formal concept of communication between humans and machines is a product of the computer age, such communication is as old as the machines themselves. The simplest tools—a hammer, a wedge, a screwdriver—do their jobs by being manipulated or, in a very primitive sense, instructed by their users. When we consider higher-order machines, whether a trusty .44 on the American western frontier, or a violin, we tend to recognize virtuosity in the use of the tool. They have a higher form of interaction. Even the crapshooter talks to the dice as they roll.

The difference between a computer and most other machines is that it talks back, often with a seeming (or real) intelligence of its own. While pushing the "start" button or dropping a deck of punched cards into a reader are forms of communication, in the context of this chapter, what we are really interested in is *interactive* human-computer conversations in which the human and the machine talk to each other, contribute to each other's store of knowledge and, often, work together toward the solution of a problem. Saint-Exupéry (1967) says, "the machine does not isolate man from the great problems of nature but plunges him more deeply into them" (p. 47).

The more "intelligent" the machine, the more it can communicate in a way that resembles human communication. Indeed, according to A. M. Turing

(1963) if a human observer was unable to tell that a series of messages came from a machine, rather than a human, then the machine was thinking. We really do not have a better definition of computer thought, even though this one clearly depends on who the observer is. Human-computer communication today can be by typewriterlike terminal (the most common) or by picture or voice. Programs —like people—vary considerably in their ability to discern the meaning of statements made to them, to cope with ambiguity, or to provide meaningful responses.

Generally, we communicate *to* a computer by giving it commands or data. Also, generally, it *responds* to us by asking questions (demands for data) or giving data in response to a demand.

As we noted above, in connection with Turing's test, the less users know about how computers work, the more likely they are to be impressed by an "intelligent" program or confused by an imperfect one. If inexperienced, users may be completely unable to discriminate between the computer and a particular program running in it, or between the computer and its software, on the one hand, and the organization (bank, school, hospital, store, etc.) that owns it, on the other. Thus, any institution that has a stake in its employees or clients using an information system would want to insure that the entire system had the kind of appeal wanted. For example, in one large American city a major bank introduced automated bank teller machines. When large numbers of clients began using these machines and depending on them to supply needed cash for the weekend, it was not uncommon for the supply of cash to be exhausted on a Friday night, after the bank itself had closed. The result was hostility toward the bank, which was seen as enticing people to rely on an unreliable machine. The problem, of course, was a minor one, easily resolved by changing some schedules for replenishment, but it *could* have had a major impact on the bank's marketing. Video games, on the other hand, seem to have found an instant, intensely loyal audience. Some of these (for example, Battleship) are the same games long played with paper and pencil, but the interaction is a clear and strong attraction.

At a more serious level, if a corporation is going to decentralize some of its operations, the new style of communication—more people involved in decisions, everyone's actions known to more people—can be threatening or appealing. Much depends on how individuals will interact with the system. Of course, much also depends on other factors, such as how management goes about "selling" the system to its people. (For discussion of decentralization see Chapters 17, 18, and 19.)

As a final example, some businesses that deal with the general public through the mail, such as credit card agencies or book clubs, could appear impervious and frustrating to a customer with a problem. But a toll-free telephone service that allows the customer to talk to someone about a problem—making the system interactive—can change the image. This is true, by the way, even when the business is an interactive one, such as one providing data communications or data-base search service.

3.2 THE BASIC MECHANICS

We often call the channel of communication between a user and a computer an *interface:* it is that part shared by two dissimilar organisms. The interface is not the same as the system, any more than a bank's teller machine is the bank. The interface is a means of getting *to* the system or of it getting to the user. The interface may be, and often is, less complex and logically discriminating than the system to which it is linked, and this is what can lead to the kind of problem where people misunderstand the system because they see no difference between it and the interface. To a user there *is* no difference, but to the designer there is, and the design can be improved if necessary. We can use as an example a visitor to a foreign country who speaks little of its language and treats everyone as simple because the language by which he communicates is simple.

In this section we discuss the basic hardware components of human-computer communication. The limitations of these devices (for example, the need for a user to communicate by typing) may impose limitations on the communication ability of the overall system. In the next section we discuss some of the ways in which we can program a computer to carry on a conversation.

We will discuss communication devices in terms of input and output. It is usually rare for the same device to serve both functions because of the way input and output units are packaged together, although it may seem to the uninitiated that this is so. A simple printing terminal, for example, is almost always two separate, copackaged devices. Occasionally they are not packaged together; instead, there is a print terminal whose keyboard is a separate unit, connected by an umbilicuslike cable. The keyboard sends signals to a modem, which sends them on to a computer, which sends *the same message* back to the printer component of the terminal. The message makes the full cycle from the keyboard to the computer and back to the printer: it does not go direct from keyboard to printer. Certainly, the action of striking keys with the fingers is considerably different from displaying or printing the corresponding characters.

We start our discussion with output devices, since there are fewer variations among these.

3.2.1 Machine-to-Human (Output) Devices

We have learned over the years that we can attach almost any kind of machine to a computer so that the latter can control the former. Well-known examples include machine tools, subway train controls, and telephone switches. But for direct communication with humans the field narrows down to communication via visual or audio channels. In terms of human comprehension it makes little difference if signals are printed on a page or displayed on what is variously called a cathode ray tube (CRT), video display unit (VDU), or video display terminal (VDT). Each presents the same shapes in the same formats. There are differences in speed of display or printing, sharpness of definition, and degree of eye strain.

Visual Display   The forms of output may be of high permanence involving the printed page, microfilm, graphic plots on paper or film, or even braille (which is decidedly not visual but serves the same purpose and is produced in a manner similar to printing—by a hammerlike device striking the page).

The most common form of display is *character-oriented*. This means that, like a typewriter, the display device can place any of a limited set of characters into any of a limited number of positions. A typewriter cannot put a character *anywhere*. It may have the ability to move up or down by a half space, to single-, double-, or triple-space lines, or to use proportional spacing between characters. But there are still restrictions, and the character must be one of those for which a typeface exists. A *graphics display* can place characters or individual dots anywhere on the screen, or at least so it seems to the human eye. Actually, it may be restricted to any one of an array of positions, typically 1000 × 1000 positions. Placing dots at positions this close together gives the impression to the human eye of a continuous line, as shown in Figure 3.1. Plotters will actually trace out a continuous curve on a page. Using a graphics display, the computer can fashion any character by "drawing" it with dots.

For character display, speeds may range from as low as 10 characters per second (cps), or approximately 100 baud, to 960 cps or 9600 baud. The lower figure suggests an obsolete but still occasionally found teletype. The higher figure represents a CRT coupled to a computer via a high-speed modem.

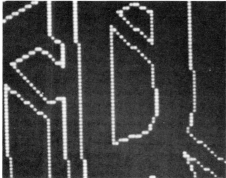

FIGURE 3.1
Each character in a graphics display is made up of tiny dots; the dots are so close together that we see a continuous line. (Courtesy Tektronix Inc.)

Microfilm can be produced at rates of up to 100,000 cps, but there is, of course, some processing delay, which may range from minutes to hours before the user can view the output.

The graphics output devices essentially draw lines or curves on the output medium or project a complete character all at once. As noted above, because of the fine mesh of possible locations, the impression of continuous lines can be given to the observer.

In recent years color displays have become common and the sophistication of the "drawings" is much increased over early systems. For example, engineering drawings can be entered into a computer as a series of flat, two-dimensional projections. These can be displayed as three-dimensional line drawings and rotated to give the viewer any aspect angle desired (see Figure 3.2).

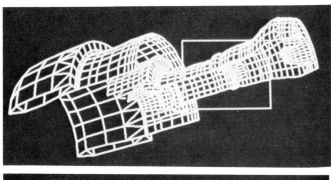

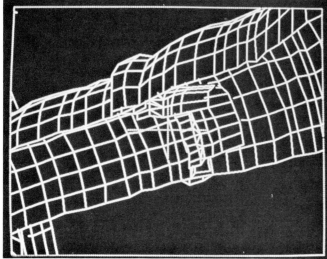

FIGURE 3.2
Engineering drawings of an object may be entered into the computer as a series of two-dimensional projections. The computer may then display the object in three-dimensional drawings and rotate the object to give the viewer any angle projection desired. (Courtesy Tektronix Inc.)

The basic difference between a character-display CRT and a graphic display is that with the latter the programmer can control the placement of a dot or character at any individual grid location. With character displays, the grid is much coarser. With a graphic display, the fine mesh enables the programmer to assemble dots into any character shape desired. With a character display, only the predetermined character set can be displayed. With a graphics terminal, the programmer can control both the size and the placement of figures. Figure 3.3 shows a rather elaborate text composition build up from basic components, with the operator, or designer, having control of such variables as size, placement, and line width of letters and figures. Character displays do not have this facility. The price that must be paid for the full graphics capability includes a higher basic hardware cost, faster communication lines, and more supporting software.

Audio Output The most primitive form of audio output is simply a tape player that can be turned on by an external signal, such as a telephone answering machine that delivers a standard message to callers. More elaborate devices can permit a human operator to communicate with the caller, then quickly switch to any of a fairly large number of prerecorded messages, depending on what the caller was asking. Such a system is used by Northern States Power Company, a Minnesota electric utility, to provide an information service that answers customers' inquiries on matters relating to energy use.

More elaborate systems use a voice synthesizer, a computer component that can convert digital character strings into their audio equivalents; for example, the stored string "hello" is sent to a voice synthesizer which produces the sound of the word. This enables a program to have complete control over a conversation, so long as the computer stays within the bounds of its stored vocabulary. While inflection can be controlled, such control is imperfect, and reconstituted messages from a computer often sound somewhat like motion picture portrayals of talking computers—rather monotonic. Most of us have encountered the telephone message, "The number you have called, 555-1234, is no longer in service." We can often hear a slight delay between the word "called" and the recitation of the number, indicating that the computer-assembled message elements do not sound exactly like a live person.

3.2.2 Human-to-Machine (Input) Communication

The input techniques roughly parallel the output, but they are not necessarily always paired; that is, print input does not always imply print output, and certainly audio output does not imply audio input. In a sense, the entry of information into computer and communications systems has progressed the least, technologically, of any of the major system components. Most data entries into computer and communication systems still require a human to strike a key (or equivalent) once for each character of data to be transmitted. By avoidance of retranscribing data (for example, retyping a letter once an error has been

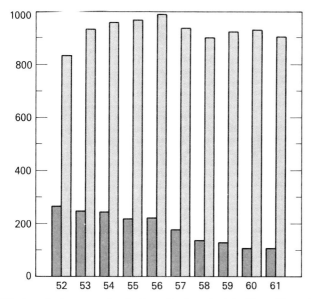

This bar chart comes directly from the bar chart facility, with no further corrections or alterations. Extra headings or keys, if any, must be supplied by the user.

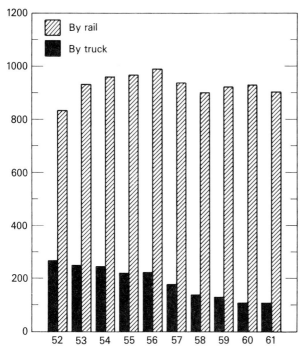

This bar chart is a copy of the one on the left, with some minor modifications. The short bars were made black in the bar chart property sheet. Then the bar chart was split, the diagonal shading was added to the other bars, the graph was heightened, and the label and key added. Note that these changes should be made after the data is entered because any further changes to the bar chart will cause the bar chart to be redrawn by the system.

FIGURE 3.3
With this text-composition unit, the designer is able to vary the size, placement, and width of letters and figures. (Courtesy Xerox Corp.)

detected by correcting a computer-stored version of it and then reprinting) we can save much time, but the original data entry is still slow. The entry of graphic data, on the other hand, can be quick.

Input of Character or Digital Information   The typewriterlike keyboard is the most common mode of entering data into a computer or communication system. Indeed, the teletype send-receive terminals (having both a keyboard and print element) was and is a popular computer data-entry service. While more modern terminals (including some of the new teletypes) can print faster, the human fingers move at about the same old rate, which is around 10 cps for professional operators, probably less than 1 cps for the unpracticed hunt-and-peck typist. For professional typists, the measurement of speed takes errors into account and should also do so for amateurs. A system that helps to reduce error increases throughput. Thus, the measurements of input speed in characters per second, given above, are not necessarily universal.

Input of Graphic Information   If a picture is truly worth a thousand words then the input of pictorial information can be very much faster than character information. However, it is really not such a simple matter because lines and curves are not entered *directly,* but as a series of points, and everything depends on how the computer is programmed to interpret the point series. There are all sorts of devices for drawing the basic curves: light pens, touch-sensitive VDT screen, electronic "pads," joysticks (popular with TV games), or the "mouse," which can be placed on any flat surface and moved, the direction and distance being interpreted as a command to move some object displayed on the VDT screen in a similar way. Exactly how to interpret these devices again depends on the program in use and the user's objectives. For example, we can move a cursor across the face of a VDT using a mouse and have this interpreted as an irregular curve. In Figure 3.4a the designer has constructed the geometric figure shown with shading and a "shadow." In Figure 3.4b, the designer enters some change commands, which result in a quickly altered figure, Figure 3.4c.

Input of Audio Information   To many people, the ultimate in human-computer interaction would be true voice interaction, so often portrayed in science fiction. We simply talk to the computer and it talks back. In fiction, it even makes jokes. Perhaps the one certain statement we can make about current capabilities is that we *cannot* now have an unrestricted conversation with a computer—that is, one in which any speaker may say anything, and all will be understood *and* in which either speaker may redefine words or give commands which the other will follow. In human conversation we can say, "What *I* mean by *natural language* is. . . .' We can also say, explicitly or by inflection, "Reverse the meaning of what I am about to say."

At the low end of the scale it is possible for a computer to understand a very limited vocabulary, even when spoken by a variety of people. An example with somewhat limited utility is a machine that can understand the digits 0 to 9.

However, some doubt that a machine can ever be built or programmed to understand the full range of natural language because language can only be understood in context, and that requires not merely knowledge of dictionary definitions of words but human experience—an understanding of inflections, analogies, and figures of speech. A more limited but still practical goal would be a computer that could simply transcribe most spoken words and return a printed

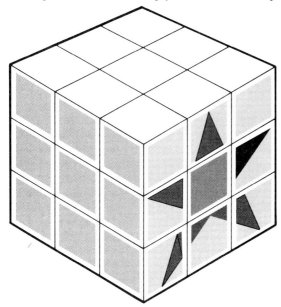

FIGURE 3.4
(a) A geometric figure shown with shading and shadow. *(b)* The designer making some changes at the keyboard and terminal. *(c)* The same figure with changes incorporated. *(a* and *c* Courtesy Xerox Corp.)

FIGURE 3-4C
Continued

or visual display—an electronic stenographer. Some error would be made by such a machine, as it always is by humans. Hence, review and editing would be required to catch those errors made by the machine because of its inability to comprehend subtleties. A machine like this would considerably reduce the cost of transcribing textual information, as well as the elapsed time required to do so.

3.3 STYLES OF INTERACTION

Regardless of how messages are physically transmitted there can be variation in the type or style of discourse between the human user and the machine. Here we omit noninteractive communication, for example, straight typing or keying in of information without some kind of response by the machine.

3.3.1 Styles of Discourse

The simplest form of discourse is typified by customer-operated bank teller machines (Figure 3.5). The human user has a small number of choices of function. Having selected a function, the user is "asked" to enter a number (account or user number, or amount of money). If the machine accepts the command it gives out money, a deposit receipt, an account status, or whatever. If it does not accept the command it says something that has the meaning "begin again." Although the machines are simple to operate, there is no way for the system to diagnose a user fault and take corrective measures. Nor is there usually

FIGURE 3.5
The bank teller machines, which may be operated by any bank
customer with a valid card, involves the simplest of human-machine
interaction. (Courtesy Wells Fargo Bank.)

any feedback as to what is wrong. In my own first use of such a machine, I
repeatedly and mistakenly tried to withdraw $0.50—an amount the machine was
physically unable to deliver—instead of $50. Since there was no diagnostic tool,
it took several tries before the error was discovered. We can represent this
primitive form of discourse by the diagram in Figure 3.6.

The telephone system, by comparison, is far more interactive. Various coded
sounds (busy or engaged, ringing) that we learn early in life give us a good bit of
feedback. Recorded voice messages provide much more specific data, for
example, that a line has been disconnected. There is, however, no way the
telephone user can talk back to these automatically generated messages. Figure
3.7 gives a summary of this simple interactive cycle.

In the case of error, the user reaction is expected to be a new action. There is
no way to ask for an explanation of the system's reaction. When no error occurs,
there is no need for any response or reaction. The caller hears the party called,
and thereafter the telephone system is transparent, that is, its actions are no
longer noticed by the user.

On a still higher level is a typical interactive computer system, whether a time

FIGURE 3.6
A representation of the simplest human-machine interaction.

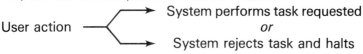

User action $\longrightarrow$ System response $\longrightarrow$ User reaction

FIGURE 3.7
A representation of human-machine interaction involving prerecorded messages.

shared large machine or a dedicated micro. Here, the conversation is almost continuous, as the user proceeds through several steps, such as:

- Log in
- Selection of programs to run (for example, RUN FORTRAN)
- Commands to the selected program (for example, a compiler)
- Entry of data through an application program

At all levels there may be error messages similar to the telephone system's, pointing out major errors of an anticipated kind but not explaining in any detail. Sometimes the computer feedback can be very specific and helpful to the user in deciding how he or she should react. For example, the statement

$$Y = X*(ZI))$$

is invalid in almost any computer language because there are two right parentheses and only one left. A computer's response to the command is usually to reject it and offer the user some explanation, which may range from a simple rejection notice (SYNTAX ERROR) to an attempt to point out exactly where the error occurred. In this case, the error is most likely to be *discovered* when the program that interprets it reaches the second right parenthesis, and some systems would send the user a message pointing to that position as the source of the error. But that is misleading in this case. There is not enough information available to know what was the cause of the error, only that there *was* an error. A likely possibility was that the user meant to write $X*(Z(I))$, but he or she could just as well have simply struck the ")" key twice, accidentally. Hence, program feedback that attempts to be too specific can be misleading. Probably the best response, in this case, would be a message stating that the parentheses were unbalanced, leaving it to the user to detected the specific error and correct it.

This computer programming example is representative of a wide range of systems in which it is possible for a computer to provide a great deal of help to a user for specific problems, often of a rather mechanical nature. These computer systems can detect errors and often suggest corrections, but they are limited in that they cannot anticipate what the user was trying to accomplish. Hence, they lack knowledge of the context in which an error was made, and this limits their ability to suggest the best remedial action.

The highest level of human-machine communication is that done without the need for interaction at the level of syntactic or mechanical detail. It is a communication of ideas. We do not include telephone conversation or the broadcasting of drama in this category because in these systems the idea communication is between people, not between a person and a machine. A common form of high-level human-machine interaction is in computer-assisted instruction (CAI), in which students' answers to questions about information found in prepared texts is analyzed by the machine, which then responds to the student in problem terms. While simple CAI systems may respond only with a right-or-wrong indication, more sophisticated ones use the cumulative record of student performance to indicate not just whether a given answer is right but the nature of the student's whole pattern of learning or failure to learn. A schematic representation of this mode of discourse is shown in Figure 3.8.

3.3.2 Style of Language

Another way to classify interactions is by the kind of language used by the human. For example, we can have the computer ask the user a series of multiple-choice questions, so that the "language" or user response is limited to the numbers of the choices. This is sometimes called a *menu* system: a limited set of predetermined choices is offered to the user, although several menus may be strung together in sequence.

The next level of language may be called, in the usage of CAI, *constructed response*. Here, the questions call for filling in the blanks: for example, NAME?————CITY?————COUNTRY?————. This form of language can pass much more information but also calls for more knowledge by the user and more elaborate software to check the validity of an item entered by a user. It is also more likely to permit an invalid entry to be accepted by the computer. For example, when we ask the user to enter NAME, CITY, and COUNTRY, we can probably verify the name of the country; that is, we can ascertain that it is on a list of names of countries known to the computer, even though there may be many variations, such as USA, U.S.A., United States, and so forth. The data element CITY is harder to deal with, there being so large a number of city or town names in the world. To expect a computer to verify the correct spelling of any personal name submitted to it is economically unfeasible.

The ultimate in human-computer communication is thought by many to be *natural language*. Whether entered through a keyboard or orally, this means that users are free to phrase their requests, commands, or answers any way they want. In general, the ability of a computer to comprehend natural language with no restrictions placed on it is limited. There are, however, a few systems, some experimental and some intended for practical use, that show signs of success (Harris, 1978).

FIGURE 3.8
A representation of complex human-machine interaction.

User action   ⟶   System assesses entire pattern of user history and responds in this context

3.4   THE SOCIAL IMPACT OF HUMAN-MACHINE COMMUNICATION

Whether dialling a telephone to make a single call or writing a natural-language question for a computer to answer, the way in which users communicate plays a major role in how effective they will be and in their attitude toward the system. Marshall McLuhan (1964) summed this up with his famous aphorism, "The medium is the message." The impact can go far beyond the performance of the immediate task at hand. It may affect the larger system of which the computer is a part, namely, users' attitudes toward use of the computer and communication systems, hence it affects the selection of tasks that users are willing to undertake. Finally, users' reactions to the interaction will affect their attitude toward the organization that provides the communicating machinery.

Effective human-machine communication requires a careful balance among four factors:

1 The level or ease of the task being performed, whether dialling a telephone or learning emergency medicine through CAI
2 The technical difficulty of achieving the desired level of interaction
3 The cost of a system
4 The negative impact on users of any failure to achieve the effectiveness goal

The first three points are fairly obvious. The fourth is akin to what happens in politics or management when people's expectations are encouraged to rise but promised performance is not delivered. A simple illustration is found in many computer systems which are interactive in that they may be used through an online connection but do not really interact with the user on content. They might simply announce the existence of errors and terminate their own operation. This tends to be much more frustrating to interactive users, because they *expect* more than do users who are simply submitting a card deck for a computer run later in the day.

Unless highly experienced in the particular system they are working with, users may not be able to distinguish between the keyboard, the communication system, or the computer software they are using, or, for that matter, between the mechanical system and the company that made or sponsors the system. At one time, the word *UNIVAC* was virtually a synonym for computer. Today, such usage is unlikely, but there are many users who think of a remote terminal as the computer or the telephone *instrument* as the telephone *system*. They may also see the bank's outdoor cash-dispensing teller machine as the bank. Thus, it behooves those who design or manage systems to bear in mind that remote access makes the whole company or service have the appearance of that user terminal—for better or worse.

REFERENCES

McLuhan, M. *Understanding Media: The Extensions of Man,* New York: New American Library, 1964.

Saint-Exupéry, A. de, *Wind, Sand and Stars,* 1939. Reprint. New York: Harcourt, Brace Jovanovich, 1967.

Harris, L. R., "ROBOT System: Natural Language Processing Applied to Data Base Query," *Proceedings of the Annual Conference of American Computer Manufacturers,* 1978, *2,* 165–172.

Turing, A. M., "Computing Machinery and Intelligence," *Mind,* 1950, *59,* 433. Reprinted in Feigenbaum, Edward, & Feldman (eds.), *Computers and Thought,* New York: McGraw-Hill, 1963.

RECOMMENDED READING

Badre, Albert, and Shneiderman, Ben (eds.), *Directions in Human/Computer Interaction,* Norwood, N.J.: Ablex Publishing Corp., 1982. (Covers research, experiments, and how-to advice on various aspects of human-computer interactive software. How to interact, as distinguished from how to compute, is a much-neglected consideration in software design.)

Meadow, Charles T., *Man-Machine Communication,* New York: Wiley-Interscience, 1970. (Written by the author of this chapter, whose view is biased, this is a not-too-technical review of how communication between computers and humans works, for example, how a graphic display is made and how a user constructs a graphic design.)

Newman, William N., and Sproull, Robert F., *Principles of Interactive Computer Graphics,* New York: McGraw-Hill Book Co., 1979. (Computer graphics have become far more sophisticated since the 1970 book. This is a computer person's view and of course more up to date.)

Raphael, Bertram, *The Thinking Computer,* San Francisco: W. H. Freeman, 1976. (A review of artificial intelligence methods and applications, not overly technical.)

Sager, Naomi, *A Computer Grammar of English and Its Applications,* Reading, Mass.: Addison-Wesley, 1981. (An advanced work for those interested in computer understanding of natural language.)

Salton, Gerard, and McGill, Michael J., *Introduction to Modern Information Retrieval,* New York: McGraw-Hill Book Co., 1983. (Modern information retrieval is a highly interactive process. Here is a review of that field. Salton is a pioneer researcher in interactive retrieval.)

Smith, H. T., and Green, T. R. G. (eds.), *Human Interaction with Computers,* London and New York: Academic Press, 1980. (A collection of research writings in the field of human-computer interaction.)

Thomas, John, and Schneider, Michael (eds.), *Human Factors in Computer Systems,* Norwood, N.J.: Ablex Publishing Corps., 1983. (The psychological aspects of the use of computers—both hardware and software.)

Weizenbaum, Joseph, *Computer Power and Human Reason,* San Francisco: W. H. Freeman Co., 1976. (There is another side to artificial intelligence. Weizenbaum questions what can and should be done.)

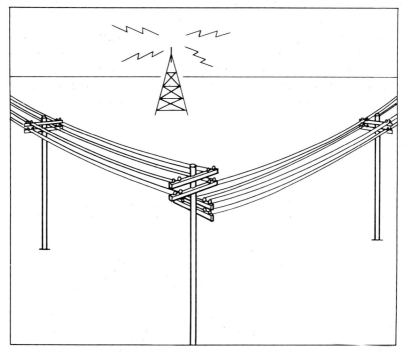

Chapter 4: Transmission

Chapter 5: The Telephone System

PART **TWO**

BASIC TECHNOLOGY

The chapters in this part describe the basic technology underlying most of the telecommunication systems of today. Chapter 4 covers transmission systems—various technologies for performing the essential task of telecommunication, that of moving information from point to point or point to area. Some of the topics from Chapter 2 are dealt with in greater depth. Chapter 5 describes the telephone system. While the telephone is an application of telecommunications, rather than an underlying technology, the worldwide system built to carry telephone messages became the carrier for most other major telecommunications systems as well. Although the degree of this dependence is now being reduced, network radio and television and digital computer networks still rely heavily on the telephone system. Chapter 6 is concerned with digital communication networks, the telecommunication phenomena that have enabled the booming use of remote computing. The final chapter of this part covers a particular form of network important to personal computer users—the local area network.

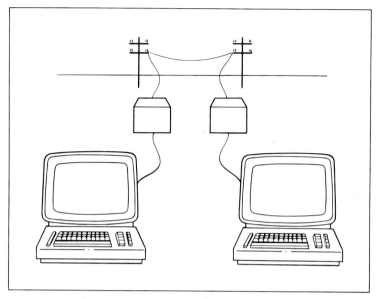

Chapter 6: Digital Communications Networks

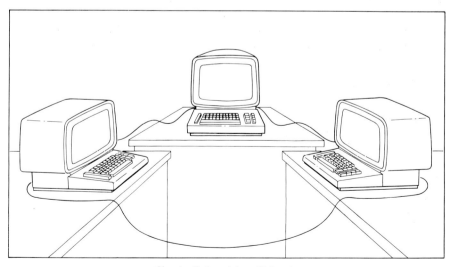

Chapter 7: Local Area Networks

CHAPTER 4

TRANSMISSION SYSTEMS

Herbert S. Dordick
Ronald E. Rice
Annenberg School of Communications
University of Southern California
Los Angeles, CA 90089

4.1 INTRODUCTION

When Agamemnon returned victorious from the Trojan War with his mistress Cassandra in tow, large mountaintop fires transmitted the news from Troy to Mycenae. This warning gave his queen, Clytemnestra, and her lover time to plot his murder. And in 490 B.C. an unknown courier ran the 26.4 miles from Marathon to Athens to signal the Athenians' victory over the Persians, thereby delivering a message and creating a media event. Somewhat more recently, the lantern lights on the Old North Church signaled to Paul Revere that the British were coming, and off he rode to warn the Minutemen.

By the 1800s, the Russians had extended semaphore telegraphy—then consisting of blades arranged on mountaintops—1200 miles, from Leningrad to the Prussian frontier. Each arrangement of the blades was confirmed for accuracy and sent back by the next station to avoid signaling errors, a very slow process. A Parisian, Charles Havas, gained considerable advantage over his journalistic competitors by using homing pigeons to deliver news from London in 7 hours. Although the homing pigeons in today's *Andy Capp* cartoon reflect his laziness, they've been most efficiently used to transmit battlefield information since the Roman era and helped Havas start the forerunner of the worldwide French press agency, Agence France Presse.

The legendary pony express was able to deliver information from St. Joseph's, Missouri, to San Francisco in 8 days if the riders escaped the Indians.

This exciting adventure in transmission by human and pony lasted only 19 months, until October 1861, when the Pacific Telegraph Company completed *its* transmission route. This is probably one of our earliest examples of the productivity of electrical communications technology; both riders and ponies were laid off!

Transmission systems have been with us throughout history. Indeed, there is no "history" before the ability to transmit knowledge of the past. These systems all have their own advantages and disadvantages, uses, and symbolic import; McLuhan's dictum that the medium is the message holds for both old and new transmission systems. Receiving a telegram nowadays in the United States has more emotional impact than receiving a telephone call. In some places in Europe, the reverse is true.

The purpose of this chapter is to discuss transmission systems. But we will emphasize electromagnetic, typically point-to-point, and instantaneous communications. Thus, we will not consider mass media such as books and newspapers or radio and television in the popular sense. It is often difficult to separate the "system" from the media used because in modern transmissions the arriving content often travels through many channels and at many rates, which can differ each time the message is transmitted and retransmitted.

First we will consider several of the basic terms of transmission that were introduced in Chapter 2, including noise, bandwidth, frequency, and analog and digital transmission. This discussion is followed by an explanation of modulation and multiplexing techniques for both digital and analog transmission. After an overview of networks and switching techniques, we will briefly introduce the major transmission systems. Finally, we will compare various attributes of these systems.

4.2 BASIC TRANSMISSION FACTORS

4.2.1 Noise

The time required for any electrical operation such as turning a current on or off is proportional to certain physical characteristics of the cable or wire. When a voltage is impressed on the wire at one end, it does not immediately appear at the other; it increases from 0 to the maximum value as the capacity of the wire or cable is charged up.

If the voltage at the transmitting end is impressed and taken away in too short a time, a very small or hardly noticeable voltage change will appear at the receiver. The signal may not be *detectable*. No signal is detected unless it is larger than a certain *threshold*. The threshold is determined both by the sensitivity of the receiving apparatus and by the magnitude of the spurious fluctuations—*noise* —which always occur on any communications channel. If it is less than the noise at the receiving end, the signal will pass undetected. Many of the major developments in communications technology over the past 30 years, including the satellite and the microprocessor, have focused on how to insure that the information sent is accurately received and, of course, economically transmitted.

One way to reduce the cost of transmission is to increase the speed of transmission. But two factors limit the speed of communications:

1 There is always noise in the communication channel. The received signal must be a certain degree larger than the spurious fluctuations owing to noise. Noise is caused by *distortion* (in the transmission system), *interference* (from extraneous but similar signals), and *random fluctuations*.

2 The received signal is always *attenuated;* that is, the received signal is always less than the transmitted signal. If the signal is attenuated too much it will not be detected through the noise.

A quantity which has been found to be very useful is a function of the logarithm of the signal power S divided by the noise power N. This quantity is usually measured in decibels as

$$\text{Signal-to-noise ratio} = 10 \log_{10} S/N$$

A signal-to-noise ratio of 10 dB means that the signal power is 10 times the noise power. A signal-to-noise ratio of 20 dB means that the signal power is 100 times the noise power. A ratio of -3 dB means that the signal power is half the noise power.

4.2.2 Bandwidth and Frequency

Bandwidth is an extremely important characteristic of a signal because the cost of its transmission is fundamentally dependent on its bandwidth. Generally speaking, higher bandwidth signals cost more to transmit. More information sent in a shorter time period requires greater bandwidth. Thus, both bandwidth and the signal-to-noise ratio constrain the system's information rate, or *capacity*. Frequency, and thus bandwidth, are measured in cycles (of the sine wave) per second, called Hertz, as discussed in Chapter 2.

Frequency is the number of cycles that an electromagnetic wave makes per second. The wave can be thought of as a sinusoidal wave, that is, a wave that goes from a peak to a valley and back to the peak in one cycle. The sinusoidal waveform is the waveform that a pendulum makes as it swings from side to side. It is nature's favorite motion.

Amplitude is the height of the cycle at the top of the waveform. It is a measure of the strength of the electrical signal.

Most telecommunications signals, such as voice or television or data, are made up of many waves of different frequencies. The difference between the highest of these frequencies and the lowest of these frequencies is the *bandwidth* of the signal. A signal may have a natural range or bandwidth; the transmission medium may allow only some of this bandwidth; or regulations may allow only portions of a natural bandwidth to be transmitted.

So, frequency equals the number of cycles per unit time, or $F = N/T$.

Conversely, $T = N/F$. Relationships between frequency, time, bandwidth and amplitude for three transmission conditions are shown in Figure 4.1.

Table 4.1 shows the bandwidths for some common signals.

FIGURE 4.1

Relationships among frequency, cycles, amplitude, and time.

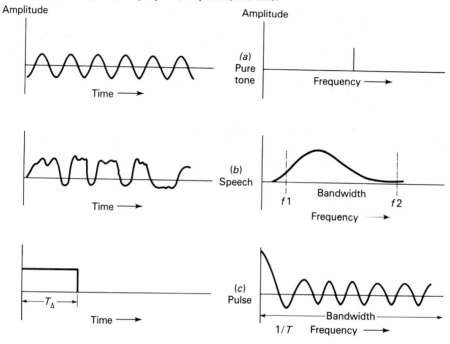

TABLE 4.1
BANDWIDTHS OF SOME COMMON SIGNALS

Signal	Bandwidth*
Telegraphy	40 Hz
Speech	4000 Hz, or 4 KHz
Hi-fi music	20,000 KHz
Color television	6 million Hz, or 6 MHz
Satellite (recent)	500 million Hz, or 0.5 GHz

*1000 hertz = 1 kilohertz; 1 million hertz = 1 megahertz; 1 billion hertz = 1 giga hertz.

Most signals contain significant components at only a small range of frequencies, but theoretically any signal with a definite beginning, that is, a sharp start, and a definite end has some component frequencies up to infinity and most of these frequencies have very small amplitudes, that is, very small power. This means, of course, that pulses such as those in a telegraph signal have numerous frequency components, and although the telegraph signal may look like a dot or a dash, a bandwidth of 40 Hz is required for accurate telegraph transmission.

From Figure 4.1(*c*) we can see that a pulse of length T has significant frequencies up to $1/T$. Thus if the pulse is shorter, that is, T is very small, a *larger* bandwidth will be required to transmit that pulse. But because bandwidth is expensive we often send signals through *filters*, which pass only a specific band of frequencies. We do that on the telephone so that the human voice, which has an enormous range of frequencies, is passed through a filter, which only allows a range of about 30 to 3400 Hz. This has been found to be quite sufficient for voice recognition and understanding. But in many countries where the telephone system bandwidth is not quite that large, it is often difficult to understand, let alone recognize, a voice by the sound alone.

A different use of the term "bandwidth" concerns the form of human communication transmitted. Print (including electronic messaging) can transmit only *linguistic* or semantic information; audio can also transmit *paralinguistic* cues such as laughter or loudness; video can further communicate *kinesic* information such as body posture and fleeting nonverbal signs; while interpersonal interaction also communicates *proxemics* such as physical closeness. These dimensions of human communication require greater bandwidth than simple transmission of text or voice alone.

4.2.3 Analog and Digital Transmission

Electrical signals are created for the purpose of sending information. *Analog* signals are signals that are "analogous" to the information; that is, they reflect the characteristics of the information to be transmitted. Thus, when you speak into the telephone, the carbon microphone vibrates as your voice vibrates and creates a signal that is analogous to your voice. The telephone typically uses analog transmission.

For a variety of reasons it is useful to digitize the signal or break it up into many pieces by sampling the original signal. The number of pieces depends on the frequency of the signal, acceptable error rate, and other factors, described below. *Digital* signals are transmitted in this manner. In modern telecommunications systems using digital transmission, each sampled signal is assigned a binary number (0 or 1).

4.3 MODULATION AND MULTIPLEXING

4.3.1 Transmitting Discrete Signals

When you broadcast a signal from one place to another there is a transmitting antenna in which a signal originates, and at a distance there is a receiving antenna or wire in which a signal is produced, similar to but weaker than in the originating wire. To transmit a telegraph signal over the air we need to produce a changing signal in our first wire; we do this with an underlying signal, or *carrier*. The carrier is in the form of sinusoidal signal and it can be made to transmit Morse code simply by turning it on and off, as shown in Figure 4.2c.

Let us now see how we send a telegraph signal (4.2a) over the air. Following the digital terminology of binary notation, we label the dash 1 and the dot 0. We know that the transmitted signal will be somewhat distorted even before it gets into the transmission system; it must pass through some wires and other devices before it combines with the carrier. So in Figure 4.2b we see the familiar shape of a signal that has been distorted by certain losses. In Figure 4.2c we see what happens when our signal is combined with or superimposed on the underlying carrier; this is called *modulation* and is the process of impressing information on the carrier in a form suited to its distribution channel. *Demodulation* is the process that recovers the original signal from the transformed one for delivery to the receiver.

Modulation is designed to match the signal transmitted to channel attributes. This matching may involve (1) matching the signal wavelength to the antenna; (2) reducing noise and interference, sometimes at the cost of larger bandwidth; (3) assigning frequencies unique to the source; or (4) overcoming limitations in the equipment by putting the signal in a more tractable frequency (Thoma, 1981).

The carrier is mediated by turning it on and off. This modulation technique is called on-off keying (OOK). We are changing the amplitude of the carrier from 1 to 0; thus on-off keying is a form of *amplitude modulation*. It is the AM on your radio and is an important way of transmitting voice.

Now assume that there is some noise on the transmission line. In Figure 4.2e we show what happens when the now noisy signal is *demodulated*, or separated from the carrier; that is, "decoded" from the previously "encoded" signal

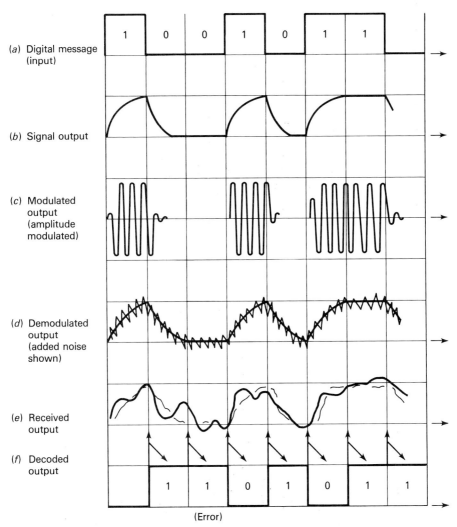

FIGURE 4.2
Noise and signal transmission.

resulting from the modulation process. This is done by a process of *filtering*. Figure 4.2f shows what the receiver sends on to the instrument the recipient will be using to read the message sent. This device is known as a *detector* because it is able to pick out the 1s and 0s from the filtered (but as-yet-not-ready) message for the recipient. Note that in Figure 4.2f the presence of noise leads to errors. One of the transmitted 0s—the second bit—is received as a 1!

Another method of sending pulses is to vary the frequency of the underlying signal or carrier as shown in Figure 4.3. The lower frequency would represent a 0, and the higher frequency a 1. This kind of modulation is referred to as

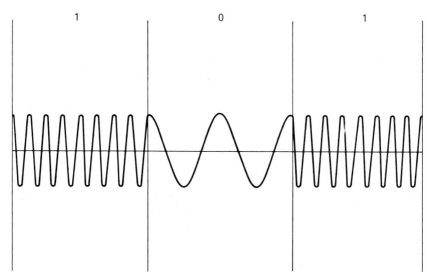

FIGURE 4.3
Frequency-shift keying.

frequency-shift keying (FSK). It is a form of frequency modulation, which is the basis of high fidelity music systems. Frequency-modulated (FM) signals are less sensitive to noise than are amplitude-modulated signals. Thus, the probability of an error is less, and consequently they are often used for data communications. But FM systems are more complicated to build and somewhat more expensive. The ability to send data via a digital signal over the telephone, which is not a digital system, is made possible through FSK.

There is a third technique for indicating a 1 or 0, involving changing the *phase* of the carrier signal, rather than its amplitude or frequency. Put simply, this involves altering the time when the signal starts moving. Note that in Figure 4.3 the 1 and 0 signals begin at the same point in the same shape of the carrier, at the top of the curve. But if we begin the 0 at the bottom of the curve and the 1 at the top, the signal is shifted to the right for the 0 and effectively to the left for the 1, as in Figure 4.4. *Phase-shift keying* (PSK) is even more immune to noise than is FSK but requires more complex equipment and is more expensive.

4.3.2   Transmitting Continuous (Analog) Signals

Modulation   Up to now we have been discussing systems for sending a discrete number of signals. What about sending more complicated signals, such as voice or television?

When we speak or sing our vocal tract produces sound waves. These waves are very complex, unlike the single frequency of a tuning fork. We can "compose" this very complicated voice signal by adding up a number of simple

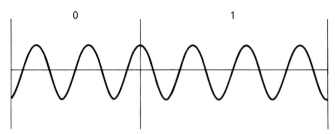

FIGURE 4.4
Phase shift keying.

standard signals, our familiar sine waves as described in Chapter 2 and shown in Figure 4.1a. The representation of a signal in terms of amplitudes, frequencies, and phases of its sinusoidal components is called *frequency-domain representation*. The sinusoidal signals in the sum all have different frequencies, and the range of values of frequencies (that is, the difference between the highest and the lowest frequencies) is, as we've discussed, called the *bandwidth* of the signal. Figure 4.5 shows how a voice signal is really made up of a number of component signals (F_n through F_{n-6}) and thus requires bandwidth in the amount of $F_n - F_{n-6}$.

Different communication channels transmit signals best at different frequencies. If we take the voice pressure of two people speaking to each other, transform it with a telephone microphone, and try to send it through the air, we would find it extremely difficult. For one, we would need very large devices (antennas) and an enormous amount of power. We have to somehow alter the

FIGURE 4.5
Bandwidth and frequency components of a voice signal.

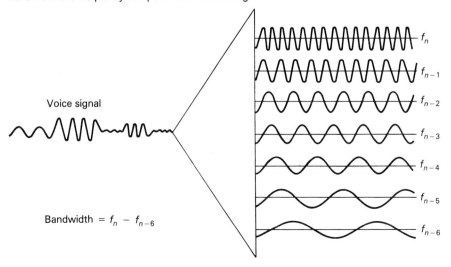

"air," if you will, and make it more amenable for the transmission of speech, or frequencies in the neighborhood of 30 Hz to 3400 Hz, an alteration we have already defined as *modulation.*

Earlier, in Figure 4.2c, we showed the process by which a digital signal is transformed by modulation and recovered by means of demodulation. Now we consider modulation in terms of analog rather than digital signals.

Figure 4.6 shows how the signal modulates the higher-frequency carrier, resulting in a modulated carrier. This is really a curious way of putting it. It would seem that the signal is modulated by the carrier, hence we say, the modulated signal. In effect, it makes little difference because what is transmitted is a modulated signal where the original signal is in the *amplitude envelope* of the modulated carrier, as shown in Figure 4.6c.

Now if we shift to the frequency domain (Figure 4.7), amplitude modulation corresponds to *shifting* the frequency of the signal. Note that the effect of multiplying the carrier amplitude by the signal, which is what we do when we modulate a carrier with a signal, or a signal with a carrier, is to produce a new signal with frequency components above and below the carrier.

The frequencies above and below the carrier, as shown on either side of the carrier in Figure 4.7c, are called the *sidebands.* In recent years engineers have learned how to use these sidebands to transmit two different signals, thereby making more efficient use of valuable bandwidth or spectrum. For example,

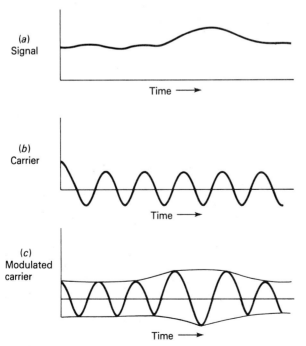

(a)
Signal

Time ⟶

(b)
Carrier

Time ⟶

(c)
Modulated
carrier

Time ⟶

FIGURE 4.6
Amplitude modulation and amplitude envelope (in time domain).

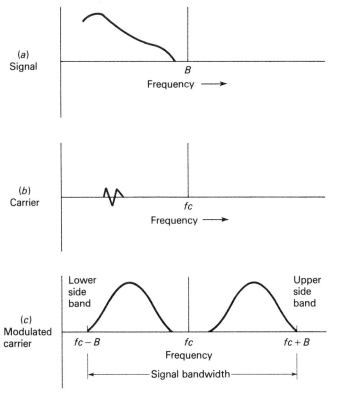

FIGURE 4.7
Amplitude modulation and frequency sidebands (in frequency domain).

agricultural and weather teletext information could be transmitted to rural farmers via the sideband of the local National Oceanic and Atmospheric Administration stations (Rice & Paisley, 1982).

The bandwidth of the resultant FM signal is more difficult to calculate than that for the AM signal. In the latter, distance between the sidebands and bandwidth can be conserved by using only one of the sidebands without losing the information in the signal. But in the case of frequency modulation, bandwidth depends on how much we choose to vary the frequency as the amplitude of the signal changes. In FM radio, stations generally choose to occupy about 150 Hz of bandwidth around their assigned frequency.

In frequency modulation the carrier *frequency* is varied with changes in the amplitude of the signal. In Figure 4.8*a* the modulating signal is a triangular one, called by engineers, for obvious reasons, a sawtooth wave. We must first produce an amplitude-modulated carrier, as shown in Figure 4.8*b,* and use it to create a frequency-modulated carrier, as in Figure 4.8*c.*

How do we choose between AM and FM? What are the benefits and drawbacks of each? Here are some general rules of thumb:

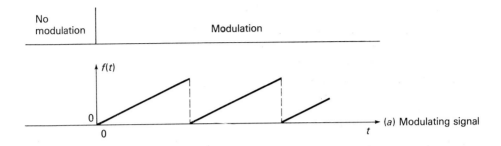

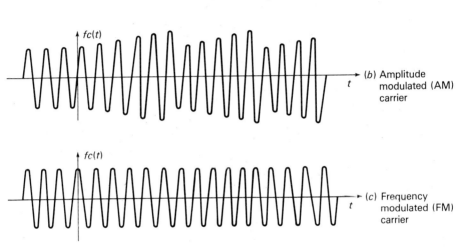

FIGURE 4.8
Amplitude and frequency modulation of signal.

• In FM the bandwidth can be increased and the signal-to-noise ratio improved without increasing signal power.
• In AM the signal-to-noise ratio can only be increased by sending a more powerful signal.
• FM receivers are somewhat more complicated than AM receivers and, consequently, more costly.
• AM transmitters are more difficult to build than higher-frequency FM transmitters.

So take your pick of benefits and costs. With the continuing reduction in the cost of electronic components, the difference in price between FM and AM receivers has become quite small, but the cost of transmission has continued to rise. Yet if a great many signals can be packed into a channel the transmission cost per signal could be low. This might favor AM, but at a cost of power.

Multiplexing Several times we have mentioned the possibility of sending more than one signal on a channel at the same time. This can be done by shifting the frequency of the signal, thereby giving each signal a different part of the channel space, or spectrum. The process of putting several signals on one channel is called *multiplexing*.

Each signal can be recovered by *demultiplexing*, which separates the various signals so that we can demodulate the signal we are after. Separating these signals is done by filtering, a process that removes the unwanted signals and leaves us with the signal, the only signal, we wish to receive. This is exactly what happens when we tune our radio or TV set. We select one of the several frequencies that are available or broadcast, by means of the demultiplexing, demodulating, and filtering processes.

If it were not possible to multiplex, our telephone systems would require an enormous number of wires, which, given the present cost of copper, would be extremely expensive. Even with extensive switching systems, we would still require a large number of wires, one for each potential simultaneous conversation between two points.

This multiplexing of signals allows for fewer wires between major population centers. Indeed, because variations in population density make telephone traffic density very different in different parts of the country it is uneconomical to provide a facility for, say, 600 channels with only 10 to 20 channels in use. But a single 600-channel system costs less than fifty 12-channel systems, owing to savings in the number of transmission lines and amplifiers. Thus, there is a need for a number of transmission systems, each optimized for a particular channel capacity. This is made possible by the technique of multiplexing. But as we increase the number of signals, we use up more and more of our precious bandwidth.

There are other ways to multiplex signals that are now becoming very popular primarily because the semiconductor chip has made equipment available that can rapidly *sample* analog signals, thereby turning them into candidates for digital transmission without seriously destroying the accuracy of the message being communicated.

Sampling We have seen how we can modulate the amplitude of a sinusoidal carrier with a signal in order to transmit it more easily. And we have seen how we can recover the original signal. We can also modulate the amplitude of *pulses*. This ability to use pulses to describe a wave form is at the heart of modern data communications. In Figure 4.9 we can see that the input signal is pretty well reflected in the modulated signal, yet there are spaces between the pulses. What if we could fill the spaces with other pulses that represent other analog signals? Wouldn't that allow us to send many different signals on the same channel?

To do so and still maintain the accuracy of the original signal at the receiving

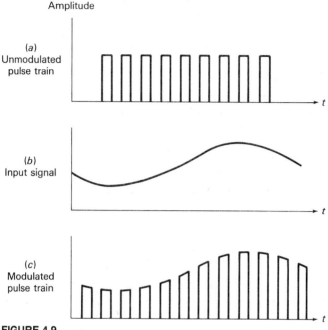

FIGURE 4.9
Pulse amplitude modulation.

end has three important requirements. First, we must determine the sampling rate, that is, the number of pulses per second we need in order to represent the signal accurately. Second, we must have the equipment that can perform this sampling rapidly and accurately. And third, we must have the facilities to recapture the original signal from the pulses accurately and, of course, in the analog form we need in order to interpret the message.

So we have turned this discussion around—from how the amplitude of pulses can be modulated to how an analog signal can be sampled for other types of modulation.

Pulse-Amplitude Modulation   Figure 4.10 shows what happens when we transmit an analog signal at different sampling rates. If we sample at a very low rate it is clear that the original signal will not likely be reproduced; or it may be reproduced in some very imaginative but inaccurate ways. Remember, the signal is not a straight line that can be determined or defined by just two points. We can increase the sampling rate by 50 percent by the adding of another point on the curve or another sample. It is more likely that the original signal will be recognizable, but there still is a great deal of room for imagination. Finally we can greatly increase the sampling rate—say, by a factor of 100. The original signal is then very clearly and quite accurately reproduced. However, sampling

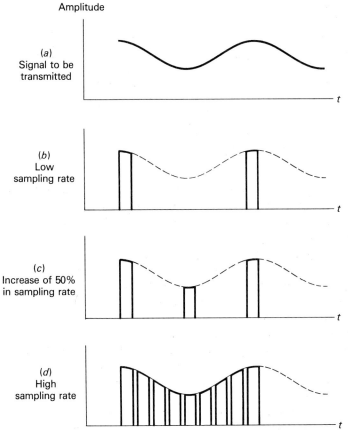

Amplitude

(a)
Signal to be
transmitted

(b)
Low
sampling rate

(c)
Increase of 50%
in sampling rate

(d)
High
sampling rate

FIGURE 4.10
Sampling for pulse amplitude modulation.

at an extremely high rate adds little to the quality of the signal. And with sampling at a very low rate we risk missing some of the variations in the signal. The key requirement is that the sampling rate, or pulse rate, be at least *twice* the highest frequency of the signal itself. For a TV signal of 6 MHz we must sample at a rate of at least 12 MHz.

Once we have the train of pulses that represent the transmitted signal, we can use this train to modulate a carrier, which will transmit the signal. This form of modulation is very similar to amplitude modulation, except that we are modulating a train of pulses rather than a sinusoid; it is called *pulse-amplitude modulation* (PAM).

Time-Division Multiplexing   As we noted previously, there are spaces between the pulses in our pulse-amplitude train. These unused spaces in time can be used to send samples of another signal or, for that matter, many signals.

Multiplexing signals in this way is called *time-division multiplexing* (TDM). *Time-division multiplexing* and *frequency-division multiplexing* are two fundamentally different ways to divide up the capacity of a channel among several messages or conversations. The latter essentially divides up a fixed narrow bandwidth continuously, while the former allocates a wider bandwidth for short periods of time. In Figure 4.11 we represent these ways of using time.

Remember that the bandwidth necessary to send a pulse-amplitude-modulated (PAM) signal depends on the width of the pulse. For a pulse of width *T,* the bandwidth is proportional to $1/T$. In order to use TDM on many signals, if we use very short pulses we must use larger bandwidths.

PAM systems are relatively simple and have become very attractive for many data transmission situations as well as for sending multiple voice signals along a single channel. PAM systems are not to be confused with digital systems; they are not completely digital, since the amplitudes of the pulses transmitted vary continously with the original analog signal variations. Very often the PAM signals are further digitized before transmission. The digital signals are encoded into any equivalent form desired.

Quantization   The process of digitizing the original PAM signals is called *quantization.* It consists of breaking the amplitudes of the PAM signals up into a prescribed number of discrete amplitude levels. Unlike the sampling process that produced the PAM signal, this results in an irretrievable (but usually inconsequential) loss of information distinguishing fine amplitude variations, since it is

FIGURE 4.11
Time and frequency division multiplexing.

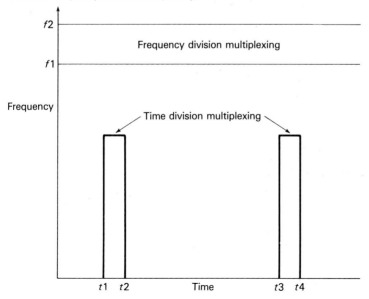

impossible to reconstitute the original analog signal from its quantized version.

The demodulated signal will differ from the derived signal and the overall effect will appear as noise. In the case of sound transmission this manifests itself as background crackle. In the case of picture transmission the continuous gradation of grays from black to white is replaced by a discrete number of grays and the picture will also look a bit noisy. This *quantization noise* can be reduced by increasing the sampling rate or by increasing the number of levels M used. Experiments have shown that 8 to 16 levels appear to be sufficient for good intelligibility of speech.

One form of TDM is pulse-code modulation.

Pulse-Code Modulation   If we transmit these quantized signal samples as pulses of varying heights, we would merely have PAM, or quantized PAM. But with discrete or numbered voltage levels each level can be coded in some arbitrary way before transmission. The ability to code these signals once they are in some quantized form allows for very highly efficient use of transmission bandwidth. This method of signal modulation is called *pulse-code modulation* (PCM).

Coding is important in data transmission for at least one significant reason; it provides the best way we know of overcoming the problem of noise. All a receiver has to do when it is listening for a binary-coded signal is to recognize the presence or absence of a pulse. The shape of the pulse is not important, just its presence or absence! Indeed, the exact amplitude is unimportant. By transmitting binary pulses of high enough amplitude we can ensure correct detection of the pulse in the presence of noise with as low an error rate as required.

Pulse-coded modulation has another benefit over other forms of modulation. As a signal is transmitted through some channel the signal becomes weaker, while noise tends to increase; the signal-to-noise ratio gets worse and worse. But with PCM transmission it is possible to place very simple devices known as pulse-regenerator circuits at intervals along the line spaces close enough to insure that the signal-to-noise ratio is fairly high at each circuit. The circuit must only determine whether a pulse is present and then regenerate a perfect pulse or, if there is no pulse present, regenerate no signal at all. The signal-to-noise ratio does not change between transmission and reception, a most important feature of PCM transmission.

An example of PCM is shown in Figure 4.12, using three different messages. We sample each of these message signals at different times and then put all of these pulses together in a string, or train. If each of these signals is of a different bandwidth, sampling will have to be at the rate determined by the signal with the *largest* bandwidth.

4.4   NETWORKS AND SWITCHING

In this section we concentrate primarily on transmission concepts and systems, leaving the bulk of the discussion concerning switching to Chapter 5. We shall,

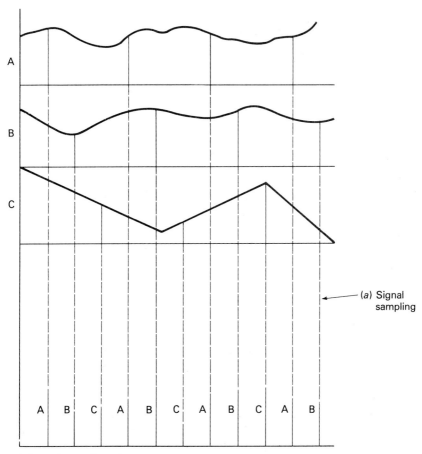

(a) Signal sampling

(b) Resultant pulse train

FIGURE 4.12
Pulse code modulation.

however, conclude this section with a brief discussion of some basic switching concepts that bear directly on the transmission of signals.

4.4.1   Networks

Establishing system performance at a given cost is constrained by the desired error rate (or subjective reception quality), bandwidth, transmission speed, and network configuration (Thoma, 1981). Network "architectures" are, in one sense, designed to accommodate different levels of system usage. For example, the telephone system was initially designed for voice conversations, which involve infrequent node usage and gaps in actual transmission through a physical circuit for the duration of the call. This requires a bandwidth of only 3 KHz or so, insufficient by itself for efficient data transmission. Packet-switched networks, designed specifically for high-speed data transmission, provide efficient, reliable routing among dispersed nodes, not by an assigned physical circuit. A variety of network topologies have developed over time to connect nodes (people, locations, etc.) in appropriate ways. Conceptually, the simplest network topology would be to provide a switch for all possible nodes (a "point-to-point" network). For n nodes, this means $n(n - 1)$ switches, or 90 switches for 10 people. Figure 4.13 shows various network configurations. A centrally switched network (a star) dramatically reduces the number of switches and the amount of linkage but requires a highly reliable and complex switch. A ring structure simply connects all nodes in a circle, which reduces errors but requires some sort of bypass at each node to lessen the ring's vulnerability to failure. A bus topology is less vulnerable to failure, since repeaters are not required at each node, as in the ring, and the bus is easily reconfigurable. But errors can be mistaken as message collisions in applications such as local area networks. The arrangement of equipment on the network is the *architecture* of the network. In practice, several of these networks are connected together to form the communication system. You might want the information to flow in a specific order, from one level to another. This system of providing levels of networks is the network *hierarchy;* it is a concept, a way of structuring the architecture.

FIGURE 4.13
Network configurations.

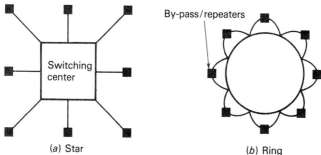

(a) Star   (b) Ring

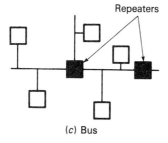

(c) Bus

4.4.2 The Public-Switched Network

The nation's telephone network is a public-switched network. Because it evolved over many years and through the development of many transmission technologies it provides an excellent opportunity to examine and compare the many modes of transmission now available for the delivery of information electronically. The network consists of three major transmission systems. A fourth is now emerging and cannot yet be considered a full member of the network, but over the next decade or so it may become a full-fledged member of the public-switched network. These four systems are discussed below.

The Local-Loop Transmission System The local-loop transmission system is the network that connects the household through the telephone headset into the local exchanges and from there to the long-distance system of transmission. Until now the major mode of transmission has been the twisted pair—telephone lines—but in recent years cable television systems have been claiming that they can also provide local-loop services. Several experimental projects have, indeed, shown that with special care and at somewhat higher cost than is required for the one-way video transmission for which cable television has been designed, it is possible to provide local-loop transmission for voice and data through the cable system. We shall discuss cable as a transmission medium in the next section.

Another candidate for local-loop services is radio, especially in the form of cellular radio. We shall also discuss this transmission medium in the next section.

Line-Haul Transmission System Line-haul long-distance, or *trunk,* circuits refer to the transmission paths needed to carry a subscriber-to-subscriber connection between local exchanges to which all subscribers are connected by local loops.

Over long distances signals are attenuated and distorted as we saw in Section 4.2 above. At some point along the long line the signal could fall dangerously near the noise in the system and be lost entirely (Figure 4.14a). If we increase or amplify the signal at points along the line, we will increase the power of both the signal and the noise (Figure 4.14b). If we choose the right time to do this, the signal will always be greater than the noise.

Figure 4.14 shows what happens to analog signals; the repeaters are amplifiers like those in your high fidelity and radio systems. But with the advent of digital systems we cannot use amplifiers; instead we use *regenerators.*

The principle of a regenerator is quite simple; since a digitized voice signal has only two levels, unlike the analog signal which can have an infinite number of levels, the digital signal can be 1 or 0 only. These signals can easily be detected. As soon as the regenerator knows that a 1 (a signal) has come down the line, no matter how weak the signal, it immediately pops forth with another one. Since noise is quite different from the well-formed 1s and 0s, the regenerator simply avoids the noise, which is effectively suppressed in the retransmission. Regene-

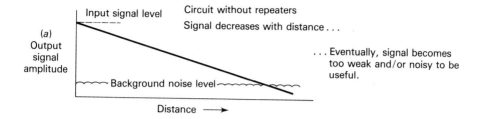

(a)
signal
amplitude

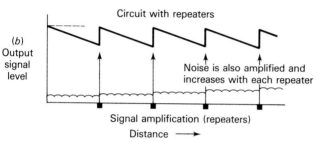

(b)
signal
level

FIGURE 4.14
Signal attenuation.

rators are usually spaced close enough to insure reliable detection, at about one mile apart for a 24- or 30-channel line-haul—trunk or long-line—system.

Because the parameters of the transmission line may distort the distinction between the 1s and 0s of the digital pulse, you could receive an almost level signal which would appear as a changing direct current, one which would be very difficult to detect. For this reason line-haul signals use *bipolar* signaling in which alternate 1s are sent with opposite polarity, as shown in Figure 4.15.

Because the use of regenerators or amplifiers in a circuit means that signals can only travel in one direction, line-haul transmission lines must have four wires

FIGURE 4.15
Bipolar coding.

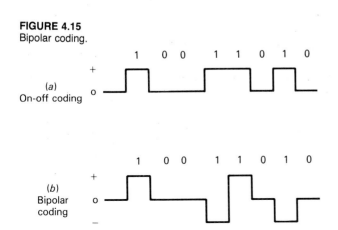

(a)
On-off coding

(b)
Bipolar
coding

or two circuits—one in each direction—for two-way communication. Local loops are two-wire and bidirectional, and it is necessary to convert between these circuits and the four-wire circuits needed in the line-haul or long-line circuits. The device to do this is called a *hybrid* and is illustrated in Figure 4.16.

Sometimes there is leakage across the hybrid and echos appear. *Echo suppressors* are voice-actuated switching devices used at each end of a four-wire circuit. They operate on the principle that when one party in a conversation is talking, the other one is listening and does not need a talking path until the roles of the two parties are reversed. In this way the echo loop is broken.

Local-Area Networks Described in more detail in Chapters 6 and 7, local-area networks (LANs) are being developed for intraorganizational transmission of multiple multiplexed channels (voice mail, telephone, data, video, electronic messaging, etc.) with programmable communication processing. We discuss them here because these networks can just as easily be used between geographically dispersed facilities of an organization and consequently could replace the local-loop network. Furthermore, cable television is currently being tested as a LAN. They allow the interconnection of otherwise incompatible peripherals without separate wired circuits for each. LANs provide these services in a *decentrailized* mode, while local private branch exchanges (PBXs) or mainframe computers can provide the services in a *centralized* switching mode. One mode of transmission access uses a *token loop,* whereby a node waits for an electronic token to approach and then transmits the message in burst mode, followed by the token to prevent overlapping messages. LAN transmission media include *fiber optics;* cable in what is called the *base-band* mode (50 megabits per second (Mbps), 2 km range—half-duplex primarily for data) and cable in the *broadband* mode (140 Mbps, 15 km range—full-duplex primarily for video and integrated services). Hybrids are already emerging, and although corporations are still treading lightly, LANs are the key for the integrated office of the future. Xerox's Ethernet and Wang's Wangnet are competing for early

FIGURE 4.16
The use of hybrids in long-haul switched networks.

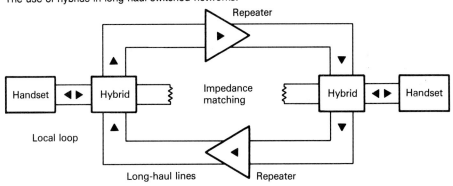

dominance in local-area networks, and IBM's entry will likely set the standards, although there are already over 12,000 personal computer local networks using the local loop of the telephone network.

The Telegraph-Transmission System   Morse is known for the development of modern telegraphy in 1837, although Wheatstone and Gohe in England also made primary contributions. Indeed electrical telegraphy was first suggested in 1753. The first public telegram was sent in 1844; soon Edison demonstrated sending messages in each direction. Modern carrier modulation makes possible the transmission of several hundred simultaneous messages. The first use of microwave transmission of telegrams, between New York and Philadelphia, showed the advantages of such technology over telegraph wires. Indeed, 18 telegraph circuits can also be sent over one telephone voice circuit; with time-division multiplexing, the number rises to nearly 200. However, even though telegraphy requires only one line (the circuit is closed by grounding to the earth), the traditional use of two wires for telephone maintains telegraph tariffs at artificially high levels. Further, modern telegraphy typically allows immediate printout by the receiving station and does not even use Morse code! Facsimile is one kind of automatic telegraphy, whereby differential current impulses transmit the intensity of shading in the original document.

The telegraph never achieved the reach in the United States that it has in Europe. Telephone quickly overtook telegraph in the United States, while in Europe switched telegraph or telex has become a major transmission system. In the United States automatic telegraphy or facsimile currently uses telephone lines, as does the telegraph. As modern telephone systems become digital, we can expect fully digital facsimile in the manner of high-speed data transmission.

4.4.3   Basic Switching Concepts

The details of modern switching will be fully discussed in Chapter 5. Here, we shall define the three general types of switching found in today's telecommunication systems (Dordick, Bradley, & Nanus, 1983).

Line-switched systems, also called circuit-switched systems, are analogous to the POTS (Plain Old Telephone Services) network, in which routing is set up prior to message transmission. The circuit is then engaged for the duration of the call. This type of network provides the lowest possible transport delay and, with the development of highly reliable digital networks, has the potential of offering relatively error-free transmission through the use of multiplexing.

Message-switched systems were developed largely to overcome the problems of error generation attendant upon the use of analog lines for digital messages. In message-switched systems, messages from each terminal are received at a buffer, which stores the transmission until it is complete. When the entire message has been received, it is sent to a concentrator, where it is given an address and coded for identification and error correction, together comprising the message's overhead. The message is then packed into the line with other outgoing messages and sent off to its destination.

Packet-switched systems are message-switched systems with the messages divided into blocks of uniform length, each of which carries its own overhead characters. While this additional burden of overhead tends to add congestion to a network, efficiencies in throughput are achieved by having the option of sending each packet by a different route. This multiple-switching scheme gives packet-switched networks the capability of effectively minimizing transport time and eliminating blocking.

4.5 CURRENT MAJOR TRANSMISSION MEDIA

In this section we shall briefly discuss the major transmission media currently in use. We begin with the wired transmission media and conclude with the over-the-air or broadcast transmission media. We shall describe the media here, and in the final section we shall summarize by comparing the media with each other.

4.5.1 Twisted-Pair Transmission

The twisted pair, such as the two copper wires connecting the telephone to the local exchange and the telegraph between its local offices, is the backbone of the nation's telecommunications system. It is simply a pair of copper wires which have been made extraordinarily versatile by the nature of the termination systems and equipment connected to it. Theoretically, there are no limits to the number of circuits these wires can carry. However, as we shall see, when used for the delivery of high-speed data or many voice channels, the higher frequencies create the undesirable "skin effect." The electrons tend to gather on the surface of the wire, and this increases the resistance or impedance of the wires, requiring many repeaters or amplifiers along the line in order to deliver quality signals.

4.5.2 Coaxial Cable

There is not much space on the surface of a ¼-in-diameter wire, so as the frequencies of signal transmission are increased in order to accommodate different kinds of multiplexing, the skin effect, that is, the resistance owing to electron crowding on the wire surface, increases.

To combat this effect two conductors were put in one cable, one inside the other, but insulated from each other. In this way more wire surface was made available and the resistance or attenuation decreased. This is coaxial cable.

Coaxial-cable transmission has been and continues to be an important long-distance (or line-haul) transmission medium. It is also the medium for cable television.

Telephone use of coaxial cable began in 1936, and the coaxial cable became an important transmission mode during World War II. A single coaxial cable can provide over 13,000 simultaneous voice channels. For cable television, recently installed 450 MHz systems can provide more than 60 channels of television. Typically cable is used to provide transmission *downstream* in residential applications, although data, voice, and video are possible upstream, either by a second cable or by multiplexing flows on one cable. However, using the telephone for responses in closed-circuit instructional applications, or for selecting program content in teletext, still seems a satisfactory and economic way to link users with the service provider.

4.5.3 Submarine Cables

Overseas radiotelephony began in 1927 by bouncing low-frequency waves off the atmosphere, but this is easily disturbed by atmospheric conditions. In 1956 the first transatlantic telephone cable carried 36 voice circuits.* Modern coaxial cable can replace 1500 twisted-pair telephone lines. Underwater cable telephony interleaves different messages from different users by means of *time-assigned speech interpolation* (TASI) to send multiple messages during natural gaps in conversation. This process increases transmission efficiency, security, and privacy but often complicates cost accounting!

The transmission costs of submarine cable are very competitive with those of satellite. Indeed, despite the attraction of the satellite (less maintenance, greater bandwidth, and often somewhat lower line costs) submarine cables continue to be laid. One reason is that while the international satellite is owned by an international organization, INTELSAT, and must share its returns with 106 member nations, a submarine cable is owned and operated by the telecommunications ministry (usually called PT&Ts—Post, Telegraph, & Telephone) of the nation and return revenues to that PT&T.

The United States, however, wishes to encourage satellite use. Because of TASI, the transmission costs of submarine cables are declining more rapidly than those of satellites, yet FCC regulation restricts the laying of such cables by U.S. companies, to foster the more expensive satellite plant.

4.5.4 Optical-Fiber Transmission†

Cable transmission, twisted-pair copper wire, and even new *millimeter waveguide* transmission (providing 230,000 to 460,000 circuits) may well be bypassed by optical fibers. Optical fibers can transmit analog or digital signals by means of concentrated monochromatic light pulses through high-quality glass fibers

---

*The first submarine telegraph cables were laid in 1858, but they failed after three weeks.

†See the 1982 September/October and later issues of *International Fiber Optics and Communications,* available from Information Gatekeepers, 167 Covey Road, MA 02146, for a directory of products, standards, and suppliers.

almost as thin as human hair. The light source can be laser or light-emitting diodes (LED) with photoelectric receptors (see Figure 4.17). The figure shows that a signal is converted to pulses of monochromatic light, which are transmitted into the optical fiber at a critical angle. This angle ensures that the light pulses are reflected completely and entirely within the fiber until received, amplified, regenerated, and decoded. Receptors, splicing, and sharp angles still provide difficulties for this infant technology, but it has tremendous advantages: silicon to make the glass is plentiful and cheap; fibers are noninductive and thus prevent cross talk from adjacent fibers, are interference-free, have low attenuation, are immune to short circuits, explosions, and sparks, and avoid spectrum-related licensing and regulation constraints. Optical-fiber transmission media can extend 26 km before repeaters are necessary and at rates of 90 Mbps. (At this speed 1342 voice channels will be provided by each optical fiber used to support Olympic communications in Los Angeles.) Speeds of 1 gigabit per second (Gbps) have been achieved experimentally. Up to 672 voice lines can be currently multiplexed simultaneously.

Although fiber-optics systems currently have high development costs, AT&T predicts an eventual growth rate of 2000 miles per year in its system. The Yankee Group predicts that the use of fiber optics by local telephone companies will compete with cable company services in 10 or 20 years. Some pilot fiber installations for CATV provide 35 GHz TV signals.

4.5.5 Radio Transmission

The first commercial radio broadcast was the transmission of the 1920 presidential election results by station KDKA in Pittsburgh, Pennsylvania. The Radio

FIGURE 4.17
Fiber optic transmission.

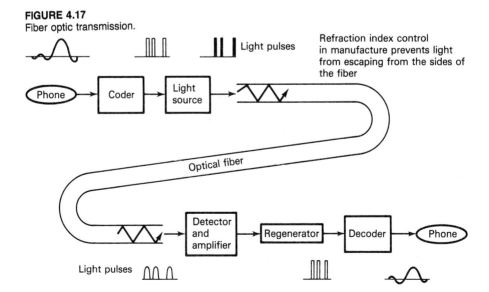

Control Act of 1927 and the Communications Act of 1934 were designed primarily to resolve frequency interference problems caused by the proliferation of new stations. But recognizing the public interest inherent in the limited electromagnetic spectrum the FCC also set forth regulatory concepts that sought to satisfy the public interest, convenience, and necessity and foster localism. Because broadcasting used scarce public resources and was therefore regulated by the market, broadcasting was regulated in the public interest.

The use of cable and microwave relays made possible the development of networks and the local affiliate structure of today's broadcasting system. More recently, a broader spectrum has been made available for a variety of point-to-point transmission services, including digital termination services (DTS) and operational fixed services (OFS). A portion of the electromagnetic or radio spectrum between citizens' band and amateur radio and VHF television was set aside for this service. Mobile radio telephone services, including paging services, are probably the fastest growing communication service throughout the world. Because of this, the narrow spectrum allocated to mobile radio or radio telephone has become extremely crowded.

The most promising means for overcoming the shortages has been *cellular radio*. Cellular radio breaks up an area (say, a city) into small cells consisting of small (less than 15-mile radius) adjacent cells within census regions but broadcasting at hundreds of different frequencies. Receivers shift from frequency to frequency as they pass through these cells. Each cell can handle over 200 conversations simultaneously. *Digital-packet radio transmission* sends digital pulses in burst mode, using the full mobile frequency band at each burst, to base stations which retransmit the pulse within the local area or distribute it via wire networks. Both developments will allow data transmission from mobile terminals and vastly increase the number of mobile radio telephone, and beeper services.

4.5.6 Microwave Transmission

When the FCC allocated spectrum to services, it recognized that new services might soon outgrow their assigned bandwidths. This did indeed occur, and there were and still are enormous pressures on the FCC to reallocate frequencies. Over the years this has been done, especially in the 1 meter and below portion of the spectrum.

This portion has seen some of the most innovative applications, including long-line telephone transmission and the nationwide distribution of video and data. AT&T provided the first nationwide microwave distribution in 1948 and before long was responsible for network video distribution until the advent of the satellite in 1972.

Microwave transmission is radio transmission at high frequencies and provides extensive backbone channels for video, radio, data, telegraph, and telephony. For example, two-thirds of all long-distance calls now travel by land-based microwave. AT&T even provides some digital service through analog microwave data links, called *data under voice* (DUV). (Indeed, telephone signals can be modulated to be transmitted over power-distribution lines.) Until recently, microwave was used primarily for local distribution, particularly for short, high-traffic routes within urban areas. Multipoint distribution services involve redistribution from satellite or cable circuits to local CATV networks or rooftop antennas. Initial costs for microwave systems are quite high, although operating costs are relatively low. Such transmission is reliable, and extra *circuits* within established capacity are inexpensive, but incremental capacity or additional routes are expensive. Owing to the high frequency, microwave links must be line-of-sight and rarely exceed 30 km.

Line-haul microwave transmission systems require numerous relays. These relays receive or accept signals at one frequency—signals that are very weak because they have come long distances. The signal is amplified and retransmitted at a different frequency; otherwise the retransmitted signal would overwhelm or blank out the received signal.

4.5.7 Video Transmission

An image-scanning device was first invented by a German, Paul Nipkow, in 1884; in the 1920s Zworkyin and Farnsworth developed successful scanning tubes. This quickly led to the first public television transmission in England in 1927, and in the United States at the 1939 world's fair.

Video transmission requires considerable bandwidth. Sideband signals correspond to the difference and sum of carrier and modulating frequencies. Radio sidebands occupy little bandwidth, so stations may be only 10 kilocycles apart. But the video frequency range is 4 MHz (400 times more bandwidth), so the additional sideband signals demand good station separation, typically 170 miles for stations on the same channel. The 12 UHF frequencies range from 54 MHz to 213 MHz, whereas the 70 VHF frequencies (added in 1952 by the FCC owing to high demand for TV station frequencies) range from 470 to 890 MHz.

Video is not often thought of as a transmission medium; video is perceived as indelibly connected to its programming and seen solely as an entertainment medium. However, as we are now learning, we can use the video transmission medium for the transmission of electronic publishing or teletext. There are other uses for this valuable spectrum. Consider, for example, the use of video spectrum during the early-morning off hours when a station is not broadcasting for the delivery of educational programs to waiting school videotaping facilities, or the use of the vertical interval for the transmission of financial information (coded, of course) to members of a banking network for storage and use the next morning. While there are certain legal restrictions in place today, the ongoing restructuring of the nation's telecommunications industry may see changes in these rules.

The high frequencies required for video transmission, as with microwave, limit transmission to line of sight. That is why the first cable systems were installed to provide service to the valleys in the Appalachian region.

As an example of the impact of bandwidth constraints, consider AT&T's Picturephone. It originally required 1 MHz, or 5.6 Mbps. Compression techniques brought this down to 1.5 Mbps. Reduction to 200 kilobits per second (Kbps) leads to the blurring of moving images; at 56 Kbps (digital voice channel) the Picturephone would be little different from *slow-scan video*. Slow-scan requires much less memory storage as well as bandwidth and indeed would serve most video conferencing needs at much lower costs (see Chapter 9). One explanation for its marketing failure is that the bulk of information transmitted between people is textual or numeric, and this doesn't require expensive large bandwidth. Various aspects of video transmission are discussed in Chapters 7 and 11.

Low-power television (LPTV), until recently used only in rural areas to rebroadcast distant signals which otherwise would have passed those areas, offers new potential for local broadcasting. These 1000-watt stations will cover only a 10- to 15-mile radius, so many more can exist than current broadcast stations requiring the 170-mile separation. Community television may develop, depending on responses by cable TV operators and FCC decisions.

4.5.8 Satellites

It was Arthur C. Clarke, known now primarily for his science fiction writing *(2001)*, who as a young engineer in 1945 suggested putting satellites 22,300 miles above the equator. They would then revolve around the Earth at the same speed as a spot on land below them, appearing stationary. Clarke now lives in Sri Lanka, and has an antenna in his yard to receive transmission from *geosynchronous* satellites.

The Russian Sputnik in 1957 was the first human-made satellite; now dozens are in geostationary orbit (see Figure 4.18). For example, Cable News Network is transmitted via Transponder 14 of SatCom satellite F3, located at 131°W, using 3.98 MHz and horizontal polarization. Auxiliary services include 1½ minutes-per-hour radio news carried on its 6.3-MHz voice subcarrier.*

Current satellites operate at 4 to 6 GHz (the C-band) and 12 to 13 CHz (K-band) (see Figure 4.18). The 4- to 6-GHz range must be shared with microwave frequency assignments, while there are only a limited number of orbital locations available because satellites must be separated by 3°, and there are only about 75° of arc over the North American continent. (The more extreme the location over the ends of the continent, the narrower the angle at the receiving end and the more difficulties in reception.) Thus the hyperpower

---

*The various issues of *Satguide*—P.O. Box 1048, Hailey, ID 83333—provides a complete listing of all current and known future domestic satellites delivering CATV. Included are frequency, polarization, latitude, transponder identification, ownership, services, and addresses. A complete commercial satellite directory is also available from Phillips Publishing, 7315 Wisconsin Avenue, Bethesda, MD 20814.

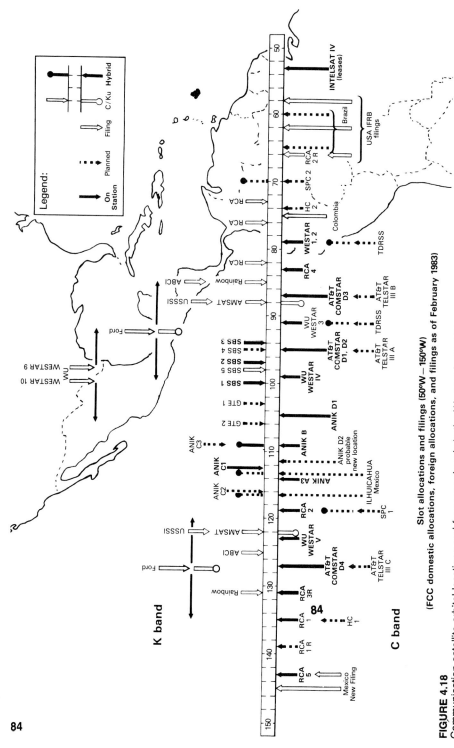

FIGURE 4.18

Communication satellite orbital locations and frequency bands in the Western hemisphere.
(*Source:* Hughes Aircraft. We thank Paul Visher for his assistance.)

satellites were designed to provide more efficient transmission. A 500-MHz bandwidth at 12-GHz transmission equals 220,000 telephone channels and 100 TV channels, using spot beams. A more powerful satellite allows the use of spot beams to provide focused transmission at a specific frequency; it also allows smaller (hence cheaper and more mobile) ground antennas. For a 12-GHz transmission, a 1-meter dish is sufficient. [See Rice & Parker (1979) for applications of high-powered communication satellites for rural areas.] These higher frequencies, however, are affected by rain and are less able to reuse the same frequency by transmitting polarized signals. Satellites are, essentially, microwave relays in space; they accept signals at one frequency and retransmit them at another.

Satellites in general have the advantage of tremendous bandwidth and are theoretically insensitive to the distance between origination and reception. Indeed, Satellite Business Systems intends to bypass AT&T entirely in delivering intercorporate communications cross-country. AT&T estimates that the point at which satellites become more economic is 3000 circuits for distances greater than 1500 miles. They are not unbiased, however, and some studies have shown economic use of satellites between points separated by only 1 mile (Parker, 1982).

Typically, signals are sent to the satellite, converted to different frequencies and amplified, beamed to a central switching station, retransmitted and re-beamed to the receiver. The amplifiers are called *transponders,* and satellites tend to have 12 to 24 of these. These "hops" create a very small delay in final reception, which is still a problem for data transmission and sometimes noticeable in long-distance telephoning.

A satellite's age (lifetimes are officially around 7 years), orbital location, power and efficiency, user categories, and the number of stations capable of receiving its signals affect its desirability and, hence, its cost. In 1980 the cost of a full circuit for 1 year was approximately $40,000 leased from COMSAT, the U.S. operator for the INTELSAT system. A domestic satellite circuit leases at approximately $12,000 to $15,000 per year. Heavy users lease an entire transponder (around $1 million per year) or even send up their own satellites. Indeed, Hughes was the first company to put a commercial satellite into orbit by means of NASA's space shuttle.

4.6 SYSTEM COMPARISONS

Communication system designers seek to provide high-quality communication at the lowest possible cost. Their task is made difficult as well as more feasible by the range of alternatives they have to work with. Not only is there a rich mix of transmission media, but there are several ways of using these media. Telecommunication engineers are always trading off bandwidth, time, distance, and cost. Further, they trade off line capacity or bandwidth against terminal hardware, for example, choosing a relatively narrow bandwidth link while using time-division

FIGURE 4.19
TRANSMISSION TIMES FOR SELECTED CONTENT.

	Typical number of bits	Lowest approximate transmission times (seconds) at 9.6 KBps*
A page or a full CRT screen of text (uncompressed)	$1-4 \times 10^4$	1–4
Facsimile image, black and white, two-tone (compressed)	$2-6 \times 10^5$	20–60
Full-page, three-color image, high quality (heavily compressed)	$2-10 \times 10^4$	200–1000
A 20-cm floppy disk, single-sided, double-density	5×10^6	500
A 720-m reel of computer tape (type 6250 BPI) or two medium-sized disk units (IBM 3310)	1×10^9	100,000 (29 hours)
One second of digitized telephone speech at pulse-code modulation	6.4×10^4	7
One second of digitized telephone speech (heavily compressed)	2.4×10^5	0.25
One second of Picturephone (moving video image)	6.3×10^4	660

*9.6 KBps is the highest commercially available transmission rate over an analog voice channel.
Source: Mandley, T. "Assessing the New Services." *IEEE Spectrum,* October 1979, 46–47.

multiplexing at a somewhat higher cost in terminals. But since copper costs money and microwave bandwidth is as scarce as satellite bandwidth will certainly become, TDM methods, despite the higher cost of terminal hardware, become more economical.

Since line costs are proportional to the distance covered, multiplexing avoids the need for separate circuits for each user. As terminal costs are fixed, multiplexing becomes more economic than individual circuits only beyond a certain distance. For a particular multiplex system, the minimum distance at which it has an economic advantage is called the *prove-in point.*

Another factor to consider are multiplexing hierarchies. These hierarchies can be considered essentially network transmission architectures designed to provide the system designer with various options for delivering information rapidly and economically. In analog or voice transmission systems, the basic architecture of hierarchy is a 600-circuit *mastergroup,* which is made up of 10 *supergroups,* which in turn are composed of 5 multiplexed *groups,* each of which multiplexes 12 voice lines. In Europe, CCITT (Comité Consultatif International de Téléphonique et Télégraphique) standards call for a 960-circuit mastergroup composed of 16 multiplexed supergroups.

The AT&T System has developed a set of building blocks for its digital architecture based on the T1 carrier. This T1 carrier, developed in 1933, can provide 24 voice signals at 1.544 Mbps. The T2 carrier uses 4 multiplexed T1 streams, while the T3 carrier uses 7 multiplexed T2 streams. Finally the T4 carrier can provide 4032 voice circuits at 274 Mbps by utilizing 6 multiplexed T3 streams. In Europe, the basic level has 30 voice channels and 2 signalling channels, at 2.048 Mbps, and is multiplexed into groups of four.

The larger-capacity multiplex systems (higher in the hierarchy) will only be economic on certain routes where sufficient trunk traffic can be concentrated to utilize the available capacity. These routes or corridors can be created by planning the network design to feed local loops into appropriate points in the line-haul system. Cost savings can be achieved even though route distances for most calls are increased for point-to-point routing. In other words it may be economical to go a longer way to reach a line-haul node that will carry local traffic cheap enough to overcome the somewhat higher cost of the local loop rather than going directly into a shorter point-to-point connection over a more expensive long-distance circuit. This may certainly be the case for satellite networks.

In the next several figures we show some comparisons for several typical line-haul possibilities. Figure 2.13 compares channels by frequency, while Figure 4.19 compares channels by transmission speed. Figure 4.20 compares some media by capacities and frequency, while Figure 4.21 graphically reveals the declining costs of these media.

Note that the most recent TD3 microwave system carries 18,000 circuits. Microwave radio has about a 3-to-1 cost advantage over cable in the same range of capacities. Enormous cost advantages accrue from satellite usage at this capacity level. But it has been argued that without the terrestrial systems provided by both cable and microwave, satellites by themselves might be considered too vulnerable to both human-made and solar-made interference and would not be depended upon so heavily.

There are, of course, other considerations of cost that must be taken into account when designing line-haul systems. For example, terrain is extremely important—the microwave radio-relay systems must operate within line of sight of each other—so usually towers are spaced at 30-km intervals. And at very remote sites there may not be any power available to operate the towers. The same holds true for long strings of cable; power is needed to operate the repeaters.

When we branch circuits off the "main stem" we have to accommodate the various hierarchies we discussed above, and this requires a considerable amount of equipment. In the design of the network—its topology—this must be taken into consideration or the benefits of multiplexing are lost in the cost of switching at the branches.

Finally, as the line-haul system becomes more and more digital, there is the problem of feeding analog signals into it. Unless the analog signals from the local loops are digitized, the electronic switching at the interfaces of the line-haul local loop with lower-cost long-distance systems cannot be used and therefore the cost

FIGURE 4.20
ADVANCES IN FOUR TRANSMISSION SYSTEMS.

Coaxial Cable Systems

Type	Date introduced	Repeater spacing	Voice-frequency channels/coax	Voice-frequency channels/route
L 1	1940	8 miles	600	1,800
L 3	1953	4 miles	1,860	16,470
L 4	1967	2 miles	3,600	32,400
L 5	1973	1 mile	10,800	108,000

Microwave radio systems

Type	Date introduced	No. of two-way radio channels	Voice circuits per channel	Frequency band in GHz
TD2	1948	5	480	3.7–4.2
TH1	1959	8	1,860	5.9–6.4
TD3	1966	12	1,200	3.7–4.2
TD4	1973	12	1,500	3.7–4.2

Transatlantic cable systems

Type	Date introduced	No. of channels	Repeater spacing (in nautical miles)
TAT 1	1956	36	20
TAT 3	1963	138	20
TAT 5	1970	845	10
TAT 6	1976	4,000	5.1

AT&T digital transmission systems

Type	Date introduced	No. of voice channels	Medium	Transmission speed
T 1	1963	24*	Wire-pair	1.544 MBps
T 2	1973	96*	Coax/shielded pair	6.3 MBps
T 4	1975	4,032*	Coax	274.0 MBps
WT4	1980s	230,000†	Wave guide	274.0 MBps
WT4A	1980s	460,000†	Wave guide	274.0 MBps

*Requires two circuits (one each direction).
†Two-way channels: 60 Frequency division channels each direction, digital modulation.

savings not realized. This requires additional analog-to-digital and digital-to-analog converters at the local loops and increases the cost of operation. But as more and more local loops become digital, cost disadvantages will disappear.

The Japanese have shown a keen interest in comparing attributes such as information cost per distance as an indication of media efficiency. A recent trend

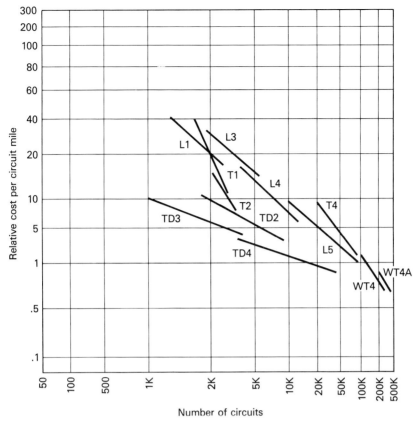

FIGURE 4.20
Advances in four transmission systems.

FIGURE 4.21
Declines in circuit-mile costs for three transmission systems. (*Source:* Ito, 1980. Reproduced by permission.)

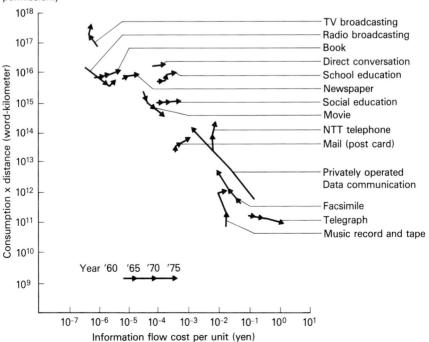

graph appears in Figure 4.22 (Ito, 1981). You can see the steady decline in movie and telegraph transmission efficiency, the equilibrium level of telephone efficiency, and the increased efficiency of video and digital transmission.

REFERENCES

Dordick, H. S., Bradley, H., and Nanus, B., *The Emerging Network Marketplace,* Norwood, N.J.: Ablex, 1981.

Ito, Y., "The 'Johaka Shakai' Approach to the Study of Communication in Japan," *Keio Communication Review,* 1980, *1,* 13–40. Reprinted in G. Wilhoit and H. de Bock (eds.), *Mass Communication Review Yearbook* (vol. 2), Beverly Hills, Calif.: Sage, 1981.

Parker, E., "Micro Earth Stations Make Business Satcom Affordable," *Microwave Systems News,* 1982, *12* (11), pp. 71 ff.

Rice, R., and Paisley, W., "The Green Thumb Videotex Experiment: Evaluation and Policy Implications," *Telecommunications Policy,* 1982, *6* (3), 223–235.

Rice, R., and Parker, E. "Telecommunications Alternatives For Developing Countries," *Journal of Communication,* 1979, *29* (4), 125–136.

Thoma, G., "Transmission of Information: An Overview," *Journal of the American Society for Information Science,* 1981, *32* (2), 1131–140.

RECOMMENDED READING

Cannon, D., and Luecke, G., *Understanding Communications Systems,* Dallas: Texas Instruments, 1980. Sold by Radio Shack.

Mandley, T., "Assessing the New Services," *IEEE Spectrum,* October 1979.

Martin, J., *Future Developments in Telecommunication,* Englewood Cliffs, N.J.: Prentice-Hall, 1977.

Pierce, J., *Signals: The Telephone and Beyond,* New York: Freeman, 1981.

CHAPTER 5

THE TELEPHONE SYSTEM

Howard R. Turtle
OCLC (Online Computer Library Center)
Dublin, OH

The telephone system represents one of the most remarkable technical and organizational achievements of the last century. Few of us are able to appreciate the complexity and scope of the system connected to the familiar instrument that allows us to speak with a business associate on another continent as easily as with our next-door neighbor. Often, we are not even aware of the extent to which the telephone system supports our everyday activities. Much of the radio and television programming could not be distributed without the telephone network, and the usefulness of computers would be seriously limited without it. Many institutions of modern industrial society simply could not function without this network.

Anyone who wishes to understand the telephone system is confronted by three basic problems. First, the amount of information to be assimilated is huge. Any understanding would require a knowledge of 100 years of scientific and engineering history, a technical understanding covering disciplines ranging from electronics to wave mechanics to aerospace engineering, a thorough understanding of business practice as applied both to small entrepreneurial concerns and to large regulated monopolies, and an intimate understanding of domestic and international politics. Second, the scope of the telephone industry is not easily defined. Third, the telephone industry is in a period of rapid change. Established monopolies are being reorganized, new technology is making existing facilities obsolete, and the demand for new telecommunication services (data, facsimile, video, etc.) is supplanting traditional voice service.

The material presented in Section 5.1 begins with a description of the history and basic operation of the telephone. Section 5.2 examines the switched-telephone network that connects telephones and other telecommunication equipment. Section 5.3 describes a selection of services provided by most telephone companies. Sections 5.4 and 5.5 review the regulatory and competitive environments in which telephone services are offered. Section 5.6 concludes with a discussion of the future of the telephone system.

Telephone systems differ from country to country. The description provided in this chapter applies primarily to the current North American telephone system unless otherwise noted.

5.1   THE TELEPHONE

The telephone is perhaps the most widely used machine in modern society. In the United States alone there are more than 170 million telephones in use. This section describes the invention and development of the telephone and the operation of a current generation telephone.

5.1.1   Invention of the Telephone

Early experimentation that led to the invention of the telephone was a by-product of efforts to improve telegraph efficiency. Telegraphy was introduced in the United States in 1844. By the end of the Civil War, roughly 50,000 miles of telegraph wire had been strung in the United States. When the first telephone patents were issued in 1876, 250,000 miles of telegraph wire covered 100,000 miles of route.

Transmission of telegraph signals employed intermittent bursts of direct current. A single telegraph wire could carry only a single one-way transmission at any given time. Two-way transmissions required that operators observe protocols that governed the order in which messages were sent (an early form of communication protocols). In 1872 the Western Union telegraph network began using a system developed by Joseph B. Stearns which allowed two-way transmission over a single wire. Stearns's "duplex" transmission system doubled the capacity of the Western Union network, and the commercial value of any mechanism that could allow more signals to be carried on a single wire became immediately apparent. Two inventors attempting to develop a multiplex telegraph system independently developed devices capable of transmitting and receiving human speech. Alexander Graham Bell and Elisha Gray filed descriptions of the first telephones with the U.S. Patent Office on the same day, February 14, 1876.

Elisha Gray was a professional inventor. In 1867 he obtained his first patent for a self-adjusting telegraph relay. Gray became a principal in the Western Electric Manufacturing Company, the preeminent manufacturer of electrical and telegraphic equipment. In 1874, Gray discovered that an induction coil could be used to convert an electrical current that was rapidly switched on and off into audible sound. Gray left Western Electric in order to devote himself full-time to exploring these "vibratory currents." He demonstrated a number of devices in 1874 and 1875 that were capable of transmitting audible tones. While Gray apparently realized that these vibratory currents could be used to transmit human speech, he was convinced that the "talking telegraph" was of little commercial value and devoted most of his efforts to multiplexing telegraph signals.

Alexander Graham Bell acquired a background in phonetics and speech therapy at the University of Edinburgh. He emigrated to Canada in 1870 and settled in Boston in 1871, where he taught at a school for deaf-mutes. While Bell had virtually no electrical or telegraphic background, he began to experiment with multiplex telegraph schemes in 1872, after reading of the adoption of Stearns's duplex system. Progress for Bell was slow at first; he had little experience in fabricating electrical machinery and lacked Gray's experience with telegraphy. By 1875, Bell had become familiar with the properties of the inductive coil that allowed pulsed electric current to be converted to sound and had fabricated a primitive instrument capable of transmitting sound.

Gray and Bell became aware of each other's work in 1874. Both men remained primarily concerned with the development of the multiplex telegraph, and both were afraid that the other might be the first to find a workable solution. Alexander Graham Bell filed a patent application for the telephone on February 14, 1876. Later on the same day, Gray filed a description of his similar device, not as a patent, but as a *caveat* or "notice of invention." Neither Bell nor Gray had successfully transmitted human voice at the time of the filing. Gray made no attempt to block Bell's patent, presumably because he remained convinced that the telephone was of little commercial value, and did not actively continue his experimentation.

Bell's patent was issued on March 7, 1876. On March 10, Bell succeeded in transmitting human speech. Further work led to the successful demonstration of a modified device in June, and commercialization began early in 1877. Bell's telephone patent, perhaps the most valuable ever issued, was eventually challenged by a number of claimants, including Elisha Gray. In the United States, Bell's patent was construed to cover the principle of speech transmission using electricity. Outside the United States, Bell's patent rights were generally restricted to the specific devices named in the patent application. Figure 5.1 shows some early telephone equipment.

5.1.2 Evolution of the Telephone

The first commercial telephones relied upon an inductive coil for both the transmitter and the receiver. A magnetic core passed through the center of a coil and was attached to a metal diaphragm. If two such devices were connected on a single battery-operated circuit, the deflections of the metal diaphragm which resulted when someone spoke into the first unit would be reproduced in the second coil unit. The transmission quality of these early devices was poor. A number of inventors produced improved transmitters, most of which were based

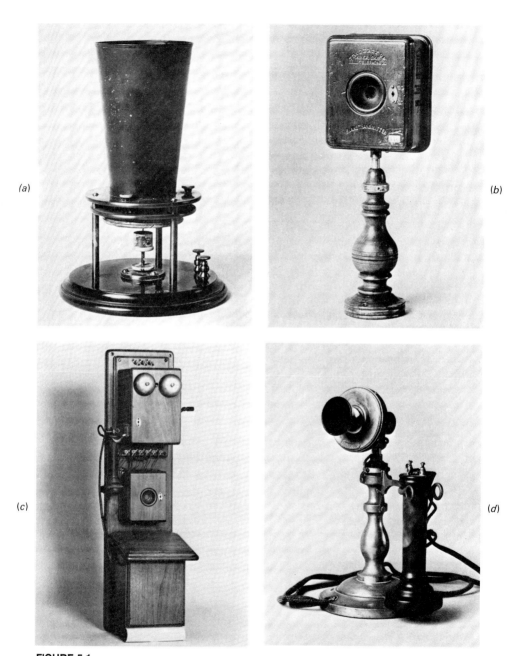

FIGURE 5.1
Some early telephone models. *(a)* Alexander Graham Bell's first telephone, 1876. *(b)* Francis Blake's improved instrument, 1880. *(c)* An 1882 wall model. *(d)* A brass telephone of 1897 that was to remain basically unchanged for over 30 years. (Reproduced with permission of AT&T.)

upon varying the resistance in the circuit in response to speech energy rather than upon induced currents. By 1878 a transmitter developed by Thomas Edison was adopted; it relied upon changes in resistance through a disk of carbon particles when compressed by the varying impact of speech energy.

The basic transmission and reception used in the 1878 telephones remained essentially unchanged until the late 1970s; a carbon-filled transmitter (microphone) varies the resistance of a circuit in response to sound energy, and an inductive coil receiver causes deflections in a diaphragm (speaker) in response to variations in electrical current passing through the coil. The major changes in telephone technology between 1878 and the 1970s were incorporated to facilitate the selective connection of the individual telephone units.

In the early days of telephony, telephones were purchased to allow communication between specific locations. If Smith and Jones felt a need for frequent and timely conversation, each purchased a telephone and had wire strung between their selected locations. If a third individual wished to talk to Jones, either Jones had to buy a second telephone or the third individual had to be added to the existing circuit. Early telephone circuits developed around special-interest groups. For example, all of the doctors and pharmacists in a town might share a single circuit, as might all lawyers and judges. A lawyer could not, however, telephone the pharmacist, who was connected to a different circuit.

The electrical current necessary to operate early telephones was obtained from batteries located near each telephone. In order to reduce the current load on the battery, a switch was incorporated in each telephone which would disconnect the circuit when the telephone was not in use. In order to signal individual subscribers that they were being called, each telephone incorporated a bell which could be rung by means of a hand-cranked magneto (which uses a coil spun through a permanent magnetic field to generate current). Since a given circuit might contain many telephones, coding schemes were used to identify individual subscribers—for example, two long rings followed by two short rings for Smith.

The obvious interconnection limitations of these early telephone circuits soon led to the introduction of switchboards to allow independent circuits to be connected. The first switchboard, or "exchange," was installed in 1878. By 1880 there were 30,000 telephone subscribers and 150 telephone exchanges in the United States. By 1887 there were 1200 exchanges in operation supporting over 150,000 subscribers.

The advent of telephone exchanges allowed other improvements in the telephone. Batteries connected to each telephone were replaced with a common battery located at the exchange. Relays were added to subscriber lines to signal the exchange operator when a telephone was off the hook, thereby eliminating the need for a subscriber to signal the operator with the magneto crank when initiating a call. Similarly, relays installed in the exchange allowed the operator to detect the termination of a call, eliminating the need for a caller to signal the operator upon call completion. As the scale and complexity of telephone exchanges grew, it became apparent that operator assistance for every call was undesirable. Almon B. Strowger developed the first successful automatic telephone switching system. His system relies upon a sequence of precisely

FIGURE 5.2
Functional diagram of an electronic telephone.

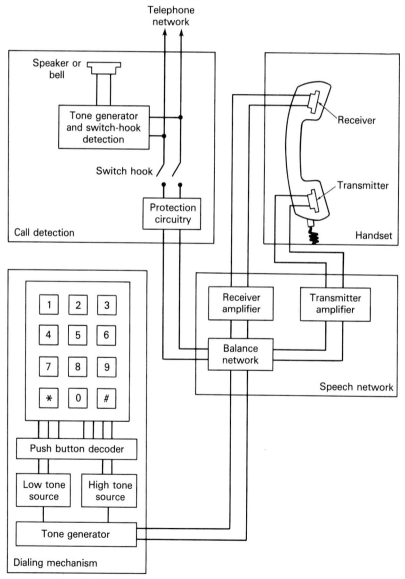

timed current pulses to automatically select a destination. The dial telephone mechanism was patented in 1898; fully automatic call routing was first installed in 1921.

5.1.3 The Modern Telephone

Until the mid-1970s, virtually all domestic telephones were manufactured and owned by the telephone companies. Since the 1976 ruling that allowed the connection of units produced by competing manufacturers, the number of telephone models and functions has expanded rapidly, and the cost of owning the basic instrument has dropped. These trends can be expected to accelerate over the next decade.

Subscriber telephone equipment is in a period of transition. The conventional instrument, which supports only voice communication, is being replaced by equipment that more closely resembles an intelligent private exchange (see Section 5.3.3), in which voice communication is one function among many. Current equipment often bears no physical resemblance to the conventional telephone. For example, equipment may be a television set that incorporates a telephone or it may be a telephone that incorporates a CRT and keyboard.

Well over 200 million telephones are in use in the United States and Canada. Roughly two-thirds of these are installed in homes, with the remaining one-third installed for business and public use. Worldwide, the number of telephones installed exceeds 500 million.

The basic telephone instrument evolved rapidly in the first 50 years of its commercial existence. The basic rotary telephone was introduced in the 1920s, and except for the introduction of push-button dialing in 1963, the 1920s telephone remained substantially unchanged until the late 1970s. Integrated circuits began to appear in telephone units manufactured in the late 1970s and have contributed to major cost reductions and performance improvements.

The telephone has four functional components: (1) a handset that contains the transmitter and receiver, (2) a speech network that connects the transmitter-receiver to the local loop, (3) a dialing mechanism, and (4) a bell or tone generator for signaling the presence of incoming calls (see Figure 5.2).

Handset The handset houses the transmitter (mouthpiece) and receiver (earpiece). In the current generation of electronic telephones, the transmitter and receiver are both realized in the form of a dynamic transducer (Figure 5.3), which replaces the carbon microphone and magnetic speaker used in conventional telephones. When it is used as a transmitter, sound waves strike the transducer diaphragm, causing the attached coil to move through a magnetic field, which then generates an electric signal. When it is used as a receiver, an alternating-current (AC) signal is applied to the coil, which causes the transducer to vibrate in the magnetic field, thereby generating sound through the attached diaphragm. The similarity between the transducer-based design and the first

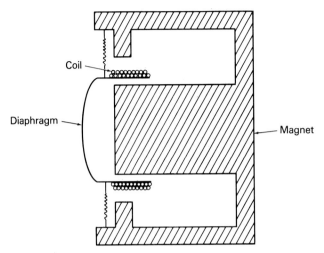

FIGURE 5.3
Cross section of a dynamic transducer.

commercial telephones is striking. After 90 years of improvement, the original design finally works.

Speech Network The primary function of the speech network is to amplify the transmitter and receiver signals. Each transducer is connected to the speech network by a pair of wires. Internal circuitry automatically adjusts amplifier gain to accommodate variations in distance to the local exchange (transmitting stronger signals for long distances; providing greater amplification for weak received signals). The speech network also controls the "side-tone" or transmitter signal fed back through the speaker's receiver and couples the tones required for push-button dialing onto the telephone circuit.

Dialing Mechanism While dial telephones that rely upon Strowger or pulsed signaling are still in common use, electronic telephones use dual-tone multi-frequency (DTMF) signaling, also known as push-button dialing or Touch Tone (a trademark of AT&T). A push-button pad is shown in Figure 5.4. Each row and column of the keypad corresponds to the frequency indicated. When a given key is pressed, two tones are simultaneously transmitted. A "low" tone selected by the key's row and a "high" tone selected by the key's column. The switching equipment at the local exchange decodes the audible harmonic into its two component frequencies to identify the digit. While DTMF signaling is designed to use sixteen keys, telephones in North America use only twelve 0–9, *, and #.

DTMF signaling is used primarily to identify the destination subscriber when placing a call. Once the call has been placed, however, the keypad can be used as a simple data entry device if the destination has DTMF decoding equipment.

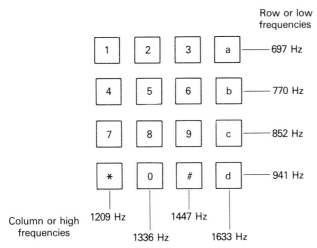

FIGURE 5.4
Push-button pad with dual-tone multifrequencies, the high and low tones generated by each button.

Push-button data entry has been used in such applications as electronic fund transfers, remote order entry, and aviation weather briefings. The keypad can be used for transmitting alphabetic information by pressing two digits to represent one letter.

Incoming Call Recognition The bell in conventional telephones has been replaced with a tone generator in electronic telephones. In response to current flow applied to the local loop by the telephone exchange signaling the presence of an incoming call, a tone generator is activated which drives a small speaker at a frequency selected to be sufficiently irritating that it encourages the listener to answer the call. When the handset is raised, the switch-hook disables the tone generator and connects the speech network to the line, thereby completing the call.

5.2 THE SWITCHED NETWORK

The switched telephone network is comprised of all the facilities necessary to establish a connection between individual subscribers. Roughly three-fourths of the total cost of providing telephone service in the United States is required to support the switched network; the remaining costs are associated with the telephones and data sets. This cost distribution is encouraging, since improvements in technology are likely to have a greater impact on the cost of the switched network than on the line termination equipment (telephones and data sets).

The switched network provides two basic facilities: transmission facilities, which actually carry voice or data transmissions between two points, and switching facilities, which select the transmission facilities necessary to complete a call. The manner in which the transmission and switching facilities are organized changes in response to the changing costs of the underlying technologies. If, for example, switching facilities were free, then the switched network would consist of a great deal of switching equipment in order to optimize the use of the transmission facilities. Similarly, if transmission facilities were free, then the switched network would be organized to eliminate as many switching facilities as possible.

5.2.1 Organization of the Switched Network

The switched telephone network in the United States is organized as a hierarchy (see Figure 5.5), with five different categories or classes of switching centers. At the bottom of the hierarchy lies the Class 5 office (also known as the end office or local exchange), to which all subscriber telephones are connected. There are over 10,000 local exchanges in the United States, serving over 100 million telephone lines. Each switching center in the hierarchy is connected to the

FIGURE 5.5
Organization of the switched network. Solid lines represent normal interoffice trunks. Dashed lines represent optional high-usage trunks.

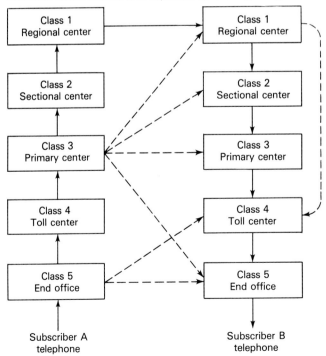

switching center above by high-speed transmission facilities or interoffice trunks. At the top of the hierarchy is the Class 1 office or regional center. The twelve regional centers that serve the United States and Canada communicate with each other over high-speed, long-distance transmission facilities.

In general, each office in the hierarchy handles the telephones in a specific geographic area; higher-level offices handle progressively larger areas and serve progressively larger numbers of telephones. A typical local exchange might handle 8000 telephone lines, while a regional center might handle over 10 million. The local exchange is involved in all calls placed from or directed to one of its subscribers; higher-level offices handle only calls to or from the areas they serve, not calls both from and to the area served by a lower-level office.

In addition to trunk connections with upper-level offices, a number of high-usage trunks are used to connect offices at all levels when the volume of telephone traffic warrants. In cities where there are several local exchanges, high-usage trunks are used to connect the individual exchanges. In these cases, the Class 4 or toll-center office serving the connected local exchanges is used only if no high-usage trunk is available. Similarly, a Class 3 or primary-center office may be connected to more than one sectional toll center and may also have high-usage trunk connections to other primary centers or regional centers.

Given the organization of the switched network, it is apparent that the number of trunks and switching centers that will be used to complete a given call can vary considerably. If we ignore the connection between the subscriber and the local exchange, a call may occupy a single switching center and no trunks if both telephones lie within the local exchange. A long-distance call may require the services of as many as 10 switching centers and 9 trunks (actually, this number can be even higher, since routing between regional centers is not always direct). Further, a call between two locations may not use the same facilities each time it is placed. The number and type of switching centers and trunks can significantly affect both the time required to complete a call and the quality of the transmitted signal.

5.2.2 Local Transmission Facilities

The local telephone exchange provides the link through which all subscriber services are delivered. The range of services available to individual subscribers is largely determined by the facilities available at their local exchange. While the description of the local exchange provided here will focus on its role in providing direct dial service, the local exchange provides additional services, which are described in Section 5.3.

Each telephone is connected to a local exchange by a "local loop." A local loop generally consists of a pair of copper wires connecting the telephone to the exchange, but other connection media (optical fibers or radio links) can be used. The length of a local loop averages 1 to 2 miles. Variations in the length of the local loop and the type of wire used affect the resistance of the circuit (one factor affecting the quality of the circuit). When long local loops are required, the circuit is usually "loaded" through the use of inductive coils to reduce signal degradation. In some data communication applications, the line termination equipment is adjusted to provide a uniform power level at the local exchange that is insensitive to the length of the local loop.

Other factors can affect the quality of the local loop. Many individual local-loop pairs are strung together in a single multiconductor cable. Electrical signals in one local-loop circuit can interfere with signals in other circuits in the same cable. This phenomenon, called *cross talk,* is more noticeable at high frequencies, and special precautions are required when the local loop is used for high-speed data transmission. Electrical interference resulting from nearby electrical power distribution systems can also degrade local-loop performance.

While a number of factors can affect their performance, local loops generally offer much higher quality than required for voice communication; data rates of 50 kilobaud have been achieved on "standard" local loops. Signal quality and bandwidth are much more seriously limited by the exchange and the switched network. The apparent inefficiency of dedicating such a high-capacity link to a single subscriber has led to the introduction of remote concentrators for use with the newer electronic switching systems. A typical concentrator combines the traffic from up to 96 local subscriber loops and is connected to the local exchange by a high-speed trunk.

5.2.3 Trunk Transmission Facilities

A wide variety of transmission facilities or "carriers" are employed to connect toll centers within the switched network. The different carriers are designed for specific transmission media and can be characterized by the distance over which the carrier can be used, the type of signal encoding employed (analog or digital), and its data-carrying capacity.

Five transmission media are commonly used to support telephone traffic: twisted-wire pairs, coaxial cable, microwave radio, optical fiber, and satellite.

1 Twisted-wire pairs, or twisted pairs, represent the most common transmission medium in use. When used to connect a subscriber to a local exchange, a twisted pair typically carries a single voice channel. When used in trunk facilities, twisted pairs accommodate between 12 and 24 voice channels when using frequency-division multiplexing, and 24 to 96 channels when using time-division multiplexing. Twisted-wire pairs are relatively inexpensive but they are susceptible to electrical interference and must be routed between connection points on poles or underground.

2 Coaxial cable is less susceptible to electrical interference than a twisted pair and has much higher bandwidth. A coaxial cable can carry between 1800 and 10,800 voice channels. High-speed coaxial links of more than a few miles typically require the use of intermediate amplifiers (repeaters).

3 Microwave radio links compete with coaxial cable for high-speed transmissions and support between 240 and 1800 voice channels per radio channel. They are attractive because they obviate the need for stringing cable between two points; their primary limitations are the restriction to line-of-sight transmissions and intermittent outages caused by heavy thunderstorm activity.

4 Optical fibers are relatively new to the telephone system but are finding widespread application. Initial problems with connecting optical-fiber links have been largely overcome. A single optical fiber provides 672 one-way voice channels. While the voice capacity per fiber appears low when compared to coaxial cable, a typical half-inch cable contains 144 fibers and supports more than 40,000 two-way channels. Optical fibers are inexpensive and immune to electrical noise, require few amplification stages, and promise much higher bandwidths in the future.

5 Satellite channels are becoming increasingly common for long-distance telephone traffic. Their capacity and cost performance have improved substantially in the last two decades. Once reserved for transoceanic use, satellite channels can now compete with land-based transmission media for transcontinental and regional use. Two characteristics are unique to satellites: (1) the cost of the channel is nearly independent of distance, and (2) a delay of roughly 270 milliseconds is experienced owing to the large distances traveled by the signals. If a two-way conversation is conducted over satellite channels, a speaker will wait an additional half-second for a reply. While this delay is of little consequence for voice or broadcast traffic, it can pose serious problems for computer-to-computer communication or for a call routed using multiple satellite channels.

5.2.4 Older Switching Technologies

The huge capital investment represented by the switched telephone network seriously limits its ability to incorporate new technologies. Any improved technology must be compatible with existing equipment, since the cost of replacing a significant portion of the existing physical plant is prohibitive. Further, the telephone companies have largely retained ownership of the equipment, much of which has been designed to achieve useful lives in excess of 40 years. A new technology rarely offers cost benefits that would make it attractive to replace an existing 20-year-old technology that is expected to function reliably for another 20 years. As a result, the replacement of switching equipment is slow. Much of the equipment installed in the 1930s and 1940s is still in operation. The rate at which the switched network is expanding, however, does encourage the introduction of new technology. The rate of new equipment installation is governed more by the demand for expanded telephone service than by the need to replace obsolete equipment.

Virtually all new installations of switching systems in local exchanges employ the electronic switching systems (ESS) described in Section 5.2.5. Of the over 10,000 local exchanges operating in 1983, 30 percent employed electronic switching. The remaining 70 percent employed the older switching technologies described here. Since the electronic systems tend to be installed in heavily populated areas, electronic switching systems handle about 50 percent of telephone subscribers in the United States. Three older switching technologies are currently in use in the United States: manual, step-by-step, and cross-bar.

Manual Switching Manual switching systems rely upon an operator to establish the physical connection, generally through the use of a switchboard. A typical switchboard consists of a series of patch cords and plugs, together with lights that signal when a telephone is in use. Each telephone connected to the switchboard is connected to one patch cord and one plug. An individual initiates a call by picking up the telephone handset, thereby signaling the operator. The operator then plugs a headset into the appropriate jack to ask the desired destination. The call is completed by connecting the appropriate patch cord if the destination telephone is handled by the switchboard or by connecting the caller to an outside line. Manual switching, although no longer widely used in North America, is not yet extinct. Its use is generally confined to small private exchanges in the United States and to rural areas in other parts of the world.

Step-by-Step Switching Step-by-step or Strowger switching was the first workable automatic switching system. It relies upon a series of electrical pulses to control an electromechanical switch housed within the local exchange. The original mechanism for generating the electrical pulses, patented in 1889, used separate wires to carry the switching signals. A dial mechanism was patented in 1898 that allowed the switching signals to share the voice lines.

In step-by-step switching a call is initiated when the telephone handset is picked up and a dial tone applied to the line to indicate that a switching circuit is available for use. Each number dialed generates a series of pulses which interrupts the circuit at a rate of 10 times per second. Each interruption causes the step-by-step switch at the local exchange to advance to the next contact position. The design of the dial mechanism ensures a delay between digits (0.6 seconds) that is significantly longer than the delay between pulses. Each digit dialed results in the selection of a single switch position corresponding to the digit. The sequence of digits dialed results in the selection of an individual circuit. The switching signal devised by Strowger had an extremely long life. Until DTMF signaling was introduced in 1963, pulsed dialing was used for virtually all direct-dial switching.

Cross-Bar Switching Cross-bar switching relies upon the same signaling techniques as step-by-step, but uses an improved switch. Cross-bar switching was introduced in the late 1930s as an improved version of step-by-step.

5.2.5 Electronic Switching

Electronic switching systems were first installed in 1965 and represent a significant departure from the electromechanical systems they replaced. Electronic switching systems differ from their predecessors in three basic ways: (1) they operate under stored program control, (2) they support additional subscriber services, and (3) they more readily accommodate digital transmission.

Stored Program Control In the earlier switching technologies, special-purpose mechanical switches respond to a sequence of electrical pulses to select the path necessary to complete a call. The manner in which a given telephone number is decoded is determined at the time the switch is designed. With the rapid development of semiconductor technology it became possible to replace the single-function mechanical devices with switches controlled by a special-purpose computer. The function of these new switches can be modified through reprogramming rather than through modification of the switching hardware. In addition to improved flexibility, the use of computer-controlled switches offered lower cost and more efficient use of existing transmission facilities.

Additional Services While electronic switching systems will allow the provision of new subscriber services, their use has thus far been aimed at improving the operation of the existing network and reducing operator-assistance requirements. Examples of services made possible by electronic switching include direct-dial credit-card calls, placing a switched-network call on hold, call forwarding, selective handling of calls based on originating number (for example, distinctive ring or call-waiting signal), and selection of special facilities for certain calls (for example, avoiding the use of satellite channels).

Digital Transmission Earlier switching systems used a single analog channel for call supervision (call establishment, routing, termination, and billing) as well as for voice and data traffic. While local-loop traffic remains predominantly analog, traffic between exchanges is increasingly being handled digitally. The use of digital signaling offers significant advantages in terms of equipment complexity and line utilization; it should also reduce setup times for long-distance calls and greatly simplify the addition of new features.

5.3 TELEPHONE SERVICES

The previous two sections have described the telephone and the manner in which individual telephones are connected. This section deals with the major services provided by the telephone network. Section 5.3.1 describes the characteristics of the switched network that affect its use for voice and other types of communication. The remainder of the material describes specialized services used primarily by business customers.

5.3.1   Service Characteristics of the Switched Network

Since most of the telephone system facilities in use today were originally designed to support voice communication, they exhibit characteristics that limit their use for other purposes, such as data communication. This section describes the characteristics of the switched network that can affect its suitability for different kinds of communication.

Bandwidth   A standard voice communication channel supports transmission of frequencies in the range of 300 to 3400 Hz. Frequencies above or below this range are sharply attenuated by normal telephone equipment. When voice channels are multiplexed onto higher speed carriers, signals are filtered to ensure that they lie within this range, so any signaling mechanism that uses the telephone system voice channels must be restricted to the 300- to 3400-Hz range. The rate at which data can be carried within this rather narrow spectrum depends upon the techniques used to encode the data. Transmission speeds in the 300- to 1200-baud range are common on voice channels, although speeds of up to 9600 baud have been demonstrated on "normal" voice channels. As the cost of the electronics necessary to encode and decode signals decreases, transmission speeds over voice-grade channels can be expected to increase.

Signaling Frequencies   When the public switched network is used, certain frequencies within the available voice spectrum must be avoided because they are used by the telephone companies for call supervision signaling. In the United States, the Bell System uses the frequencies of 2400 Hz and 2600 Hz for supervisory signals. As a result, data communication signals are usually restricted to a usable frequency range of roughly 500 to 2400 Hz. Telephone systems in other countries may use other frequencies for supervisory signaling. In Great Britain, for example, the usable frequency range is usually restricted to 1000 to 2000 Hz.

Direction of Transmission   The distinction between half-duplex and full-duplex transmission is somewhat confusing when applied to the telephone system. The confusion results from a common failure to distinguish between the physical characteristics of a transmission facility and the use made of it. The common twisted-wire pair, for example, is inherently half-duplex; any transmission which required the full bandwidth of the pair would be strictly one way at any given time. If a full-duplex channel is required, two twisted pairs are necessary (four-wire service), one pair transmitting in each direction. Virtually all long-haul trunks use separate transmission paths for each direction and are thus four-wire circuits (the terms *two-wire* and *four-wire circuit* are still commonly used to describe the physical distinction between half- and full-duplex transmission facilities, even when there are no wires involved, for example, in fiber optic, microwave, and satellite). The local loop, which connects a subscriber to the local exchange, is generally a twisted pair and is thus inherently half-duplex. The half-duplex local loop can be used as a full-duplex channel, however, by dividing the available frequency spectrum into separate send and receive channels, which can operate simultaneously. In high-performance data communication applications, which require the full-frequency spectrum for full-duplex operation, private-line service can be obtained that provides four-wire local loops.

Call Setup Time   The time required to place a call using the switched network has three primary components: (1) time to receive a dial tone after the subscriber unit goes off-hook (the handset is raised), (2) time to dial the phone number, and (3) the switching time necessary to establish the connection. Call setup time statistics usually exclude the time required for the called party to answer. While the actual delays are dependent upon a number of factors (type of switching equpment used, traffic load, DTMF versus pulsed dialing, etc.), average setup times for a local (7-digit) call in North America typically range from 14 to 22 seconds and are dominated by switching delays (typically 9 to 13 seconds). Call setup times are relatively short when compared to the length of an average telephone conversation but can be a significant factor when automatic dialing equipment under computer control is used for data communication.

Traffic Capacity   The switched network is intended to provide sufficient capacity to allow a high percentage of all calls attempted during periods of heavy load to be completed. The level of service denial ("busy" or "engaged" signal) during peak load hours varies considerably, but a failure rate of 1 to 2 percent is common in the United States. Service denial owing to insufficient capacity results in a busy signal when the called telephone is not actually in use.

The traffic capacity provided by the telephone company has two components: transmission capacity and switching capacity. A typical residential telephone system provides sufficient transmission capacity to allow the origination of calls by roughly 10 percent of its subscriber population at any given time. Telephone systems serving predominantly business subscribers often provide higher capacity. It is worth noting that the transmission capacity required in a given area is heavily dependent upon the characteristics of the traffic being supported. A telephone system that supports 1000 simultaneous calls with an average length of 3 minutes requires roughly the same transmission capacity as a system supporting 100 calls to a time-sharing service with an average call length of 30 minutes.

The switching capacity of a telephone system usually supports a relatively small number of simultaneous subscribers. A residential telephone system that provides transmission capacity to simultaneously support 10 percent of its subscribers might provide switching capacity for less than 1 percent. Thus, a telephone system with 10,000 subscribers might allow 1000 of its subscribers to be engaged in calls they originated, but it would allow only 50 to 100 subscribers to be simultaneously dialing a call. This switching capacity is adequate for normal voice traffic, but service could be seriously degraded if automatic dialing equipment was installed that occupied more than 10 percent of the systems switching capacity.

Transmission Losses and Noise   There are several sources of noise (for example, cross talk between cables, dirty mechanical switch contacts, atmospheric disturbances, and inadequately filtered battery supplies), and the design of the telephone system is intended to minimize its effects. For voice traffic, noise shows up as static and distorted transmission. For data traffic, noise shows up as transmission errors.

Transmission losses arise from the normal attenuation of signal energy during transmission. All of the transmission media described in Section 5.2.3 have transmission loss characteristics which determine the number of amplification states (repeaters) required to transmit a given distance. High-loss transmission media adversely affect noise characteristics because each stage amplifies any noise present.

One of the primary advantages of digital transmission is its relative immunity to noise. While an analog repeater amplifies any noise present on its input, a digital repeater sends an entirely new copy of the received signal from which any noise has been removed. If a digital repeater can recognize its input at all, it can transmit a noise-free copy to the next repeater.

Line Termination   The physical connection between the subscriber's telephone equipment and the local loop is referred to as the line termination. Any equipment that is to be connected to the telephone network must use an approved line termination in order to ensure compatibility with the existing network. Prior to 1968, all telephone equipment was owned by the telephone companies. From 1968 to 1976, equipment not supplied by the telephone companies could be connected to the network only through a direct-access arrangement (DAA), special protective circuitry provided by the telephone company. Since 1976, non-telephone company equipment can be connected if it is approved by the FCC. For standard voice telephone service, the line termination is housed within the telephone itself. For data communication applications, the line termination is usually incorporated in a modem or data set that encodes and decodes digital signals for transmission through the network.

5.3.2 Private-Line Service

The description of the telephone system provided thus far has dealt with what are commonly referred to as switched or direct-distance-dial (DDD) services. Switched service is by far the most common; all telephone service that makes use of the telephone company switching facilities is of this type. Private-line service (also known as leased- or dedicated-line service) makes use of the telephone company transmission facilities but not the switching facilities; it is used when the performance characteristics of the switched network are inadequate or when the high volume of traffic between two points makes use of the switched network uneconomical.

Unlike switched telephone circuits, in which the route to be used is short-lived and determined at the time the call is placed, a private line represents a permanent connection between two or more points and does not use the normal switching equipment. The route is usually established when the private line is installed and is changed infrequently thereafter.

Private lines can offer the following advantages:

1 No call setup is required, since the connection is permanently established. As a result, no automatic dialing equipment is required, the call setup delays are eliminated, and no contingencies are required for frequent busy signals during times of heavy telephone system load. If the traffic volume or frequency of connection is high, the cost of a private line may be lower than the cost of using the switched network. A number of variables affect the break-even point: required line speed, distance between the connected points, number of hours per day that the connection is required, and, most importantly, the applicable telephone company tariffs.

2 Private lines can be "conditioned" to provide higher-quality transmission than is available through the switched network. Conditioning can be used to achieve higher transmission speeds and lower error rates. When line conditioning is requested, the telephone company guarantees the minimum-performance characteristics of the circuit. The actual performance characteristics of a private line may fluctuate, since the telephone company is free to use whatever transmission facilities it deems appropriate as long as those facilities provide the guaranteed level of performance.

3 Transmission over private lines can use a wider range of frequencies than is possible over the switched network, since there is no need to avoid the frequencies reserved for call supervision. The availability of a wider range of frequencies can result in higher transmission speeds.

4 Private lines are less susceptible to noise than switched lines. The switching equipment itself is a major source of noise in the switched network. Private lines eliminate most switching noise.

The performance advantages of private-line service will diminish as the quality of switched-network service improves. Electronic switching equipment, for example, eliminates most of the noise advantage of private lines. While private-line service will remain attractive to high-volume subscribers for the foreseeable future, the costs of private-line service can be expected to increase as the sophistication of the telephone companies' switching and multiplexing equipment increases. The cost of a private line is ultimately tied to the revenue potential that it would represent if it were used to handle switched-network traffic.

5.3.3 Special Communication Services

Several other types of communication services are available through the telephone system. This section describes four widely used services: wide-area telephone service (WATS), foreign exchange (FX) service, telex service, and private exchanges.

WATS WATS is a special long-distance service designed for high-volume users. WATS service has been a topic of active regulatory debate recently, but current tarrifs provide two basic kinds of WATS service: inbound and outbound.

Inbound WATS (now called 800 service) provides a special telephone number that can be called without charge to the calling party. Inbound WATS is widely used for advertising, customer service, and data collection operations. In the past, separate 800 numbers were required for intra- and interstate traffic, but an extra cost option now allows use of a single number. Other options allow the call to be routed to different destinations based on calling location or the time at which the call is placed.

Outbound WATS provides a bulk discount on calls placed to specific geographical areas, but no itemized billing is provided.

FX Service FX service provides a private-line segment that is connected to telephone switching equipment on one end. FX service may cost less than WATS or DDD service if an organization has a sufficiently high volume of long-distance traffic between two cities that can make use of the FX line. FX service can offer more flexibility than normal dedicated-line service if dial access capability can be used effectively.

FX service is available in two forms: inward and outward. Inward FX service allows a subscriber unit located in city A to be connected to the local exchange in city B. Thus subscribers in city B can call the subscriber in city A by placing a local call. Outward FX service allows the subscriber in city A to place local calls to any subscriber in city B. The charges for FX service depend upon the distance between the cities and the charges for business telephone service in effect at each end point.

Telex Telex is a low-cost service for transmitting typewritten messages between locations equipped with specialized terminals. Available worldwide, telex is operated in the United States by Western Union International. There are roughly 140,000 telex subscribers in the United States and 1.5 million worldwide.

Telex uses a sub-voice grade channel (50 to 150 baud) to offer what is essentially a form of electronic mail. Subscribers are equipped with terminals that can be used to transmit typed messages to other subscriber terminals through a switched network. Telex traffic has been growing rapidly; its cost per message is extremely low when compared to voice. Optional features allow the user to request delivery of telex messages as telegrams, cablegrams, or by U.S. mail (mailgram).

Private Exchanges   The rates charged for telephone company service are largely designed to recover the costs incurred to provide that service. In the case of a local subscriber loop, the major cost components include the installation and maintenance of the telephone equipment and the local loop, and a portion of the costs associated with the switching and transmission facilities. When a large number of telephone circuits are required in one location (for example, an office building or manufacturing facility), significant cost savings can be realized by installing a private telephone exchange. A large number of acronyms have been spawned to describe the variety of private exchanges available: PBX (private branch exchange), PAX (private automatic exchange), PABX (private automatic branch exchange), CBX (computerized branch exchange), etc.

Private exchanges are available from telephone companies and from independent manufacturers. Private exchanges range in complexity from simple jack-plug switchboards, in which all calls require manual operator intervention, to sophisticated computer-controlled systems which handle hundreds of circuits of varying bandwidths and provide a variety of automated services not available through the switched network (see Figure 5.6).

In a typical private exchange, all telephones within a building are connected to the private-exchange switching equipment. Calls within the private exchange are handled directly, usually using 3- or 4-digit extensions in place of the full 7-digit telephone number. The private-exchange switching equipment is connected to the switched telephone network using tie lines. Calls to locations outside the private exchange generally require that an extra digit (most often 9) be dialed to obtain access to a tie line, followed by the telephone number which

FIGURE 5.6
Representative PBX functions.

Direct inward dialing	Calls from outside the private exchange can be routed to phones inside the exchange without operator intervention.
Direct outward dialing	Calls from inside the private exchange can access the public telephone network without operator intervention.
Call restriction	Individual phones can be limited to certain kinds of calls (e.g., no long-distance or WATS access).
Call forwarding	Calls to a given phone can be automatically routed to another phone. Forwarding can be permanent or used only when the called party doesn't answer.
Call pickup	Calls to a given phone can be answered by nearby phones.
Conferencing	Several phones can participate in a single conversation.
Call waiting	A user already engaged in a conversation is notified that another party is calling.
Automatic dialing	Frequently used numbers can be dialed with a two- or three-digit code.
Least-cost routing	The type of facility to be used for an outgoing call can be automatically selected by the PBX. This feature is extremely useful for organizations using WATS lines, private lines, or specialized carriers such as MCI.

will be handled by the local telephone company exchange. Incoming calls may access individual PBX extensions directly or may require operator intervention, depending on the kind of service in use. Private exchanges can be connected to communications services other than the switched network. In large organizations, the private exchange provides a direct link to their private lines, WATS service, FX lines, telex facilities, other specialized services, and other private exchanges.

5.3.4   Directory Services

The importance of the directory services provided by the telephone companies is often overlooked. The annual preparation of the Yellow and White pages is a massive publishing effort.

The White Pages contain nearly 80 million listings of residential, business, and government customers. Prior to 1971, the White Pages were prepared manually. Since that time most of the preparation has been automated to provide a number of directories, including the White Pages, automated directories for directory assistance operators, and specialized directories for neighborhood use.

The Yellow Pages represent a major advertising medium for local businesses. It is estimated that AT&T realized revenue of $2 billion in 1982 from Yellow Pages advertising.

The high cost of providing directory services has led some European telephone agencies to experiment with computerized directories in the home as an alternative to printed directories.

5.4   REGULATORY ENVIRONMENT

The competitive telecommunication environment in the United States is atypical and has led to a much more complex structure charged with formulating and administering telecommunication policy than is found in other countries. In Europe, for example, the government agency that provides telecommunication service is also responsible for formulating and administering telecommunication policy. In the United States, however, telecommunication policy is formulated and administered by government agencies, while telecommunication service is provided by competing enterprises. In Europe, telecommunication policy addresses questions about what services should be offered, how the services should be implemented, and when they should be introduced. In the United States, telecommunication policy is concerned with controlling the competitive environment in a manner that encourages the emergence of appropriate services and equitable rate structures.

The regulatory environment in the United States is further complicated by the existence of multiple levels of regulation. While the FCC regulates interstate carriers, each state has a similar regulatory body which controls intrastate communication services. Further, several organizations, such as the Justice Department and the federal and state courts, exercise legal control over the telecommunication industry. Others, such as the American National Standards Institute (ANSI), the Electronic Industries Association (EIA), and the Institute of Electrical and Electronic Engineers (IEEE), establish standards governing the use of telecommunication facilities.

Regulation at the international level is somewhat less dispersed. A single body, the Comité Consultatif International Téléphonique et Télégraphique (CCITT), is charged with establishing standards for the international telecommunication industry.

5.4.1 U.S. Regulatory Environment

Twenty years ago, regulation of the telecommunication industry in the United States was more straightforward than it is today; the FCC and other government bodies were primarily concerned with striking an equitable balance between the corporate needs of the public telephone utilities and the consumer and with preventing counterproductive competition within the telephone industry. This stable regulatory environment was possible because (1) the services provided by the telephone industry were relatively homogenous, their main function being the provision of voice communications, (2) both in research and development and in the manufacture of telephone equipment, the telephone companies appeared to enjoy major economies of scale, and (3) the telephone industry was easily identifiable—there was little difficulty distinguishing between the services provided by the telephone company and those of a computer manufacturer, a publishing company, the postal service, or a radio broadcaster. However, the accelerating pace of technological advance over the last two decades has changed the situation; the conditions underlying the stable regulatory environment no longer exist.

First, the demand for telecommunication services is no longer homogenous. Transmission facilities must carry a number of different forms of information in addition to voice, including text, graphics, facsimile, and video signals. To further confuse the issue, voice is increasingly being treated as a digital data stream rather than an analog voice signal. A number of companies now offer specialized transmission facilities that are optimized for specific applications. In short, the demand for telecommunication service is no longer homogenous.

Second, the dramatic reductions in technology costs and improvements in capabilities have eroded the technological advantages once enjoyed by the telephone companies. In 1960 a satellite earth station cost $3 million dollars; today it is closer to $3000. The cost of a satellite circuit has dropped by a factor of 1000 since 1964. A small computer that cost several million dollars in 1962 could be replaced with a modern personal computer costing under $1000. The outstanding research and development capability of AT&T is no longer unique; rather, it is being challenged by industries ranging from the traditional oil and chemical companies to relatively new industries such as semiconductor, aerospace, and software development. In manufacturing, the erosion of productivity advantages is even more pronounced. Relatively small companies can now compete for a share of the telephone equipment market.

Third, the distinction between industry sectors and markets has become blurred. Western Electric competes with companies ranging from Corning Glass to IBM to Intel. Modern transmission facilities depend upon the aerospace, radio, and cable television companies. The boundaries which separated the telecommunication industry from other industrial sectors no longer exist.

Not surprisingly, the telecommunication regulatory environment is in a state of flux. Regulatory decisions over the last 20 years have shown a strong tendency to deregulate the telecommunication industry and to encourage competition. Both the continuing rapid pace of technological change and the ideological underpinnings of the free enterprise system argue in favor of complete deregulation. The preponderance of monopolistic telecommunication agencies in the international community, the desire to preserve telephone service as a public utility, and the need for compatibility among telecommunication carriers argue in favor of continued regulation of at least some sectors of the telecommunication industry.

5.4.2 Regulatory Environment Outside the United States

Outside the United States, telecommunication services are predominantly state-owned; frequently called *PTTs* (Postes, Télégraphs, Téléphones), they offer a more limited range of services and exhibit markedly different rate structures. In 1980 many countries did not allow data transmission using the switched network, did not allow digitized voice traffic, did not support private-line service, and did not allow private exchanges to access international lines.

Understandably, PTTs do not enjoy dealing with the diversity of American telecommunication providers. If, for example, a French PTT wishes to expand its capacity to Japan, it need only negotiate with the Japanese PTT. If the French PTT wishes to expand its capacity to the United States, however, it may have to negotiate with a half-dozen organizations, each with its own rate structure.

5.4.3 International Regulatory Environment

At the international level, no regulatory body exists which approves tariffs or sets rates. Coordination among the various national carriers results from voluntary compliance with recommendations published by CCITT. Strictly speaking, the CCITT has no legal authority. It neither issues regulations nor sets standards; it simply recommends. In practice, however, CCITT recommendations are almost universally accepted; in many countries, PTTs are required by law to comply with CCITT recommendations.

CCITT is part of the International Telecommunications Union, which is, in turn, a part of the United Nations. The CCITT membership consists of representatives from the telecommunication communities in the United Nations countries. These representatives convene working groups charged with developing and maintaining recommendations covering an aspect of international telecommunications. The recommendations of the working groups are reviewed at plenary assemblies held at four-year intervals. CCITT recommendations cover virtually all aspects of international telecommunications.

Other international standards bodies, for example, the International Standards Organization (ISO), generally accommodate CCITT recommendations when formulating related standards.

5.4.4 Rate Structures

The services offered by telecommunication carriers are described in documents called tariffs. In the United States, all interstate telephone services are covered by tariffs approved by the FCC, and all intrastate telephone services are covered by tariffs approved by state regulatory bodies. Telephone rates for a service described in a specific tariff document are generally approved by the controlling regulatory body. While interstate rates are applied uniformly throughout the United States, rates associated with intrastate tariffs vary considerably from state to state. To further complicate matters, it is not always easy to determine what tariffs apply to a given service. The cost of a private line covering 50 miles, for example, will depend upon whether the connected points lie within the same state or in two different states.

A description of the actual charges used for telephone services is well beyond the scope of this chapter; further, the interval between telephone rate changes is small when compared to the interval between manuscript preparation and publication. Two characteristics of the U.S. rate structures, however, have had a major impact on the development of telephone services; rate-of-return pricing and the shift from pricing based on value to pricing based on cost.

Rate-of-Return Pricing   The telephone rates charged by U.S. common carriers are regulated to allow a controlled rate of return; essentially, revenue is indexed to the book value of the installed equipment. As a result, telephone companies tend to capitalize as much of their physical plant as possible, use straight-line depreciation over long periods, and prefer to use extremely reliable and expensive equipment in order to minimize maintenance expense. These practices are difficult to defend in periods of rapid technological change and have led the FCC to establish regulations aimed at accelerating the depreciation on some classes of telephone company equipment. While accelerated-depreciation schedules are more consistent with modern business practice and should lead to lower operating costs in the long run by increasing the rate at which obsolete equipment is replaced, in the short term they mean higher subscriber rates.

Service Value versus Cost of Operation   Historically, telephone rates have been partially based on their value to different classes of subscribers. The notion of service value is poorly defined, but the intent has been to provide uniform pricing that masks variations in the cost of providing service. For example, telephone subscribers in a rural setting pay the same rate for telephone service as subscribers in a nearby city, even though the cost of providing the service is much higher in sparsely populated areas. Similarly, rates for different types of services are somewhat artificial; long-distance rates were once artificially high and effectively subsidized local telephone service. As the current trend toward decreased regulation and increased competition among common carriers continues, rate structures are beginning to more nearly reflect the cost of providing the service. The increasing use of measured service, in which telephone charges depend upon the number of calls placed, and the lower long-distance rates offered by specialized carriers such as MCI (see Section 5.5.2) represent two examples of the changes taking place.

5.5   TELEPHONE COMPANIES

Telephone service has come to be viewed as an essential public service. In most industrialized nations, governments attempt to ensure widespread availability of uniformly high-quality telephone service. Major capital expenditures are required to provide this service; uncontrolled competition, which results in widespread incompatibility or duplication of facilities, would result in unnecessarily low-quality or high-cost telephone service. The desire to control the development of telecommunication facilities derives from the view that, in at least some aspects, they are inherently monopolistic. Arguments for or against telecommunications as a monopoly tend to be ideologically based and have resulted in state ownership in some countries and state regulation in others. In all countries, some form of regulated monopoly or oligopoly exists.

As previously discussed, the telephone system in the United States encompasses a number of telecommunication providers. The major organizations involved (Figure 5.7) may be loosely classified as common carriers (Section 5.5.1), specialized carriers (Section 5.5.2), international record carriers (Section 5.5.3), and satellite carriers (Section 5.5.4).

5.5.1   Common Carriers

Common carriers provide basic telephone services. They install and maintain telephones, operate local exchanges, and provide long-distance and various other services. The common carriers are what we think of as telephone companies; in 1982 they accounted for roughly 90 percent of the revenues generated by all telecommunication carriers in the United States.

AT&T has been the dominant common carrier in the United States since the invention of the telephone. In 1982, AT&T controlled 80 percent of the

	Common carrier	Specialized carrier	Satellite carrier	IRC
AT&T and Regional Bell Companies	x		x	
GTE	x	x†		
Western Union	x		x	
Rochester Telephone Co.	x			
United Telecom	x	x†		
Continental Telecom	x		x	
Central Telephone and Utility	x			x
ITT World Communication				x
Tymnet		x		
COMSAT			x	
RCA			x	x
Southern Pacific		x	x	
MCI		x		x†
American Satellite Corp.			x	

†Through a subsidiary.

FIGURE 5.7
Major telephone companies and their functional roles.

telephone market and had revenues of $45 billion, assets of roughly $160 billion, and 1 million employees.

Initially formed as the Bell Telephone Company in 1877, the company was reorganized as the American Bell Company in 1879, following an agreement with Western Union which disallowed competition by Western Union for the duration of the initial telephone patents. During the period 1879–1894, American Bell had monopoly control over the telephone market and worked actively to establish its dominance. During this period it acquired Western Electric to become the sole manufacturer of telephone equipment and formed the American Telephone and Telegraph Company to develop long-distance service. In 1900, AT&T became the parent corporation when American Bell was bought with AT&T stock to bring the corporation under New York law from Massachusetts.

The basic Bell patents expired in 1893 and 1894. The period 1894 to 1907 saw a number of independent telephone companies established that were able to compete successfully. By 1907, although Bell still dominated long distance and service in large cities, independents controlled 49 percent of the telephones in the United States.

AT&T's market had been significantly eroded by 1907, and it decided to acquire a telegraph company and independent telephone companies through merger. AT&T acquired a controlling interest in Western Union and, by 1912, had cut independent market share to 42 percent. In 1910 the Interstate Commerce Commission (ICC) began to regulate telephone companies. Under threat of antitrust action, AT&T was forced in 1913 to agree (1) to divest itself of Western Union stock, (2) to allow independents to connect to AT&T facilities, and (3) to refrain from further acquisition of direct competitors. The merger prohibition was relaxed in 1921.

The period from 1910 to 1934 was characterized by a lack of competition, the gradual formation of geographical telephone monopolies, and the gradual acquisition of independents by AT&T. By 1934, AT&T controlled roughly 80 percent of U.S. telephones and virtually all long-distance lines. The Communications Act of 1934 created the FCC, which took over the regulatory functions of the ICC. During the period 1934–1956, AT&T operated as a regulated monopoly; its 80 percent market share and dominance of the long-distance market remained unchanged.

In 1944, the Justice Department filed another antitrust suit against AT&T. AT&T was able to delay action for several years; the suit was eventually settled through the negotiation of the 1956 Consent Decree. The Consent Decree left the Bell System intact, but it restricted future business activities to regulated common carrier services and required Bell to license its proprietary patents.

The period 1956–1982 was characterized by regulatory pressure to stimulate competition. The 1968 "Carterphone" decision allowed nontelephone company equipment to be connected to the telephone network, which stimulated competition in commercial telephone equipment manufacture. Connection restrictions were further relaxed in 1975 and 1976, which stimulated competition in the home market. Specialized carriers began to compete with AT&T in 1969.

In 1974 the Justice Department again filed an antitrust suit against AT&T which eventually resulted in the 1982 negotiated settlement calling for a major restructuring of AT&T which took effect in 1984. Figure 5.8 compares the anticipated pre- and post-divestiture organization of AT&T. The major components of the predivestiture organization include:

1 Western Electric, AT&T's vertically integrated manufacturing unit.
2 Bell Laboratories, AT&T's highly regarded research and development unit.
3 AT&T Long Lines, which provides all long-distance service.
4 Bell Operating Companies (BOC), consisting of 22 separate telephone companies providing service to specific geographical areas.
5 AT&T International, which is responsible for all international telephone service.
6 American Bell, a new organizational unit charged with handling unregulated and competitive services. American Bell began operation in 1983 as a result of a 1980 FCC ruling allowing AT&T to reenter the competitive market through a separate subsidiary.
7 Advanced Mobile Phone Service, another new organizational unit charged with developing and marketing mobile telephone service.

The divestiture will result in two visible organizational changes. First, AT&T Long Lines will become AT&T Communications and will provide intrastate

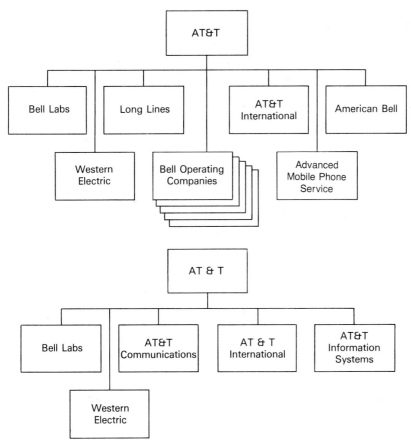

FIGURE 5.8
Pre- and post-divestiture organization of AT&T.

interexchange service in addition to its current interstate service. Second, Bell Operating Companies will be restructured to form seven regional corporations that are organizationally independent of AT&T. In addition to these visible changes, the roles of existing units will change. Western Electric, for example, will no longer be the sole supplier of equipment to the operating companies.

While the structure shown in Figure 5.8 is current at the time of this writing, further changes can be expected.

5.5.2 Specialized Carriers

The specialized common carriers offer public access to telecommunication facilities that are tailored to specific applications. MCI and ITT World Communications, for example, offer low-cost sub-voice-grade circuits. GTE Telenet,

Tymnet, and United Telecom's Uninet offer packet-switched data communications services. MCI and Southern Pacific Communications offer low-cost, long-distance voice-grade service.

The number of specialized carriers can be expected to grow during the next decade. While a number of proposed specialized carriers (for example, Datran) have failed since the 1969 FCC decision allowing specialized carriers, a number of specialized data communications networks which use common carrier transmission facilities are expected to enter the market as second-tier carriers. (First-tier carriers own and lease telecommunications lines; second-tier carriers use the first-tier lines and add services to meet the needs of a specific market segment).

In 1969, MCI Communications Corporation became the first specialized common carrier when it received FCC approval to build and operate a microwave link between St. Louis and Chicago. The FCC ruling marked the end of a 6-year legal battle in which AT&T contended that MCI would be unfair competition, since it would offer profitable services in profitable geographical areas, while the common carriers were forced to offer services in less profitable markets.

MCI's initial business offering consisted of leasing microwave channels to large commercial users; pricing was attractive and their network expanded rapidly. In the early 1970s, MCI began to expand services to commercial users by developing enhanced long-distance voice offerings and later by offering complete network management services under which MCI managed all of an organization's telecommunication needs.

More recently, MCI and other specialized carriers have begun offering long-distance voice service to the general public at rates below those charged by the common carriers. These new services employ the local facilities of the common carriers to allow subscribers to access the long-distance facilities of the specialized carriers. The specialized carriers must pay the local exchange an access charge for the use of their facilities. The common carriers have long maintained that the access charges paid by the specialized carriers do not cover the cost of providing the access service. Since it appears likely that access charges will increase and that common carrier long-distance rates will decrease, it is uncertain whether long-distance voice will remain a lucrative service for the specialized common carriers. MCI and others are experimenting with ways to provide subscriber access to their services that avoid common-carrier facilities by using radio or cable television networks.

MCI has continued to expand the capacity and geographical coverage of its network by adding both microwave facilities and newer technologies, such as fiber optics.

5.5.3   International Record Carriers

In the past, international telecommunication traffic was divided into voice traffic and record traffic (telex, facsimile, data, etc). All international voice traffic was handled by the common carriers (specifically AT&T) under operating agreements with individual PTTs. All record traffic was handled by a relatively small number of international record carriers (IRCs) under separate operating agreements with the PTTs. While the distinction between voice and record traffic has largely disappeared, the regulatory distinction remains. AT&T and the IRCs now handle both forms of traffic; since 1982 the IRCs have been allowed to offer domestic services.

Twenty years ago, international telecommunication traffic was carried by undersea cable, whose capital requirements limited the number of international carriers. The rapid development of satellite telecommunication over the last two decades and the emergence of the satellite carriers have reduced the capital and technical barriers preventing entry of additional IRCs. While new carriers can be expected, significant regulatory and political barriers still exist.

5.5.4 Satellite Carriers

The satellite carriers are relative newcomers to the telecommunication industry but already carry a high percentage of long-distance voice, video, and data traffic. Experimental and military communications satellites existed as early as 1958, but commercial telephone traffic did not begin until 1965. The Communications Satellite Act of 1962 created the Communications Satellite Corporation (COMSAT) as the U.S. carrier for international satellite communications, which effectively precluded the use of satellites for domestic telephone traffic. The creation of COMSAT was followed shortly by the formation of the International Telecommunications Satellite Organization (INTELSAT) in 1964. Commercial use of the INTELSAT series of satellites began in 1965.

In 1970 the Office of Telecommunications Policy recommended the commercial use of satellites for domestic communication. In 1971 the FCC indicated, through its open-skies policy, that it would consider applications to operate domestic satellite facilities. Western Union launched the first U.S. satellites used for domestic telecommunication in 1974, followed closely by other satellite carriers.

The advances in satellite telecommunication have been impressive. The first INTELSAT satellite had a capacity of roughly 240 voice channels (or 1 television channel), provided two-way service between Europe and North America, and had a design life of 1.5 years; each voice channel cost $23,000 per year. Current satellites handle in excess of 15,000 voice-grade channels, provide communications between dozens of earth stations, and have a design life of 10 years; each channel costs roughly $30 per year.

The satellite carriers originally served the common carriers and the IRCs. Like other segments of the telecommunication industry, the role of the satellite carriers is changing; they now package their transmission facilities in a number of ways to serve specialized markets. COMSAT, for example, continues to lease channels to major common carriers (AT&T and GTE) who use them to support transmission of voice, television, teleconferencing, and some data. American

Satellite Company specializes in data and voice traffic transmitted between small earth stations located at customer sites. Western Union has integrated its satellite channels and its terrestrial microwave network to provide private-line service between selected cities and to support its telex and mailgram services.

5.6 FUTURE OF THE TELEPHONE SYSTEM

We can confidently assert that the telephone system will undergo substantial change over the next decade. The difficulty of predicting the nature of this change arises not from the difficulty of predicting changes in the underlying technologies but from the difficulty of predicting the regulatory environment and distinguishing between "basic" telephone services and related services in which competition will be allowed.

5.6.1 Regulation and Competition

As a result of the FCC Computer II decision of 1980, basic telephone services will continue to be regulated and offered by the common carriers, while enhanced services and terminal equipment will be offered on an unregulated and competitive basis. AT&T and GTE will be allowed to compete in the unregulated market only through independent subsidiaries. The precise distinction between basic and enhanced services will remain unclear for some time and the situation is further complicated by the 1982 antitrust settlement, which is not entirely compatible with Computer II. Despite current uncertainties, the trend of the last decade can be expected to continue, thereby favoring competitive service offerings in the domestic market.

The international regulatory climate is less clear. While some countries (notably, Great Britain) are moving toward increased competition, most others are opposed to the U.S. policy of encouraging competition. While foreign opposition will have little effect on the U.S. domestic market, it will tend to preserve the market shares of the current international voice and record carriers and will discourage competitive international rate setting.

5.6.2 New Communication Technology

The telephone industry has traditionally been a high-technology field. Indeed, some of the world's most advanced telecommunications research and equipment are produced by Bell Laboratories and Western Electric. Despite the technical sophistication of telephone research and manufacturing, the rate at which new technology has been incorporated in the telephone system has lagged; the huge capital costs of replacing or upgrading subscriber equipment or switching equipment in low-volume exchanges are prohibitive.

At a time when the technical sophistication of the telephone network is lagging, both the market for improved services and the number of organizations capable of providing them are growing. The technical sophistication of semiconductor, computer, and other potentially competitive organizations equals or exceeds that of the telephone companies; the accelerating demands of the new information industry have outstripped any single organization's ability to supply.

As a result of increased competitive pressure and the opportunity for significant technological improvements in the telephone system, the next decade will witness major improvements in the function and cost performance of the telephone system.

1 The cost of telephone service will become nearly distance-insensitive as a result of increased satellite and radio transmission capacity and improved multiplexing of terrestrial transmission.

2 Digital transmission will largely supplant analog signaling, thereby offering better error rates, substantially simplified computer-to-computer communication, and greater flexibility.

3 Intelligent telephones will become common; future telephones will more closely resemble small computers that facilitate access to the variety of communication services available to the home.

4 Subscriber telephone service will increasingly allow communication over CATV and radio channels in addition to the local loop.

5 A variety of new computer-based services will be offered through the telephone system (for example, videotext, electronic mail, security, and medical-alert systems).

6 The cost of basic telephone services will rise, but the cost of enhanced services will fall.

The changes wrought by increased competition and improved technology will not be without cost. The useful life of telephone equipment will shrink from decades to a period more closely resembling a computer terminal or expensive video game (1 to 4 years). Further, the rates charged for new services will necessarily attempt to recover development costs over short and speculative lifetimes.

RECOMMENDED READING

Brock, G. W., *The Telecommunications Industry,* Cambridge: Harvard University Press, 1981.

Brooks, J. *Telephone, the First Hundred Years,* New York: Harper & Row, 1975.

Hills, M. T., *Telecommunications Switching Principles,* Cambridge: MIT Press, 1979.

Lighthill, Sir J., Eastwood, E., May, C. A., and Cattermole, K. W., *Telecommunications in the 1980's and After,* London: Cambridge University Press, 1978.

McNamara, J. E., *Technical Aspects of Data Communication,* Bedford, Mass.: Digital Press, 1977.

Pool, I. de S., *The Social Impact of the Telephone,* Cambridge: MIT Press, 1977.

Pool, I. de S., *Forecasting the Telephone, a Retrospective Technology Assessment,* Norwood, N.J.: Ablex, 1982.

Povey, P. J., *The Telephone and the Exchange,* London: Pittman, 1979.

CHAPTER 6

DIGITAL COMMUNICATION NETWORKS

Alan E. Negus
Consultant
Biggleswade, Bedfordshire SG18 8DU
United Kingdom

6.1 HISTORICAL INTRODUCTION

In the earlier chapters we learned about the ways in which signals are transmitted, and something of the different requirements for analog and digital transmission. We have also seen how the telephone network developed and how it operates today. It is now time to take a look at digital communication networks—why they exist, how they operate, and what they have to offer.

Put quite simply, digital networks exist today to improve the quality and capabilities of communication between and with computers. Actual transmission of digital signals was covered in previous chapters. Often the transmission medium will be the public switched-telephone network or private wires leased from the common carrier or PTT; even where it is privately owned and maintained, for example, within one site or building, the same transport media—twisted pairs, coaxial cables, optical fibers, microwave radio links, etc.—will be used.

It is important to distinguish between the transmission techniques used, the purpose for which the transmission service is provided, and that for which it is used. Thus, more and more voice lines are being provided, at least between switching centers, or exchanges, by digital techniques, because there are certain advantages in doing so. For example, the capacity of a given physical channel can be increased, the need for repeater stations can be reduced, and the quality of each voice channel can be maintained at a higher level with less effort. But this does not make such circuits part of a digital communication network in the sense in which it is being discussed in this chapter.

Communication networks for the transmission of digital signals have existed for many years, and in one sense they predate the telephone networks, with early telegraphy being a type of digital transmission. And, of course, telex and teletypewriter exchange service (TWX) are also digital networks dating from the earlier part of this century.

With the proliferation of computers and computer systems in recent years, digital networks have become far more important. At first, remote access to computers was mainly aimed at obtaining computer power which could not be obtained locally, but in recent years, perhaps over the last decade, the prime motivation has been slanted toward access to data as lower costs have brought sufficient power within the reach of more and more potential users.

6.1.1 Why Digital Networks

Before considering networks in detail it is necessary to look at some of the reasons why they exist—what advantages they offer over the public switched-telephone network, or leased lines, for example.

When a single connection between two computers or between a terminal and a computer is required, the only real advantage in using a network intended for digital transmission is that the integrity of the transmitted data is likely to be better, owing to the characteristics of the network with its inbuilt error detection and correction facilities. Costs, too, may be different, but this is really incidental because of utilization levels and general policy decisions rather than the presence of the digital network *per se*. The real benefits come when it is necessary to connect more than two machines, perhaps not at precisely the same instant but certainly on a routine and frequent basis.

However, the main benefits of digital communication networks are, perhaps, best appreciated when shown in the form of a simple list:

1 Transmission costs are lower, particularly at higher speeds.
2 Data is less liable to become distorted during transmission.
3 Sender and receiver need not operate at the same speed.
4 Sender and receiver need not use the same character codes.
5 The range of devices which can communicate with each other is increased.

There are several distinct types of digital network in use today, with different techniques used for the transmission and routing of signals. For practical purposes the only distinction necessary for the reader to understand is that between public networks, that are usually based on packet switching, and local area networks providing a service to link a number of devices, typically within one site.

6.1.2 Early Digital Networks

The early digital communication networks, telex and TWX, operate on the principle of circuit switching, with a continuous communication channel being established for the duration of a call and dedicated to that call, whether or not any data is actually being transmitted. The regular telephone service is also circuit-switched: once a telephone is being used for one call, no other calls can be made, or incoming calls received. When plans were first being made for digital networks to carry computer-to-computer traffic, several telecommunications administrations (*administration* is used here to mean a PTT or a recognized common carrier) seriously considered the provision of circuit-switched high-speed digital transmission networks. One such service was the Caducée circuit-switched network operated by the French PTT in the early 1970s, offering speeds of 2400 to 9600 baud and even 48 or 72 kilobaud in certain localized areas. However, there are now few who would consider providing such a service, except in very special circumstances.

Clearly, in many instances the full capacity of a communication channel is only used for a small increment of the time that a call occupies. This is manifestly true in the case of normal telephone conversations—although there are those cases where both parties talk at the same time. It is also true of much communication with computers, particularly with interactive services. A method of using this fact to increase the utilization of communication channels—particularly important for expensive long-distance links—has been developed and is now widely used for digital networks. This technique, *packet switching*, may be regarded as a particular and formalized version of message switching, whereby a communication link is only used for as long as data is actually being transmitted, rather than being made available, and therefore unavailable for use by any other party, for the whole period of time during which the parties wish to interact.

An early and readily understandable example of a message-switching system for digital transmissions is the torn-tape relay, which was used on a worldwide scale by Societé Internationale de Télécommunications Aeronautique (SITA). SITA was formed in 1949 with 11 member airlines; it had the simple aim of providing better, more cost-effective, interline communication between airlines and from sales offices to central offices. At the time most airlines lacked the traffic to justify leased circuits on any but a few routes, and the public switched networks were slow in the absence of international subscriber dialing on either telex or telephone. From the beginning the SITA network used message switching as opposed to circuit switching in the communications centers on its trunk circuit network. Originally, leased telex lines were used between the centers, which naturally contained a number of telex terminals. Messages were transmitted onward from originator to recipient by the simple expedient of punching incoming messages at each center onto paper tape and then sending the same message, using the paper tape as input, over the next dedicated link. Messages could easily be sent to two or more destinations from appropriate centers in the network. Of course, manual switching using paper tape has now been replaced by automatic switching and store-and-forward computer centers, but the principle remains the same.

Packet switching takes this concept one stage further. Instead of each message

FIGURE 6.1
A military "torn-tape" teletype relay center of the 1940s. Incoming messages were recorded on punched paper tape, and the tape was carried from an incoming receiver to a transmitter connecting the relay center with the destination or another relay station. (Courtesy U.S. National Archives Trust.)

being forwarded from point to point until it reaches its ultimate intended destination, a message is split into fixed-length segments which are forwarded separately and reassembled at the destination. The maximum size of each segment is fixed arbitrarily and is quite independent of message length.

6.1.3 Emergence of Packet Switching

The concept of packet switching was first proposed in the mid-1960s by Paul Baran (1964a; 1964b) in the United States and independently by Donald Davies (Davies et al., 1967) in the United Kingdom. The first experimental link was between the TX-2 computer at Lincoln Laboratory and the AN/FSQ-32 computer at the System Development Corporation (SDC) in 1966 (Marrill & Roberts, 1966). Following this, the U.S. Advanced Research Projects Agency (ARPA) decided to fund an experimental network, and the first tests with a 4-node network were made in 1969.

The ARPAnet, as it came to be known, developed quickly during the early 1970s as the necessary techniques were refined and permitted useful resource-sharing activities by mid-1971, which may be regarded as the date at which the first operational packet-switched network of the sort we know today became operational (Roberts, 1974; Roberts & Wessler, 1970).

Although ARPAnet was primarily a network connecting computers in universities and research institutions and allowing remote terminal access to those computers, there were some commercial time-sharing machines connected to the network and, most importantly, it demonstrated the clear advantages of packet switching and set the pattern for future developments.

There are other techniques that can be used with digital networks, message switching mentioned above being one, and some of these are mentioned in Section 6.8 and in Chapter 7, where local area networks (LANs) are discussed. However, for public digital networks it seems that packet switching does and will predominate, message switching and circuit switching having been examined by some authorities and, for the time being at least, discarded.

6.2 PACKET SWITCHING

Before going on to look at some of the ways in which packet-switched networks can be used, and the specific benefits that can be obtained from what has come to be known in some areas as a *value-added network,* that is, one that offers more than normal telephone companies and authorities, it is necessary to understand how they operate and to consider why they are attractive and what makes them possible.

6.2.1 Basic Principles of Packet Switching

An outline of the philosophy behind packet switching has been given above, using the torn-tape relay as an illustration. But, of course, the realization of an operational and reliable network is far from simple.

The basic components of the network are the computers comprising the nodes of the network, to which computers and terminals alike must connect, and the transmission links between the nodes. The internode transmission links are typically leased lines provided by telephone administrations (who may themselves operate the packet-switched network) and may physically be any of the methods mentioned earlier and described more fully in Chapters 4 and 5. Of course, the capacity of those links need not concern the network user, except in extremely rare circumstances. Normally they will be more than capable of satisfying user requirements.

Network nodes consist of computers which must handle a number of functions to ensure the smooth and reliable transmission of data. Before looking at these functions it is necessary to consider, in broad terms, what is involved. First, there is a calling party and a called party, which may both be computers, although often one will be a terminal. In the language of telecommunication administrations, both these fall into that class of devices known as data terminal equipment (DTE). Perhaps the most helpful distinction is that made by British Telecom between a packet terminal, that is, an intelligent device such as a computer, and character terminals such as simple visual display units or teletypewriters. It is important to note that this distinction must be applied to the manner in which a device is in fact connected to a packet-switched network, rather than to its inherent, but perhaps unused, capabilities. Thus an "intelligent" or "smart" terminal will often operate as a character terminal, although it is potentially capable of operating as a packet terminal, given suitable software. In this chapter, the term *computer* is often used to indicate a mainframe or minicomputer operating in packet mode, or at least connected to the network in packet mode, perhaps via some interface device. The word *terminal* is used to indicate a device, be it a simple character-mode terminal or a sophisticated microcomputer, operating in character mode when connected to a packet-switched network.

The actual connection of the DTE to the network will be through some sort of data circuit terminating equipment (DCE)—a modem or acoustic coupler, for example—and a dialed or leased line. In other words, the boundary of the network is at the DCE.

During any connection, messages of varying length will be sent at unpredictable times, as far as the network is concerned, and either DTE may originate a message.

Additionally the two DTEs in communication may wish to transmit data at different speeds, possibly using different codes. Naturally, each device will wish to know where each message originates, just as it would if a dedicated circuit were used for the duration of the session or permanently.

Against this background, the functions that must be provided to operate the network become clearer.

Within the network, packets must be correctly forwarded to the correct final destination, so that at each node there must be provision to examine the source and destination of each packet and deal with it accordingly. The breaking of each message into packets, and reorganization of received packages to reform the message, could be carried out by the sending and receiving DTE, of course, but this would result in a rather primitive and limited network as far as users were concerned, so these functions, too, must be present in the network. These tasks are performed by a packet assembler-disassembler (PAD).

In a packet-switched network, each packet transmitted through the network must travel complete with addresses of originator and destination. Already we have seen that the need to provide this information with each packet is taken away from the user. However, it is not particularly attractive if the user must provide this information with each message. Particularly in the case of interactive use from an online terminal, many of the messages sent by the terminal are extremely short, maybe only one or two characters, and the terminals used are often very simple, or "dumb," and would be incapable of providing any assistance to the user who would have to key in the appropriate information repeatedly. This mode of operation, where each message must be addressed individually by the sender, is often known as a datagram service.

For most networks, since much of the traffic will be interactive, rather than communication from mainframe (or mini) to mainframe, additional facilities are needed whereby originators can identify themselves and the destination for the duration of a session. This is often known as a *virtual-call facility,* whereby the network will add the necessary information to each packet as it is created from input messages.

6.2.2 Connection to a Network

At each of its nodes the network must allow for different forms of connection appropriate to different types of equipment. For terminals this will generally mean the provision of modems to handle low-speed transmission at, say, 300 to 1200 baud and possibly the ability to handle different character sets, for example, ASCII or EBCDIC. It may also be necessary to allow for terminals operating in full-duplex (echoplex) and in half-duplex.

For more powerful devices, that is, computers, more sophisticated capabilities may be provided, as the computer has the ability to meet the characteristics of the network more precisely. Thus a computer may connect to the network via a "black box" which makes the network look like a set of, say, 1200 baud asynchronous lines, or it may connect more directly, using its own front-end processor to format messages according to the protocols of the network. Most networks today conform to CCITT recommendations, which specify the interface between DTE and network. Recommendation X25 is perhaps the most widely known of these (CCITT, 1981a, 1981b).

An additional range of facilities whose complexity is unseen by the user, although its effects are not, is necessary once a network operates commercially. No matter what method is chosen, quite complicated internal accounting procedures are necessary. Thus, for each call set up the network must be able to identify the originator of the call as an authorized user and store details of the source and destination, the duration of the call, and the volume of data sent, as all of these are needed either to calculate the charge or for identification purposes. Additionally, where reverse charging is used, the called party must be notified of the calling party in a form recognizable by the called party. (Reverse charging is a procedure where the called party pays the network operator; it is precisely the same as calling collect or reversing the charges with a normal telephone call, except that there is no operator intervention. It should be noted that reverse charging is not permitted by some administrations.) The called party may or may not pass this charge on to the originator of the call.

The basis of charging may vary from network to network, although a charge based on duration and volume is becoming more and more usual. There will often be an initial registration fee and a small standing charge in addition to usage charges.

6.2.3 Benefits of Packet Switching

The most obvious benefit is that packet switching increases the effective capacity of transmission channels, as these no longer have to be solely dedicated to one connection for the duration of that connection whether or not anything is actually being transmitted. However, this increase in the effective capacity is partially offset by the cost of the computing power that must be present in the network. The steady decrease in the costs of computer power, at the same time as costs for transmission links have continued to rise (although not as rapidly as they might have done, owing to growing use of microwave links, satellites, and optical fibers), has made packet switching viable.

There are other advantages as well. Because the network has intelligence, in data handling at least, it is possible to allow more flexibility. For example, it is not necessary that the speeds of both communicating devices be the same; indeed, they may not be forced to use the same code for representation of data. Error detection and correction procedures can reduce or almost eliminate the chance of incorrect data being received. High-speed transmission over long distances becomes particularly cost-effective when only relatively short leased lines are needed to connect from a user's site to the nearest access point of the network. And alternate routing, which can be carried out on a packet-by-packet basis if really necessary, can give almost absolute reliability to a developed packet-switched network.

6.3 MORE ABOUT ARPAnet

ARPAnet was introduced briefly in Section 6.1.3 as the first operational packet-switched network. A deeper examination of the network is instructive in giving greater insight into the methods of operation of a packet-switched public data transmission service, although there are, of course, some differences between what is possible—or, indeed, required—with what is essentially a research network. The original purpose of the ARPA network was to permit resource sharing between computer centers, and the original design reflects this goal. The basic requirement was that users of any one machine connected to the network should be able to access the facilities available on other machines. In other words, primary access for the user would be via one of these machines, or *hosts,* as they came to be known. In fact the term *hosts* has now become common usage for a computer attached to a digital communication network.

Strictly speaking, the ARPA network consisted of the communication subnet, together with all the computers attached to the network, and properly, ARPAnet should be used in this sense. Often, however, the term is used to refer to the communication network only. Initially, the communication network

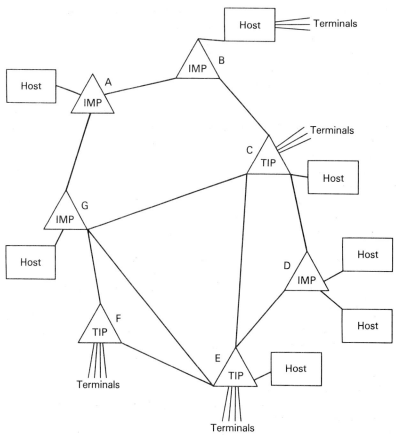

FIGURE 6.2
Schematic of an ARPAnet network showing use of interface message processors (IMPs) and terminal interface processors (TIPs) to connect hosts and terminals. Redundancy in connections between nodes allows alternative routings to cope with congestion or breakdown. Thus, packets from *A* to *E* could follow routes such as *A-G-E, A-B-C-E,* or *A-G-F-E.*

consisted of a network computer, known as an interface message processor (IMP), at the site of each host, and connected to the host, with IMPs being connected together using 50-kilobaud leased lines. Later, higher-speed lines were used on some routes. The topography of the network showed the first deviation from earlier data networks, although it should be noted that the arrangement adopted was exactly the same as that used by providers of telephone services. Nevertheless, it is noteworthy that ARPAnet did not use a star configuration with one central control unit through which all messages must pass. Instead, each IMP was connected to neighboring IMPs, with messages between two different points passing through several intervening IMPs, perhaps. Multiple connections provided alternative routes, invaluable in the case of either line or IMP failure, or network congestion.

In hardware terms, IMPs were rather simple devices, comprising Honeywell DDP-516 minicomputers with 12K words of 16-bit memory and a teletype and a high-speed paper tape reader for maintenance, debugging, and system modification only (Heart, et al., 1970). Each IMP could accommodate up to four hosts, and 60 outgoing lines (63 if there was only one host). In practice, the limits were seldom approached. Messages from the host were broken into packets with a maximum size of approximately 1000 bits, and reassembled by the destination IMP for delivery to the receiving host. Addressing was carried out initially by the sending host, which added a leader to each message. A header, derived from this leader together with some other information required for network purposes, was added to each packet by the IMP. Being individually transmitted, each packet in a message could follow a different route, and IMPs therefore had the capability to reassemble packets in their correct sequence before delivery. IMPs clearly have a finite capacity, so the IMP software contained routines to ensure that overflow could not occur and packets become lost. This was aided by having only one message on a link at any one time—a message having a maximum size of 8095 bits, and a link comprising a conceptual path between two points. After one message had entered a link, that link was blocked until the sending IMP was notified by the destination IMP that all the message had been received. This notification was done by sending a special control message known as Ready for Next Message (RFNM). Packets themselves contained sequences of check digits to enable error detection. On acceptance in error-free form, acknowledgment messages were sent, retransmission being used when appropriate. Thus a message would move on, packet by packet and step by step, from one IMP to another, until it reached the destination.

With the original ARPA network, it was necessary for users to be connected to one of the hosts attached to the network in order to be able to reach any of the other hosts. The actual transmission of messages was then carried out by the network, but other matters, such as dealing with differences in terminal capabilities and characteristics, would be carried out by the local host, in effect. To overcome this limitation and allow direct connection of terminals to the network, the *terminal interface processor* (TIP), was developed (Ornstein, 1972). A TIP used a Honeywell H-316, with 20K words of store, and was able to handle up to 63 terminals, which could be local to the TIP or connected via a modem. Additionally, a host was able to connect to a TIP in the same way as to an IMP. TIP handled terminals with varying characteristics, being able to identify and accommodate a variety of speeds and character sets by analyzing characters sent by the terminal at the time of establishing the connection. How this appeared to the user is shown in the following section on the Telenet network.

6.4 THE TELENET NETWORK

Arguably the first commercial packet-switched network set up purely to provide data communications for third parties was Telenet. (Earlier data services were set up originally for a specific purpose, and were based on message switching rather than true packet switching. For example, Tymnet was created to provide access to time-sharing services).

Telenet was based firmly on ARPAnet and was in fact founded by Larry Roberts, previously the head of ARPAnet. Service began in a limited form in 1975 and had expanded to offer local access from nearly 200 U.S. cities by 1982. Telenet Communications Corporation has now been taken over by GT&E to form GTE-Telenet, but, essentially, network operations and capabilities remain unchanged. Telenet does not in fact own or operate transmission lines—these are leased from other common carriers—but only the computer nodes that make up the packet-switched network. It is, therefore, a *value-added network,* that is, one that operates on top of the facilities offered by the telephone companies and adds extra value to them.

The techniques used with Telenet to determine routing, deal with errors, and so forth arise from those used with ARPAnet, although modifications have been made in the light of operational experience. However, these parts of the network, and the fact that alternative routing can be used, remain invisible to the user, who is really only concerned with setting up a call. It is rather easy to set up a call using Telenet, because first, it is a national network, second, it operates on the basis of reverse and third, it is used largely for remote-terminal access rather than computer-to-computer communication. Having dialed the nearest Telenet node the user enters two consecutive carriage-return characters which the network uses to identify terminal speed. Telenet responds with a message confirming the connection and requesting that the user identify the type of terminal being used by entering the appropriate code selected from a list supplied by Telenet. The network responds by printing @, at which point the user enters a short code number to identify the computer he or she wishes to access. Each of these user inputs is terminated by carriage return. When a session with a host has been terminated, the user is normally returned to the network, which confirms that the connection has been terminated and issues another @ so that the user may connect to another computer. Connection to the network is normally terminated by ending the telephone connection to the network node, that is, by hanging up.

6.5 THE EURONET NETWORK

Euronet was set up on the initiative of the Commission of the European Communities, Directorate General XIII, Information Market and Innovation by a consortium of the then nine European PTTs (Purser, 1982). Euronet really sprang from a decision of the Council of Ministers, made in July 1971, to promote better use of scientific and technical information throughout the EC countries. Real planning for the communication network got under way in 1975, and the network became fully operational in 1980. As is the case with ARPAnet, there is some confusion over the use of the term *Euronet.* This was originally used to mean the total service, the packet-switched network, and the hosts offering information services over that network. However, with the separation of responsibility, hosts being operated by independent bodies quite separate from the PTT consortium, Euronet became the term for the communication network itself. The name DIANE (Direct Information Access Network for Europe) was coined to identify hosts collectively, with the term Euronet-DIANE being used for the total complex of services. Nevertheless, in spite of this clear distinction, the different terms have been used indiscriminately by many commentators. In fact, any host computer may connect to the packet-switched network Euronet no matter what services, if any, are offered. Also, several computers are connected for private access only, the traffic to such hosts being designated third-party traffic.

Euronet was created as an international network conforming to all the relevant CCITT recommendations and is thus somewhat more complicated to use than is Telenet, for example. Initially, Euronet consisted of nodes in Frankfort, London, Paris, and Rome, with remote-access concentrators in the other countries of the European Communities. It has been extended since then, first to Switzerland, and then to other countries, including Greece, Sweden, Finland, and Portugal. The network is fully compatible with and based on the technology of the French national packet-switched network, Transpac.

As national networks develop, parts of Euronet are disappearing as a separate network and being replaced by links between other national networks which conform to the same protocols, the method by which a user contacts a given host remaining essentially unchanged.

Euronet is used both for the purpose for which it was initially sponsored—that is, remote-terminal access to online information retrieval systems providing a public service—and for private traffic and computer-to-computer communication.

Tariffs are set by the national PTTs, who provide the service in their own jurisdictions. They are distance-independent, being based on duration of call and volume of data transmitted, although there are variations from country to country and special rates may apply in special circumstances, for example, off-peak usage or bulk transfer. In general, reverse charging is not allowed, the originator of the call being billed by the national PTT.

Establishing a call on Euronet involves the entry of two major components: the network user address (NUA) to identify the destination and the network user identifier (NUI), a personal password to identify the caller. NUAs are numbers made up of components to identify the country in which the destination DTE is situated, the network to be used, and the specific DTE. It is constructed thus in accordance with CCITT recommendations designed to allow for full international interworking in the fullness of time.

Having called the local Euronet node, the user of a character-mode terminal must first enter a letter H to allow the network to adjust for the speed of the terminal (unless a single speed port has been called). The user must then enter the letter N, followed by the NUI, followed by a hyphen, the NUA, a letter D or P followed by information to be transmitted to the host, for example, the host name, ending this sequence with a carriage return. Connection is confirmed by the network before the called DTE responds.

On Euronet, and indeed other networks, users are permitted to change a number of so-called PAD parameters. Some parameters may be changed by both calling and called parties, while alteration of some may be restricted to one or the other. For example, it is possible to specify the conditions that should be met in order to send a packet when the DTE is a character-mode terminal. The network can be set up to transmit under what the operator considers are sensible conditions: after 64 characters have been entered (although the packet size is 128 characters on Euronet, charging is based on segments of 64 characters), or a carriage return has been entered, or the terminal has been inactive for a set period, such as 5 seconds. It may be necessary, with certain systems, to have a particular character, such as *escape,* recognized as the end of message symbol by the DTE and thus initiate the sending of a packet. If a terminal wishes to operate in full-duplex with a host computer, it will be necessary to send each entered character in a separate packet. (This practice is not recommended. Not only is it expensive, but there will certainly be some delay between hitting a key, and the character appearing on the screen—a most disconcerting phenomenon, which can also occur when operating in full-duplex via a satellite link.) Such changes can be made by either party, although it is more usual for them to be made by a time-sharing computer, for example, to ensure that input is received and interpreted correctly.

6.6 OTHER PUBLIC NETWORKS

Many other public networks are in operation or about to be introduced, the vast majority of them packet-switched. An important feature of this growth is the interconnection of different, usually national, networks, either directly, or via international gateways (Casey, 1982; "National Networks Interaction," 1982). Thus, the first true international network (as opposed to networks in North America, or remote access to American networks from Europe), Euronet, is being replaced by interconnecting of national networks, with the immediate benefit that it will become accessible via a local call or a short leased circuit from all those points served by nodes of a national network—a situation that has existed in France for some time, access to Euronet being via Transpac.

Some more important networks are:

Belgium—DCS
Canada—Datapac
Canada—Infoswitch
Finland—Finnpak
France—Transpac

Japan—DDX-P
Mexico—SCT
Netherlands—Datanet
Norway—Norpak
Spain—RETD
Sweden—Telepak
Switzerland—Telepac
United Kingdom—PSS
United States—Telenet
United States—Tymnet
United States—Uninet
West Germany—Datex-P

International gateways include:

Australia—Midas
Canada—Teleglobe
France—NTI
Japan—ICEA, Venus-P
New Zealand—Oasis
United Kingdom—IPSS
United States—ITT, RCA, WUI, FTCC

The capabilities of the vast majority of these networks will be similar to those of Euronet, as most will conform to CCITT recommendations. Tariffs, of course, will vary between administrations, but there are signs that the distance independence pioneered by Euronet will be maintained over relatively large areas. (Transatlantic traffic will remain more expensive, however.) Costs are likely to decrease in real terms as network availability expands and usage increases.

The full capabilities of packet-switched networks are only beginning to be realized by both users and providers, and there is sure to be rapid and impressive expansion in the coming years.

6.7 STANDARDS FOR PACKET-SWITCHED NETWORKS

Communication with and between computers can be an extremely complex process, and it is always necessary to have a number of rules or protocols to govern such communication (Scott, 1979). Packet-switched networks are no exception to this general rule, and each must have its own protocols, both for communication within the network and for connection of computers or terminals. Further protocols must be agreed to for the connection of one packet network to another. Protocols can be agreed to at the local level, of course, but this militates against free working across and between networks, so for full interworking to be possible, standards must be adopted. There are a number of bodies responsible for the making of standards or recommendations, as well as the many national organizations. Those responsible include the International Standards Organization and the International Electrotechnical Commission, but the body responsible for protocols for packet-switched networks is the CCITT, which is part of the International Telecommunications Union (ITU) located in Geneva. The special recommendations for packet-switched networks form the X series of CCITT standards (CCITT, 1981a, 1981b), the most important being X25, which specifies the connection of packet DTEs to the network, the format of network messages, etc. Other protocols are X3, X28, and X29, which govern working of terminals with a PAD, X75 which covers the connection of networks, often called a gateway, and X21, which sets out the international numbering plan for public data networks.

A full listing of all relevant protocols should be available from the operators of data networks.

6.8 LOCAL AREA NETWORKS

It would not be possible to leave the discussion of data communication networks without mention of *local area networks* (*LANs*).

The networks discussed earlier in this chapter are intended, by and large, for communication over long distances. LANs, on the other hand, are intended to provide interworking between computers in a restricted area—typically, a single site. However, they are far more than a physical network to provide terminal access to a local mainframe, even though such a network may be specially set up using digital techniques.

The purpose of LANs is to allow a number of different intelligent devices, for example, microcomputers, minicomputers, or word processors, to connect to each other and possibly to a local mainframe and to share data, processing capacity, and specialized devices such as large-capacity disc stores or high-quality printers. In other words they are more than the network used to connect the work stations of a shared-logic word-processing system, for example.

A number of differing techniques have been and are in the process of being developed (Lane, 1981), and it is too early to say which will and will not be successful. Most are proprietary products, and the user must be careful to distinguish between those intended to allow communication between the products of a single manufacturer, such as Wangnet, and those intended to interconnect products of different manufacturers, such as Ethernet or Cambridge Ring systems.

In essence, the basic requirements of a LAN should be that simple protocols are used, thereby reducing the limitations that must be placed on connecting devices, and that the capacity must be sufficient to accommodate expected traffic. Data rates on LANs can range from, say, 9600 baud, the maximum that many terminal devices equiped with a serial interface can handle, up to 10 or more megabaud. Another characteristic which distinguishes local area networks is that none of the connected computing equipment takes on the role of the master or central point in the system. Instead, there is a continuous transmission system, or cable, to which all devices are joined in the same manner, no one device being more important than the others. (This is not to say that there is not any control in the network!)

Messages are sent into this transmission system together with information to identify the destination device, which in time receives the message. Clearly, such a system requires techniques to ensure data integrity and to manage traffic on the LAN efficiently. In addition, communicating devices must be provided with software, or a black-box connector, so that they can handle the necessary communication protocols. Two techniques are the Cambridge Ring and Ethernet systems, although others are important. For example, IBM favors a token-passing scheme which is likely to form the basis of an IEEE standard.

6.8.1 Cambridge Ring

A Cambridge Ring, as its name implies, consists of a loop of wires; it was developed by a team at Cambridge University (Banerjee & Shepherd, 1982; Needham, 1979; Wilbur, 1980). Data is placed on the ring at one point, the source, and removed at another, the destination. Data is inserted into the ring in an *information packet,* containing the following information:

Bit position	Use
1	Start of packet
2	Full-empty indicator
3	Monitor passed once
4–11	Destination address
12–19	Source address
20–35	Data bits
36–37	Response bits
38	Parity bit

In this example, the packet is 38 bits long, the ring being padded out to its working length of 50 bits by "gap" bits.

A working Cambridge Ring consists of a monitor station, repeaters, work stations (that is, connected computing equipment), a ring power supply, and a length of twin twisted-pair cables. The monitor station initializes the ring on starting and enforces the packet structure, as well as detecting and counting errors. Each work station has a repeater station attached to it to encode and decode the data stream from the ring. Repeater stations are also needed at intervals of 100 meters to amplify the signal.

Packets make one complete circuit of the ring before they are freed for use by other work stations. When a source sends a packet, it is marked as being full, and the response bits cleared. When the packet is detected by the destination (corresponding to the destination address entered by the source), the response bits are set to indicate whether the message was received correctly or rejected. The packet then continues round the ring to the source, which checks for any errors and marks the packet as empty. When a packet passes the monitor the monitor-passed-once bit is set. Any packets arriving at the monitor with this bit set and the packet marked *full* must be in error, not having been cleared by a source, or, perhaps, received by a destination. They are, therefore, freed by the monitor station.

Work stations can select only packets sent by one particular source, rejecting all others, or select all packets, or, indeed, reject all packets. This clearly gives considerable versatility in an operational environment. It should be noted that sources know when a destination will not accept their data by the state of returning packets.

6.8.2 Ethernet

Ethernet is a single coaxial cable, called the *ether,* to which communicating devices are attached. Transmission speeds up to 3 megabaud can be achieved over distances of up to 1 kilometer. Like the Cambridge Ring, data is transmitted in digital packets; but unlike the ring, there is no control or monitor device. Instead, each device listens all the time to passing packets, which have a common format and contain a destination-device address. A packet of data is broadcast onto the ether and is heard by all stations. The packet is copied at those stations selected by the address bits.

The ether is a totally passive broadcast medium with no central control. All stations contend for use of the ether until one acquires it for packet transmission.

A packet is detectable through the presence of a carrier signal on the ether. Thus a station listens to the ether as it transmits, to detect any other carriers that appear on it. This situation leads to a potential collision of packets because of propagation delays, that is, distant stations may see a quiet state on the ether and start to transmit at the same time. If a collision is detected, transmission is aborted and a jam signal sent out to notify all other stations. A random time delay is introduced to avoid a repeat collision. This technique is known as *carrier sense multiple access with collision detection* (CSMA/CD).

Ethernet was developed by the Xerox Corporation about 1975 and is now available with products from both Xerox and other manufacturers (Crane & Taft, 1980; Metcalfe & Boggs, 1976). By 1982 some 20 major computer companies had pledged support for Ethernet-like systems as defined in standards for the physical and data-link layers issued by the European Computer Manufacturers Association as ECMA TC 24/82/54 and TC 24/82/56. The IEEE 802 local-area-networks committee worked closely in cooperation with both ECMA and Xerox to ensure that all versions would be fully compatible.

Ethernet systems can be interconnected and can also, through appropriate gateway devices, communicate with the outside world via the public-switched network or X25-based packet-switched networks, for example.

REFERENCES

Banerjee, R., and W. D. Shepherd, "The Cambridge Ring: New Advances in Distributed Computer Systems," *Proceedings of the NATO Advanced Study Institute*, Dordrecht, Netherlands: Reidel, 1982, pp. 223–237.

Baran, P., "On Distributed Communication Networks," *IEEE Transactions on Communication Systems*, 1964, CS-12,

———, Boehm, S., and P. Smith, "On Distributed Communications," Santa Monica, Calif.: Rand Corporation, 1964 (series of 11 reports).

Casey, M., "Packet Switched Data Networks: An International Review," *Information Technology Research and Development*, 1982, (3), pp. 217–244.

CCITT, *Data Communications Networks: Services and Facilities, Terminal Equipment and Interfaces, Recommendations X.1–X.29* (Yellow Book, Volume VIII-Fascicle VIII.2). Geneva, Switzerland: International Telecommunication Union, 1981.

CCITT. *Data Communication Networks: Transmission, Signalling and Switching, Network Aspects, Maintenance, Administrative Arrangements, Recommendations X.40–X.180* (Yellow Book, Volume VIII-Fascicle VIII.3). Geneva, Switzerland: International Telecommunication Union, 1981.

Crane, R. C., and Edward A. Taft, *Practical Considerations in Ethernet Local Network Design*. Paper presented at the Hawaii International Conference on System Sciences, January 1980.

Crocker, S. D., et al., "Function-Oriented Protocols for the ARPA Computer Network," *AFIPS Conference Proceedings*, 1972, *40*, pp. 271–279.

Davies, D. W., et al., "A Digital Communication Network for Computers Giving Rapid Response at Remote Terminals," *Proceedings of the ACM Symposium on Operating System Principles*, 1967.

Heart, F. E., et al., "The Interface Message Processor for the ARPA Computer Network," *AFIPS Conference Proceedings*, 1970, *36*, pp. 551–567.

Lane, J. E., *Communicating with Microcomputers*, Manchester, England: National Computing Centre, 1981.

Marrill, T., and L. Roberts, "Towards a Cooperative Network of Time-Shared Computers," *AFIPS Conference Proceedings*, 1966.

McQuillan, J. M., et al., "Improvements in the Design and Performance of the ARPA Network," *AFIPS Conference Proceedings*, 1972, *41*, 741–754.

Metcalfe, Robert M., and David R. Boggs, "Ethernet: Distributed Packet Switching for Local Computer Networks," *Communications of the ACM*, 1976, *19*,(7).

"National Networks Interconnection," *Diane News*, no. 26, April 1982, p. 8.

Needham, R. M., "Systems Aspects of the Cambridge Ring," *Proceedings of the Seventh Symposium on Operating Systems Principles*, New York: Association for Computing Machinery, 1979.

Ornstein, S. M., et al., "The Terminal IMP for the ARPA Computer Network," *AFIPS Conference Proceedings*, 1972, *40*, pp. 243–254.

Purser, M., "The Euronet DIANE Network for Information Retrieval," *Information Technology Research and Development*, 1982, *1*(3), pp. 197–216.

Roberts, Lawrence, G., "Data by the Packet," *IEEE Spectrum*, February 1974, pp. 46–51.

——— & Wessler, B. D., Computer network development to achieve resource sharing. *AFIPS Conference Proceedings*, 1970, *36*, 543–549.

Scott, P. R. D., *Introducing Data Communications Standards*, Manchester, England: NCC Publications, 1979.

Wilbur, S. R., "Low-Level Protocols in the Cambridge Ring," *Data Networks: Development and Uses: Proceedings of Networks 80*. Northwood Hills, England: Online, 1980.

RECOMMENDED READING

Fitzgerald, Jerry, and Tom S. Eason, *Fundamentals of Data Communications*, New York: Wiley, 1978.
Martin, James, *Telecommunications and the Computer,* 2d ed., Englewood Cliffs, N.J.: Prentice-Hall, 1976.
Tannenbaum, Andrew S., *Computer Networks*, Englewood Cliffs, N.J.: Prentice-Hall, 1981.

CHAPTER 7

LOCAL AREA NETWORKS

Juan Bulnes
Xerox Office Systems Division
3450 Hillview Avenue
Palo Alto, CA 94304

In the previous chapter, we learned about computer networks and touched briefly on the subject of local area networks (LANs). This type of network constitutes a major evolutionary step, because it uses relatively new technologies to provide an innovative, cost-competitive solution to the problems of large-scale office and industrial automation. One possible approach to understanding a new technology is to start by examining the factors and opportunities that motivated its development. Against that background, we can see why the new methods became necessary, and how they must differ from previous solutions to communications problems.

7.1 THE MOTIVATION

As a workplace is filled with a plethora of increasingly intelligent devices, the need for communication increases exponentially. Most of the information exchanges happen, however, over relatively small distances, i.e., within a building or a campus. A rule of thumb says that typically 80 percent of the interactions occur between devices in the same local environment while 20 percent involve communications with remote machines. (*Introduction to Local Area Networks*, 1982)

At the same time, a proliferation of interconnected devices in the local environments gives rise to new opportunities for the effective sharing of expensive resources. For example:

1 Those required for the storage of large amounts of information (typically called *file servers*)

143

2 High-quality printing devices (*print servers*)

3 Minicomputers that link the local environment to other, possibly remote environments (*communication servers*)

4 Systems that facilitate communication with an especially popular class of computers which do not have the capability of being connected to the specific LAN because of systemic incompatibility (*application gateways*)

5 Devices that implement a shared access point for a number of low-intelligence devices, so that simple terminals or electronic typewriters can enter the network while sharing the cost of the access system (*terminal servers*)

6 Minicomputers that act as a "postal service," receiving, distributing, routing, and delivering electronic mail between users (*mail servers*)

This list cannot be exhaustive; in fact, it keeps growing all the time. The successful introduction of the technology for distribution of functions in a LAN has created a new marketplace for an unlimited number of specialized services that enhance the overall usefulness of the network.

Paradoxically, although this distribution of functionality represents a major increase in the complexity of a network, it works to the advantage of each individual user, who sees a simpler system, specialized for the functions that constitute his or her job. Three examples will illustrate how this is so:

The user of a shared printing device should not be encumbered with having to remember a number that tells the machine where to find or how to access the printer.

The user of an electronic message system should not have a message returned as undeliverable because the addressee's office was moved to a different location.

The user of a local database machine should not even notice that the machine was moved to another building (if the machine answers, why should the sender care?).

In other words, the intelligence required to increase the user-friendliness of the system is another shared network resource (Bulnes, 1983). The distribution of functionality also results in higher reliability of the network: critical functions can be replicated; unreliability of individual resources can be dealt with by layers of software that are invisible to the user; and temporary unavailability of a resource may result in the temporary impossibility of performing a specific task without any degradation of the network's ability to perform other tasks that are not related to that particular resource.

In summary, the most important motivations for the development of LANs are:

1 To offer cost-competitive solutions to the interconnection of large numbers of devices over short distances, i.e., within a building or a campus

2 To exploit opportunities for resource sharing in these highly automated local environments, resulting in cost savings as well as increased quality of service

7.2 THE REQUIREMENTS

Resource sharing, especially, differentiates the LAN solution from the classic network of the 1970s. Two principal differences are in the bandwidth and in the architectural design of the network. Other differences arise from the mode of usage of the networks, and concern simplicity, flexibility, expandability, ease of installation, and maintenance. There is a strong emphasis on standards, in order to provide for compatibility between different vendors' equipment.

7.2.1 High Bandwidth

The extent to which it is possible to share resources, and the type of resources that can be shared, critically depend on the speed and on the bandwidth of the communication between endpoints, that is, on the quantity of information that can be transferred in a given unit of time between two partners of a "conversation." At the same time, since the network must carry many simultaneous conversations between different users, the available bandwidth must be shared, and yet it must be sufficient for the needs of each individual user under most traffic load conditions (i.e., almost all of the time). Typical long-haul communication media operate at speeds of a few thousand bits per second (i.e., kilobits/s), while the media used in LANs operate at a few million bits per second (i.e., megabits/s).

A study of the behavior of the first experimental 3 megabit/s Ethernet, which connected 120 devices, showed that in an average day this network was transporting about 300 million bytes, and that this load is roughly equivalent to half the average daily load for the entire Arpanet network. Yet the goal of resource sharing makes the LAN network much less tolerant of communication delays; the higher bandwidth is actually needed, and it can be provided at a reasonable cost, whereas the same bandwidth would be prohibitively expensive for long-haul communication.

7.2.2 Tightly Coupled Architecture

The classic long-haul network was designed as a means of communication between basically stand-alone computer systems. In a shared-resources network, the importance of the communication function is much higher; in fact, many of the LAN devices, such as workstations and servers, are specifically designed as components of the network, rather than stand-alone systems. The structural design of these devices is, therefore, very tightly coupled to the structure of the network.

At the same time, a tightly coupled design permits a more effective utilization of the communication media, for which this design is specifically intended. LANs are carefully optimized at the levels of the physical transmission medium, the access control method used to share the medium, and the size and the format of the packets that are exchanged between the stations on the network.

Finally, because an effective LAN is carefully optimized for a class of problems, it implies a whole architectural concept. Thus, there is room for tailoring the architecture to a specific class of problems; this gives rise to a variety of LAN designs that are optimized for different applications.

7.2.3 Layered Architecture

The structural design of the network is customarily called *network architecture.* The intended meaning is exactly what we normally understand in everyday English ["*Architecture:* the science, art, or profession of designing and constructing buildings; a style of construction," "*Structure:* something composed of parts (in a definite pattern of organization)"].* However, the state of the art or practice gives rise to jargon, so that "network architecture" carries the additional implication of layered architecture, because networks are typically built in layers. The lower layers are those close to the physical transmission medium, and the higher layers are those close to the human-computer interface. A layered approach to network design is characteristic of all networks, local or not. But the explosive development of LANs has caused a renewed emphasis on layered design. We will see more of this when we discuss standards.

7.2.4 The Mode of Usage

A typical LAN network is actually a microcosm of a classic, long-haul computer network, in the sense that it handles a comparable number of network nodes

Webster's New World Dictionary of the American Language, College Edition, Cleveland, World Publishing Co.

FIGURE 7.1
The classical long-haul networks may consist of any number of nodes and any number of connections among them.

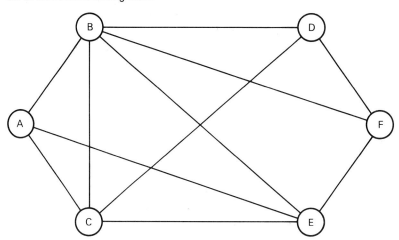

(typically a three-digit number), as well as a roughly equivalent average traffic load. It should not surprise us that a LAN has the same networking capacity as a large network or more. But LANs cost much less, and their cost is steadily decreasing. There already are in operation several hundred LANs of several different types, and most of them are privately owned. We are witnessing the emergence of a burgeoning new marketplace, with off-the-shelf network components and products. So, although the total capacity of a LAN has been increased, there is a certain decrease in complexity by sticking to simple design concepts. (For example, compare the network design in Figure 7.1 with that in Figure 7.3).

Ease of installation and maintenance is a majo. competitive feature in this market place. It is desirable that a user can start small and grow the network as needs dictate, without having to plan the whole network in advance. As employees and equipment are continuously moved between offices, it is desirable that the procedures for dealing with these moves be as simple as possible. The same considerations apply to the initial installation procedures.

7.2.5 Standards

Although a LAN product requires a tightly coupled design of all its components, we are witnessing a tremendous market pull for compatibility among the products of different vendors. As users grow their networks with an ever-richer array of new devices, they naturally want to shop for each device, rather than being tied to the offerings of one network supplier. As a result of this unprecedented situation, we are witnessing an equally unprecedented flurry of activity in the national and international standard-making organizations. Never before have we seen a system approach to standards, where there is already an international standard that tells how to subdivide the problem into standardizable parts ("Information Processing Systems," 1982; Zimmerman, 1980).

7.3 THE CHARACTERISTICS OF LANs

LANs differ from other networks mainly in the characteristics of the lower architectural layers. We will examine the principal LAN designs. All of them use packet switching, about which we learned in previous chapters. But they differ in their choices of transmission media, demultiplexing techniques, algorithms for control, access and allocation of the network channel, and topology (that is, the spatial arrangement of the components, in relationship to each other and to the network channel). We will start with network topologies because it gives a vantage point for the discussion of the other aspects.

7.3.1 Network Topology

The topological arrangement of a network is like a graph: the network nodes are the vertices of the graph, and the connections between nodes are its edges.

Here, one could be speaking of physical or of logical topologies, meaning the actual physical relationships or those of a logical nature. We will take a quick look at some of the terms related to network topologies.

The classical long-haul networks are normally unconstrained in their topologies. They consist of many nodes and a number of connections between them, where the connections do not follow any predetermined pattern, as shown in Figure 7.1. When the route between two points involves intermediate nodes, these relay the messages and have some means of knowing how to route them. There may be several routes between the two nodes, and it is possible that the same message arrives by more than one of those routes. There is a large body of literature dealing with the control of this type of networks, including such matters as preventing endless looping of a message, dealing with the failure of intermediate relays, and congestion control. These complex methods are justified because of the cost of connecting distant nodes. For a LAN, however, simpler solutions are necessary.

One approach to simplicity could be to eliminate the need to make routing decisions by having a single path between any two nodes, as in Figure 7.2. In such a network, a message from A to F has to go through all the intermediate nodes: B, C, D, and E. This approach would not be satisfactory from the point of view of network reliability, because the failure of any intermediate node would destroy the connectivity of the network. Neither would this network be able to cope well with traffic congestion.

A more successful approach to simplicity is the *multipoint* or *multidrop link,* also called a *bus.* This is a line shared by a number of nodes as a single channel for all transmissions, as shown in Figure 7.3. Many LANs are bus networks. If the two ends of this line are welded together, we have another commonly used topology, the *ring.*

A *star topology* is the paradigm of a PBX, where a central branch exchange handles the switching between all nodes and all routes pass through this central

FIGURE 7.2
A single path among nodes has the advantage of eliminating routing decisions among nodes, but the reliability of the network depends on its weakest link.

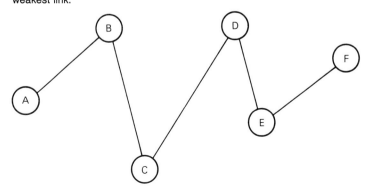

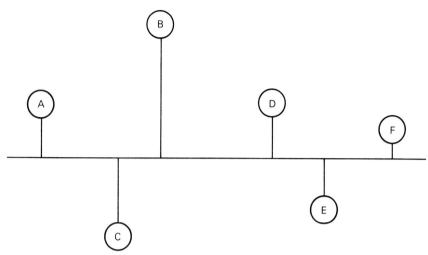

FIGURE 7.3
The bus network is also simple in structure, yet enables any node to communicate with any other one, even in the case of failure of some other nodes.

point. This is also the topology exemplified by a large number of terminals attached to a powerful computer mainframe. The central node constitutes a single point of network failure, so this topology is not frequently used in LAN design, except when the transmission medium is the PBX itself.

7.3.2 Transmission Media and Demultiplexing Characteristics

We already learned about coaxial cable in Chapter 4. Fiber optics bears some promise to become a choice medium, with better performance and cost characteristics. At present, however, most LANs continue to use coaxial cable, and they are said to be "baseband" or "broadband," depending on whether the cable carries all messages in one base frequency or uses a range of frequencies in which the messages can be modulated. Polemics between the proponents of these two methods often overlook the fact that the ability to transport bits between stations, though necessary, is an insufficient measure of network capability. Both techniques are usable, and each has its own areas where it is better suited than the other.

In a baseband network, the frequency channel must be shared using time division demultiplexing (TDM, which was introduced in Chapters 2 and 4). The most commonly used baseband frequency is 10 megahertz, yielding a bandwidth of 10 megabits/s. Using only one frequency leads to simple components for the attachment of devices to the medium (medium attachment units, or "taps"), and it also leads to a robust system that is highly insensitive to changes, such as the addition or removal of stations.

In a broadband network, there is a range of frequencies on which different messages can be modulated simultaneously. This range is divided into a number of channels; thus the medium is shared by the use of frequency division demultiplexing (FDM). In this type of network, stations are connected to the cable via modems. A modem is said to be "frequency agile" if it has the ability to be switched between frequencies; the effective use of FDM requires these agile modems. Both ends of a transmission must be in agreement about the channel to be used, lest one will not hear the other. If 1000 stations are sharing 50 channels using FDM, the problem of channel allocation and control becomes quite complex. One approach to solving this problem has been to have a master station that assigns channels, upon request, typically for a limited time slot, to the stations that wish to transmit. Another approach has been to combine FDM with a secondary demultiplexing method, such as TDM: a particular channel, or several of them, are shared by a TDM scheme.

7.3.3 Channel Allocation and Access Control

We introduced this subject in the last paragraph. Now we will look at some alternatives for sharing a channel among a number stations. These TDM methods, by which stations share access to the channel, resemble the familiar ways for managing conversations among large numbers of people.

First, one can distinguish between polling and contention methods. Polling means managing the order in which stations take turns to transmit, so that contention for the medium is avoided at all times; then, each station can use its turn for a limited time. Polling can be centralized or distributed.

Centralized polling requires a master station administering the channel access; it is like managing a large meeting where people must raise their hands and wait for the chairperson's permission before speaking. The drawback of centralized polling is that there is a single point of failure: when the master goes down, so does the whole network.

Distributed polling is usually implemented by passing a token, in a predetermined order, among the stations. The owner of the token has exclusive use of the channel and must pass the token without delay when its time is up or as soon as it no longer has a transmission to make (whichever comes first). This method is sometimes used on social occasions: the most common variant takes place when people sit at a round table and take turns around the table. A round arrangement is not strictly necessary if the order can be determined by a list, for example, by alphabetical precedence; then it is enough that each participant remembers from whom it has to receive the token and to whom it has to pass it. In the LAN jargon, the two schemes are also called *token ring* and *token bus,* because in the first case the stations are attached to a circular cable, and in the second to just a cable which acts as a communication bus.

Slotted rings are another variant of the token ring passing scheme. Here the token consists of several slots, usually a fixed number of frames of fixed size. In each frame, one bit is used to indicate whether it is empty or is carrying a message. These frames circulate around the network, like a train. When a station sees them passing, it can place messages in empty slots, and it can copy any messages destined to its address into its buffer, thus emptying the frame.

All token-passing networks must resolve the problem of initializing the circulation of the token, first when the network is set in operation, then after each interruption of its operation. Usually there is a single station charged with this task.

All the methods just described are designed to avoid conflicts between stations wishing to transmit. In a contention method, these conflicts are allowed, anticipated, resolved when they occur, and actually constitute an integral part of the design that permits fair sharing of the channel among the stations. The most popular contention scheme, *carrier sense multiple access with collision detection* (CSMA/CD), is described in detail in the next section.

7.4 ETHERNET

The Ethernet system uses the CSMA/CD method which can be compared with the rules by which people informally manage their conversations at a small party, namely: (1) listen before you talk, and defer if someone is talking; (2) when nobody else is talking, you start; (3) if two persons happen to start talking simultaneously, both must stop, wait a random moment, and then try again. A few more details will be discussed below.

"Carrier sense" means each station's ability to sense whether anyone is using the channel. This is the first rule: Listen before you talk. "Multiple access" refers to each station's right to transmit upon detecting a free channel, the second rule above. The following point requires more precision: In a party, guests do not start speaking immediately after guessing, or knowing, that somebody has just stopped talking. People allow a prudential time so that everybody realizes that the previous speaker has stopped, and everyone can get ready to attend to another speaker. In a CSMA/CD network, there is a minimum time of silence between transmissions. Each station actually listens all the time to the channel, regardless of its intention to transmit, and none will transmit without having observed silence on the channel for this minimum time, called *interframe spacing*.

Finally, "collision detection" means each station's ability to sense whether its transmission has collided with someone else's. It does this by sensing the energy level in the channel; a collision causes a change in this energy level. Here, we have another rule, concerning collision enforcement. When a collision occurs, each station involved in that collision sends a jam signal, a short burst of noise, in order to ensure that every station involved actually noticed the collision. After this jamming, each station aborts its transmission. In our analogy, this means that if you sense a collision after you start speaking, you must shout "Collision!" then stop.

A fine point concerns the channel acquisition time: collisions occur because stations that may be a couple of kilometers apart may start transmitting at roughly the same time. However, if a station has transmitted for a time sufficient for it to be heard at the other end of the network, plus the time required for the possible jam signal to come back from the other end, then the station can be sure that its transmission has not and will not collide. Then the station is said to have "acquired the channel," and this channel acquisition time is equal to the worst-case round-trip delay of a signal travelling between the farthest points on the network, including the delays necessary to travel through the cables that connect the stations to the main trunk. For example, for a 10 mbit/s network with a maximum speed of $0.77c$ (where c is the speed of light), this time is 46.38 μs. These are the actual numbers used in the Ethernet and in the Institute of Electrical and Electronics Engineers (IEEE) 802 standard for CSMA/CD networks (*Ethernet*, 1982; Draft, IEEE Standard 802, 1982).

By a transmission, we mean the sending of exactly one packet. CSMA/CD standards define a minimum packet size of 64 bytes and a maximum packet size of 1518 bytes. The minimum packet size ensures that a valid packet is always larger than a collision fragment, i.e., an incomplete packet whose transmission was aborted by a collision. The maximum packet size is engineered for good throughout and fair channel utilization by all stations.

Other points requiring additional precision are the rules for retransmission after collisions. If a station collides, it will, after finishing the jam signal, wait for a random amount of time, which must be at least as large as the interframe spacing, and then retransmit if the channel is free. If it collides again, it will wait a somewhat larger, random amount of time before retrying. If this random waiting time is roughly doubled after each unsuccessful attempt, the scheme is called *exponential backoff*. The CSMA/CD standards call for a maximum of 16 retransmission attempts with exponential backoff. After 16 consecutive collisions, the station is required to discard the packet without transmitting it. After any successful transmission, the collision count goes back to 0 again. Like a post office, CSMA/CD networks make a "best effort" attempt to transport a packet from source to destination, but they do not guarantee or acknowledge its actual delivery. The overhead of acknowledging each packet is not justified at this architectural level, especially in view of the fact that actual delivery by the network is not necessarily the same as actual reception by the program that will eventually consume the packet. In the next section, we will see how some functions are better dealt with at higher architectural levels.

7.5   FUNCTIONAL INTEGRATION

A LAN's capability to transport packets of bits between network hosts is only the first prerequisite for systems integration. The mere transfer of information, however, constitutes less than 10 percent of the system intelligence required for useful functionality. (Metcalfe, 1981) Drawing an analogy from the field of computer mainframe design, we can compare the ability of system elements to exchange packets on a LAN with the ability of a computer to use a random-access memory: a powerful computer needs several layers of system superimposed on its random-access capability. Similarly, an effective LAN architecture requires several layers of protocols built upon its basic ability to exchange packets.

The first example of a desirable higher-level integration is the ability to "glue" a number of heterogeneous networks, which use different, incompatible protocols, into one logical network (called the *internetwork*). This is achieved by superimposing one internetwork protocol on top of the protocols used by the various networks.

By way of analogy, imagine a multinational corporation that uses one common mandatory envelope for its internal memos all over the world; thus, anybody wishing to transmit a message must "encapsulate" the message into the envelope. When these memos are transported, however, they may go by a variety of carriers, such as Federal Express; each carrier requests that the company standard envelope be again "encapsulated" in another, carrier-specific envelope, such as a Federal Express envelope. Imagine also that some messages must be carried with one carrier part of the way, then taken out of that carrier's envelope and sent with another carrier for another part of the way. If this hypothetical corporation establishes an efficient system of relays to handle the transport of these messages, and if it establishes an adequate worldwide addressing system for its internal offices, it should be clear that the sender of a message need not be concerned with the actual geographical location of the recipient.

An internetwork protocol functions exactly like that. It is a "higher-level" protocol, whose "envelopes" must again be encapsulated when they are transmitted on the "lower-level" transport media (Dalal, 1982).

Another example of desirable functionality is the ability to transport any amount of information, large or small, and to be assured that the information is received reliably in the proper sequence and without duplication of any of its parts. Most "lower-level" LAN protocols do not offer this possibility directly, because packets are limited in size, packet delivery is not always guaranteed, and transmission is not necessarily free of errors. It is not difficult, however, to design a protocol that numbers the packets, keeps track of those sent and received, and resends lost packets (White and Dalal, 1982).

These functions, the integration of multiple LANs into one logical internetwork and the information transport capability, still constitute no more then the necessary foundation for developing integrated applications. In addition, LAN users want to do such things as sending and receiving electronic mail, transferring files between heterogenous devices, and printing documents on miscellaneous printing devices. All these require further layers of protocol (Bulnes, 1983).

7.6 OPEN SYSTEMS INTERCONNECTION

With the explosive development of LANs, there has come an especially strong market pull toward an "open architecture," which would require equipment

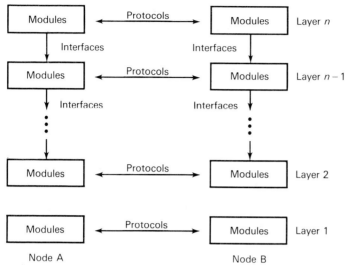

FIGURE 7.4
A model of network communication. Peer modules communicate via protocols. Interfaces allow a module to use the services of the module below in the hierarchy.

manufacturers to adhere to commonly agreed standards in order for the buyers to be able to mix and match equipment on their networks.

This unprecedented movement towards standardization has met with remarkable success. The International Standards Organization (ISO) Reference Model for Open Systems Interconnection (OSI) has laid a foundation for a systems approach to the standardization process. (Zimmerman, 1980) This model views networks as a seven-layer hierarchy of protocols. Communicating entities in a network will consist of modules that perform defined functions, specified by the architecture. Modules residing in the same network host (e.g., in a workstation or a computer) stand in a strictly hierarchical relationship to each other, and they communicate with each other by interfaces. These interfaces implement the services from one layer to the next layer above, called the "client" of the layer below. These concepts are depicted in Figure 7.4.

7.6.1 The Seven Layers of the OSI Model

The ISO reference model for open systems interconnection (OSI) postulates the following seven layers (Figure 7.5):

1 The *physical layer* provides mechanical, electrical, functional, and procedural characteristics to establish, maintain, and release physical connections for the purpose of transmitting physical impulses that are interpreted as bits of data.

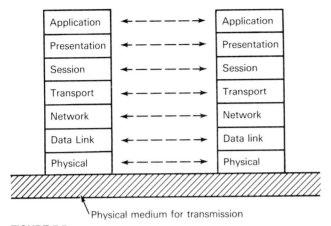

Application	◄ ─ ─ ─ ─ ─ ►	Application
Presentation	◄ ─ ─ ─ ─ ─ ►	Presentation
Session	◄ ─ ─ ─ ─ ─ ►	Session
Transport	◄ ─ ─ ─ ─ ─ ►	Transport
Network	◄ ─ ─ ─ ─ ─ ►	Network
Data Link	◄ ─ ─ ─ ─ ─ ►	Data link
Physical	◄ ─ ─ ─ ─ ─ ►	Physical

Physical medium for transmission

FIGURE 7.5
The open system interconnection model. Modules physically
communicate with those immediately above or below in the
structure, but logically there is communication between peer
systems at each level.

2 The *data link layer* transmits messages between network nodes attached to
the same physical channel; this layer typically frames the messages for transmission, checks integrity of received messages, and manages access to, and use of,
the channel. The contention and polling algorithms previously described are an
essential part of many data link layer protocols.

3 The *network layer* manages transmission of messages between nodes on a
network; these nodes may be connected not by one but by a variety of physical
channels, intermediate nodes, and intervening relays. This layer routes messages
and controls traffic flows, so as to provide the means for end-to-end delivery of
messages.

4 The *transport layer* allows network nodes to exchange data reliably,
sequentially, and independently of the location of the intervening nodes and of
the quantity of data that must be exchanged.

5 The *session layer* manages the dialogue between communicating entities
and provides synchronization and resynchronization facilities to assist in the
support of their interactions.

6 The *presentation layer* manages the encoding and decoding of data into
formats which enable display on terminal screens and printers, and it manages
the exchange of structured data items.

7 The *application layer* is the highest layer of the OSI model; all lower layers
exist solely to support this layer. At the application layer, we find protocols that
directly support user tasks, such as file transfer, printing on a variety of devices,
electronic mail, database management, etc. In addition, this level contains
protocol to manage these applications and the network.

7.7 THE FUTURE OF LANs

We have taken a bird's eye view of an emerging technology that is undergoing rapid evolution. At the lower architectural levels, there already is sufficient stability to say that the CSMA/CD, token ring, and token bus access methods will stay with us for many years. They have become or will become international standards within a year. We can forsee new technologies for transmission being applied with these same methods, for example, CSMA/CD on fiber optics. Thus the bandwidth of LANs will continue to increase.

On the area of higher-level protocols we foresee a fair amount of evolution as the standards are being developed. There is intense activity by the International Standards Organization (ISO) and by the Consultative Committee of the Telephone and Telegraph (CCITT) toward these application standards. Eventually, computer networks are going to have a most pervasive role in our lives, much like the telephone system does today.

Many new types of products and services will be made possible by that technological basis; any attempts to characterize those new products would bring us into the slippery field of social and technological forecasting, or perhaps even into science fiction.

REFERENCES

Bulnes, J., "Beyond Ethernet: Integration of Office Functions in the Xerox 8000 Network System." *Conf. Proc. Northcom. '83,* Northwest Computer Conf., Portland, May 1983.

Dalal, Y. K., "Use of Multiple Networks in the Xerox Network System," *IEEE Computer Magazine,* vol. 15, no. 10, October 1982, pp. 82–92.

Draft, IEEE Standard 802.3: *CSMA/CD Access Method and Physical Layer Specifications,* The Institute of Electrical and Electronics Engineers, Inc., revision D, December 1982.

Ethernet, A Local Area Network: Data Link and Physical Layer Specifications, Digital Equipment Corp., Intel Corp., & Xerox Corp., Maynard, Mass., Santa Clara, Calif., and Stamford, Conn., version 2.0, November 1982.

"Information Processing Systems—Open Systems Interconnection—Basic Reference Model," ISO/DIS 7498, International Standards Organization, 1982.

Introduction to Local Area Networks, Digital Equipment Corporation, Maynard, Mass., 1982.

Metcalfe, R. M., "A Strategic Overview of Local Computer Networks," *Proc. of the Online Conf. on Local Area Network and Distributed Office Systems,* London, May 11–13, 1981, pp. 1–10.

White, J. E., and Dalal, Y. K., "Higher Level Protocols Enhance Ethernet," *Electronic Design,* vol. 30, no. 8, April 15, 1982, pp. ss33–ss41.

Zimmerman, H., "OSI Reference Model—The ISO Model of Architecture for Open Systems Interconnection," *IEEE Trans. Comm.,* vol. 28, no. 4, April 1980, pp. 425–432.

Chapter 8: Television in the Corporate Environment

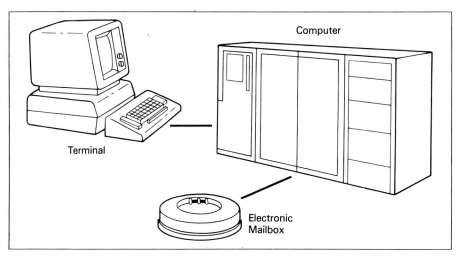

Chapter 9: Electronic Mail

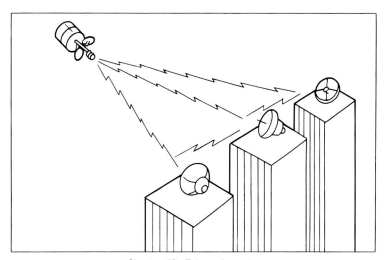

Chapter 10: Teleconferencing

PART THREE

THREE

APPLICATIONS

In this part of the book we examine five telecommunications technologies to gain insight into their adaptability to management. In Chapter 8 television is explored. The emphasis is on the technology as a system of visual communication. Comparison is made to other electronic visual communication systems. In Chapter 9 the technology and organization of electronic mail are explored. Chapter 10 is dedicated to teleconferencing in its various forms: audio, video, and computer. A brief case study of the Allstate Insurance experience with teleconferencing is included. Mobile communication is the subject of Chapter 11 in which the mobile telephone, radio paging, and cellular radio are reviewed. In Chapter 12 videotex is examined. Emphasis is placed on system design and the likelihood of adoption of videotex in business environments.

Chapter 11: Mobile Communication

Chapter 12: Videotex

CHAPTER 8

TELEVISION IN THE CORPORATE ENVIRONMENT

Albert S. Tedesco
WWSG-TV
Philadelphia, PA 19128

8.1 INTRODUCTION

That we live in a "visual culture" is a given of 20th century American civilization. It is no surprise, then, that the communication of information in visual form is increasingly the concern of business managers. In this chapter we examine the technology of television and its application to the managerial environment.

Private television systems are used in private- and public-sector organizations to communicate with employees, customers, shareholders, and other constituents. Private television is different from the mass media we are accustomed to because it is limited to a very small group of receivers, namely those already associated in some way with the senders.

In this chapter the subject of private television in the corporate environment is addressed in the following way. First, the scope and significance of private television as an industry are assessed. Next, a taxonomy of *electronic visual transmission* systems is presented to guide the reader's evaluation of the appropriate role of television in the corporate setting. In the final portion of the chapter, the "nuts and bolts" of television systems are reviewed.

8.2 THE SCOPE AND DEVELOPMENT OF CORPORATE TELEVISION

Today corporate video specialists produce more hours of television programming each year than ABC, CBS, and NBC combined, according to a recent study conducted for the International Television Association, the industry group which has a membership of 6000 nonbroadcast video professionals from 11 countries ("CCTV Paced by Business Video," 1983a).

In 1981 more than 3000 organizations spent about $1.5 billion for equipment to produce more than 18,000 hours of video programming, a figure expected to reach $3.6 billion by 1984, reflecting a 30 percent growth rate ("Corporate Video Net," 1983b).

But how are such resources allocated? Corporate video systems have found many different applications; the ten most frequent applications are ranked here (D. Brush, 1980).

1 Basic skill training
2 Specific job training
3 Employee orientation
4 Supervisory training
5 Employee information
6 Management communications
7 Management development
8 Sales training
9 Safety and health information
10 Employee benefits

According to D/J Brush Associates, budgets for corporate television, including salaries, facilities, equipment, and related production and program acquisition expenses rose 87 percent between 1977 and 1980, from a median of $72,000 to a median of $135,000. This change was attributed to real growth in the development of distribution networks, the use of supplemental services to enhance production values and acquire special programming, and the production of higher-quality programming. At the same time, the median number of programs produced dropped between 1977 and 1980, reflecting an increase in the quality of production (J. Brush, 1980).

While corporate video managers once worried primarily about justifying their existences to top management, the locus of their concerns has shifted to new areas: the industry's current concerns revolve around the adoption of new technologies such as video teleconferencing, interactive video, and the identification and adoption of new cost-effective systems for distributing programming by means of cable and other new technologies (Meigs, 1983). Faced with such new conditions, adopting and implementing appropriate technology has become the central concern not just for the video manager but for those to whom they report.

8.3 A TAXONOMY OF ELECTRONIC VISUAL TRANSMISSION: A GUIDE TO ADOPTION

The decision to select an electronic medium to transmit information can be thought to take place within a three-dimensional conceptual framework in which cost, complexity of image, and perishability of information are the critical variables (Figure 8.1).

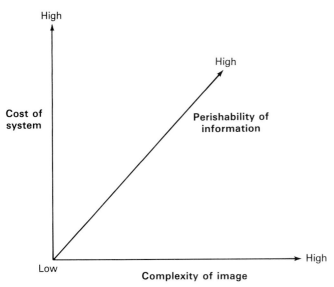

FIGURE 8.1
A taxonomy of electronic visual information systems.

The *cost* of systems is a fundamental consideration. For example, if the daily transmission of static (unanimated) graphic information is all that is required, then a relatively low-cost facsimile system that reproduces images in black and white may be sufficient.

However, if animated-graphics capability as provided by full video is important, then cost becomes a significant factor. The question then becomes: How much should be spent to send the information?

A second dimension is the *complexity of the image*. This dimension is composed of several factors. The first of these is *resolution*. The user must determine how complex the visual image to be transmitted is. What is needed to do the job? Is color essential? Is great detail (high resolution) important? Each electronic visual transmission (EVT) system, for example, has the capacity to transmit a given level of resolution. For instance, compare these two frames from a demonstration of standard (NTSC) American television with a proposed standard for high-definition television (HDTV) (Figure 8.2). The difference in resolution (clarity) between the two pictures is the result of the application of double the number of scanning lines and, of course, a concomitant increase in bandwidth for transmission (Roizen, 1983). The difference in the resolving power of the two systems gives rise to a question that management must decide: Does the difference in resolution affect the communication of information? Is the difference sufficient to justify the choice of one system over the other (Sandbank & Moffat, 1983)? If the information to be transmitted requires high resolution, for example, the design of microprocessor circuits, then the adoption

of high resolution might be deemed cost-appropriate. If, by contrast, the video information consists of clips from a new commercial which would be transmitted by standard television in its final form, then the lower-resolution system would be deemed cost-appropriate.

The next factor is *action* (movement). Does the visual information require movement to be effective? On the surface this appears to be easily resolved. In fact, it is not such a simple question. Take, for example, the case of a video teleconference. Is it mandatory that the participants see movement, the transmission of which requires full video at 30 frames per second?

Or will less frequently transmitted video, say, 1 frame every 5 to 10 seconds suffice? The difference between the two requirements is the difference between standard video and slow-scan systems. In one case, the full bandwidth of video is required, while in the other, using video compression techniques, the still frames of video can be transmitted via telephone lines or as ancillary signals on standard FM or television channels (Kelleher, 1983).

Composing requirements are also important factors. How easy is the medium to use? Does it require special training? Some systems, such as facsimile or telewriting, are very easy to use, require little formal training, and can be accessed rapidly with little or no advanced planning beyond installation of the technology itself. Others, such as broadcast level video, require a clear understanding of the language of the medium, the support of a professional staff, and advance planning and preparation to use effectively and offer only limited access.

Some EVT systems require a thorough grasp of the communications techniques associated with the technology to guarantee that the messages sent are compatible with the average level of expectation among receivers about sender competence in using the technology. Such is the case with corporate video, for example, where demanding production standards are set by network television to which all users (senders and receivers alike) are exposed.

Compare such constraints as these with facsimile, where no special talent is required to operate the system to its maximum efficiency.

One can reasonably expect that users of facsimile systems (senders and receivers) have similar skills and comparable expectations about the product.

The third dimension for consideration is the *perishability of the information* to be conveyed by the system. In the case of facsimile, the information is present at the receiver and sender for as long as it needs to be retained. For example, contracts can be exchanged and reviewed with the certainty that both parties are looking at exactly the same language. In the case of a live video teleconference, by contrast, the information is more perishable: the video data are presented in a continuous flow which, although it may be recorded, is generally thought to be useful as a "real-time" (meaning perishable) exchange of information.

FIGURE 8.2
A comparison of standard American television (NTSC-525 lines, right) and the high-definition television system (HDTV-1125 lines, left) proposed by Sony. (Courtesy of Sony Corp.)

In Figure 8.3, three-dimensional space shows how the dimensions of this taxonomy interact.

8.4 MOTIVATIONS TO USE ELECTRONIC VISUAL TRANSMISSION SYSTEMS

Many motivations justify the interest of managers in EVT systems. These include (1) the value of electronic media in accelerating the communication-transportation trade-off; (2) the quality of verisimilitude exhibited by electronic media which have the capacity to emulate "reality" and thereby facilitate interaction and transaction; (3) the relatively low cost of producing and transmitting electronic messages, and (4) the acceptability of electronically transmitted visual information among generations of managers acculturated at an early age by televised images and, more recently, direct experience with home video games and personal computers.

8.4.1 The Communication-Transportation Trade-Off

In the age of energy scarcity it is axiomatic that telecommunications systems represent the means to trade communication for transportation. That it will be more cost-effective in the future to transmit information than to transport people is the crux of this argument (Berlo, 1975). The application of EVT technology to teleconferencing, intra- and extra-organizational communication, marketing, training, and like tasks are all offered as examples of arenas in which this trade-off will occur.

FIGURE 8.3
A three-dimensional array of electronic visual media characteristics.

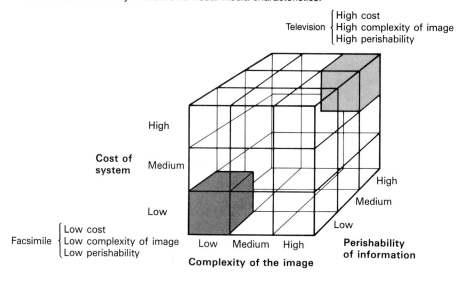

The economics of this trade-off are just now beginning to be understood. Major barriers to adoption of such systems include the economic, psychological, and institutional investments in existing systems of face-to-face information delivery that individuals and corporations have made.

Lag in adoption of new telecommunications systems often has more to do with an organization's misconception of the potential of such systems effectively to trade face-to-face for mediated communication than it does with the cost of adoption.

8.4.2 The Quality of Verisimilitude

EVT systems represent materials and events—"real things"—and thereby foster interaction and transaction. For example, facsimile reproduces "hard copy" to provide visual and tactile reinforcement in the exchange of ideas. Legal transactions illustrate this well: both parties can exchange amendments and modifications without loss of detail, thereby encouraging resolution of issues too complex to convey in an audio channel alone.

8.4.3 The Relatively Low Cost of Transmission

Video transmission represents a relatively cost-effective option: there are economies to be gained from the use of video today which were not possible 10 years ago. These include less expensive equipment and transmission networks such as cable, multipoint distribution service (MDS), operational fixed service (OFS), and satellite. Video equipment and resources need not even be housed within the corporation to be used regularly: an entire production industry has come into existence in part to support corporate video at a reasonable cost. Overall, however, television still remains expensive when compared with other EVT systems.

8.4.4 Acceptability of Televised Images

Television is the dominant medium of public communication in the United States from any perspective we choose to view it—audience size, advertising revenue, variety of service, or number of daily viewing hours per household. Because of this, the *language of television* is well understood. When applied in a new way, such as for the purpose of training or delivering information via closed circuit to large numbers of people, it requires no new skills of its receivers but does demand that the basic grammar of the medium be learned by those who want to employ it effectively (Mattingly, 1979).

8.5 AN OVERVIEW OF SPECIALIZED EVT TECHNOLOGIES

While television is the principal concern of this chapter, four other related technologies are identified here for the sake of completing the inventory of

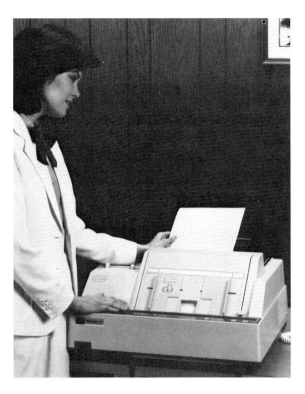

FIGURE 8.4
This high-volume digital facsimile transceiver features an autodialer and automatic document feeder. It can transmit a business letter anywhere in the world in less than 30 seconds. (Courtesy of 3M)

significant EVT technologies in use in the corporate environment. We are concerned here with facsimile, videophone, slow-scan video, and telewriting.

Facsimile is a system by which graphic and written materials and still pictures may be transmitted by means of wire or wireless links from point to point. The product is hard copy. The standard transmission system employs a drum on which the material to be transmitted is placed. The drum is rotated and the material is scanned by a narrow beam of light. Variations in the intensity of the reflected light are translated into electrical impulses by a photoelectric cell and sent through a telephone wire or other network. At the receiving end the process is reversed: the received signal is converted into a beam of light which is directed at a rotating drum holding sensitized paper. The beam of light reproduces the image on the paper. Generally, 800 rotations are made for each inch of picture area. Transmission time is generally 3 to 6 minutes; in digital systems, the time is significantly shorter (Hellman, 1983).

The utility of facsimile is found in its rapid and exacting transmission of materials such as contracts and other documents, hard copies of which are needed in a hurry.

Facsimile was widely adopted by the newspaper business, where it rapidly became the extension of the wire services, which employed it for photo transmission (Costigan, 1971). Facsimile is now found throughout the office environment (Figure 8.4).

The *videophone* was first conceived as a personal medium. It was designed as a desktop unit capable of transmitting animated video and audio. It contained a small 5-inch screen and a carefully concealed camera. It used the two-wire-pair telephone system for transmission, with some modification to the transmission network to accommodate the video signal (Dickson, 1973). The subject of considerable experimentation, videophones have yet to be deployed on a large scale (Figure 8.5).

Slow-scan video technology transmits single frames of video information in sequence, with what broadcasters describe as a "wipe" (left-to-right movement) between frames. Slow-scan television is also called *narrow-band video* or *freeze-frame video.* It is employed to transmit still video images inexpensively and conveniently via telephone lines; it may also be carried on radio, microwave, and satellite channels.

In regular television transmission, the viewer is exposed to 30 pictures or frames per second (NTSC/U.S. standard). Each of these frames consists of 250,000 picture elements. Such a system is referred to as wideband or full-motion video. In slow-scan television a standard closed-circuit camera which generates 30 pictures per second is used to pick up the picture information. The signal generated by this camera is a full 30-frame picture. It is fed to a *scan converter,* which slows these 30 frames per second to match the channel capacity of an audio circuit, such as a telephone line. Using the audio line, the

FIGURE 8.5
The video telephone consists of a picture display unit (containing the camera, picture tube, and loudspeaker), a control unit (containing the control buttons and knobs and a microphone), a 12-button TouchTone telephone, and a service unit (containing the power supply, logic circuits, and transmission equalizing circuits). (Courtesy of AT&T)

narrow-band picture is then transmitted to its destination, where a second scan converter reconstructs the picture for display on television monitor.

The speed of transmission varies with the channel used and level of resolution required in the picture; it can take only a few seconds by satellite or a minute by phone. Because 30 frames of video are not being transmitted each second in a slow-scan system, the cost of such narrow-band transmissions is far below band transmission ("Slow-Scan Television and Tele Medicine").

Slow-scan video has found application in diverse environments ranging from general communications to highly specialized uses. In general communications, slow-scan is used for person-to-person exchanges of graphic information, the transmission of engineering and scientific data, and the remote viewing of ad layouts, news photos, real estate, construction sites, and product lines. It has been employed by insurance claim adjusters, to provide schedules to remote locations, as a silent paging system, and, of course, as an important adjunct to teleconferencing (Kelleher, 1983).

Other applications include remote sensing in weather observation, the monitoring of ship movements and highway traffic, meter reading, and smoke detection. In the security field, slow-scan has been used for signature verification, face and fingerprint identification, gate observation, area surveillance, intrusion detection, and malfunction analysis.

In medicine, slow-scan video has been used for remote diagnosis with nuclear, infrared, ultrasound, x-ray, and visible-light diagnostic technology. It has also been used to transmit images in emergency patient care and for computerized image analysis. Slow-scan video has found application in educa-

FIGURE 8.6
A basic slow-scan system including video camera, scan-converter, and video monitor showing video frame as sent. (Courtesy of Colorado Video, Inc.)

tion and broadcasting, where it has been used to carry special programs and data on FM signals and to provide a national news service, *UPI Newstime,* for cable television (Figure 8.6). It has also been used to transmit images in emergency patient care and for computerized image analysis.

Telewriting is a technology which permits the transmission of written information in "real time" via telephone lines or satellite channels. The use of telewriting as a supplement to teleconferencing is one of its obvious applications. In this mode it becomes a communal scratch pad on which graphic elements which support or advance the teleconference may be displayed (Figure 8.7).

8.6 TELEVISION: THE DOMINANT EVT TECHNOLOGY

Television's history is older than radio's. The earliest television experiments were electromechanical in nature and involved a spinning disk and light-sensitive switches. Mechanical systems were the precursors of all electronic systems which use electronic-beam scanning to break images into transmittable impulses that, once received at some distant point, are recognizable to the receiver (Barnouw, 1966).

The technical development of radio and television, but not their commercial exploitation, is historically parallel and owes much to the same intellectual and theoretical sources: The same motivation which drove the Marconis of this world to create the technology of radio was behind the development of television: the desire to communicate at a great distance—to telecommunicate.

Marconi's early radio experiments in the late 19th century culminated in his transmissions across the Atlantic from Newfoundland and Wellfleet to Great Britain in 1901 and 1903. The rapid deployment of Marconi wireless equipment among mariners lead to the historic reporting of the sinking of the Titanic by David Sarnoff of the Marconi Company (1912); no single event in the early history of radio so captured the public imagination and contributed so much to the excitement about this new medium.

The 1920s and 1930s in the United States were characterized by the rapid diffusion of radio stations and receivers and the parallel growth of networking and the regulatory framework. The 1940s saw the application of radio and fledgling television to wartime uses. The late 1940s saw the emergence of television as an entertainment medium. The 1950s saw the growth of network television, and the parallel reduction in movie attendance. At the same time, radio met the challenge of television by changing its format (Barnouw, 1968). The 1960s witnessed the growth of television in the corporate environment and the introduction of satellite technology and inexpensive videotape systems (Barnouw, 1970). The 1970s have seen the rapid deployment of multichannel broadband systems (cable television) and satellite networks and the application of these new technologies to corporate communication. Developments in the

FIGURE 8.7
Graphics drawn on a pressure-sensitive blackboard are transmitted over ordinary telephone lines (private or switched network voice grade facilities) for display on remote video monitors. For group usage, a portable conference telephone equipped with microphones and built-in speaker may be used to permit open discussion between the point of origin and audience. (Courtesy of AT&T)

1980s so far reflect the deregulatory environment, in which the rule of thumb thus far has been to allow the evolution of new technologies to take place in the marketplace without excessive government regulation. It is in the 1980s that we are likely to see the rapid growth of corporate applications of television technology.

8.7 THE TECHNOLOGY OF TELEVISION

To those who have contemplated using television as a medium for communicating within or between institutions, large public entities, or diverse publics, television has often appeared to present formidable obstacles because of its technical complexity and the fact that good television is a marriage of art and science.

Television has been viewed by managers as an expensive, difficult-to-use medium because it appears associated with high expectations linked to our experience with the entertainment and news programming of the commercial and public networks.

Today the cost of television technology, while still considerable, is dropping all the time, making it more accessible. At the same time, there is growing appreciation among top corporate management that television can make a major contribution to corporate goals ("Corporate Video Net," 1983).

8.7.1 The Camera and Its Operation: The Source of Video

Television cameras convert what the eye sees into electronic signals. They do this by means of light-sensitive pick-up tubes or charged coupled devices (CCDs). Television cameras are no mystery to the general public, which has available a variety of low-cost equipment for use in home videography; nor need TV cameras be a mystery to the manager who must decide about components for a corporate video system. While this section is not designed to provide a buyer's guide to equipment (these are readily available from such industry sources as *Broadcast Management and Engineering*), it is designed to demonstrate how the pieces of television systems fit together.

Television cameras are generally of three types: (1) the light-weight, portable electronic news-gathering type (Figure 8.8), (2) the electronic field-production camera (Figure 8.9), and (3) the studio camera (Figure 8.10).

The portable *ENG camera,* which can be hand-held and used comfortably by one person holding it on his or her shoulder, permits quick access to remote situations. It is commonly used in conjunction with a portable videotape recorder (VTR). (New equipment reflects the marriage of camera and videotape recorder in one hand-held unit, as in Figure 8.11.) Portable videotape recorders (the renowned Sony Portapak is a good example) have been in widespread use since the late 1960s and have found application in corporate communications

FIGURE 8.8
An ENG (electronic newsgathering) camera with portable videotape recorder (VTR). (Courtesy of RCA)

FIGURE 8.9
An EFP (electronic field production) camera with viewfinder. (Courtesy of RCA)

FIGURE 8.10
A broadcast studio camera with Teleprompter. (Courtesy of RCA)

programs as an integral part of employee news and management television networks (Marsh, 1974).

The second camera configuration is that of the *EFP* type, which is similar to the ENG camera except that it generally comes with a studio viewfinder. In this configuration the camera is tripod- or dolly-mounted in the field and is used for studiolike set-ups, in documentary or commercial production where fixed position is required.

Studio cameras are designed for use in studios or as part of large, mobile television production vans dispatched to cover major sporting events, parades, concerts, and the like for which multiple cameras, sophisticated special effects, and complex video control systems are required (Paulson, 1981). They are generally found in installations where broadcast quality is desired. (While studio cameras come in all price ranges, we refer here to broadcast-quality, high-end equipment). Studio cameras are designed to produce high-resolution pictures and do so at relatively lower light levels and with higher resolution than EFP and ENG cameras, although in many instances the performance of ENG and EFP cameras is technically equal to broadcast studio cameras. Studio cameras are also more costly owing to the complex circuitry and set-up configurations required for "balancing" that must be done to "match" cameras so that shots taken of the same object by three different cameras have the same light values.

FIGURE 8.11
An RCA Hawkeye camera and videotape recorder (one-piece assembly for electronic newsgathering applications). (Courtesy of RCA)

This is important because studio cameras are generally used in groups of two or more; cutting between shots produced by different cameras reveals differences in color values, should any be present, with a resulting unpleasant visual jolt.

The camera types reviewed here are all capable of producing high-quality color pictures. (Black-and-white cameras have generally disappeared from use except for video graphics and special high-resolution and digitizing applications.)

In addition to cameras, there are two other principal sources of video information in a television system. One of these is the *telecine* or film chain (Figure 8.12). This device consists of a camera mounted permanently to pick up images from slide and motion picture projectors. Visual information of this sort may also be provided by digital storage devices which store frames of video information for recall. These are called *digital-frame store devices.*

Another source of video information is the *character generator* (Figure 8.13). This device, sometimes referred to by its common trade names, such as Chyron or Vidifont, is a keyboard device used to type characters on the screen for insertion as headlines, title inserts, sports scores, captions, and the like. Some graphics systems, like the Dubner, have sophisticated animation capabilities in addition to their use as character generators.

Once the image has been produced by video cameras, it is mixed, in the case

FIGURE 8.12
A telecine or film chain island for
origination of film and slides.
(Courtesy of RCA)

of real-time multicamera productions, by means of a *video switcher,* which permits live editing of shots, including special effects transitions. Special effects consist of everything from a simple dissolve between two shots, where the first image melts into the second and disappears, to complex zooming, shrinking, enlarging, and rotating of images.

When video pictures are shot single-camera style, they are edited in postproduction with sophisticated editing equipment that provides video editors with considerable flexibility. Since video images cannot be seen when the tape is examined, electronic time codes (SMPTE Time Code) are used to mark the position of each frame of video, and it is this code which is used as the reference for computer-based video editing systems, as shown in Figures 8.14 and 8.15 (Paulson, 1981).

8.7.2 Audio

Television sound is an area that has in the past received relatively little attention compared with video. This is changing. Today, broadcasters pay more attention than ever before to audio because of the increased sophistication of the viewing audience which has grown accustomed to high-fidelity stero recordings and FM stereo broadcasts. With the advent of stereo simulcasts (telecasts of musical events in stereo over cooperating FM-stereo radio stations) the public has begun to expect high-quality audio from television. Such service already exists in Japan.

FIGURE 8.13
(a) A Vidifont character generator keyboard. *(b)* A representative character/graphics display produced by a Vidifont graphics system. (Courtesy of Thomson-CSF Broadcast, Inc.)

High-fidelity stereo audio is also finding its way into the corporate environment, where two-channel audio capability is often employed for bilingual transmission or for supplementary information.

Audio for television production may be as simple as associating a microphone with a performer or as complicated as taping a multitrack version of a live orchestra performance and mixing the channels for rebroadcast. (See Figure 8.16.)

Audio is also added to the production of television by means of taped music and sound effects. These techniques provide additional audio information, which further illuminates the video.

8.7.3 Video Recording

In the early days of television all recording was made via kinescope, a system in which a film camera made a record directly from the television screen. By 1956

FIGURE 8.14
A production video switcher. (Courtesy of RCA)

the Ampex Corporation demonstrated a magnetic tape recorder system based on 2-inch tape, which, until recently, was the industry standard for broadcast television. The advent of high-quality 1-inch, 3/4-inch, and 1/2-inch videotape recording systems for use in ENG settings (see the RCA Hawkeye) has made tape the preferred recording medium in most television productions (see Figures 8.17 and 8.18).

These systems have lowered the cost of videotape production to a level where it is less expensive than film, and because of sophisticated editing techniques they can be used to produce effects which are on a par with those that could only be achieved by film not so long ago.

Videotape recording, even more than the evolution of low-cost video cameras, has moved television into the corporate environment. It has made video a low-cost tool in the audio-visual mix available to the manager. Because of its accessibility and relative low cost, videotape has made the production of local company news and information programs a viable choice for corporate programmers (Marsh, 1974).

The availability of programmable 1/2-inch formats like Beta and VHS and computer-controlled playback of videodisks, for example, has opened the door

FIGURE 8.15
Three-quarter-inch editing station with two videorecorders, joystick time-code editor, monitors, and video switcher. (Courtesy of JVC Company of America)

to new applications for video production—applications which permit in-house production of training materials and the use of in-house systems for internal communication (Smellie, 1979; Szilak, 1979).

8.7.4 Transmission

Television in the corporate environment makes use of a variety of distribution systems. In many corporations part or all of the physical plant is wired for closed-circuit delivery of video information. (SmithKline/Beckman in Philadelphia distributes a regular news show via such an internal network.) However, it is likely that the most common mode of transmission for some time to come will be the physical distribution of video materials on cassette or disk. This requires only compatibility between origination and playback systems; many companies have found it cost-effective to purchase production and playback facilities as part of a package deal and to distribute playback systems among their several locations (Van Deusen, 1979).

Of course, there is much discussion about the use of other transmission

FIGURE 8.16
Television audio in an electronic newsgathering (ENG) setting. (Courtesy of RCA)

systems for delivery of corporate video programming. Johnson & Johnson as a result of the Tylenol tragedy in 1982, effectively used an ad hoc 30-city satellite network to create a national news conference dedicated solely to that company's plans to restore Tylenol to its market share in the wake of the Chicago murders (Moore, 1982).

In a clever bit of corporate video, the company created an environment in which its new marketing concept was introduced, including full details of safety packaging, and at the same time fielded questions about its responsibility and the ethical stance it took following the events in Chicago. It was an effective use of video for a novel situation and demonstrated how a company could use the technology of television to focus attention where it wanted it focused. Interestingly, the Johnson & Johnson strategy was to eschew advertising of Tylenol, which it felt would irritate consumers, in favor of making news about their remarketing plans, which were given prolonged nationwide news coverage. In effect Johnson & Johnson used television to create a media event which was redistributed as news by network and local media.

Another area where external networks have played a role is the application of ITFS to continuing professional education. ITFS is a system of microwave television frequencies, similar to those which carry HBO to homes in many markets, dedicated to instructional applications and licensed to schools and universities.

Early experiments by the Moore School of Electrical Engineering at the

FIGURE 8.17
The Type C one-inch videotape recorder, which is gradually replacing older two-inch Quad recording equipment in broadcast and industrial applications. This RCA TR-800 VTR is microprocessor-controlled, and the studio console shown here includes an editing system, waveform monitor, vectorscope, and picture monitor bridge with audio loudspeakers.

University of Pennsylvania and General Electric Company illustrated the effectiveness of such systems. In the early 1970s, the General Electric Corporation was able to link its King of Prussia campus (30 miles from Philadelphia) to the classrooms of the University of Pennsylvania for interactive sessions on advanced topics in solid-state physics and related engineering disciplines (Figure 8.19).

In the future corporations will take advantage of newer media like the multichannel capacity offered by cable television and its ability through business and "institutional networks" to provide channels of information to business users in its franchise areas (Furlotte, 1983) and satellite networks (Rice, 1983).

8.7.5 Reception

Video distribution must terminate somewhere. Herein lies a critical element in the design of video systems for corporate environments. The use of standard

FIGURE 8.18
Half-inch videotape editing
session showing two RCA
Hawkeye consoles, one being
used to record audio channel.
(Courtesy of RCA)

FIGURE 8.19
Moore School of Electrical Engineering video classroom, University of Pennsylvania. (Courtesy
of Dr. O. M. Salati, Univ. of Pennsylvania)

monitors is the most obvious outlet for these programs. But the development of large screen displays has made it possible to address large audiences simultaneously, as in the case of the Tylenol news conference, which used large-screen projection in every major market. The availability of retrieval by tape has allowed ready access to the material produced by corporations in other display modes, including video lounges and specialized learning carrels which lend themselves to self-paced retrieval and instruction.

8.8 TRADE-OFF ANALYSIS: VIDEO VERSUS OTHER MEDIA

The choice of video as a communications medium must be based on full assessment of its potential and shortcomings. It is at its best in the delivery of instantaneous perishable information (the corporate network model), where there is a sense of urgency about the information to be communicated. From the perspective of cost effectiveness, it may be at its worst in the delivery of materials which can be transmitted better by still pictures. However, the advent of videodisks used for training programs and married to interactive computer programs can make the difference in favor of video for training, where before other media like slides and audio tape would have been the first choice.

The following criteria should be employed to assess the applicability of video to corporate environments:

1 *Resolution:* Does the video image provide the level of information resolution needed? Does motion help or hinder the presentation? Will stills suffice? Would some other EVT system be better matched to the needs of the presentation? What about the audio associated with the video? Is it what is called for?

2 *Speed of transmission:* In the case of instantaneous delivery of information, as in the national network teleconference, does the speed of transmission which "live" television provides really add to the presentation? Is the information so perishable that it must be transmitted in "real time"? Would video be better used on a delayed basis or on cassette or disk?

3 *Display:* Does the available (or desirable) method of display meet the needs of the presentation? There may be instances in which video displays are less useful than other means, such as slides or print materials. Because CRT displays are still bulky, and because the technology of flat-screen television is not yet commonplace, considerations must be given to the fit of information to display mode. The context in which the display takes place is also important. Is the information intended for large or small groups or for individuals?

4 *Future developments:* The assessment of video as a tool for management information must also consider new developments, such as three-dimensional and high-definition images. Where three-dimensional television enhances the data (as when physical models or products are displayed), the additional cost may be justified. Similarly, the evolution of high-definition television (HDTV), with 1000 or more scanning lines, will provide resolution comparable to the quality of 35mm motion picture film and, for some kinds of data (engineering, medical, technical), will lend itself to projection and other large-group presentations far better than is the case with the now standard 525 or 625 line systems (Roizen, 1983; Sandbank, 1983).

   5   *Cost:* Television is expensive. Networking by satellite, cassette distribution, internal closed circuit, MDS, ITFS, OFS, or broadband cable all entail considerable costs which must be laid off against competing media (Van Deusen, 1979).

8.9   INSTITUTIONAL PERSPECTIVE

Whether applied to the delivery of entertainment programming or management information television as a communication medium has been affected by recent changes in the regulatory environment which reflect laissez-faire values. In this setting the opportunity for new applications of video to management information delivery appears bright; not only are new channels for delivery such as low-power television (LPTV) coming on line, but existing systems such as UHF and VHF television are being given the freedom to redefine their roles in the telecommunications marketplace.

   Commercial television stations, formerly limited in this regard, may now scramble their signals so that only sets with decoders receive them. In the scrambled mode such stations may address programming to paying audiences. (Regulations which limited the delivery of scrambled signals by market were lifted by the FCC in 1982.) The application of scrambled signals to delivery of management information and training materials has not yet been attempted by broadcasters who, in the future, may find such programming profitable when delivered in off hours to audiences interested in continuing professional education. (A version of this system has been proposed by ABC and Sony to deliver entertainment programs; scrambled signals will be decoded and taped on the user's videocassette recorder for replay at the convenience of the user.)

8.10   TELEVISION IN THE MANAGEMENT ENVIRONMENT: AN OVERVIEW

There are three principal areas in which EVT systems will play a role in management strategies. The first of these is the training of personnel. Here visual information can readily be adapted to the task of socializing new employees into the corporate culture. Its use in retraining older employees for new positions under conditions of technology-induced change will also be significant.

   A number of interesting applications of video to corporate training have evolved. In one instance, Phillips Petroleum has used its corporate video system to train executives to respond effectively to the unexpected in television news interviews. In such training sessions, company executives spend a "TV day" simulating interview formats, including panel interviews, the two-person stand-up interview, on-the-scene interviews, and the talk-show interview. Their training also includes an "ambush interview," in the style of CBS's *60 Minutes,* where they are caught off guard by a probing, persistent reporter (Carlberg, 1980).

Many reasons can be cited for the use of video in corporate training, including the motivation of learners who, overall, respond well to the medium and to the drill and practice which taped programming facilitates (Onder, 1979).

The second area of application is special corporate networks, in which distribution of information about short-term activity or decision making is shared internally, often simultaneously, with key decision makers who are geographically dispersed. Whether the focus of the network is the implementation of new policy or the introduction of new products, the special corporate video network will be commonplace in the future.

The March 1983 meeting of the chief executives of the Holiday Inn Corporation provided a good example of the use of a special corporate network. Using Holiday Inn's Hi-Net teleconferencing network, the company conducted a review of 1982 business for 16,000 employees and guests in North America, Europe, and Asia. The 90-minute program, which originated at the company's headquarters in Memphis, included a full-motion satellite-delivered videoconference and a telephone link for feedback from each of the locations. In this way, those present at the meeting were able to put questions directly to corporate managers. The network incorporated 131 domestic and 3 foreign venues, including Hong Kong, London, and Frankfurt (Wiley, 1983).

The third area of application of video technology is the regular but limited video network. In this system the focus is on employee communication designed to associate the corporation with the interests of employees and their lifestyles and concerns. Just as television exposure conveys status in society at large, so does exposure on corporate television within the microsociety of the company. As SmithKline/Beckman has demonstrated, for example, employee news programs are a valuable tool in furthering company-employee relations.

Another example of the successful application of regular internal video networks is the Mary Kay Cosmetic Company. Faced with rapid growth, this company established a weekly 8-minute "newscast," using large screen video displays to update management on upcoming events in manufacturing. The programs include materials supplied by managers, accountants, and technicians and contain location footage which presents pictures of new machinery and industrial processes for all to see. The weekly newscasts are now supplemented by how-to pieces. High retention rates are reported for video material presented this way, and such data reinforce management's willingness to use television as a reliable channel of internal communication ("Corporate Video Net," 1983).

8.11 CONCLUSION

In this chapter a broad outline of the function of EVT in the corporate environment has been drawn. It is clear that the current role of EVT technologies is evolving. It is also clear that the corporate video manager will confront a variety of challenges as champions of technologies new in the 1980s compete with television for limited corporate resources.

Corporate video managers, as well as those who must make policy to govern the use of video in the corporate environment, will find themselves, as D. Brush (1980) has argued, pressed hard to evolve existing systems into something more than video-centered communications services: these systems and the people who manage them will be part of new developments merging information technologies, including personal computing, videotex, videodisk, videotape, and new distribution systems. They will become part of the data processing and word processing revolution.

REFERENCES

Barnouw, Erik, *A Tower in Babel: A History of Broadcasting in the United States to 1933,* Volume 1, New York: Oxford University Press, 1966.

———, *The Golden Web: A History of Broadcasting in the United States, 1933–1953,* Volume 2, New York: Oxford University Press, 1968.

———, *The Image Empire: A History of Broadcasting in the United States from 1953,* Volume 3, New York: Oxford University Press, 1970.

Berlo, D. K., "The Context for Communication," in G. J. Hanneman and W. J. McEwen (eds.), *Communication and Behavior,* Reading, Mass.: Addison-Wesley, 1975.

Brush, D. P., "Is Television Dead? It May Be As We Know It," *Educational and Industrial Television,* 1980, *12*(12), pp. 50–51.

Brush, J. M., "Corporate Video Progresses—Some New Figures," *Educational and Industrial Television,* 1980, *12*(11), pp. 68–70.

Carlberg, S., "How to Prepare Your Company's Executives for TV Interviews," *Educational and Industrial Television,* 1980, *12*(8), pp. 40–44.

"Slow-Scan Television and Telemedicine," Colorado Video, 1983.

"CCTV Paced by Business Video," *Communications News,* 1983, *20*(4).

"Corporate Video Net a Key to Success at Mary Kay Cosmetics," *Communications News, 20*(4).

Costigan, D. M., *Fax: The Principles and Practice of Facsimile Communication,* Philadelphia: Chilton, 1971.

Dickson, E. W., *The Video Telephone: A New Era in Telecommunications,* Ithaca: Cornell University Press, 1973,

Furlotte, N., "Cable TV for CEO's," *Cable Marketing,* 1983, *3*(2), pp. 22–26.

Hellman, H., "Facsimile," in *The Electronic Edition of Grolier's Academic American Encyclopedia,* Danbury, Conn.: Groliers, 1983.

Kelleher, K., "Move the Expertise Not the Expert with Slow-Scan Videoconferencing," *Communications News,* 1983.

Marsh, K., *Independent Video,* San Francisco: Straight Arrow Books, 1974.

Mattingly, G., "Video Grammar," *Educational and Industrial Television,* 1979, *11*(1), pp. 36–39.

Meigs, J., "Corporate TV at the Crossroads," *Videography,* 1983, *8*(5), pp. 32–33.

Moore, T., "The Fight to Save Tylenol," *Fortune,* November 19, 1982, pp. 44–49.

Onder, J., "Why to Use Television in Management Training," *Educational and Industrial TV,* 1979, *11*(3), pp. 57–61.

Paulson, C. R., *BM/E's ENG/EFP/EPP Handbook: Guide to Using Mini Video Equipment,* New York: Broadband Information Services, 1981.

Rice, H., "Satellites Are a National Resource to Educate/Train Corporate America," *Communication News,* 1983, *20*(3), pp. 80–81.

Roizen, J., "Setting the Sights on HDTV Standards," *Broadcast Communications,* 1983, *6*(4), pp. 62–65.

Sandbank, C. P., and M. E. B. Moffat, "High Definition Television and Compatibility with Existing Systems," *SMPTE Journal,* 1983, *92*(5), pp. 552–556.

Smellie, D. C., "Videodiscs in the Classroom," *Educational and Industrial Television,* *11*(5), p. 33.

Szilak, D., "Interactive Tape Cassettes for Industrial Training," *Educational and Industrial Television,* 1979, *11*(4), pp. 43–44.

Van Deusen, R. E., "How to Set Up a Videocassette Network—Part 1: Planning," *Educational and Industrial Television,* 1979, *11*(1), pp. 31–34.

Wiley, D., "Video: The Eye of the Information Age Focuses on Entertainment Plus Business," *Communications News,* 1983, *20*(4), p. 56.

CHAPTER **9**

ELECTRONIC MAIL

**Ruann Pengov
General Electric Information Systems
Rockville, MD 20850**

9.1 HISTORICAL INTRODUCTION

Historically, mail has been used when other forms of communication are too expensive or when a written record of the communication is required. The ideal mail system should transfer information—text, data, pictures, etc.—between receiver and sender according to speed and privacy requirements of the sender and at an acceptable price. Electronic mail is a mail system which passes information electronically from sender to receiver. There are many examples and definitions of electronic mail systems. In its broadest sense, it includes telegraph and telex communications, facsimile *(FAX)*, computer-based messaging services (CBMS),* communicating word processors, computer conferences, voice messaging systems, and others. In the long term, the model electronic mail system ought to allow a user to communicate information regardless of the source (fax machine, word processor, computer), the format (text, data, graphics, voice), or the destination (local or remote) of the information.

Figure 9.1 shows graphically the existing range of equipment and forms of information with which the current office user must contend. Rather than interfacing and communicating individually with each piece of equipment or having a separate electronic mail system for each piece of equipment, an integrated electronic mail system will allow the user to transmit information to and from various types of equipment through a single user interface (hardware and software). Hence, any message could have a voice component, a text component, an image component, a graphics component, and so forth. An electronic mail system should act simply as an electronic envelope for all of these forms of information, and it should forward the information to and from various pieces of equipment, performing the necessary translations of forms of data.

---

*A CBMS system uses computers to receive, store, route, and control electronic messages or electronic "envelopes."

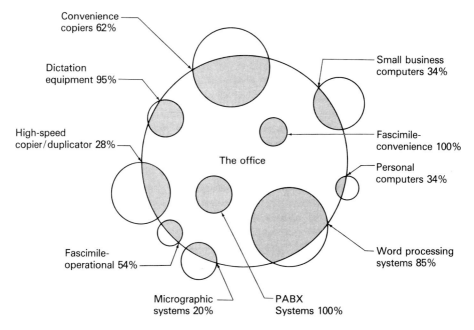

Note: White areas within equipment circles represent non-
office use, %'s indicate office use.
Size of circles indicates proportionate market
share of office expenditures.

FIGURE 9.1
Office equipment. (Courtesy of Creative Strategies, 1979)

Electronic mail has a long history and currently has many forms in the market place.

9.1.1 Telegraph

The telegraph was the very first electrical mail system. Western Union, a company formed in 1851, currently has a registered trademark for the term *electronic mail*. The telegraph met the criteria of its day for rapid communication. Its most notable drawback was the requirement to manually convert between English and Morse code. Since messages were not recorded, operators were required on both ends. Additionally, the user could not control the message destination; since Morse code was sent down a line, it could be picked up or received by multiple unknown individuals.

9.1.2 Teletypewriter

Teletypewriter units, or teletypes (TTY) as they are often called, offer two key advantages over the telegraph. First, message text can be entered from a keyboard, and second, a physical conduit is established between the sender and the recipient to control the message destination. The teletypewriter unit converted the characters keyed in at the keyboard to digital signals similar to Morse code. The chief drawback of the teletype system was that both teletypes, one at the sending and one at the receiving end, had to be active at the same time. This meant that both operators had to be present at the same time in order to communicate. Nonetheless, traditional teletype services provided for immediate message delivery when the operators were present.

With the development of paper tape as a means of recording and transmitting teletype messages, it was not necessary for the operator to remain at a particular station during the entire time a message was being received or transmitted. Operators could control a large number of stations. See Figure 6.1 for an illustration of a torn-tape teletype relay station. A keyboard-only unit (requiring an operator) is called a *keyboard send-and-receive* unit (KSR), while a device capable of sending and receiving using paper tape as a medium is called an *automatic send-and-receive* unit (ASR). In addition to requiring fewer operators, the tape relay system had the advantage of enabling an operator to type the message onto paper tape and then, when its correctness was assured, transmit it at a much faster rate of speed, thus economizing on the use of transmission facilities.

9.1.3 Telex and TWX

In the early 1960s, store-and-forward message systems were introduced. In these, a computer, rather than paper tape or a buffered terminal, is used to store a message at an intermediate location in a relay center until it is ready to be forwarded to the other end. Although an improvement over the early teletypewriter systems, these still require the users to manually check the reliability of the messages and to number and log them in as they arrive. The method for addressing other users is complicated enough that a trained operator is required to handle all of the technicalities of a system.

9.1.4 Facsimile

Although the classical facsimile system was developed in 1875, the usefulness of facsimile for business came about with the introduction of a low-priced, plain-paper desktop facsimile unit in 1966. (However, see Chapter 18 for a discussion of facsimile's use in news service well before this time.) Like telex and TWX systems, most older facsimile systems require simultaneous communications from sender to receiver; more modern ones overcome this limitation.

Facsimile works by identifying whether each point or pixel* on the page is dark or light, and then transferring this information across a traditional

---

*A *pixel* is the smallest fragment of a picture, typically about 1/10,000 of the area of a page, that is sampled or read by picture processing machinery.

telephone line. Initially, the transmission for a page could take as long as 6 minutes. Currently, there are three groups of units. Group 1 services are essentially analog devices like those introduced in 1966 for transmitting a page in 4 to 6 minutes. Group 2 devices employ data compression techniques to achieve transmission times of 2 to 3 minutes per page, although they still transmit analog data. These devices can be automated or not. Group 3 devices reduce the information transmitted, usually by digital techniques, and send a page in 1 minute or less over normal telephone lines. The future of the digital facsimile devices appears to be very bright because of the capacity which these devices have for processing and adding intelligence to the page being transmitted. As of 1980, over 255,000 facsimile devices were installed in the United States, a growth rate of 15 percent per year (Yankee Group, 1981).

The strongest advantage of facsimile systems is that they can send images (graphics, alphanumeric information, etc.) in addition to text. This is especially good with material such as the Japanese character set where it is very difficult to encode the many characters in digital form. The trade-off with facsimile is generally cost versus transmission time and ease of use. High-speed devices are more expensive but reduce telephone charges and length of operator attention per page. Ease-of-use features like automatic page feeders also add to the cost. Facsimile devices cost approximately $110 to $500 per month to rent or $5000 to $20,000 to purchase, depending on the volume (Yankee Group, 1981).

The major vendors in the facsimile marketplace have been Xerox, Quip (an Exxon Enterprises product), Graphics Sciences (a Burroughs Company), and 3M in the United States. Both Graphics Sciences and 3M have digital capability. Recently the Japanese have actively entered the digital market. The leaders are Hitachi, Nippon, Rapicon (a Ricoh company), and Panafax. In addition, NTT (the Japanese equivalent of AT&T) has a network for public facsimile transmission.

Facsimile users want the capability to transmit to more than one user at a time. Additionally, they would like to be able to transmit directly to the terminal screen rather than to a hard-copy output device. These types of user requirements are being addressed by current products under development today. They are harbingers of trends which will see facsimile integrated into work stations at both the sending and receiving ends of a facsimile system. Such systems will also enjoy the benefits of the electronic mail systems described below. The key is not only development of the technology but also development of standards which will allow connection across computer-based message systems (see Section 9.22). One of the major unsolved problems with facsimile is the incompatibility of different vendors' equipment.

9.1.5 Communicating Word Processors

Without going into a full discussion of the evolution and state of the art of the word processing marketplace, it is important to note the role of word processing in electronic mail systems. Word processors are computers that permit users to enter, store, retrieve, edit, reformat, and display text. Although initially developed as stand-alone devices, they can now communicate with each other, passing the digital representation of documents back and forth to similar equipment and, many times, through software translations to dissimilar equipment from multiple vendors. When they operate in this manner, communicating word processors are a form of electronic mail carrier. The word processing operator directs documents to be forwarded to other systems where they are printed out or distributed directly to another user's workstation. The communicating word processors generally do not have all of the value-added capabilities characteristic of electronic mail systems, such as automatic storage and forwarding of messages. Many of the communicating word processing vendors offer computer-based electronic messaging systems and are incorporating the word processing linkage into their electronic mail systems. Common among these are Wang, Xerox, IBM, and Datapoint.

9.2 ELECTRONIC MAIL

More than half of the Fortune 500 companies are looking at, designing, or implementing electronic mail. The major reason is to increase productivity and improve profits. As Bittner (1982) has observed:

> The existing decline in white collar productivity will have dire consequences on this country where more than 50% of the work force consists of white collar workers—a figure that is growing 20% faster than the workforce as a whole. In dollars, this figure represents a cost of some $13 billion each week according to recent estimates. Against this background, executives are being bombarded with questions:
>
> What can be done about the declining productivity spiral in which an estimated 25% of the top managers' time is spent waiting for information?
> How can rising labor costs be reduced in the labor intensive workforce?
> What can be done with the workforce in which fewer and fewer people will be available to perform the more routine tasks?
> How can business get information out on time?
>
> Some people may not realize it and others will do everything they can to deny it, the answer is simply—automate. (pp. 63–65)

9.2.1 Costs and Benefits

Figure 9.2 historically reinforces the perspective introduced above. It shows that 40 percent of the productivity growth in the United States from 1929 to 1978 came from technological innovation. More specifically, automation of the mail process has brought costs down. The cost of preparing and mailing a single letter has been estimated at $6.63 as shown in Figure 9.3.

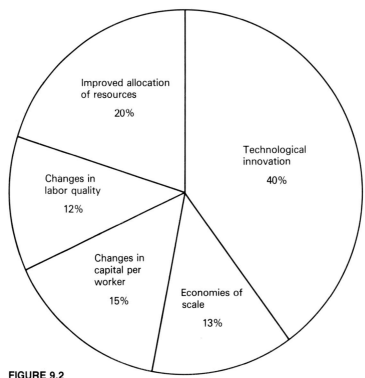

FIGURE 9.2
Sources of productivity growth in the United States (1929–1978). (Courtesy of Yankee Group, 1981, p. 10)

In 1982, American first-class postage alone was $0.20 and conventional mail lacks both speed and dependability. The cost of a typical telex or TWX message or long-distance phone call is around $1.50. Computer-based electronic mail systems can send the mail for approximately $0.25 to $1.00. Some computer-based message systems can send messages for less than $0.05 where there is high message traffic (Ulrich, 1980).

Bair (1979) lists the following benefits of electronic mail to the individual user:

    1 A reduction in "telephone tag" (a series of calls back, with the destination person always being out) and increased efficiency in communications. A high percentage of such communication is one way. Only 28 percent of phone calls are completed the first time, and it can take an average of three to six calls before two busy people connect, while 100 percent of electronic mail messages are completed. That computers are somewhat less reliable, mechanically, than the voice telephone network may reduce the likelihood of delivery somewhat. The potential saving is about 30 minutes per day per user.

    2 Reduction in interruptions because the users read the messages at their convenience rather than every time the phone rings. Interruptions and restarts of work are eliminated. The potential saving from this aspect is about 60 minutes per day.

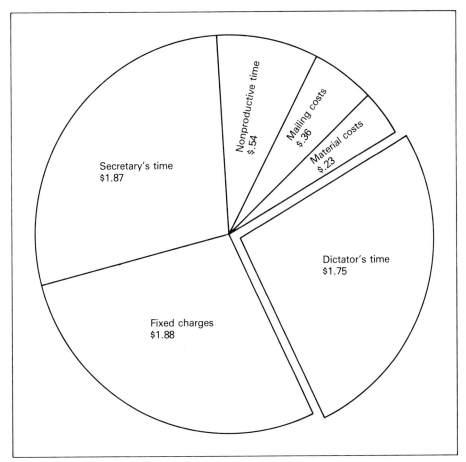

FIGURE 9.3
Cost of a letter. (Courtesy of Management World Magazine, 1981, p. 12)

3 Elimination of time-zone differences.

4 Faster, more timely communication because the typing, proofing, copying, and traditional mailing steps can be skipped for many types of communication.

5 As much as 2 hours saved per day per business professional with the use of a good electronic mail system.

Figure 9.4 summarizes the payoffs from a computer-based message system as opposed to a traditional telephone system. It results from an analysis at a very detailed level of office work. There are many other similar examples. Figure 9.5 shows the potential impact on management productivity of electronic mail and other office automation uses.

The importance of making office communications more effective and efficient is highlighted by the fact that most managers and professionals spend over half

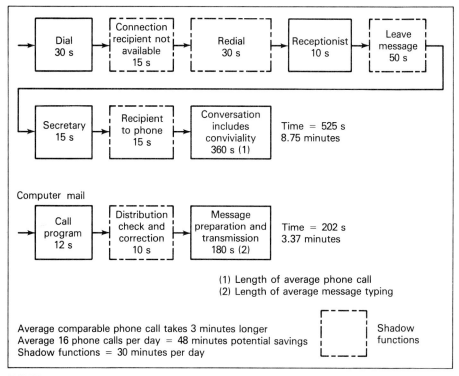

FIGURE 9.4
Potential time-saving CBMS versus telephone. (Courtesy of Bolt, Beranek, and Newman, 1981, pp. 1–24)

their time communicating. Other studies show (1) productivity increases for the past decade to be 5 percent for office workers compared to the 90 percent average for all other industries and (2) capital investment per worker in the office of approximately $2000 compared to $25,000 as the average in all other industry sectors (Uhlig, Farber, & Bair, 1979). These figures offer evidence that the time is right for providing new tools to help individuals working with information (office workers) to be more productive. Electronic mail offers such potential.

A few organizations are implementing sophisticated electronic mail and office automation systems: most are beginning to explore their potential. Those who do not may well find themselves falling behind their competition.

9.2.2 The Office of the Future

In 1978 relatively few people had heard of office automation, the office of the future, or the electronic office. Today, "integrated office systems" are being heralded as a means of reversing the white-collar productivity slump and achieving productivity gains in the office similar to those achieved in other areas

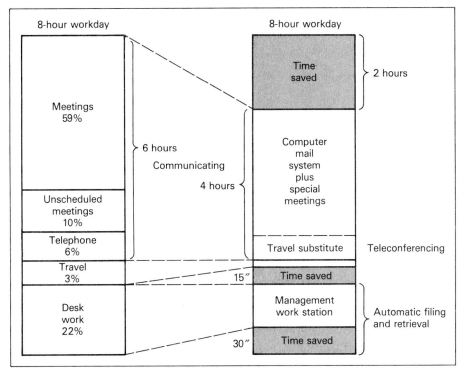

FIGURE 9.5
Office automation potential impact on management productivity. (Courtesy of Bolt, Beranek, and Newman, 1981, pp. 1–26)

of industry. Office systems will eventually affect the way people work, the kind of work they perform, and the social interaction with fellow employees. Given the central functioning of communication of information in any office, electronic mail will be a central capability in any office system.

Key to the successful use of electronic mail or any of the other new tools provided for office systems is a keen understanding of what the users are doing currently and how new tools can help them be more effective at their work.

This view begins with a list of office activities for which an innovative end user might consider computer assistance. These activities can be categorized into four broad office areas, which are all new to the traditional data processing main. These categories are document management, organizational communication, decision support, and personal support.

Document management includes the creation, editing, formating, printing, filing, and searching of electronic documents. Such documents will include a wide range of information forms (data, text, image, voice, graphics, video, etc).

Organizational communication includes such everyday tasks as the sending of a message or document, phoning and leaving a message if no one answers, or the presentation of information in graphic form in meetings.

Decision support includes the ad hoc retrieval, analysis, and presentation of information drawn from files throughout the organization.

Personal support includes the storage and manipulation of information for private use. Examples include tickler files, to-do lists, and calendars.

Although communication falls in one quadrant of analysis of the functioning of an office user, Figure 9.6 shows the key role of electronic mail as the communications "nervous system" of office systems.

Computer-based messaging systems evolved in the 1970s. In these, the message is entered by the sender and stored in digital form by computer for subsequent delivery to one or more recipients. Most often, a CBMS message is initiated from a keyboard on one terminal and received on the display screen or on paper at a second terminal. Between the two terminals, however, is a computer which actually receives the message, processes it in some way, and then routes it to the recipient.

Because the computer is involved in receiving and forwarding the message

FIGURE 9.6
Components of the existing office. (Courtesy of Hewlett-Packard Co., *HPMAIL Electronic Mail,* 1982)

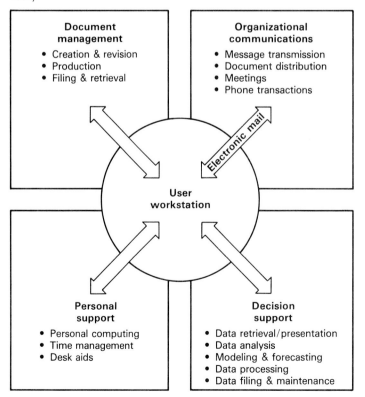

much added value can be provided in this electronic mail system over earlier teletype, TWX, or telex systems. The computer serves both as post office and as postal delivery service by sorting and distributing messages. The full power of the computer can be brought to bear with the following added cabilities:

1 *Message preparation features.* Text editing capabilities and even full word processing capabilities can be provided in a mail system to assist the sender in creating the message or in sending a document created previously in a word processing environment.

2 *Maintenance or distribution of lists.* The computer can allow for creation of specialized distribution lists along with storage and on-demand recall of such lists for sending messages.

3 *Message confirmation.* CBMSs provide for confirmation to the sender that the message has, in fact, been sent and received by the recipient.

4 *Utilization logging.* The computer can keep very detailed statistics on the exact number of characters sent by any sender, the time sent, etc. This information can be used for billing systems or for tracking messages.

5 *Message filing.* CBMSs allow for storage and retrieval of messages previously sent or received.

6 *End-user–end-user addressing.* The more sophisticated CBMSs require the sender only to identify the names of the recipients on the distribution list; no knowledge is required of the computer system or the terminal location of the recipient. The CBMS itself maintains tables and directories of all the users of the system.

7 *End-user–end-user communication.* When the mechanical system is simple enough and when terminal equipment is properly distributed within the office, CBMSs allow the parties to a conversation to enter information directly, without the need for the time or expense of dealing with intermediaries. Not only can this save money, but it also makes long-distance digital communication more informal.

8 *Mailbox capability.* With this capability, recipients need not be present when mail is sent to them. All messages are collected in users' electronic mailbox; users simply sign on to their terminal when they wish to receive mail messages. Some systems even allow for notification by a signal—a light, bell, etc.—at users' terminals when a message is received.

9 *Offline paper delivery.* For those users who are not yet on the CBMS or who do not wish to use it, most CBMSs allow for creation of paper output of the messages for delivery through the traditional paper mail system.

10 *Multiple computer capability.* Some CBMSs allow for message distribution to users who are on multiple computer systems for connecting computers to each other. Figures 9.7 and 9.8 show simple configurations of CBMS with one computer and with multiple computers. In Figure 9.7, the user terminals are connected to the computer by typical transmission media such as twisted-pair telephone lines (for a local device), leased and dial-up telephone lines, value-

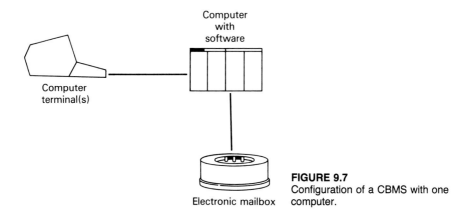

FIGURE 9.7
Configuration of a CBMS with one computer.

added public data network, etc. In Figure 9.8, the same situation applies, except that the two computers or multiple computers are connected to each other and pass messages as needed to other computers in order to transmit them to the correct end user. In the latter case, more sophisticated electronic-mail software is required in the computers to handle the message transfer. In Figures 9.7 and 9.8, a key component of the computer-based message system is the software in the computer which adds the intelligence to perform the user functions such as message preparation, filing, etc.

11 *Security.* CBMS can provide for multiple levels of security to ensure that only those people who should have access to messages do indeed have access to them.

12 *Support of a variety of terminals.* The most flexible CBMSs allow for use

FIGURE 9.8
Configuration of a CBMS with multiple computers.

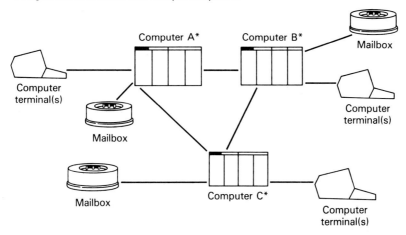

*All with electronic mail software

of almost any type of terminal to send and receive messages. The computer handles terminal-specific information.

13 *Options for message disposition.* Most CBMSs offer the capability for disposition of messages upon receipt. These include having a designate read it, "throwing" the message away, adding a note to the message and forwarding it to others, filing the message, leaving the message in the mailbox, etc.

14 *Storage efficiencies.* The more efficient CBMSs store a message only once per computer even though it might be sent to hundreds of individuals' mailboxes; this saves storage space.

15 *Ease of use.* The most successful systems follow a model which is natural and familiar to the end user in terms of the office functions performed. Not only should the use be almost intuitive, but the initial encounter with the system should require no more than 30 minutes (preferably less than 10) for the user to learn to send and receive simple messages. This is probably the area where most systems have been less than successful; in their attempt to provide full functionality they have often developed a cumbersome and unnatural user interface which requires the unsophisticated user to learn many commands and sequences in order to perform the functions within the computer-based message system.

16 *Forms capability.* A state-of-the-art computer-based message system will provide the electronic equivalent of a fill-in-the-blank form that is common in today's offices for all types of applications such as expense reports, purchase orders, etc. Forms handling capabilities and other computer applications can add intelligence in the handling of information (for example, checking the contents of a given field for a range of values, taking further steps based upon the contents of a field, etc.).

17 *Ability to send any type of information.* The advanced computer-based message system will provide an electronic envelope into which the user puts any type of information (a document, a message, a graph, a data file, a voice message, a facsimile page, a video message, etc.).

18 *Integration with other office functions.*

9.3 ELECTRONIC MAIL DELIVERY SYSTEM

A large number of computer-based messaging systems are in the market today, each providing its own individualized mix of the features and capabilities reviewed above. Systems can, however, be categorized by delivery method: time-sharing service or in-house system.

9.3.1 Time-Sharing Service

With the time-sharing service system, users buy mailbox space and electronic mail service from a time-sharing computer vendor and use their own terminal to access the mail system. Neither computer nor storage capabilities are required at the user site and users generally pay according to the number and length of

TABLE 9-1
MAJOR PROVIDERS OF CBMS

Company	Product
General Electric Information Services Co.	Quick-Comm
Dialcom	Automated Office Systems
GTE Telenet	Telemail
Tymnet	On-Tyme
Computer Corp. of America	Comet
CompuServe	Infoplex
MCI	MCI Mail

messages transmitted and stored. Some of the major providers of time-sharing CBMSs are shown in Table 9.1.

9.3.2 In-House Services

The second major category of systems are those which are provided for installation on an in-house computer, that is, a computer at the user site. The majority of the offerings in the category are provided by equipment vendors who sell computers, terminals, and disk storage units, along with CBMS software. In this situation, users must be concerned not only with the terminal and its link to the computer but with the installation of the computer itself, the storage devices required for the mailboxes, and the software and communication links between computers if multiple computers are involved. Some of the major suppliers of in-house CBMSs are:

Data General Corporation
Data Point
Digital Equipment Corporation
Four-Phase Systems, Inc.
Hewlett-Packard
IBM Corporation
Prime Computer
Wang Laboratories, Inc.

In 1981–1982 most major computer companies announced product strategies if not actual product offerings for office systems. A key element of such strategies in all cases is a computer-based message system.

Several configurations exist for in-house CBMSs. With a single-site system, electronic mail resides in one computer. While other remote computers may exist in the user's network or organization, they have no electronic mail functions except perhaps to link users to the system that handles the electronic mail. In a distributed mail system, electronic mail software exists in several computers. Each computer handles locally as many functions as it can; when mail is designated for users at a different site, the local computer transmits the mail to software residing in the designated remote center.

In another configuration, one computer acts as a central switching and distribution and collection point for all mail from all systems. Each system has electronic mail software, but when it receives mail destined for another site, it sends the message to the central computer for rerouting rather than sending it directly to the remote computer.

The appendix to this chapter offers a sample dialogue from a computer-based message system.

9.3.3 Advanced Computerized Voice Communications

Current sophisticated telephone switching equipment, often called *private automatic branch exchanges* (PABXs) provide some or all of the following features to a business customer: "Conference calling, call holding, call forwarding, chain calling, answer any station . . . secretarial hunt, paging access, call recording, traffic measuring and storage, optimal and alternate call routing and lots more" (Ulrich, 1980). Vendors will soon be offering CBMS that are integrated with the telephone systems—this marriage is inevitable. Integration of these communication offerings is exciting, since it will tie together the capabilities of CBMSs while utilizing the most common workstation in the office today—the telephone.

9.3.4 Voice Mail

Unlike PABXs, voice mail systems are computer-based systems developed specifically to handle voice store-and-forward communications. As such, they are indeed a computer-based message system with the message itself stored in voice format. The user can enter messages, send them to predefined distribution lists, store them, reroute them, dispose of them, etc., using the telephone as a workstation terminal. Most systems are not integrated with the PABX systems or with other computer-based message systems (that is, the user cannot mix voice and text messages), and they are generally quite expensive—over $100,000 for the initial purchase price. The most notable vendors offering voice store-and-forward systems today are IBM, EMS (a Texas-based firm), and Wang.

As mentioned above, the natural next step is for voice message elements to be integrated with digital computer-based message systems.

9.3.5   Other Computer-Based Message Systems

There are many other forms of CBMS. Computer conferencing, discussed at length in Chapter 10, is a special form of CBMS where multiple users can simultaneously communicate with each other to emulate a conference or meeting of individuals. One of the most capable computer conferencing systems is offered by Infomedia, Inc. (Johansen, 1979).

In computer conferencing, the user docs not have a general mailbox but rather receives information already presented by the topic of interest or according to the group of people in the conference. Unlike video conferencing, computer conferencing does not necessarily provide simultaneous communication.

Another form of electronic mail is that offered by the U.S. Postal Service, electronic computer-originated mail (E-COM). It is a service by which computer-readable tapes are delivered to the post office; the tapes are then read and the messages electronically distributed to other E-COM postal centers throughout the United States. At the destination center, they are printed out and delivered through the local mail system, thus avoiding the delay of long-distance mail transfer. The issue in the E-COM offering is the appropriate balance between public and private services offered in the area. Should the Postal Service spend public funds to develop such systems? More specifically, private vendors such as AT&T, MCI, General Electric, and value-added networks such as Tymnet, Telenet, etc., will most likely compete with E-COM. If the Postal Service does not offer competitive service, the competitors could divert mail flow and potentially raise first-class mail rates. A study by the Congressional Office of Technology Assessment (1982) offers a thorough discussion of the technology and public policy issues in this area.

9.4   COMPARISON OF SYSTEMS

The advantages and disadvantages for each of the various types of electronic mail systems are summarized below:

9.4.1   Telex and TWX

The advantages here are the universality of service and standardization, particularly internationally. This service is the main international service connection between the United States and European countries. The major disadvantages are the slow transmission capability, the lack of user friendliness, and the inability to transmit anything but a very limited character set (for example, no pictures).

9.4.2 Facsimile

The obvious advantages of facsimile are that no keyboarding is required and graphics as well as text can be transmitted. The disadvantages are the lack of standardization across facsimile equipment, the requirement for manual intervention of operators at either end, and the lack, at least in most systems, of intelligent processing or value-added capability.

9.4.3 Communicating Word Processors

The advantages here are the high capability in document preparation and the very sophisticated user-oriented interface, particularly when linked with a CBMS from the same vendor. Disadvantages are that the stand-alone word processors generally do not have the sophisticated data management, communication, and other office systems capabilities provided by computer vendors, and there is generally only local communications (from one terminal to another on the same word processor).

9.4.4 PABX and Voice Mail

The advantages here are the elimination of typing and the use of the telephone as a terminal. The disadvantages are that such systems are not suitable for formal correspondence and generally there is no integration with the data processing and CBMS systems.

9.4.5 Computer-Based Message Systems

A sophisticated CBMS offers the speed of a telephone with the hard-copy output of a letter. Users are free from telephone tag. With the problem of the time zones and work shifts, they can read and respond to messages as desired rather than as dictated by others. The speed of communication is also an asset, as is the reduction of paper flow and information float (time lost while paper is passed from person to person). A CBMS helps to distribute information immediately to all people who need it rather than passing the paper from desk to desk.

The advantages of the time-sharing service are that start-up requires minimal capital investment and time; also, the user is not locked into any particular vendor. The disadvantages are the higher costs for large volumes of usage and the lack of integration with in-house data processing applications, word processing, or other office systems capabilities. Other concerns are security, consistency in response time, and control.

The advantages of choosing an in-house system are the potential for growth and integration with data processing, word processing, and other office systems capabilities. Additionally, data security, response time, control, etc. are in the hands of the user company. Disadvantages are initial lock-in to a particular vendor, costs of on-site installation, the need for knowledgeable individuals for implementation, and the costs of continuing operation, maintenance, and upgrade.

The extensive capabilities of CBMSs are their greatest advantage; the complexity of implementation may be their greatest disadvantage.

9.4.6 Implementation

Implementing electronic mail systems is not easy. Many times failure to address the human and organizational concerns may make electronic mail implementation unsuccessful. A clear idea of the needs of the individual user community is essential to successful implementation. Specifically, this includes:

1 Understanding the company, the environment, and the culture into which the electronic mail system will be placed.

2 Understanding the needs of the group of people who will be users of the electronic mail system.

3 Recognition of potential user resistance and need for attention to the human element and the change process.

4 Monitoring and carefully understanding the paper mail and other communication systems currently in place to use as a basis for design of an integrated electronic system.

5 An initial awareness of the limitations of the computer system.

6 Formation of a planning and design group to monitor, spearhead, and evaluate the implementation.

7 Formation of a strong support group within the organization to handle administrative functions, user training, and so forth.

8 Formation of a pilot system as a test prior to full-scale implementation.

9 Continuous user needs refinement for the system.

10 Integration of electronic mail system with other functions and capabilities in office systems and the general management information systems environment.

11 Provisions for growth and addition of capabilities. Companies such as Texas Instruments, Digital Equipment Corporation, Xerox Corporation, Hewlett-Packard, Manufacturers Hanover Trust, Westinghouse Corporation, Northern Telecom, and many others have studies showing the benefits of computer-based message systems in their organizations (Bolt, Beranek, and Newman, 1981). They and many others are or will be implementing electronic mail systems.

9.5 THE FUTURE

The market projection for electronic mail in the United States shows high annual growth rates (see Figure 9.9). The merger of office systems capability with data

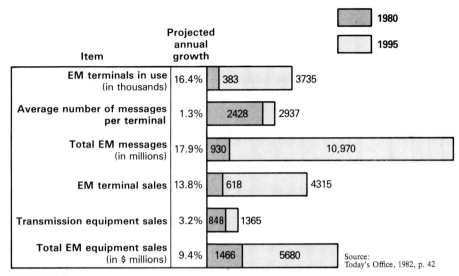

FIGURE 9.9
U.S. electronic mail market.

processing capabilities and messaging systems will form an integrated information management system for the end user (see Figure 9.10).

The goal is to help the user get at the information needed—in the form in
which it is needed, when it is needed—to help improve productivity. Referring

FIGURE 9.10
Integrated information management.

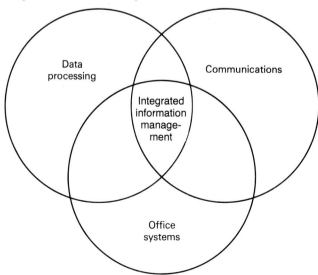

back to Figure 9.1, we might visualize the user sitting in the center of an office and having access to all the varieties of equipment capabilities without having to know that the different equipment exists. Users would simply interface through their computer-based message systems and their multifunctional workstations to access integrated information originating from many different types of equipment throughout the organization. The potential for productivity improvement is great.

REFERENCES

Bair, J. H., "Communication in the Office of the Future: Where the Real Payoff Will Be," *Business Communications Review,* 1979.

Bittner, P., "Electronic Mail," *Computer World Office Automation,* 1982, *16*(8A), pp. 63–65.

Bolt, Beranek, and Newman, *Electronic Mail: The Message Systems Approach,* Cambridge, Mass.: Information Management Corporation, 1981.

Facsimile and Electronic Mail, San Jose, Calif.: Creative Strategies International, 1980.

Johansen, Robert, Jaques Vallee, and Kathleen Spangler, *Electronic Meetings: Technical Alternatives and Social Choices,* Reading, Mass.: Addison-Wesley, 1979.

HPMAIL Electronic Mail, Document #5953-82-54, Cupertino, Calif.: Hewlett-Packard Company, 1982.

Management World Magazine, June 1981.

Office Automation, San Jose, Calif.: Creative Strategies International, 1979.

Office of Technology Assessment, U.S. Congress, *Implications of Electronic Mail and Message Systems for the U.S. Postal Service,* Washington, D.C.: 1982.

Today's Office, "Electronic Mail: A New Medium for the Message," August, 1982.

Uhlig, Ronald, David Farber, and James H. Bair, *Office of the Future Computers and Communications,* North Holland, N.Y.: 1979.

Ulrich, Walter E., "Introduction to Electronic Mail," *AFIPS Conference Proceedings,* 1980, pp. 435–488.

Yankee Group, *The Report on Electronic Mail* (2d ed.), 1981, Cambridge, Mass.

————, *The Report on Electronic Mail,* 1982, Cambridge, Mass.

RECOMMENDED READING

Connell, Stephen, and Ian A. Galbraith, *Electronic Mail: A Revolution in Business Communication,* White Plains, N.Y.: Knowledge Industry Publications, 1982.

Kerr, Elaine B., and Starr Roxanne Hiltz, *Computer-Mediated Communication Systems —Status and Evaluation,* New York: Academic, 1982.

Mullins, Carolyn J., and Thomas W. West, *The Office Automation Primer: Harnessing Information Technologies for Greater Productivity,* Englewood Cliffs, N.J.: Prentice-Hall, 1982.

Ulrich, Walter E., "Electronic Mail—Introduction and Genealogy," *IEEE 1980 National Telecommunications Conference,* New York: Institute for Electrical and Electronics Engineers, 1980, 60.1/1–3, pp. 435–488.

APPENDIX: Sample Dialogue from a Computer-Based Message System

HP3000 / MPE IV.C.OV.20   FRI, OCT 1, 1982   8:52 AM
:hpmail

HP36579A.00.01 HPMAIL (C) Hewlett-Packard Co. 1982

IND (Marketing/Support). (CSP10046)

Please type your name: richardson . . . . (common last name
                                    user identification)

Please type your password:
Beth Richardson signed on.
Signed on recorded at 0853 on 10/01/82.
Last signed off 1155 on 09/30/82.

HPMAIL

Beth Richardson

You have two new messages. . . . . (prompts for new
                                      mail)

Select 1 IN TRAY — Read your incoming mail
       2 OUT TRAY — Send messages
       3 PENDING TRAY — Track messages you have sent
       4 WORK AREA — Create new work
       5 LIST AREA — Create new distribution lists
       6 FILING CABINET — Look in your folders
       7 ADMINISTRATION
       8 LEAVE HPMAIL — Sign off and end the program
       9 Sign off and sign on as someone else

Please type a number to indicate your choice.
Type HELP if you need help at any time . . . . (on-line HELP always
                                      available)

HPMAIL > 1

IN TRAY of Beth Richardson   10/01/82 0854.

6 messages.

(Automatic In-Tray Summary—Mail messages are summarized so you can see at a glance which items need immediate attention. Now you can prioritize and organize the way you work.)

Item**	Subject	From	Received	New	Ack	Pri	Urg
1	CBMS standards	Langford, Vic	08/31/82				
2	hpmail	Gross, Gail	09/21/82		*	*	*
3	training class	Gross, Gail	09/23/82			*	
4	mail orders	Wing, Trevor	09/23/82				*
5	HPMAIL Brochure	Wing, Trevor	09/25/82	*	*		

**(Common-sense sequential numbering of contents)

IN TRAY > read 5 . . . .
      (Familiar User Commands — simple commands based on familiar office
      tasks we used so your established way of working stays the same.)

Message.   Dated: 09/27/82 at 1249.

Subject: HPMAIL Brochure

Sender: Trevor Wing / HP1600/02

To: Beth Richardson / HP6600/EO

Beth, I expect 10,000 flyers and 10,000 datasheets to be delivered here at CSP by the end
of the week. We will send these to the US ASAP.

We don't need to reprint the HPMAIL brochures as field marketing still is stocked and we
have plenty here to replenish the field until November or December.

Cheers, Trevor
P.S. HPMAIL orders in July were over quota, nice going . . .

End of Item 5

IN TRAY > send to Ruann Pengov . . . .(Plain English, no location address
                              needed if properly configured.)

Subject: Staff Meeting

I won't be able to attend our regular staff meeting this week as I'll be out of the office.

The message is now ready to be MAILed.

MESSAGE > acknowledge 4
Read acknowledgement set. . . . .(Can choose levels of acknowledgement to
                              check on progress of mail.)

MESSAGE > private
Security set to PRIVATE. . . . .(If a message is private the recipient will
                              be required to sign on with a password
                              to view it.)

MESSAGE > mail

Mailed on 10/01/82

(Convenient Message Tracking: The pending tray allows you to request various levels of acknowledgment and check on message progress. Acknowledgments are returned automatically without requiring any extra actions on the part of the receiver.)

IN TRAY > forward 2 . . . .(Say forward and the message item number)

To: Ken Hess

cc: Chris Kocher

Comments: . . . . can add comments

I thought that this information might be of interest to you. It may help you in answering phone message on HPMAIL.

(The forwarded message is now ready to be MAILed.)

FORWARD > mail . . . . (Items only leave when you request them to be mailed.)

Mailed on 10/01/82 at 0915. . . . .(System confirms desired activity occurred.)

(Efficient Message Forwarding: HPMAIL lets you forward a message you have received to one or several other users without having to leave your in tray.)

IN TRAY > file

Existing in the IN TRAY

FILING CABINET of Beth Richardson 10/01/82 0904.

3 folders

Item	Label	Created	Contents
1	Incoming	06/27/82	4 parts
2	Outgoing	06/27/82	6 parts
3	HPMAIL	07/27/82	7 parts

CABINET > Leave Mail

Beth Richardson signed off.

Thank you for using HPMAIL

(Personalized Electronic Filing: You can create your own filing system to suit your personal needs. The information you need to do your job efficiently is always available in seconds.

Flexible File Folders: Folders may contain ANY kind of information which is valuable to you: reference documents, business graphs and charts, data files as well as MAIL messages!)

CHAPTER **10**

TELECONFERENCING

Patrick S. Portway
Applied Business Communications
San Ramon, CA 94583

10.1 THE GROWTH OF TELECONFERENCING

Teleconferencing is not a new concept, but recent developments have engendered a renewed interest in the use of telecommunications to replace travel as a means of holding meetings. Some of these changes have been the result of technical advances, but simultaneous economic and social changes have further supported the application of the new technology.

The energy crisis or, more precisely, the increased cost of fossil fuels has driven travel costs higher and higher, while concerns for white-collar productivity have focused interest away from the automation of data entry and toward the costs of executive meetings.

All these factors combined have resulted in predictions like those in Gnostic Concepts' market research report of 1982—that user expenditures will grow from $50 million to $900 million between 1980 and 1990 (see Figure 10.1).

10.1.1 Quantitative Justification

Typically, managers spend about 47 percent of their time in meetings (Figure 10.2). The value in dollars per meeting hour to carry on these meetings is significant, but of the $290 billion spent by U.S. business on meetings in 1981, $195 billion was spent on getting the people to the meetings (Figure 10.3). Savings in travel costs, including salaries, constitute the most easily identifiable benefits from teleconferencing. In fact, frequently the only significant justification for installing audio or freeze-frame teleconferencing is the travel savings.

While costs of travel, including air fares, hotel rooms, and restaurant meals,

213

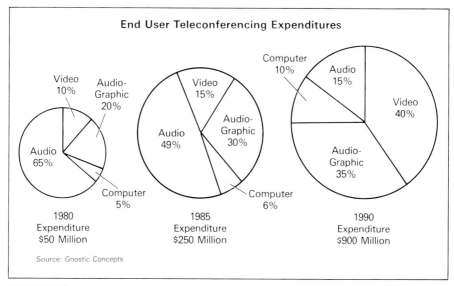

FIGURE 10.1
End-user teleconferencing expenditures (1980, 1985, 1990).

FIGURE 10.2
Managerial time allocations.

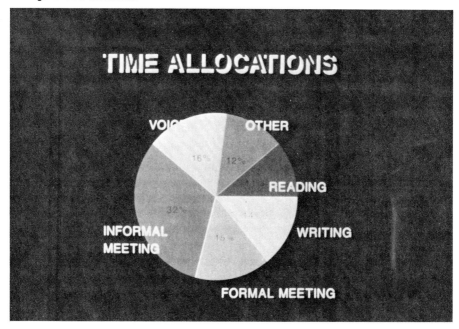

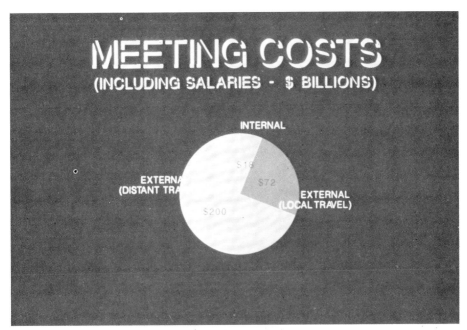

FIGURE 10.3
Meeting costs including salaries.

have been rising at a rate of approximately 40 percent per year (Figure 10.4), the costs of technology, electronics, and communications bandwidth have actually been declining, as illustrated by the cost of computing power (Figure 10.5). The combination of computers and telecommunications, as discussed under the section on technological developments, has resulted in digitally compressed video that requires less than one-sixtieth of the communications bandwidth used by today's broadcast television signals. This reduction in the capacity required to transmit video and the proportional reduction in costs make private video practical for business communication applications.

10.1.2 Qualitative Justification

Teleconferencing has traditionally been viewed by business managers as a poor substitute for face-to-face meetings, acceptable only because of travel budget constraints. Recent studies have shown, however, that in some cases teleconferencing is really better than face-to-face meetings.

One reason is that it is faster. Executives tend to delay decisions to be made at meetings until they are to travel to the location concerned. This "batch processing" of decisions puts off the resolution of problems and compounds the delay to major projects such as product development, product introduction, new

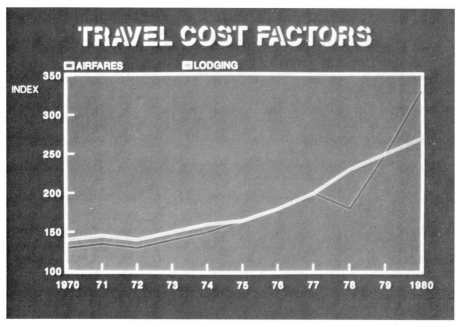

FIGURE 10.4
Travel cost factors.

FIGURE 10.5
Computer costs.

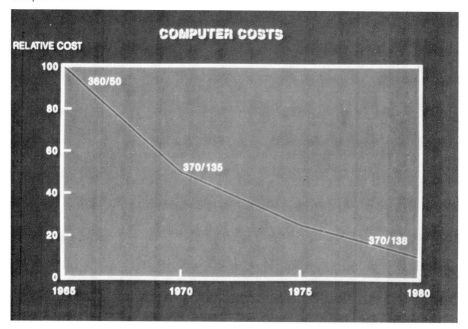

software, upgrades, etc. Teleconferencing, by contrast, allows real-time decision making that can speed the entire process of the program. As one IBM executive put it, "We saved $1 million in travel, but more importantly, we cut our product development cycle by one-third."

Another justification for teleconferencing is increased participation. As American businesses become more sensitive to quality circles and other forms of expanded participation in the decision-making process, teleconferencing offers the opportunity to open to everyone who will need the information, meetings that were previously restricted to a few key people because of travel costs. Often, those who attend a meeting have to hold yet another meeting when they return to present the results of the first session. Now, through teleconferencing, everyone concerned is able to hear the information firsthand.

It is also more businesslike. Although the lack of face-to-face contact may depersonalize meetings, it has the benefit of reducing extraneous conversations or unrelated social exchanges. Teleconferences tend to be more intensive and to focus on the subject at hand. Much of the cost of meetings is hidden (hours in transit, lost productivity, etc.), but communications costs are clearly identifiable. Thus it is more meaningful to say that it costs $450 per hour for a full-motion video teleconference than to total the costs of travel and salary for all who attend a face-to-face meeting. As proof of the superior planning and execution of teleconferences, users have indicated in surveys that they have experienced a reduction of one-half in the time required to carry on the same amount of business.

The final justification of teleconferencing is primarily meaningful to frequent business travelers. Young executives may view business travel as a perk, an opportunity to see new places. But when they make their sixth trip from California to Cleveland, Ohio, they find that such travel has lost its glamor. When fuel costs increased, families phased out costly auto travel and airlines sought to increase margins by reducing flights and increasing loads per plane. Much of the pleasure went out of business travel. Users of Allstate Insurance's early teleconferencing system (referred to later in this chapter) found that the reduced travel was a real benefit which allowed them more time with their families.

10.1.3 Market Awareness

Three major forces in the marketplace have created greater awareness and interest by major corporations in teleconferencing. These are the marketing efforts of AT&T and Satellite Business Systems; the availability of ad hoc or special event teleconferencing; and the highly visible commitments to teleconferencing by early leaders such as ARCO, IBM, Allstate, and Citibank.

Marketing of Major Common Carriers AT&T committed significant resources to the development of the Picturephone Meeting Service, which gave the public access to video teleconferencing facilities under a one-year experimental tariff in 1980–1981. This by-the-hour offering introduced a number of key executives to the potential business uses of video communication for small group meetings. In 1982, AT&T offered the service on a fully tariffed basis, allowing companies to install private on-site rooms that could connect with AT&T's public rooms throughout the United States. AT&T's national advertising program and their account executives in major corporations helped further awareness of teleconferencing as a business tool.

Satellite Business Systems (SBS), a partnership of IBM, Comsat, and Aetna Insurance, undertook a $7.5 million research program which stimulated and helped fund the development of several new products in the video teleconferencing field. SBS combined the latest available technology in two full-motion video teleconferencing demonstration rooms in 1981. SBS's seed money and large corporate marketing program, in conjunction with its private satellite network offering, stimulated teleconferencing interest across the country.

Ad Hoc Teleconferencing   A number of corporations have used private broadcast programs via one-way satellite video to introduce new products, hold press conferences, or communicate to field organizations at low cost. One-way video with two-way audio (using phone lines to send questions back from receive sites) allows interactive communication from one organization site to many temporarily equipped receive sites. The temporary or ad hoc network can be created whenever needed and disassembled when not in use. Hotels or convention halls with projection screens and TV receive-only earth stations (TVRO) can receive the video and audio in 2 or 200 sites, display them to hundreds of people, and allow questions by phone line back to the origination site. Although sales meetings via ad hoc video teleconferencing can become large productions, the savings in travel and lost time achieved by satellite distribution make them very cost effective. The instant return and identifiable benefits of this mode of teleconferencing have led several companies who have experienced the benefits of a one-time meeting to explore permanent, dedicated teleconferencing facilities.

Corporate Leaders   The highly visible commitments of major corporations to teleconferencing have provided encouragement to others to explore seriously its potential for their use. Allstate Insurance was the first corporation to install the SBS design on site in 1981, and its experience is detailed as a case study later in this chapter. IBM installed seven freeze-frame video teleconferencing facilities in the early 1980s and expanded the network to more than 23 facilities. Its $1.5 million in travel savings generated interest in lower-cost facilities.

A 1980 *Business Week* article on the commitment of Atlantic Richfield's chairman, R. O. Anderson, to the use of full-motion video teleconferencing and the company's subsequent development of a private satellite teleconferencing system utilizing new technology captured the imagination of progressive business leaders in late 1982.

All of these factors have combined to double the annual expenditures on teleconferencing and the growth of teleconferencing facilities. Even faster growth is projected for the mid-1980s.

10.2 TYPES OF TELECONFERENCING

10.2.1 Audio Teleconferencing

The simplest form of teleconferencing is the use of amplified speaker phones to join groups of people at each end of a telephone conversation. Sophisticated audio teleconferencing equipment, such as conveners with speakers and improved microphones, can improve the quality and utility of audio meetings. The Darome Convener[tm] pictured in Figure 10.6 is an example of the kind of equipment.

10.2.2 Audio Bridges

An audio bridge connects several phone lines together to allow a participant to communicate with 5 to 24 locations. Just one call to the bridging location connects all the locations and balances the differences in volume between them to assure that all participants can hear one another. Bridges can also be used to broadcast analog facsimile and freeze-frame signals from one location to many locations.

FIGURE 10.6
The simplest form of teleconferencing is the use of amplified speaker phones to join groups of people at each end of a telephone conversation. Pictured is the Darome Convener[tm] which works over ordinary telephone lines and includes microphones and an amplifier with a control panel in the front, making for high quality audio reception and transmission. (Courtesy of Darome, Inc., Harvard, Ill.)

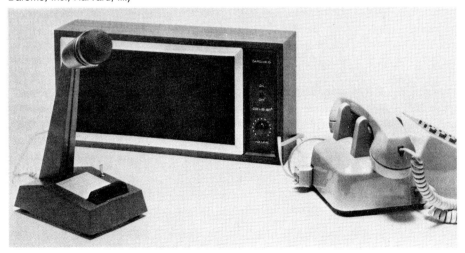

Audio is a component of every form of teleconferencing, and audio quality —the conditioning of facilities to eliminate echo and improve clarity—is a significant factor in any of the forms of teleconferencing described in this section.

10.2.3 Audio with Graphics

The addition of facsimile equipment to transmit documents and the use of equipment to illustrate, such as the AT&T electronic blackboard, Gemini, add significant capability beyond voice-only teleconferencing. Today it is possible to illustrate with lines, graphics, or drawings what it is that is being discussed. Facsimile allows detailed text to be transmitted both prior to and during the meeting.

One clever way of combining audio, graphics, and the mails is to use standard phone lines and 35mm slides sent the day before by expedited mail service to carry on a meeting. Audio, as well as control signaling to a slide projector in a distant room, is carried over a standard phone line; and the presentation in the remote darkened room is nearly the same as if the speaker were present.

10.2.4 Freeze-Frame or Slow-Scan Video

Video transmission of one frame at a time over analog phone lines or data lines adds a dimension of interactivity not possible with facsimile and provides greater detail than is possible with line drawings.

Freeze-frame video can be transmitted in black and white or color at a variety of resolution levels. These characteristics and the data rate available determine how fast a frame can be transmitted, as shown in Figure 10.7 below. The application and user tolerance determine how appropriate the rate is for use in truly interactive meetings.

Freeze-frame combined with a pointer capability or real-time annotation

FIGURE 10.7
Slow-scan speed of transmission. (Courtesy of Colorado Video)

Configuration	TV line rate	525				625			
	Memory	256x256		256x512		256x256		256x512	
	Grayscale	6-bit	8-bit	6-bit	8-bit	6-bit	8-bit	6-bit	8-bit
Clock rate (bits/s)	2400	156	208	311	415	166	221	331	442
	4800	78	104	156	208	83	111	166	221
	9600	39	52	78	104	41	55	83	111
	40.8K	9.1	12.2	18.3	24.4	10	13	20	26
	500 K	.75	1.0	1.5	2.0	.9	1.1	1.6	2.2

Scan time in seconds

capability (available over a coordinated phone line) can often be sufficient for technical meetings or other exchanges of data.

10.2.5 Computer Conferencing

The preceding discussion has involved conferencing forms that include audio transmission, in some cases augmented by video. Another form of teleconferencing is entirely based on digital, or character, information transmitted through a computer with an elaborate store-and-forward message-handling system. This is called *computer conferencing*—a somewhat misleading term since, as we have seen, other forms of teleconference are mediated by a computer. However, that is the common expression for this form of conference, which may be considered an elaboration of electronic mail (discussed in Chapter 9).

In a computer conference, participants need not be involved simultaneously. It is, in effect, a teletype conference call. A member of a conference may send a message at any time, and it can be read by others whenever they have time. Thus, a member of a conference can interact directly and immediately with others or can drop in and out, say, while traveling, and still not miss what others are saying or the opportunity to contribute.

In electronic mail, an individual typically stores a message with an explicit address, referring to an individual or a group. Thus, it is one-to-one or one-to-many communication. Typically, when a message is delivered by electronic mail ("delivered" meaning received by the addressee), it is then deleted by the mail system, although it may be stored in a personal file of the recipient.

A computer conference is basically a group activity. A group of people elect to join a conference. Their geographic location is immaterial, so long as each has access to a digital communication network leading to the computer that will handle the conference. In its simplest form, a computer conference will allow each participant to input messages and to read any input by others. Messages are not deleted when they are read. In this way, any member, even one joining at a later time, can catch up with the conference, review all communication by others, and add new messages or comments.

A typical computer conference will have the features listed below. Like a computer programming language, the actual features available are dependent on the particular software in use, and there is normally considerable variation among software packages and different versions of a given package. The usual functions include signing up and entry, classification, and reading of messages.

Signing Up Membership may be restricted to members of a group—a university class, a group of professional colleagues, anyone interested in joining. The minimum requirement is physical (and perhaps fiscal) access to the conference computer. There must always be some sort of signing up procedure. This may be as simple as entering a single statement that the sender wishes to join an indicated conference. At the other extreme, membership may be permitted only as the result of an action initiated by the conference controller, namely, by invitation.

There is normally a leader or controller whose duties will include initiating the conference, specifying rules for membership, deciding when to purge the conference record, or portions of it, deciding when to create a subconference or committee (or to terminate one), setting deadlines for task groups, and terminating the conference.

Payment for the conference may be handled by the conference leader, as would be typical of an intracompany conference, or by individual participants, as in a public conference in a widely available system such as The Source.

Entry of Messages   A conference member will ordinarily be allowed to enter a message at any time. Entry of a message is quite independent of whether anyone else is entering one at the same time. Members *can* all talk at once, but this does not block sequential reading or inputs by others.

Classes of Messages   Most messages are comments, opinions, suggestions— at any rate, unstructured text. Some may be formal votes, openings or closings of subconferences, signing on or leaving subconferences, etc. Most messages are "public," within the boundaries of the conference, but some systems allow one member to send a message privately to another, much as participants in an in-person conference may pass notes or side comments to each other.

Reading Messages   This is one of the key variables in conference design— how members can read the conference record. Usually, there are a number of controls, which might include:

1 All messages that arrived since this member's last reading session
2 All messages from a given other member
3 All messages
4 The first few lines of all messages, or any other definable subset of records
5 A call for a vote or poll, which would go to all members
6 A proposal for a new subconference or committee
7 A proposal for disbursing or terminating a subconference or the entire conference

Probably the major disadvantage of computer conferencing is the lack of personal contact. For some, the requirement to express themselves in writing, through a keyboard rather than orally or even in handwritten form, can be even more inhibiting. These are highly personal and subjective considerations.

The advantages are more formal and universal. With the exception of telephone conference calls, computer conferences involve the fewest equipment and location restrictions of all the teleconferencing forms. The same transportation savings apply as with any form of teleconferencing. The lack of special equipment (this, of course, presumes that computers and terminals are already part of an organization) makes the cost quite low. Finally, a record of conference proceedings is automatically made in a form that can easily be computer-edited into a printed proceeding.

A somewhat unexpected benefit for many but not all is that participants have time to consider their responses to what has gone before, whether this takes a few minutes or a few days. Rhetoric and dazzle can still be used, as in any form of conference, but the deliberate, considered response which characterizes computer teleconferencing is not a characteristic of most face-to-face meetings.

10.3 ALLSTATE LEADS THE WAY: A CASE STUDY

Where Are We in Implementing Video Teleconferencing

On January 12, 1982, the *Wall Street Journal* reported that 84 percent of the Fortune 500 companies have "imminent plans for installing teleconferencing systems." Since that time, many companies have expanded their audio conferencing. It is useful to review where we are in implementing private corporate video teleconferencing.

There is one full-motion, interstate, corporate video teleconferencing system in operation. Allstate Insurance has two rooms, based on the Satellite Business Systems (SBS) design, communicating between Northbrook, Illinois, and Menlo Park, California.

There are some other full-motion teleconferencing systems operating under special circumstances or over limited distances. Ohio Bell operates a full-motion system for its own use within the state of Ohio. NASA operates one in conjunction with the space shuttle program, and several systems are being tested across single cities or between buildings.

Boeing in Seattle, Procter & Gamble in Cincinnati, the U.S. Department of Energy in Washington, D.C., and Aetna and Citibank in the New York City area are all testing full-motion systems over limited distance without the use of satellite channels.

There are several full-motion systems under development, such as the Atlantic Richfield ArcoVision system, and expansion plans which would add distant cities to the local networks described above. By the end of 1982, there should be a dozen full-motion networks and more than 250 freeze-frame systems operating in the United States.

Allstate's communication system over the SBS network service is justified against voice and data applications, as well as against video teleconferencing. Thus, the costs of communication facilities for video teleconferencing are not charged totally against teleconferencing.

The rooms installed at Allstate Insurance headquarters in Northbrook, Illinois, and the facility in Menlo Park, California, are very nearly duplicates of the SBS demonstration rooms in McLean, Virginia. The only major difference is a reduction in the control systems from the PDP-11-based system selected by Allstate.

The per-room cost of approximately $600,000 probably represents the highest cost for installing such rooms (in constant 1981 dollars) that will ever be incurred by Allstate or by any future corporation for which a network will be built.

According to Sandra Foy, associate communications manager of Allstate, "The design of the room encompasses not only the equipment, but human factor considerations as well. Its special features are a reflection of research on the nature of communications in typical Allstate business meetings. The room is sized for meetings involving up to seven primary participants. There is additional seating in the back of the room to accommodate six or more additional attendees." As the photograph illustrates (Figure 10.8), the room layout, furnishings, and lighting are similar to those of a typical conference room.

One criticism of this early design, which is not typical of a business conference room, is that the Allstate rooms have exposed cameras on the side walls to make possible close-ups of individuals seated around the trapezoidal table. These side cameras have associated monitors that are intended for viewing of the distant room while an individual is the subject of a close-up. This unnatural orientation of speaking to a television set and a lens makes eye-to-eye contact very difficult.

To reduce the bandwidth required for nearly full-motion video, Allstate uses NETEC X-1 (Nippon Electric Television Encoding and Bandwidth Compression Unit), which reduces bandwidth from 60 Mbps to 1.5 to 3 Mbps. The NEC

FIGURE 10.8
Full motion video teleconferencing room. (Courtesy of Applied Business Communications)

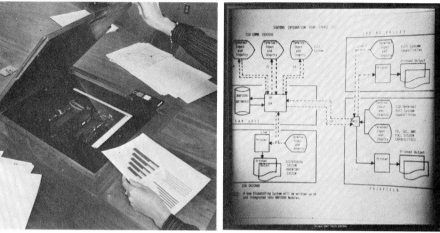

FIGURE 10.9
High-resolution graphics display system for teleconferencing. (a) Rapicom's document scanner
built into the conference room table. (b) 8 1/2- by 11-inch documents displayed on a
4-foot-square screen at 1024 lines of resolution. (Courtesy of Rapicom)

interframe encoding technique produces a slightly less natural motion when in a
close-up mode than when the view is of the entire room and each person is
smaller than life-size. In close-up shots, movement often appears less smooth
when large body movement occurs but adequate for most business applications.

Those who have visited the SBS demonstration center and the Allstate rooms
consider the most significant advance to be the high-resolution graphics subsystem. The system, built by Rapicom, provides a resolution of graphics that is
about twice the standard television resolution (1025 versus 525 lines per inch).
The high-resolution graphics document scanner is completely recessed in the
conference table. The high-resolution display screen pictured in Figure 10.9
displays the documents placed on the tabletop scanner. A document can be
scanned, displayed locally, transmitted, and received at the remote location in
less than 10 seconds. An associated printer automatically produces a paper copy
at either location in approximately 6 seconds.

The control system requires one participant in the meeting to exercise control
through a control console. The control screen displays menus of different
selection screens. By touching the proper symbol of the menu, all the features
and functions of the room can be individually activated. Menus provide a single
convenient source of initiating, conducting, and terminating a video conference.

According to the SBS tariff, demand transmission charges are currently
priced at $1080 for the 3-Mbps transfer rate and $540 for the 1.5-Mbps transfer
rate for each hour of use. The high-resolution graphics system, which has a
transfer rate of 448 Mbps, currently costs $161 per hour.

Room amortization at Allstate is based on a cost of $170,000 per room based on a 10-year depreciation schedule. Twenty-one work days are used for the calculation, arriving at an hourly charge per room of $8.43 or $16.87 for a two-room hook-up.

RECOMMENDED READINGS

Johansen, Robert, Jacques Vallee, and Kathleen Spangler, *Electronic Meetings: Technical Alternatives and Social Choices,* Reading, Mass.: Addison-Wesley, 1979.
Hiltz, Starr Roxanne, and Murray Turoff, *The Network Nation: Human Communication via Computers,* Reading, Mass.: Addison-Wesley, 1978.

CHAPTER 11

MOBILE COMMUNICATION

Jerry Orloff
Communications Group, Motorola Center
Schaumberg, IL 60196

11.1 HISTORICAL INTRODUCTION

Mobile communication is an exchange of information between two or more parties who are free to walk, run, drive, fly, or sail in separate directions as they communicate with each other. The medium is radio. It enables a moving communicator to share a distant vehicle, vessel, aircraft, or spacecraft with a co-communicator. Co-communicators may be human, using oral language. They may be human, using a nonhuman interface: a teletypewriter or a computer. They may be a human and a machine. They may be a machine and a machine.

Mobile communication can help reduce a business's capital requirements. Fewer road trucks, fewer lift trucks, fewer switching locomotives, fewer loaders and material handling tractors, fewer farm tractors are needed to attain productivity goals when their operators can be directed by mobile communication. Less actual time and fewer work hours are needed. Fewer people are needed to perform many tasks; mobile communication can be instrumental in transforming waiting time and idle time into working time. When a human and a machine finish a task at one part of the plant, mobile communication can instantly direct them to another part of the plant for another task. Without such a tool, management would have to hire another person and buy another machine.

Employees who are physically alone are never out of touch when their supervisors, subordinates, and peers can reach them by mobile communication. Their separate movements can be combined in a single economic social purpose. The advantages of mobility combine with the advantages of instant communication, occurring at the speed of light through lightproof barriers.

Heinrich Hertz produced radio waves in 1889. It occurred to Guglielmo

Marconi that such waves could be used in communication. He demonstrated mobile radio in 1898 by following the Kingstown Regatta in a tug and flashing the results to the office of a Dublin newspaper. A radio SOS brought aid to the crew of a sinking lightship in 1899, to the passengers of the distressed steamship *Republic* in 1909, and to the passengers of the *Titanic* in 1912. But the idea of radio communication from a conveyance smaller than a ship was not immediately pursued.

The first broadcast-band automobile radios were installed in the late 1920s. Radio pioneer Daniel Noble found that FM was more reliable than AM in mobile communication, and he developed a two-way system for the Connecticut state police. During World War II he was a leader in the design of the walkie-talkie military two-way radio, which was said to have been the most essential piece of communication equipment in the Allied invasion Normandy and the subsequent conquest of German-occupied Europe. After World War II, the way was clear for the production of FM two-way radios for police, taxi, and transportation. Subsequent developments in the 1950s included a car telephone, complete with a dial to interconnect with telephone company lines, the pocket paging receiver, and the widespread use of transistors.

In the 1960s new manufacturing techniques improved the stability and reliability of the mobile equipment. By replacing old vacuum tubes with solid-state devices, principally transistors, manufacturers were able to reduce the size and weight of their units. They were able to make compact multi-channel radios. They were able to develop a mobile teleprinter, which provided hard-copy readout in a vehicle. Later printers also had keyboards for data entry.

In the 1970s there was a sizable growth in the mobile communication of digital data. A police officer, for example, would feed data into a base station computer, and the computer would feed data to the teleprinter. This eliminated the need for a human being to translate voice to data, to record oral information and enter it into a computer. In addition, a frequency could carry more information per second in the form of data than in voice form.

The 1970s also saw the widespread use of multilayered printed circuit boards, replacing the labor-intensive, space-consuming, soldered wiring of prior years. Plug-in hybrid modules took the place of discrete components. With a system of guides keyed to prevent the incorrect insertion of modules, the newest radios were reliable and serviceable.

Another development of the 1970s was the use of integrated circuits and microprocessors in such sophisticated products as the portable radiotelephone, a hand-held instrument that was entirely self-contained. In a prototype cellular system developed during the late 1970s and early 1980s, the portable radiotelephone enabled a person walking down a street of Baltimore or Washington, D.C., to communicate to or from any one at any land-line phone. Another prototype cellular system worked successfully in Chicago. (Cellular radiotelephone is defined and discussed later in this chapter.)

11.2 THE SYSTEM

Mobile human-to-human communication usually involves *two-way radio,* so-called because each instrument can transmit and receive. In day-to-day business, many mobile communications turn out to be multiway radio, in which several mobile parties transmit to each other. The space these parties occupy becomes a mobile conference room. The walls, the floors, and the face-to-face contact of a conventional room are unnecessary. The time and fuel needed to bring the conferees to a convention table can now be used to raise the quality or lower the price of their product or service.

But a mobile communication system is not necessarily a conference room or a party line. In certain two-way radios, the speaker is silent until a transmitted tone or digital signal opens the receiver to a sender's message. There are selective two-way systems that activate a small group of receivers out of a population of many. There are selective one-way systems, reaching a single pocket-size radio pager with an audible tone or a tone-and-voice message. There are radio pagers with digital displays to show telephone numbers or other data. There are vehicular or wire-line phones.

The radiotelephones use a *duplex* system; that is, both parties can talk or listen at the same time. Most two-way mobile systems are *simplex,* with push-to-talk buttons. At each unit, pushing the button activates the microphone and transmitter while shutting off the receiver and speaker. Releasing the button reverses the condition; the operator can now listen. The push-to-talk arrangement conserves power, since the receiver's consumption is much less than that of the transmitter.

The mobile communication of business and government is carried out principally on FM radio, on frequencies which the FCC limits to certain classes of users. For example, there are sets of frequencies for public safety, manufacturing construction, agriculture, forestry, trucking, railroads, utilities, petroleum producers, and miners. The FCC must restrict not only the allocation of frequencies but also the radios' transmitting power to minimize interference and give access to as many legitimate users as possible.

Mobile communication is normally of limited range: within the plant, within the property, within the city or county. But the communication is not necessarily direct, from radio to radio. In some systems, a two-way radio will transmit to a *repeater*—a radio which automatically retransmits the message at higher power to other two-way radios in the system.

Mobile communication, then, increases the ability of management to manage its mobile people.

It should be noted that mobile communication is not an electronic tether. It cannot prevent wandering of mind or body; it cannot prevent inefficiency. But, in the hands of motivated people and motivated organizations, mobile communication is invaluable. It brings mobile minds together. It increases the value of each mind, the productivity of each person, and the return on the organization's investment in its people and property.

11.3 CLASSES OF MOBILE COMMUNICATION SERVICE

Table 11.1 is a list of FCC classifications of service. Consideration of this list will give the reader an idea of the widespread use of mobile communication in business and government.

A fuller list of mobile communicators would at least include the federal and state governments, all utilities, the public transit system, and such industries as airline and marine transportation, telephone, mining, and construction. But while applicability would seem to be infinite, the portion of the spectrum available for mobile communication is finite.

Land mobile communication takes place at 25–50 MHz (low-band), 132–174 MHz (high-band, otherwise known as very high frequency or VHF), 403–430 and 450–512 MHz (ultra high frequency or UHF). During the 1970s the band from 806 to 870 MHz was also allocated to mobile radio users.

The low band is widely used by county and state law enforcement units, long-haul truck and bus lines, pipeline operators, electric and gas utilities, and other organizations that require long-range mobile communication. Low-band range may be as high as 50 miles in flat terrain, less in hilly terrain. But it has disadvantages, such as skip interference, in which user's transmission skips far beyond its normal range. Low-band systems on opposite coasts of the United States have been known to cause mutual interference.

The high band is used by those whose operations are generally within an urban area. Range may vary from 5 to 25 miles, although greater ranges are often experienced.

TABLE 11.1
FEDERAL COMMUNICATIONS COMMISSION
CLASSIFICATION OF MOBILE SERVICES

Public safety service	Industrial radio service
Fire radio	Business
Forestry conservation	Forest products
Highway maintenance	Manufacturers
Local government	Petroleum
Police	Power
Special emergency	Special industrial

Land transportation	Common carrier
Railroad	Wireline car telephone
Taxicab	Radio common carrier car telephone
Other transportation	

The UHF band is ideal for urban communication. It provides a clear two-way radio link, even in skyscraper canyons.

Much of the data transmission, cellular communication, and other sophisticated systems and equipment are designed for frequencies above 800 MHz. Frequencies above 900 MHz have been allocated for cellular radiotelephone.

11.4 THE USERS

Who uses mobile communication? In the United States, the federal government is the largest user. The automobile makers are major users; in an assembly plant, for example, there may be a channel for maintenance, with the appropriate employees tuned to it. The airlines are major users. Among their ground personnel, two-way radio expedites baggage-handling and passenger service. The railroads use radio to communicate between train and wayside stations, and the wayside stations may repeat the message (voice or data) via microwave or wire line to a central dispatcher hundreds of miles away. The trucking companies' radio saves time and fuel, particularly in local pickup-and-deliver service. On the inland waterways, for example, marine radio provides a link between a tug and its barge crew. A radio signal may control a bow thruster, a power unit that helps steer the front barge. And on a railroad, in a long train, a radio signal from the lead locomotive may control an auxiliary locomotive. The utilities and the energy producers use mobile communication extensively.

So do the smallest of small companies. Its effect has been shown, for example, in Columbia, Missouri, in an informal 1978 survey. Two-way radio, "actually enables us to provide better service without raising our prices," a plumber said. "The first thing our customers ask when they call for someone is, 'Can you get them on the radio?' " a homebuilder's receptionist said. "To be competitive, you have to be able to provide good service; and radio helps us do that," an insulation contractor said. "In two years, I have never delivered a wrong load; and radio is my assurance that I won't in the future," a building-material dealer said.

Mobile communication enables management to direct its mobile employees. The medium is FM radio on channels dedicated to management's particular class of service, as defined and licensed by the FCC. In contrast, the *citizens band* (CB) of frequencies is open to anyone over 18 years of age, and the medium is AM radio. CB equipment is low-cost, but congestion may be high, and AM is more interference-prone than FM. The business that depends on mobile communication is likely to use the heavy-duty commercial equipment and an appropriate commercial frequency.

Many businesses use the services of a *radio common carrier* (RCC). Just as a wire-line common carrier provides telephone service to the public, so does an RCC provide radio service. An RCC will extend a wire-line call to mobile radiotelephone in a customer's car. Or the customer may dial his or her radiotelephone and be connected automatically, through the RCC's interface, into the wire-line system. An RCC will provide one-way paging service, activating a customer's pocket pager, or "beeper." Some RCCs also provide a two-way mobile radio-dispatch service.

The radio common carriers' trade association, Telocator Network of America, said at the end of 1980, that the nation had approximately 550 RCCs serving 750,000 subscribers in 1200 communities. Most of the RCCs are small businesses: independent companies, rendering a communication service under license by the FCC. They generally own, operate, lease, and maintain the pagers and radiotelephones. The wire-line carriers also provide this service in several areas.

11.5 THE CAPABILITIES OF MOBILE COMMUNICATIONS EQUIPMENT

Here is an overview of the capabilities of mobile communications equipment: the mobile and personal two-way radio, radio repeaters, radio pagers and paging encoders, monitors, control centers, base stations, digital voice protection systems, data communication equipment, radio control equipment, and cellular radiotelephone.

A unit designed for vehicular installation is called *mobile two-way radio* (mobile radio). The microphone, with its push-to-talk button, is shaped to fit the human hand. A coiled cord connects the microphone to the *control head,* containing the on-off, volume, frequency selection, and squelch controls. A simple *squelch* circuit minimizes the reception of messages that are not meant for the listeners. A more sophisticated squelch circuit keeps the speaker silent until a brief sequence of inaudible tones opens the circuit and lets the message through. Typically, a user's transmitter begins each transmission with the tone sequence that opens the squelch circuits in that user's vehicles only. A more advanced system is *digital squelch,* which uses digital codes instead of tone codes.

In the most economical FM two-way mobile radios, the control head, transmitter, receiver, and speaker are all in a single housing (Figure 11.1).

In the more common configuration, the transmitter and receiver are in a separate locked case, installed under a seat or in the trunk of a vehicle. The speaker also is separate from the control head. This allows room for the components that provide particularly high power (within FCC-mandated limits), high selectivity (reducing adjacent channel interference), low distortion, and clear audio output. It also allows room for the various optional functions (Figure 11.2). In addition to the squelch they may include a *busy light, a time-out timer, and selective signaling.*

The *busy light* is a signal that goes on when the frequency is being used by other people. Without a busy light, the user of a vehicular two-way radio has to *monitor* the frequency, that is, open the squelch circuit and listen before transmitting to be sure the frequency is not being used. When drivers transmit without monitoring their frequency, they may obliterate parts of another user's

FIGURE 11.1
A mobile radio, combining the transmitter, receiver, and control head in one housing. (Courtesy of Motorola)

FIGURE 11.2
A mobile radio with a more sophisticated control head. The "mode select" buttons enable the operator to select the transmit and receive frequencies, the squelch codes, the priority scan frequencies, and other optional capabilities. (Courtesy of Motorola)

message. If the obliterated message concerns a life-or-death emergency, such carelessness may have a fatal consequence.

Another possible problem can be the inadvertent keying of the transmitter in the vehicle. The microphone may have been put into place carelessly, jamming the button and causing the errant transmitter to interfere with all two-way radios in the system. As a solution, the unit may have a *time-out timer,* which shuts off the transmitter after a predetermined period.

The "party-line" aspect of mobile communication has its disadvantages. Hearing every two-way communication all day may increase driver fatigue and make drivers less sensitive to their own messages. And in many operations, one driver's job is of no concern to another. The solution is *selective signaling.* It enables a base station operator to contact a single driver or group of drivers. Various tone codes or digital codes act as keys that unlock certain receivers, either individually or in groups. The user thereby combines the mobility of radio with a degree of address exclusivity. And if a driver happens to be out of the vehicle when a selectively signaled call comes in, a "call received" light on the decoder's panel stays on until the driver removes the microphone from its hang-up box.

Some selective signaling equipment will sound a vehicle's horn (briefly) or turn on the headlights as a reminder that a call has come in.

A *channel-scan monitor* is a device that sequentially samples each channel of a multichannel system and stops automatically when it detects the presence of a carrier or a message. One channel is designated as the priority receive channel, and if *that* channel receives a signal during a scan, the receiver automatically reverts to it.

A *single-tone encoder* enables the driver to transmit a tone pulse that actuates a relay at a receiving unit. The driver can turn on and off pumps, generators, motors, and lighting systems; open and close gates, and so on. This is a mobile device that enables a human to use radio to operate a machine.

Another device, a *mobile speech-scrambler* uses the frequency inversion method of audio scrambling to provide privacy over two-way systems. A more sophisticated method, digital voice protection, is described later in this chapter.

In the realm of selective mobile communication, a recent development has been *trunking.* This is the sharing of a few channels (pairs of frequencies) in the 800 MHz band by several radio users. A specialized mobile radio (SMR) service may own the repeaters and the system controller, while the user owns the mobile radios and control stations, which are designed specifically for trunked service.

When a driver picks up the microphone, a microprocessor instantly scans all the channels (as many as 20, in one manufacturer's system). It picks out a clear channel and locks out all other talkers. If all radio channels are busy, the driver hears a "talk prohibit" tone and a "busy" light comes on. The request to talk is automatically placed in an order-waiting line, so there is no need for the driver to monitor repeatedly for a clear channel. When a channel becomes available, a tone signals that the driver can now begin to talk. Waiting callers are selected on a first-in, first-out basis.

By means of code plugs in the control heads, users can set up groups of vehicles as subfleets; for example, those driven by supervisors (subfleet 1) or by service persons (subfleet 2) or by management persons (subfleet 3); dispatchers can then address a single subfleet to the exclusion of others. An SMR can establish various fleets and subfleets among its customers. Or a big user of mobile radio—for example, a public utility—may elect to set up a private trunk system.

The earliest mobile two-way radios had vacuum tubes, which had to be mechanically cooled and which failed frequently. The latest units are completely solid-state, that is, free of moving parts, heated filaments, or vacuum gaps. Some are resistant to dust, shock, and vibration and are so weatherproof that they can be mounted outside the vehicle. The earliest units required crystals to establish their transmitting frequency. Many still do. But in the newest mobile two-way radios, the crystal has been replaced by an electronic *frequency synthesizer.* To change or add frequencies, the user replaces the memory module of the radio's microprocessor control system. The synthesizer's stability represents a significant improvement in the transmission of voice and particularly in the transmission of data.

11.5.1 Portable Two-Way Radio

Today's radios bring mobile communication wherever a human can go. The human has complete freedom of movement—and yet is never alone, never without direction, never without access to authority, to assistance, to the full resources of the organization and of society beyond.

Society's basic unit of labor is the human on foot. A lone person on security patrol in a hazardous plant or a hazardous neighborhood, is always part of a much larger force because of the mobile radio. The refinement of the two-way, hand-held portable radio has, in fact, changed the basic technique of law enforcement communication. Yesterday the radio was only in the patrol vehicle, and police officers were tied to it when they needed to stay in touch. Today the radio is on the officers. They are never on their own, unless they choose to turn their radio off. The option of using the "off" switch has been available to radio users ever since the days of Marconi.

To a user of portable two-way radio, weight is no problem. A multifrequency radio with battery and digital squelch may weigh less than 1.5 pounds (Figure 11.3). Some recharge in as little as one hour; some are designed and approved for use in specific hazardous atmospheres; some give their operators a choice of four frequency channels with the turn of a single knob; some allow them to communicate on as many as eight frequencies. Some are available with noise-canceling headsets, allowing users to speak and listen with their portables in extremely noisy areas. At least one model slips into and out of a case mounted under a dashboard. When users are in their vehicle, they have true mobile radio, complete with a mobile microphone, speaker, antenna, and a connection to the automobile battery. When they are about to leave the vehicle, they take out the

FIGURE 11.3
Portable two-way radio goes
wherever a human can go. This
unit operates on any of four
frequencies. (Courtesy of
Motorola)

portable, which instantly becomes a self-contained two-way communication
device.

For emergency medical communication, there is *coronary observation radio*.
It is, essentially, two-way radio equipped for telemetry: it transmits the patient's
life signals back to the hospital, where a doctor analyzes the data and transmits
instructions to the paramedics. They and the patient may be in a remote field, or
in the ambulance, or at the hospital's emergency entrance. The radio continues
to monitor the patient and the paramedics continue to receive instructions until
the hospital personnel take over (Figure 11.4).

Standard telephone-type Touch Tone buttons are mounted in some hand-held
portable two-way radios. They enable a user to enter a number and be

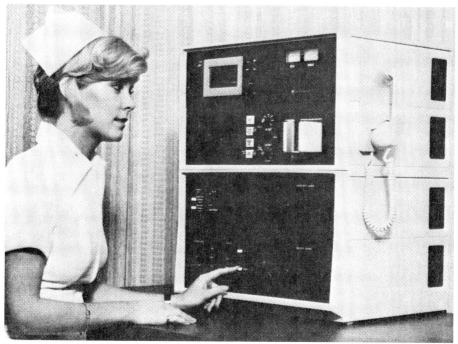

FIGURE 11.4
Hospital console contains radio and telemetry control, electrocardiograph monitoring unit, and a tape recorder. (Courtesy of Motorola)

connected to any telephone through an interconnection at the user's base station. The button can also provide a signal to operate certain remote equipment that has a digital radio interface. Or the holder can use the push buttons to enter information into a computer. A hand-held portable computer terminal with alphanumeric keyboard will be discussed later in the chapter (Figure 11.5).

Before the invention of portable two-way radio, there were hand signals: between locomotive engineers and their brakemen; between high-rise construction supervisors and their crane operator; between road construction flagmen; between surveyors; between lifeguards at stands on a crowded beach. The radio has made their communication more precise, more rapid, more dependable. It has made these employees more productive, lowered the cost of their goods and services, and saved human lives.

11.5.2 Repeaters

How can low-cost mobiles, portables, and base stations operate in a system that requires communication over a wide area, even an area containing hills, valleys,

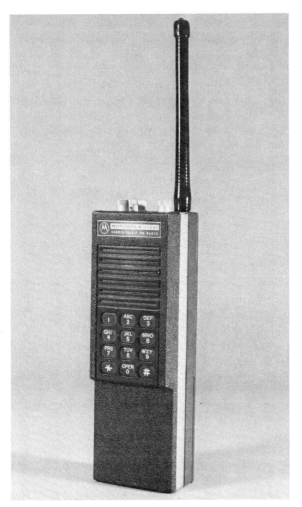

FIGURE 11.5
This portable two-way radio can access a telephone number, enter computer data, or operate radio-controlled switches. (Courtesy of Motorola)

and tall buildings? The answer is in the use of radio repeaters, sensitive receivers which pick up weak signals and feed them to tramsitters, which repeat them at higher power.

In many cities, a *community repeater* is at the top of a building. It picks up signals from several users and retransmits them at the user's assigned frequencies. A user's base station may be connected to a rooftop dish, which beams the signal at the repeater antenna many miles away. A rooftop antenna is advantageous because FM transmission takes a line-of-sight path; it does not follow the earth's curvature, as AM transmission does.

Repeaters may be owned and operated by individual users. The stationary repeaters—one or more—may be located on the user's property or in a remote building. Or they may be microwave or wire line to a *satellite receiver voting system* at the main base station. When, for example, a signal from a portable is picked up by two or more of the repeaters, the system evaluates all the signals and "votes" for the strongest, which it then feeds into the transmitter of a repeater. A recent refinement of this is the cellular system, which will be discussed later in the chapter.

Some repeaters are mobile. A police department, for example, may bring one into a remote area to increase the range of its vehicle-to-vehicle and vehicle-to-base communication.

Some repeaters are designed for operation over inaccessible terrain: mountains, swamps, or other areas where land-line power is not available. They operate on low current from batteries or solar cells.

Many repeaters can also be used as base stations. And one model of repeater can be carried in an attaché case. It runs on batteries or line current and is designed for rescue operations and law enforcement.

11.5.3 Radio Paging

A pager is a compact radio receiver that emits an alerting signal when a unique tone code activates the receiver's tone-sensing circuitry. A *tone-only pager* emits a signal only; a *tone-and-voice* pager allows a voice to follow the signal. *Digital-display* beepers show the number to be called in a liquid crystal display on the surface of the beeper. Most pagers are about the size of a cigarette package and weigh 6 ounces or less. (Figure 11.6).

Some telephone companies rent them out as part of a radio paging service. Each pager has its own telephone number. When the number is dialed, the pager sounds a tone, signaling the user to call the home or office. Some radio and wire-line common carriers also offer the paging service but without the direct dial-a-pager interconnection.

Many two-way radio users have radio paging as part of their own communication systems. Pressing a series of buttons at the control center will signal a single pager. The operator can signal a group of pagers—or all the pagers—in systems that have group-call or fleet-call capability.

Pagers may have an extra-loud tone (85 dB) for extra-noisy environments; or may be listed by Underwriter's Laboratories as intrinsically safe for use in certain hazardous atmospheres; or may be approved by the Mining Safety and Health Administration for use in coal mines with methane gas atmospheres; or may be resistant to drop damage, water-spray damage, and dust contaminants in heavy industrial use.

It may have a push-to-listen button; users hear the voice message only if they push the button. It may be able to receive a page without sending an alert; later, pushing a button will retrieve the stored signal. Or the signal may come through immediately, not as an audible tone but as a touch-sensitive vibration; this is useful when the user is in a conference, in a hospital, or in a noisy area. Or the

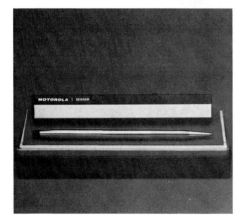

FIGURE 11.6
A radio pager, or "beeper," is a compact receiver. It emits an alerting signal when a unique tone-code activates the receiver's tone-sensing circuitry. The model in the upper left delivers a voice message. Some radio pagers have alphanumeric displays (top right). Miniature pocket pagers are no longer than a ballpoint pen and fit comfortably in jacket pockets (lower left). (Courtesy of Motorola)

pager may be capable of a tone that is either pulsating (say, a signal to call the office) or steady (a signal to call home). From an array of paging products users can find the unit that fits their work style and environment.

A *monitor* is a pager that enables the listener not only to hear his or her own tone-and-voice message but also, by flipping a switch, to monitor all conversation on the frequency. Some table-models monitors are tuned to emergency frequencies. They may be used by schools, for example, to carry tornado and blizzard warnings.

11.5.4 Communication of Data

Data communication transcends the limitations of the human memory, the human voice, the human ear, and the ballpoint pen. It gives mobile users direct access to the memory of a distant computer. And it gives management an up-to-the-moment report of its mobile units' activity and productivity.

For example, police officers can enter a license-plate number and get full alphanumeric display of information from local, regional, and national data banks. In such a routine communication, the data system reduces the possibility of garbled, forgotten or misunderstood messages. Police officers can ask the operator for message formats and fill them out on the CRT, thus reducing the time they would otherwise spend on paperwork and communication. A data system gives the law officer more time for law enforcement. In other fields as well it justifies its cost by giving employees more time and information with which to perform their jobs.

A typical mobile keyboard display terminal provides a 240-character message display in a 6 × 40 format, for example, and may have an alphanumeric keyboard and several functional keys (Figure 11.7). It sends and receives through the vehicle's mobile radio and the system's base station. To and from the base station, the data flows through a mobile communication processor, a central processing unit, and the system's control console. A *mobile communication processor* controls all the functions required to encode, decode, check and correct messages in a mobile data terminal system. It transforms outbound messages from digital to analog and inbound from analog to digital.

In the vehicle, an alternative to the complete mobile terminal is a *status-message terminal* (Figure 11.8). It has several push buttons, each of which sends an abbreviated routine message that gives the vehicle's status and helps the dispatcher manage the fleet. In transit-mix concrete delivery, for example, such messages might include "charging," "enroute to site," "waiting," "discharging," and "empty." The system saves time for the driver and dispatcher; it gives management up-to-the-moment information on material flow; and it makes the briefest possible use of the channel. Adapted to public safety, the status-message procedure can speed the processing of fire and public dispatches. It can be part of a data system in which, for example, the dispatcher enters a fire alarm type

FIGURE 11.7
A mobile data terminal gives the driver a direct access to computer files. A mobile data printer can be attached. (Courtesy of Motorola)

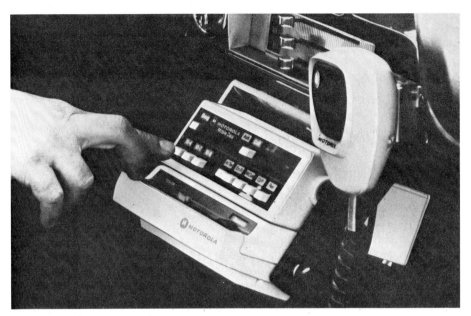

FIGURE 11.8
A status-message control head. Each button sends a routine piece of information in digital form.
(Courtesy of Motorola)

and zone; and the computer presents a response plan, based on current information about equipment availability and location.

Radio communication of data is also being used in bus dispatching. When a city bus passes a *radio signpost*—a roadside transmitter, designed as part of the system—the signpost transmits its location digitally to the bus's mobile radio unit, which repeats the information (along with digital identification) in a message to the base station. The data then flow through a mobile communication processor to the central processing unit. With that information on display, a dispatcher can speed up, slow down, or reassign various buses, so that the city gets the maximum return on its investment in equipment and labor and the public gets good service. Another advantage: a driver who is about to be robbed or wants to make a silent report of any other emergency situation can press a hidden alarm button that signals the dispatcher, who will direct the police to the bus.

The radio signpost system can also be applied to material handling. It can show a dispatcher where each lift truck is, whether it is loaded, unloaded, or overloaded, moving or stopped, low on fuel, low on oil pressure, high on engine temperature, and other readings, all with automatic vehicle identification.

There is a hand-held, *portable two-way data terminal,* which sends and receives through a hand-held portable radio (Figure 11.9). The terminal has a

FIGURE 11.9
A portable two-way data
terminal. It sends and receives
through a hand-held portable
radio. (Courtesy of Motorola)

complete alphanumeric keyboard. It can enter information instantly into the computer and even display a line of data. Process management, freight-traffic management, and material handling and load-distribution management are among the areas where a portable data terminal can be valuable.

11.5.5 Digital Voice Protection

Public safety communication becomes too public when a criminal can listen in to avoid detection of apprehension. The system for preventing such eavesdropping is called *digital voice protection* (DVP). It converts speech into its digital equivalents, which are scrambled through a multiregister nonlinear combiner algorithm. A DVP message contains no voice components. All the eavesdropper hears is a signal that sounds like constant-level random white noise.

The number of available DVP codes is equal to 2.36×10^{21}. The user inserts a code and changes it at any time. No code has characteristics that provide even a partial output for any other code. DVP circuitry can be built into the transmitters and receivers of mobile radios, portable radios, base stations, and repeaters. The flip of a switch converts the radios to ordinary voice mode.

11.5.6   Base Stations

Base stations are the nonmobile transmitting-receiving radios through which management or its representatives communicate with people in the field. A base station may be self-contained in a desktop cabinet, complete with controls and a microphone connection. Or the base station may be a remote-control model; a control console and the microphones or desk sets may be elsewhere. Some base station systems have telephonelike desk sets with push-to-talk buttons instead of a microphone and speaker. The base station may be both local and remote, operated as a local-control station by day and a remote-control station at night, accessible by ordinary wire-line telephone from a management person's home, which would also have a control console. Or, as a combination base station and repeater, it would transmit and receive for the base units and repeat for the field units.

11.5.7   Control Consoles

These units control the more complex base station functions. While a simple *control station,* a desktop unit, may determine the receive-transmit, squelch, and frequency selection, a floor-based control console contains an array of controls. In a typical public service installation, for example, the console may have the frequency-selection switches for two fire department channels, two police channels, and ambulance channel, and a supervisory channel (Figure 11.10).

Most consoles have a modular design, which makes customization economical. Various switch panels may fit into various console bays and cabinets which, when assembled, comprise a control center. In this way, the center can grow with the organization. A fully equipped console may have vehicle status indicators, an illuminated map, a system of spotting lights (to spot vehicles' positions on the map), a paging encoder, tape recorders, an intercome station, and more.

For emergency medical service, special consoles have been designed. Such a console may have a voice-coupling device that enables a person (say, a doctor) at a telephone to talk to a person (say, a paramedic) at a mobile radio. It may also have an oscilloscope, a heart-rate meter, an electrocardiograph strip recorder, and a tape recorder.

11.5.8   Cellular Radiotelephone

For a long time car telephone channels have been congested. During the 1970s and at the beginning of the 1980s users who wanted a car telephone had to put

FIGURE 11.10
Mobile communication control center combines several modules to meet the user's requirements. For example, this configuration would be appropriate for a public safety agency. (Courtesy of Motorola)

their name at the bottom of a long list. After waiting between 1 and 10 years, they would get a telephone that was technologically up-to-date but hampered by the scarcity of mobile telephone channels. Only 51 channels were available. In a metropolitan area, each would handle only one call at a time. This was because a single high-powered base station would serve an entire city and its suburbs (Figure 11.11).

The response to this shortage is *cellular radiotelephone,* which makes several hundred channels available within a metropolitan area. The system operates on 800 and 900 MHz bands that are dedicated to cellular service. It uses a network of low-powered base station transmitters and receivers, which are connected to the public wire-line telephone network. These base stations handle transmissions to and from mobile and portable telephones in the area surrounding each station. Such an area is called a *cell* (Figure 11.12).

The system's data processing equipment determines which base station will handle the communication and when the conversation will be "handed off" to another station. The equipment also makes possible a prompt reassignment of every frequency, so that each channel can be used at near capacity.

Users who are two or three cell diameters apart can make simultaneous use of a single channel. And, as a cellular system adds subscribers, the carrier can "split" cells, add new cells, and increase the system's capacity. By splitting cells,

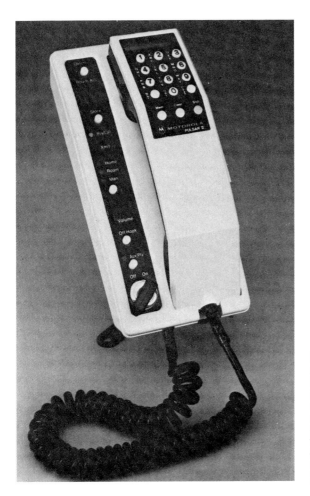

FIGURE 11.11
A mobile radiotelephone. It has its own number and can make and receive telephone calls, to and from wire-line phones. This unit also has an automatic channel scan, which secures the first available channel. In some cities, it may be part of a cellular radiotelephone system. (Courtesy of Motorola)

a carrier can, for example, serve over 100,000 customers in the Baltimore–Washington, D.C. area.

That is where a radio common carrier, American Radio Telephone System (ARTS), began to build a demonstration system in 1977. In the same year, the world's largest wire-line common carrier, AT&T, began a demonstration system in Chicago. Both systems went into operation shortly thereafter and they continued to operate into the 1980s. The ARTS system used equipment made by the Communications Group of Motorola, Inc.. The AT&T system used equipment made by its Western Electric subsidiary and by other suppliers.

The most attractive feature of cellular mobile communication is its use of the truly *portable telephone,* an attainment of one of yesterday's seemingly impossi-

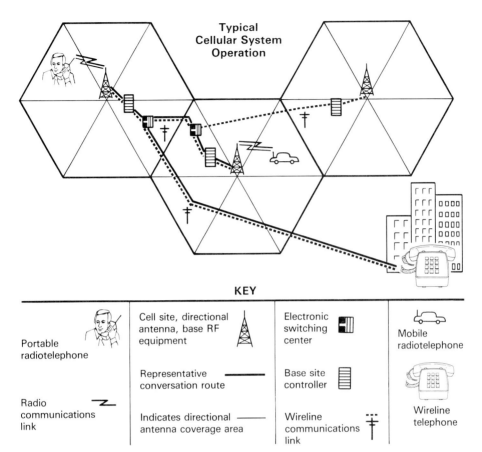

FIGURE 11.12
Typical cellular system operation. (Courtesy of Motorola)

ble goals. Fitting easily into a briefcase or purse and weighing under 2 pounds, the portable telephone increases the productivity of an organization's key people, wherever they may be. The telephone actually rings: on the sidewalk, in the restaurant, in the elevator. The holder receives calls and makes calls, just as he or she would on a mobile radiotelephone or on an ordinary land-line phone (Figure 11.13).

"People need to communicate with people, not vehicles, and that's the key to the marketability of portable phones," said Motorola's president, John Mitchell, in a 1980 interview. "I think the concept of portable telephones is the most exciting thing I've come across in my 33 years in the Bell System," said Louis Weinberg, AT&T's director for business exchange and mobile systems, also in 1980. "At 980 MHz, most buildings are transparent," said Martin Cooper,

FIGURE 11.13
Hand-held radiotelephone
transmits and receives through a
low-power base station that
serves the cell where the user is.
The cellular base stations have
an interface with the wire-line
telephone system. (Courtesy of
Motorola)

Motorola's vice president and director of research and development, commenting on the omnipresence of the telephone signal within a particular cell. He pointed out that cellular radiotelephone technology has been the latest development in a continuing evolution—an evolution that Hertz and Marconi began and that has not ended.

RECOMMENDED READINGS

Bowers, Raymond, Alfred M. Lee, and Cary Hershey, *Communication for a Mobile Society: An Assessment of New Technology,* Beverly Hills, Calif.: Sage, 1978.

CHAPTER 12

VIDEOTEX

Albert S. Tedesco
WWSG-TV
Philadelphia, PA 19128

12.1 HISTORICAL INTRODUCTION

Videotex is the generic term for a class of electronic text services which use CRT displays, including the home TV set, and transmission systems such as TV broadcast frequencies and the telephone network to transmit pages of text which can be retrieved at will by the user. While definitions vary from author to author and organization to organization, in this discussion the family of videotex services is defined as consisting of two classes: teletext and viewdata.

Teletext is that class of text services delivered over standard television signals by insertion in the unused portion of the video signal called the *vertical blanking interval* (VBI). Teletext is a one-way service. Communication between user and system is pseudointeractive, that is, users appear engaged in an interactive process through which they may retrieve pages of information as part of a "search." In fact, they retrieve bits of data from a stream of information from a source that they have no real control over. Examples of teletext systems include CEEFAX (United Kingdom), ANTIOPE (France), TELIDON (Canada), and KEYFAX (United States).

Viewdata is a two-way service, distributed by telephone network or cable system. Viewdata systems are truly interactive in that users access complicated hierarchies of information directly. The major difference between viewdata and teletext is that viewdata systems support *transactions,* and teletext systems do not. Viewdata-type systems include PRESTEL (United Kingdom), VISTA (Canada), TELETEL (France), and VIEWTRON (United States). Sample teletext and viewdata pages are shown in Figure 12.1.

A pioneering videotex system with professionals as the target market is

FIGURE 12.1
Teletext and videotex pages. (a) A sample page from Taft Broadcasting's 100-page Electra teletext service transmitted over Channel 12, WKRC-TV in Cincinnati, showing one in a series of pages describing a local event. (Courtesy of Taft Broadcasting) (b) An advertising page from Knight-Ridder's Viewtron videotex service in Coral Gables, Florida, showing an advertisement for Southeast Bank and offering a menu of additional pages. (Courtesy of AT&T)

Lockheed's DIALOG Information Retrieval System, which was established in 1969. DIALOG is the largest online system with more than 180 data bases containing more than 40 million records which provide references to technical reports, conference papers, newspapers, journal and magazine articles, patents, and statistical data.

The evolution of consumer-oriented videotex services began in the early 1970s in the United Kingdom, when British Broadcasting Corporation (BBC) engineers developed a teletext system to carry captioning for the deaf as an ancillary service to a conventional video signal ("Examining European Videotex Standards," 1983).

The BBC soon extended the horizons of the project to encompass a more broadly based service—one that was capable of providing not only captioning for the deaf but also a magazine of text services for other users. This project became CEEFAX, a 100-page video magazine; its counterpart in the British commercial television service (ITA) was called ORACLE (Sigel, 1980).

The concept behind videotex was simple: in the case of broadcast text service (teletext), the engineering goal was to find new uses for the unused portion of the broadcast television signal, VBI; and in the case of viewdata, the goal was to increase use of the telephone network.

FIGURE 12.2
Vertical blanking interval (VBI) showing teletext data. The data appear in the lower third of the vertical interval (the black horizontal bar in the middle of this TV picture, which has been misadjusted to reveal the text data). The teletext data can be seen just above the picture (they are the white area immediately above the reporter's head). (Courtesy of Joe Roizen, Telegen)

Examining the conventional television signal provides some insight into the electronics of teletext. Each video picture is a randomly interlaced signal which, in the United States, consists of 525 scanning lines. The unused (unseen) portion of the television picture consists of lines numbered 1 to 21. Half of line 21 in the United States is used to carry captioning for the deaf (see Figure 12.2).

In both American and British versions of teletext the goal was to use the unused portion of the system to generate a text magazine consisting of pages of information, each page being a single video frame. These frames would provide an entirely new ancillary service working in parallel with the main program service, either to enhance it or to provide a separate, stand-alone service (Spongberg, 1975).

12.2 VIDEOTEX SYSTEM COMPONENTS

Videotex systems have several system components in common: (1) the host computer system, (2) the composing or data entry system, (3) the transmission system, (4) the display system, and (5) the user retrieval system (decoder).

12.2.1 The Host Computer System

Each videotex system has a host computer. The size of this computer system varies, depending on the number of users needing simultaneous access, the amount of storage, and the speed of access required to service them.

In teletext systems, minicomputers such as the PDP-11 have proven sufficient to support 100 to 200 pages of information and to provide access to 4 or 5 composing terminals. Because teletext systems are generally viewed as one-way pseudointeractive systems, the principal task of the computer system is to provide a cycle of data (conceived of as a wheel of pages) at a standard rate (10 pages per 25-second period using two lines in the VBI), which is then retrieved by the user at his or her station (Tydeman et al., 1982).

Users of teletext are on the receiving end of a bit stream from which they retrieve preformatted pages of data. The limitations on host computer size are determined more by the transmission speed of the television channel than by other factors. Transmission speeds vary with the number of lines employed— full-channel teletext using most of the 525 scanning lines can offer over 25,000 pages of text every 30 seconds (Tydeman et al., 1982).

In the case of viewdata services, however, the host computer can be considerably larger, often an entire mainframe with large storage and fast CPU, capable of accommodating thousands of users simultaneously. Examples of such large-scale viewdata systems include Lockheed's DIALOG, Compuserve, The Source, Prestel, and Viewtron. The Source, for example, operates several host computer systems which handle demand for the 24-hour service via time-sharing networks (Source Telecomputing Corporation, 1981).

12.2.2 Composing and Data Entry

The process by which pages of text are composed and entered into videotex systems is a major shortcoming. When entry is done manually, formatting each page may require several minutes or as much as an hour depending on complexity of the graphics involved. Some systems incorporate digitizing pads which permit page creation similar to drafting; such methods promise to save time and money.

Of course, as systems become more sophisticated, graphics will improve so that they equal or exceed those of current television graphics systems such as Chyron or Vidifont, both in font styles and resolution (Brenner, 1983).

12.2.3 The Transmission System

This is the means by which data are transmitted from host computer to users. In the case of viewdata, transmission systems generally consist of telephone or broadband cable lines; in the case of teletext, UHF, VHF, FM/SCA, MDS, or satellite channels are the means of transmission (Sigel, 1980).

12.2.4 Display System

Display systems consist of a CRT monitor (a picture tube in either black and white or color) or a printer. Consumer-oriented text services in Europe and the United States have been designed to provide color videotex service. A significant issue is the nature of the display: CRTs, especially home video receivers, were never designed for flicker-free, up-close viewing, the most common mode of videotex usage. When used to deliver videotex data, CRTs can cause eyestrain and fatigue. Moreover, there is concern about the potential health hazards of nonionizing radiation emitted from CRTs. Such issues have become part of collective bargaining agendas in data processing industries in California recently. One solution to the radiation threat may be found in flat screen displays such as those currently being introduced in the computer field.

12.2.5 User Retrieval System

Users employ a decoder to retrieve information from the system. It consists of a calculatorlike touch pad (in the case of teletext) or terminal keyboard (in the case of viewdata) which is used to select pages of text from the system or to communicate with the system interactively (see Figure 12.3).

Teletext decoders select and store one page of text at a time. Some decoders

FIGURE 12.3
(a) This Zenith teletext decoder enables consumer television sets to receive a teletext magazine by means of standard television signals. Pictured is a Zenith teletext decoder (top of set) and full-function remote control device which viewer uses to select "pages" of teletext information on demand. (Courtesy of Taft Broadcasting Company) (b) The viewer is using a full electronic keyboard to interact with the Viewtron videotex system provided by Knight-Ridder to subscribers in Coral Gables, Florida. The two-way link between user and the Viewtron host computer is provided by the local telephone company. (Courtesy of AT&T)

are capable of storing several pages at a time, thereby enabling the teletext system to appear to respond quickly because whole blocks of related pages can be stored in memory for fast retrieval (Roizen, 1980).

12.3 VIEWDATA SYSTEM DESIGN AND ARCHITECTURE

In Figure 12.4 is shown the basic system architecture for a viewdata system. There are four basic components: (1) the system itself, (2) the transmission lines, (3) the information providers, and (4) the users.

12.3.1 The System

Viewdata systems consist of routines for control, processing of data, and charging and housekeeping functions, as well as online storage of information pages. The computer center—in fact, the system itself—is transparent to the content of the data. This means that the operator of the system retains no right to

FIGURE 12.4
Viewdata system architecture.

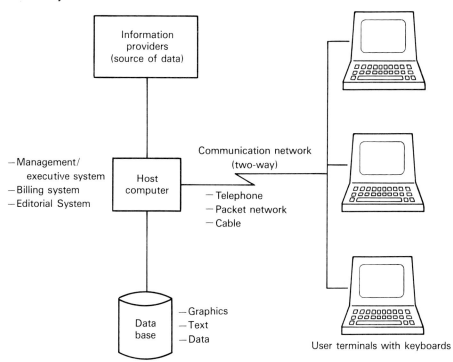

censorship over the system, except where the legality of the content is in question (Commission on New Information Technology, 1980).

It is also the case that system operators provide a major service to the IPs in that they guide IPs applications and assist in the implementation of technological advances which affect the format, creation, and distribution of pages.

12.3.2 Transmission System

The viability of viewdata services lies in their capacity to distribute data over many different kinds of channels. The origin of videotex systems within the British Post Office, for example, suggests that the telephone company is a natural locus for the distribution of the service. However, cable TV systems, dedicated two-way microwave, and other kinds of two-way links can be used as well (Sigel, 1980).

12.3.3 The Information Providers

These are sources of data. They may be corporations, individuals, the government, or any other entity with information to distribute, either free or for a fee. Essentially, information providers (IPs) are external to the operating system.

12.3.4 User Groups

A variety of users can be identified, including government, corporations, individual users, educational users, cultural institutions, and the like. While users of information, these groups may also be information providers in a viewdata system.

12.4 TELETEXT SYSTEM DESIGN AND ARCHITECTURE

Figure 12.5 shows how teletext services work. The system components consist of (1) information providers, (2) the broadcaster who holds the license for the frequency over which teletext will be transmitted, (3) the host computer and data storage system, (4) the insertion system, (5) the television transmitter, and (6) users (see Figure 12.5)

12.4.1 Information Providers

Most observers agree that broadcasters will be the principal information providers as teletext services mature. There are two reasons for this. First, the scope of teletext service will be limited by the number of available lines in the vertical blanking interval; this limitation means that relatively few pages of text (100) can be transmitted in a 25-second interval if only two lines in the VBI are

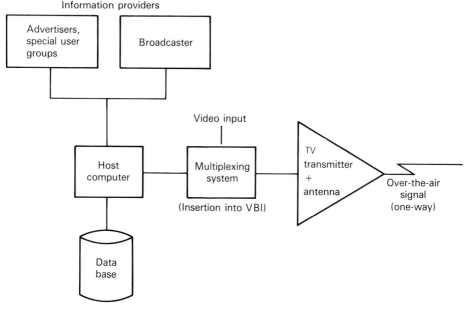

Information providers

FIGURE 12.5
Teletext system architecture.

used (Tydeman et al., 1982). Given such limitations, broadcasters are likely to retain full control over all pages for their own purposes.

In its 1983 ruling the FCC decided to allow broadcasters to carry teletext on lines 14 to 18 and 20 of the vertical blanking interval, with use of lines 10 to 13 to be phased in between 1988 and 1991. In the same ruling the FCC also decided to limit content for the time being to that which could be displayed on the screen, leaving open for future discussion the use of the vertical blanking interval for paging. The FCC cleared the way for a viable teletext service when it waived all logging requirements. At the same time, however, the FCC ruled that cable system operators could strip out broadcast teletext if they so desired, a decision which met with instant resistance from broadcasters ("FCC Approves Teletext Transmission," 1983).

Second, broadcasters are likely to see teletext either as a threat which, if inevitable, must be controlled, or as a means for extending their medium. In the case of commercial broadcasters, there is one rule of thumb which will determine the kind of teletext service they will deliver: if teletext threatens the profitability of the commercial message, it will not be carried or will be modified to reduce the "negative" impact of the text on the commercial. Broadcasters don't want advertisers, who pay for the privilege of addressing the broadcast audience, to become disenchanted because the very broadcaster who sells them

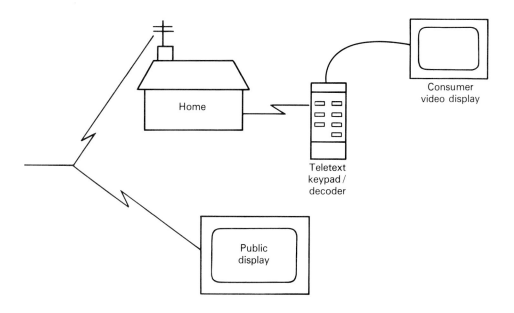

audience attention also provides a means (teletext) for that audience to avoid the commercials. To prevent this, broadcasters may choose not to run text services during commercials. Such a policy would guarantee the uninterrupted delivery of commercials (Tedesco, 1980).

Of course, the broadcaster is likely to enhance the commercial by using teletext to increase product information available to the viewer. In another context (Tedesco and Bushman, 1979) it has been proposed that "caption cueing" would permit the broadcaster to insert a signal (perhaps something as simple as a flashing asterisk in the upper right-hand corner) to alert viewers to search for additional information about the product. A page number would be flashed with the asterisk to indicate the direct route to retrieve the data. To prevent switching to text during commercials, broadcasters might offer such text data only after the commercial block had finished, during the program.

The cardinal rule of broadcasting is that the broadcaster is in the business of selling time; in fact, the *attention of the audience* is being sold as the principal product (Melody, 1975). But the key issue is, Does the audience stay tuned long enough to view the commercial? For these reasons, it is highly unlikely that broadcasters will use teletext service for much beyond enhancement of commercials and programming if they feel it will diminish the impact of commercials. In news, additional pages of text might be presented for use by readers who want additional information about fast-developing stories, but the cost of providing such data would be met by advertising revenues (Gordon & Mermigas, 1983).

There is one other way that broadcasters are likely to use teletext as an enhancement, and this is as a program-listing service, an electronic *TV Guide,* if you will. This would permit broadcasters far more flexible schedules and would give viewers instantly accessible program information. Experiments along this line have been run on KCET in Los Angeles (Mahony, DeMartino, & Stengel, 1980).

In sum, it is unlikely that private entrepreneurs will have access to broadcaster-delivered text services unless they already buy commercial time on the station. Moreover, it is unlikely that the broadcasters offering teletext will ever be willing to treat it as a common carrier service which would allow the development of a public teletext service to which any person or group would have access both as information providers and as users (Tedesco and Bushman, 1979).

12.4.2 The Broadcaster

Broadcasters hold the key to both the display and application of teletext services. If they adopt teletext, the flow of information will be under their control solely because traditionally they closely control all broadcast content. They will not function as transparent hosts, as most videotex system operators are likely to do. This attitude may change as the regulatory environment changes: as broadcasters become less accountable for program content, they may become more willing to carry a "transparent" teletext system, over whose content they have little or no control.

12.4.3 Host Computer and Storage

This part of the teletext system is essentially like those used in viewdata. However, because of the smaller transmission capacity of teletext and its one-way characteristic, the size of the system and storage capacity will be smaller than that used in viewdata systems.

12.4.4 Transmission System

The transmitter and antenna of the broadcast system are the means by which broadcasters transmit teletext, which, in the broadcast context, is an ancillary service embedded in the vertical blanking interval. Of course, broadcasters could decide during off hours to deliver full-channel text service, using all 525 scanning lines for that purpose. They would then have the capacity, by one estimate, to deliver as much as 25,000 pages of text in a 30-second period (Roizen, 1980). At these levels of throughput teletext service begins to look like viewdata, especially when sufficient decoder memory is present to permit the local storage of enough information (pages) to allow rapid retrieval of related tiers of data.

According to one analyst (Woolfe, 1980) there are three levels of exchange foreseen in videotex systems: (1) *retrieval* (one-way); (2) *interactional* (two-way searching with direct feedback from the host system); and, (3) *transactional* (actual transfer of money or information from user to host computer, or from one computer to another). Teletext systems are placed in category 1.

The data from the broadcaster's computer are fed into an encoding device which inserts them into the vertical blanking interval. The broadcast transmitter sends data out embedded in the video signal. The data reach every receiver capable of displaying the standard signal, subject to the vagaries of digital signal transmission in areas where ghosting is a factor or where terrain-related or atmospheric interference and environmental conditions (such as foliage) affect signal reception.

12.4.5 Users

The teletext user is likely to be a member of the general public, although it is not inconceivable that broadcasters might target small (closed) user groups. The French (SOFRATEV), for example, employ a UHF channel to carry text services for the electric company.

However, the BBC's early experience with CEEFAX has established a framework for future applications so thoroughly embedded in a public service orientation—a general-audience focus—that the users are most likely to be conceived of as the mass public which will use teletext for general information and programming enhancements, including the commercial embellishment that American broadcasters are likely to introduce.

One final word about transmission links is appropriate. Teletext as described here is really confined to the broadcast channel. In the United States we currently have an application using one-half of line 21 for closed captioning for the deaf, generated by the National Captioning Institute in cooperation with most of the major networks, which the FCC has decided to retain in the near term ("FCC Approves Teletext Transmission," 1983).

12.5 RETRIEVAL CHARACTERISTICS: WHAT THE USER CONFRONTS

In order to grasp what videotex service really is, the fundamental retrieval characteristics of the system must be examined. To use a videotex service (either type), the user must employ a terminal of some sort which addresses the system. At minimum, the user can retrieve information from a stream of data in constant circulation (like a carousel)—teletext—or at maximum, the system allows the user to transact business (exchange money or information) with the viewdata host system. The device (terminal) in use is tailored to these needs. In the case of teletext, a simple calculatorlike touch pad, similar in design to a Touch Tone keypad is used. In the case of viewdata systems, the user employs a full typewriter-type keyboard which permits an alphanumeric exchange with the host computer. Menu structures provide the key to access. (See Figure 12.6.)

As technology has improved, viewdata terminals have grown "smarter,"

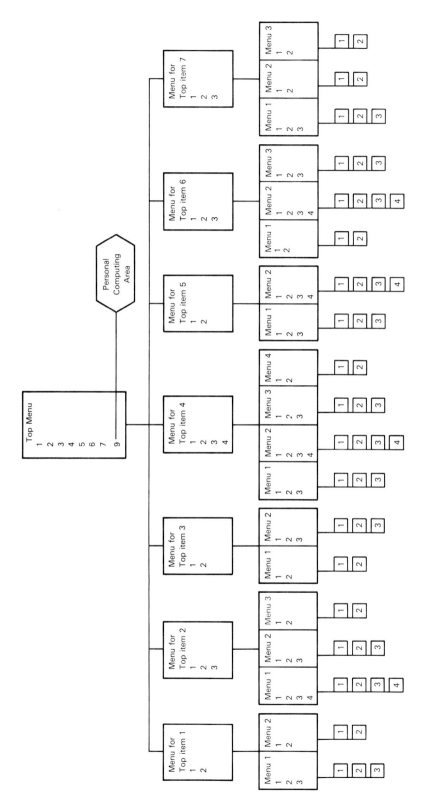

FIGURE 12.6
Menu structure. Using a menu structure, videotex systems, like Compuserve, provide lists of available items to guide the user's choice. This diagram illustrates how it is possible to move through several menus and layers of information to reach the exact information desired. It is also possible to exit the menu structure to gain access to other services such as the personal computing area. (Courtesy of Compuserve)

combining the characteristics of a simple terminal with those of a personal computer, and function as either videotex terminal or personal computer without difficulty.

Videotex systems operate under one of two competing display formats: *alphageometric* and *alphamosaic*. These differ in the degree of resolution offered and in cost. The alphageometric system is a more graphics-oriented delivery system which composes images using a geometry to create large areas of the design at one time. The alphamosaic system relies on cursor-directed design of each picture element (see Figure 12.7). The alphamosaic World System Teletext (WST) decoder is reported to be $200 cheaper, in quantities of 10,000, than its alphageometric competitor, North American Broadcast Teletext Specification (NABTS) ("Teletext Battle Surfaces in Las Vegas," 1983).

The difficulty with all videotex displays is that they provide relatively low picture resolution compared with standard television images, and much lower levels than full-color print advertising, a significant shortcoming of concern to advertising agencies.

There is also the related question of whether the level of resolution is sufficient to justify extended use of standard CRTs, around which most videotex systems have been configured, or if the inherent flicker of the CRT will cause fatigue so as to prohibit extended use.

Moreover, there is a delay in retrieval of data which affects the user's perception and attitude toward the system. CEEFAX users, for example, were reported dissatisfied with delays in excess of 12 seconds (Carey, 1981). In Compuserve and The Source viewdata systems, response is generally faster, although lag time between request for data and display increases as the number of users online increases, a common experience with time-sharing systems.

12.6 IMAGE-CREATION CHARACTERISTICS

All pages in videotex systems, like their counterparts in traditional print media, must be composed. Herein lies the central labor-consuming cost of such services—the creation of pages of data, each of which must be input by a person. The costliness of data entry affects the profitability of the service. Digitizing tablets and sophisticated transfers from existing data bases, such as Reuters and Dow Jones, will decrease the cost of page creation and increase profitability.

Production of pages of text for videotex services is less expensive than either video or print media with which videotex service has been compared, promising that new user groups not now using either video or print because of cost may be enfranchised by videotex.

In the Knight-Ridder Viewtron experiment, for example, the charge to advertisers to input a color frame was $15, or $45 if the frame were created by the Viewtron designers. Updates were $5 each. These costs compare favorably with the costs of preparing black-and-white art work for print publication (Brenner, 1983).

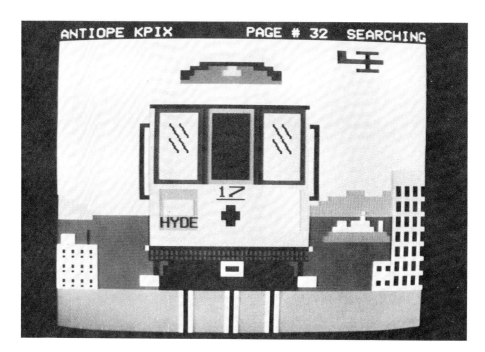

FIGURE 12.7
Comparison of Alpha-Mosaic (World System Teletext-WST) and Alpha-Geometric [North American Broadcast Teletext Specification (NABTS)] frames. (a) The Alpha-Mosaic method of creating graphics. Note the rough outline of the cable car roof which is typical of this system. (b) A frame showing Alpha-Geometric graphics. Note the relatively smooth lines in the title and illustration. (Courtesy of Joe Roizen, Telegen)

12.7 USER APPLICATIONS

One way to look at potential videotex applications is represented by the three-dimensional space in Figure 12.8.

Four classes of patrons for videotex services are identifiable: business, government, private (nonprofit), and consumer (public). The first online *business* videotex services have been pioneered by the British Post Office under the names VIEWDATA and PRESTEL, both targeted initially and primarily at business users, and secondarily at the home (consumer) market. Still in their formative stages, these services place heavy emphasis on transactional and interactional data.

Sending either *perishable* (stock market) or relatively *permanent* data (train schedules, for example), is part of the versatility of these systems; videotex systems are readily accessible to both commercial users, who will employ them to retrieve business-related data, and to the general public, to whom advertisers will offer information to spur the purchase of products and services. Delivery of specialized services such as electronic mail is also envisioned, especially for closed user groups.

Government applications include delivery of timely data designed to facilitate use of public systems such as mass transit. Widespread use of videotex systems to deliver public information will depend on the government's granting access to

FIGURE 12.8
A taxonomy of videotex application.

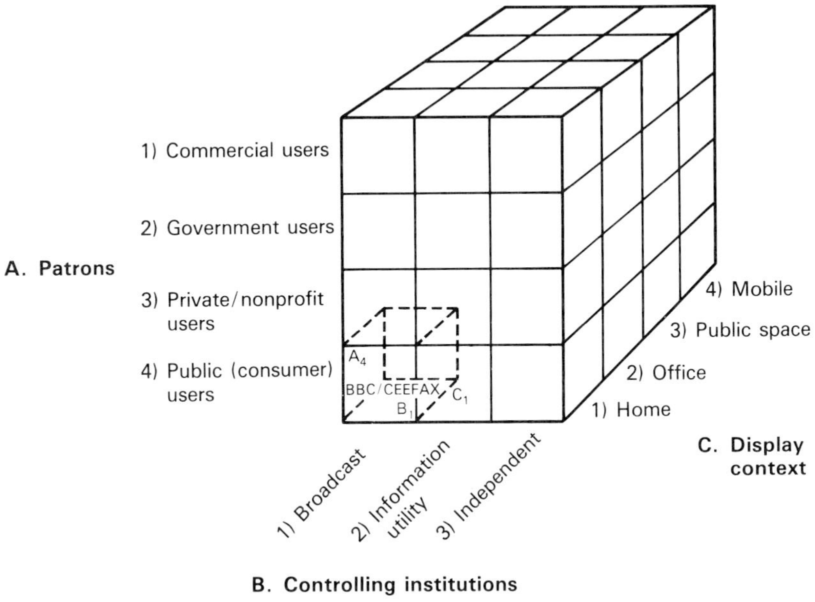

A. Patrons
1) Commercial users
2) Government users
3) Private/nonprofit users
4) Public (consumer) users

C. Display context
4) Mobile
3) Public space
2) Office
1) Home

B. Controlling institutions
1) Broadcast
2) Information utility
3) Independent

data it controls and the public's perception that making such data available is a useful public function which justifies the cost.

Videotex in *educational* settings (private and/or nonprofit) has been the subject of experiments in the United Kingdom, South Africa, and the United States, at San Francisco State University. Some form of videotex will find a home in the enhancement of recorded and live-broadcast educational programs, allowing users to take quizzes and reveal answers or to conduct searches for information which supplements the main program.

Examples of public (consumer) videotex services include The Source and Compuserve.

Both services offer electronic mail, some transactional services, access to information sources like the UPI wire service, *The Washington Post,* and many other financial and business services, game packages, and educational programs.

Videotex in *direct marketing* is an application that has advertising and marketing executives interested. While advertisers will use it to enhance existing message systems and may develop new technologies with it, marketers will use videotex to exchange information (product description and personal-preference data) and to conduct transactions. Consumer protection agencies and public interest groups will become involved in the development of the service, as will grassroots organizations.

Local community uses may evolve into viable local information networks, including, but not limited to, an electronic real estate market. Community bulletin boards will carry disparate information such as the frequency of neighborhood burglaries, actions taken by local citizen groups, directory of local services, local electronic mail, etc. Public videotex displays are likely to be commonplace ("HVC Tries Videotex in Dallas," 1983).

Another way to look at videotex services is as a product of the interaction of three characteristics: interactive capacity, determinant of content, and perishability of information (Figure 12.9).

Videotex systems may be thought of as supporting three *levels of interaction:* noninteractive (electronic billboard with no user interaction); quasiinteractive (one-way teletext); and fully interactive (two-way via telephone or cable).

The second dimension is the *determinant of content:* Who programs the system? In the first instance, all content is source-determined. In the second instance, user and source contribute jointly. In the third case, users create the data base.

The third dimension is *perishability of information.* Data are either perishable, meaning of short-term utility, or permanent.

An example of the interaction of these dimensions may be seen in train-delay information which is displayed on a CRT at a station as a noninteractive electronic billboard, the content of which is determined solely by the source (transportation authority) and which is perishable because the same information will not likely apply in a few minutes.

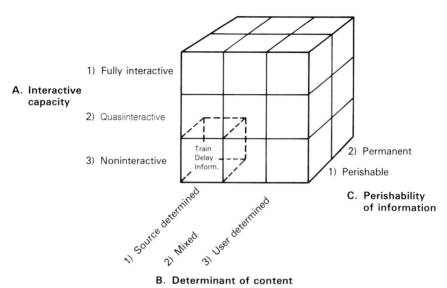

FIGURE 12.9
A three-dimensional differentiation of videotex characteristics.

12.8 BARRIERS TO ADOPTION

Many factors will affect the rate of adoption and diffusion of videotex technology. There are questions of competing standards. Historically, government has identified and standardized operating parameters for new telecommunications technology. But there are drawbacks to government-imposed standards when the ultimate shape and potential of the technology are not clear. All too often, such standards have grown out of political considerations and reflect successful lobbying rather than the best possible technical or market data. An example is the politics of adoption of a color television standard for France (Crane, 1979). Standards battles are also related to vested corporate interests and willingness of new entrants to incorporate the dominant systems into their new design. No new telecommunications technology can be built without some reference to the adaptability of the system to widespread diffusion.

Cost is also a major consideration and is often closely tied to the question of displacement of other technologies: Is the new system sufficiently worthwhile and innovative to justify displacing what is already in use? This is a significant question considering that older technologies, like newspapers, are run by new entrants in the videotex field who may adopt or reject electronic text—electronic publishing, based on a cost-benefit comparison with print.

In the decision to adopt videotex services, businesses must evaluate carefully their investment in existing computer-based data retrieval systems. Privacy and security are also key factors in the adoption of videotex systems: business and other users must be certain that transactions and information exchanges within videotex systems are secure (Commission on New Information Technology, 1980).

Another apparent barrier is the positioning of videotex vis-à-vis competing technologies. Adoption often hinges on skills needed to operate a new technology. Moreover, there is concern over the level of complexity and cost associated with the adoption of a new infrastructure to manage the new technology.

There are also a variety of legal barriers to adoption, including copyright protection, regulatory controls, and the general history of territorial domains in telecommunications. The question of copyright is most significant because storage and retransmission of pages protected by copyright, the pirating of data, is a potential of videotex systems. Any videotex terminal equipped with disk storage can be used to record and, if desired, retransmit pages of text out of the control of the copyright holder. Political barriers are also relevant. The U.S. regulatory framework reflects the party in power in the White House and Congress. Current regulatory decisions are affected by the laissez-faire marketplace orientation. So far marketplace forces with an interest in these technologies have created proposals, including a joint North American videotex standard evolved by AT&T and others and two competing teletext standards (WST and NABTS). It is unlikely that the federal government will be compelled to create a single standard for teletext and viewdata in the near future ("FCC Approves Teletext Transmission," 1983).

Long-term projections suggest that should videotex grow into the multibillion-dollar industry some see as its potential, then the need for government regulation to guarantee standards will be seen. However, the market will act long before the government does.

12.9 BUSINESS AND PUBLIC POLICY ISSUES

Is there a business in videotex in the long term?

The answer appears to be yes. After more than a decade of experimentation videotex services are now seen by advertisers as viable delivery systems for commercial messages, and by direct marketing professionals as a new avenue for "instant gratification" (Brenner, 1983). One estimate ("Changes by Banks," 1983) is that by 1990 4.7 million households, or 5.2 percent of all U.S. homes will pay for interactive services including telebanking. Compared with numbers of current subscribers to videotex services—Dow Jones has 67,000; Compuserve, 44,000; and The Source, 35,000—the projections appear quite optimistic, yet possible.

However, several important steps will have to be taken to overcome consumer inertia. As Carey has argued, selling teletext to the average television viewer requires that we recognize the difficulty people already have dealing with complex gadgets in the home. We must confront not only the technological barriers that are likely to put the public off but those created by the format of information display and retrieval, as well (Carey, 1981).

Some systems will grow up to meet specific needs, as in the case of agriculture's Green Thumb Project and similar services like AGNET (Bissel, 1983). Other systems, like Viewtron and general-purpose teletext magazines now evolving, will target broader interests.

Educational applications seem appropriate as well, especially since videotex systems provide relatively low-cost channels for direct-to-the-home delivery of learning materials, thereby overcoming a major barrier to continuing personal and professional education.

The advent of these systems has awakened concern over public policy questions. Just who will guarantee the privacy and confidentiality of transactions conducted through such systems? Will those who need but cannot afford information from videotex data bases be subsidized by the government? Will there be sufficient access for the public, not just as users but as information providers? Will the free market be the best mechanism for directing the growth of databases, or will government intervention and planning be required? Issues like these are being debated now (Commission on New Information Technology, 1979; Jones, 1981; Tedesco and Bushman, 1979) and will evolve along with videotex technology itself.

12.10 A FINAL WORD

If videotex services are to be viable, a variety of institutions, organizations, and individuals must adopt them either to displace some existing delivery systems (print or other) or to enhance an existing service (commercial television, for example).

Information providers must be willing to use these new technologies. As one communications economist, Gordon Thompson (1979), has pointed out, there is a clear difference between eletext and viewdata in that the latter offers a "public good," which is generally available and offered free to each user, and the former offers a "private good," which is for sale. While distinctions between viewdata and teletext will blur as technology vests teletext with more of the characteristics of viewdata, especially larger memory, the use of both services will no doubt eventually be on a pay basis.

Ultimately, the cost of development and deployment will fall on the consumer, for whom the initial cost of the terminal and recurring fees to access data will be the price of entry. If the present industry trend is carried to its logical conclusion, both the initial and the continuing market for videotex will be among personal computer owners, who now form the nucleus of videotex users.

REFERENCES

Bissel, Kathy, "American Farmers: Pioneers in Videotex," *Today,* 1983, pp. 12–15.
Brenner, Elizabeth, "Knight-Ridder Puts Video Future on Line," *Advertising Age,* 1983, *54*(21), pp. 1, 44, 53.

Carey, John, "Selling Teletext to Archie Bunker," in M. L. Moss (Ed.), *Telecommunications and Productivity*, Reading, Mass.: Addison-Wesley, 1981.

"Changes by Banks, Retailers Critical to Growth of Videotex," *Electronic Media,* 1983.

Commission on New Information Technology, *New Views: Computers and New Media—Anxiety and Hopes,* Stockholm, Sweden: 1980.

Crane, Rhonda J., *The Politics of International Standards,* Norwood, N.J.: Ablex, 1979.

"Examining European Videotex Standards," *Today* 1983, pp. 47–48.

"FCC Approves Teletext Transmission," *Broadcast Week,* 1983, *1*(20), p. 1.

Gordon, Richard L., and Diane Mermigas, "Teletext Arena Grows," *Advertising Age,* 1983, *54*(15), pp. 1, 72.

"HVC Tries Videotex in Dallas," *Electronic Media,* 1983, p. 12.

Jones, Mary Gardiner, "Consumer Information Data Bases: How Can They Best Be Developed?" in Mitchell L. Moss (Ed.), *Telecommunications and Productivity,* Reading, Mass.: Addison-Wesley, 1981.

Madden, John C., "Prospects for Videotex and Teletext," in Mitchel L. Moss (Ed.), *Telecommunications and Productivity,* Reading, Mass.: Addison-Wesley, 1981.

Mahoney, Sheila, Nick DeMartino, and Robert Stengel, *Keeping PACE with the New Television,* New York: VNU Books International, 1980.

Melody, William, *Children's Television: The Economics of Exploitation,* New Haven: Yale University Press, 1973.

Roizen, Joseph, "The Technology of Teletext and Viewdata," in Efrem Sigel (Ed.), *Videotext,* White Plains, N.Y.: Knowledge Industry Publications, 1980.

Sigel, Efrem (Ed.), *Videotext: The Coming Revolution in Home/Office Information Retrieval,* White Plains, N.Y.: Knowledge Industry Publications, 1980.

Source Telecomputing Corp. *The Source User's Manual,* McLean, 1981.

Spongberg, Robert C., *Ancillary Signals for Television: Innovations and Implications,* Denver: Denver Research Institute, 1975.

Tedesco, Albert S. and F. Anthony Bushman, "Teletext in the Public Interest: The Case of New Consumer Information Services," in *Teletext and Viewdata in the U.S.: A Workshop on Emerging Issues,* Menlo Park, Calif.: Institute for the Future, 1979.

Tedesco, Albert S., "Perspectives of the Marketplace: Outlook for New Information Technologies," *Videotex Services,* Washington, D.C.: National Cable Television Association, 1980.

"Teletext Battle Surfaces in Las Vegas," *Broadcasting,* 1983, *104*(16), pp. 108–112.

Thompson, Gordon B., "Memo from Mercury: Information Technology Is Different," *Teletext and Viewdata in the U.S.: A Workshop on Emerging Issues,* Menlo Park, Calif.: Institute for the Future, 1979.

Tydeman, J., H. Lilinski, R. Adler, M. Nyhan, and L. Zwimpfer, *Teletext and Videotex in the United States,* New York: McGraw-Hill, 1982.

Woolfe, Roger, *Videotex: The New Television-Telephone Information Services,* London: Heyden and Son, Ltd., 1980.

Chapter 13: Cost-Benefit Analysis in Telecommunications Management

Chapter 14: Regulation of Telecommunications in the United States

MANAGEMENT OF TELECOMMUNICATIONS

Since this book is for managers, we will turn away from the technology here to cover some of the more strictly managerial aspects of telecommunication. The first of these, Chapter 13, is on cost-benefit analysis, which is a requirement of management in any context. This chapter is included because managers today are so often faced with making decisions on telecommunication equipment and use with which they are personally unfamiliar. Hence, there might be more reliance on formal decision-making procedures than would otherwise be the case. Telecommunication is a heavily regulated industry or service all over the world. The laws and issues in the United States differ from those in other countries; hence we have two separate chapters, Chapter 14 on regulation in the United States and Chapter 15 on international telecommunications. The section concludes with a description of the typical duties and problems of the manager of telecommunications in a large corporation.

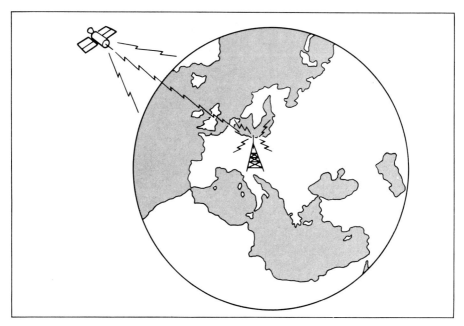

Chapter 15: International Telecommunications

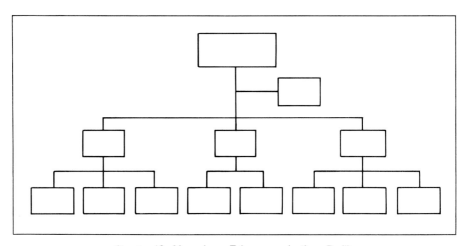

Chapter 16: Managing a Telecommunications Facility

CHAPTER 13

COST-BENEFIT ANALYSIS IN TELECOMMUNICATIONS MANAGEMENT

Lawrence F. Young
College of Business and Administration
Drexel University
Philadelphia, PA 19104

13.1 COST AND BENEFIT IMPACTS ON THE ORGANIZATION

New technology is often threatening because it requires us to consider moving into unfamiliar and therefore less predictable and controllable circumstances. Faced with the need to react simultaneously to innovation and to its associated risks, human beings often find themselves paralyzed with indecision. Benjamin Franklin proposed a remedy for these kinds of indecision, which, he said,

> are difficult chiefly because while we have them under consideration all the reasons pro and con are not present to the mind at the same time; but sometimes one set present themselves and at other times another, the first being out of sight. . . . To get over this, my way is to divide half a sheet of paper by a line into two columns; writing over the one "pro" and other "con." Then during three or four days' consideration I put down under the different heads short hints of the different motives that at different times occur to me for and against the measure. When I have thus got them all together in one view I endeavor to estimate their respective weights; and where I find two, one on each side, that seem equal I strike them both out. If I find a reason pro equal to some two reasons con, I strike out the three. If I judge some two reasons con equal to some three reasons pro I strike out the five; and thus proceeding I find at length where the balances lie . . . and come to a determination accordingly. And, though the weight of reasons cannot be taken with the precision of algebraic quantities, when each is thus considered separately and comparatively and the whole lies before me, I think I can judge better and am less liable to make a rash step; and in fact I have found great advantage from this kind of equation in what may be called moral or prudential algebra. (Doren, 1941)

Franklin's "prudential algebra" is not unlike aspects of cost-benefit analysis. The introduction of a new technical device into a work system often has unforeseen results. Telephones, computers, copying machines, terminals, word processors, and other kinds of office equipment have had impacts on the social and psychological aspects of organizations, as well as on more directly economic outcomes derived from the technological characteristics of these devices. In some cases, expected cost savings could not be documented because the introduction of the new devices created new and unplanned types of usage. The value of this new usage often could not be assessed. Users of these devices were often willing to pay more for new services even though benefits were not measured in monetary terms. The mere availability of some new devices seems to create its own, sometimes seemingly insatiable demands.

Despite the difficulty of anticipating all organizational impacts and because we have often seen greater impacts than had been foreseen, it is important to attempt as thorough an analysis of costs and benefits as is feasible. Because of uncertainties it is also advisable to monitor and reexamine the results of systems changes as they become available. Cost-benefit analysis of telecommunications systems, as well as of all other aspects of an organizational system, should be considered to be an ongoing *control* process as well as part of *planning* new systems.

The fundamental concern of cost-benefit analysis in both the planning and control stages is to identify and quantify all of the significant impacts—positive and negative, direct and indirect—on the organization. The intent is to measure all of these impacts in monetary units wherever possible, so that a given project or system design can be seen to provide either a net gain or loss, indicating either a go or a no-go decision. There is nothing really new, sophisticated, or complex about this concept, although carrying it out can be difficult. It is just good business sense. In the public sector, where the public good rather than profitability is the objective, the application of this approach was a new idea. The term *cost-benefit* (or sometimes *benefit-cost*) was coined to identify the analog in the public sector of the private sector's profitability analysis (Anderson & Settle, 1977).

However, the attention resulting from efforts to elaborate upon and (summarize) the methods used to carry out cost-benefit analysis in the public sector also renewed the interest of many managers of corporate enterprises. They, too, began to see that many decisions with significant economic impacts on the firm were being made by seat-of-the-pants methods. New attention was therefore directed to analytical methods, and thus the term *cost-benefit analysis* found its way into the standard vocabulary of management in the private as well as the public sector.

While wending its way from private business to public policy and back again, the cost-benefit concept did seem to acquire a new emphasis on system thinking. That is, viewing the organization as a system placed new emphasis on the dynamic, long-term, and indirect impact on economic outcomes as well as the more obvious, direct, and short-term economic results. Furthermore, practical-minded managers saw a need to take into account impacts that could not be translated into monetary units of measure without expending large amounts of time, effort, and cost on the analysis. Thus, a judgmental kind of cost-benefit analysis is often done on the task of doing a cost-benefit analysis itself, and no more cost is expended in the analysis than is profitable. But this does not mean that important impacts can be ignored because they require too much analysis. Instead, it implies that all important impacts should be identified: some will be measured more precisely, others less precisely, and still others will merely be judgmentally categorized. The final decision to implement a system or not will therefore not always be made on the basis of a single net-profit-or-loss measurement. This practical managerial approach to cost-benefit analysis is the outlook we will take in describing methods of evaluating the organizational impacts of the telecommunications system.

13.1.1 Economic Impacts

If all of the costs and benefits resulting from implementing a system could be measured in monetary units, the economic impact of the systems could be evaluated within the following framework:

1 Estimate the acquisition and set-up costs required for such items as site preparation, purchase of equipment, testing, initial recruiting and training of personnel, development of new procedures, controls, etc.

2 Estimate operating costs for items such as equipment rental and line leasing, maintenance fees, operating personnel, space charges, supplies, power, etc.

3 Estimate benefits, such as displaced personnel time costs, other displaced costs, avoided costs, increased revenues, etc. This involves a comparison of the estimated costs, revenues, and other economic outcomes that would result from the new system with the corresponding outcomes that would result if the present systems were retained.

4 In subtracting the costs of the proposed new systems from the cost of the present systems, comparable time periods must be considered. The benefits (3) and operating costs (2) should be estimated period by period over the entire expected life of the system. Net benefits for each period must then be converted to their present values using a selected rate of return.

5 If the present value of all benefits exceeds the one-time acquisition and set-up costs in (1), then the new system is deemed a worthwhile investment.

Another way of stating the last step is to find the rate of return at which the present value of all net benefits would equal the one-time costs. If that rate of return is acceptable, then the proposed systems can be said to have passed a cost-benefit test.

An alternative or additional criterion could be to examine the payback period (the time it takes to recoup the initial set-up costs) and decide whether or not that period is acceptable.

In carrying out rate-of-return calculations, managers can use either tables and formulas in a standard text on engineering economics (Grant, 1950) or, more conveniently, an interactive computer routine. Such computer routines are found in many financial planning decision support systems packages for time-sharing or personal-computer use.

The procedure described above, however, represents only a partial picture of an analysis of costs and benefits. It can take into account both long- and short-term economic impacts—fixed and variable economic impacts—and can even be applied to more than one estimate of each impact, such as high and low estimates or an entire distribution of estimates. But it is limited in the following respects:

1 Rough estimates of indirect, hard-to-measure costs and benefits cannot be considered in the same way as more easily measured economic impacts.

2 It is incapable of adding in outcomes that are valued by management but are not normally measured at all in monetary units, that is, risk, prestige, market share, social service contribution, work satisfaction.

3 As stated, it only examines a single proposed alternative against the status quo. Even if more than one alternative is assessed, the above method does not offer any assurance that some other unexamined alternative might be far preferable if it were identified.

The first two limitations are similar, although the first refers to economic impacts and the second refers to noneconomic impacts. They are similar because they are both problems of obtaining consistent measurements. Ways to overcome these limitations are discussed in the next section on noneconomic impacts (13.1.2).

The third limitation, however, requires a discussion of decision-making methods, and how the previously described method fits into a wider spectrum of such methods. This topic will be discussed subsequently in Section 13.2.3.

13.1.2 Noneconomic Impacts

Let us assume all significant costs have been identified for a new proposed system and compared to those that would be incurred if the present system were maintained. We can also assume that estimates of the message volume and channel capacity requirements for the future life of the system have been estimated. Taking these requirements into account we have, we assume, a result that indicates that the proposed system will be only slightly less expensive on an annual basis. At this marginal reduction in cost, the payback period will exceed the 10-year criterion usually applied. If no additional benefits can be taken into account, the proposed system would be rejected. However, management recognizes that other impacts may result that cannot be assessed economically. These may be simply noted and assessed judgmentally in combination with the economic aspects. A display of impacts such as those shown in Table 13.1 can be considered.

TABLE 13.1
A DISPLAY OF IMPACTS, INCLUDING NONECONOMIC IMPACTS

Impacts	Proposed system	Present system
All economic	2% less cost	(Base for comparison)
User population	95% of all management and engineering staff	All managers, 50% of engineers
Flexibility	Will provide more flexible data base manipulation (show examples)	Fixed format data displays

The direct economic benefits are not sufficient to justify the change, but the other benefits may tip the scales in favor of the proposed system because of the subjective judgment that economic payoffs will result from these factors even though they have not been specifically quantified now. These noneconomic factors could possibly be assessed for their economic impact if we were willing and able to invest the time and money required to carry out suitable experiments. But management has concluded that the costs of more extensive analysis would exceed the value of having quantified benefit estimates. This is a rational way to approach the analysis, not only on commonsense grounds, but also according to the more formal framework of decision theory.

According to decision theory (Emery, 1950), additional information can only have a net value if all of the following are true:

1 We would make a different decision if we had the information.

2 The payoff of such a decision would exceed the payoff resulting from the decision made in the absence of such information.

3 The relative payoff advantage would exceed the cost of acquiring the information.

Applying these rules to the above comparison of the alternative systems, we might ask the following questions. Do we believe that the unquantified impact factors will have any ultimate economic payoffs? If the answer is yes, then we can ask: Will we prefer the proposed system regardless of how much the ultimate economic payoffs of these factors will be? If the answer to the second question is also yes, then clearly the value of more information about these payoffs is zero according to decision theory because we would have made the same decision with or without this information.

Suppose, however, that the situation was not a matter of one last straw, no matter how light, sufficing to tilt our preference toward the new system. In this case, the analysis would be similar, but the questions we could ask ourselves would be somewhat different. First, how much additional economic benefit would the proposed system have to have in order for us to decide to implement it? This would be the difference between currently estimated annual savings and the savings level that would result in just passing the acceptance criterion, expressed in payback period length or return of initial investment. Second, do we believe that the unquantified impacts will be worth at least as much to the firm? If the answer to this question is yes, then we should prefer the new system.

This procedure enables the decision maker to narrow the area of subjective evaluation by first quantifying those factors that can be easily quantified.

Note also that we need not consider only economic (albeit unmeasured) impacts. If the impact is thought to be not so much economic but rather a more intangible benefit, such as "a greater sense of reliability and confidence" or "a more satisfying work situation" or merely convenience, the question would have a slightly different meaning. It would mean: How much are we willing to pay to obtain these noneconomic impacts? This way of assessing value is sometimes called *value analysis.*

In either case, the analysis can take the unquantified benefits into account after the more formalized economic portion of the cost-benefit analysis is completed.

13.1.3 Experience, Wisdom, and Decision Support Criteria

Another way in which the area of subjective judgment can be narrowed without carrying out a costly experimental investigation is to search the historical records, including our own and those of others in similar situations. It may also be helpful to search for previously expressed "wisdom" or the judgments of others. Both these kinds of information may help management to assess its own situation.

For example, in considering the benefits of "more and faster communication between managers and others," we might accept this effect as a qualified benefit. It is, after all, part of the conventional wisdom that problems are often caused by lack of communication. On the other hand, it has been observed that "more" and "faster" do not always equate with "better." Sometimes increased-capacity communication channels and more messages can be prime confusion creators. As Murray Bob (1982) pointed out in his guest essay in *The New York Times,* "Saying nothing may be the administrative analog of the medical commandment, 'Above all, do no harm.' " The ability of the communicators to use the additional capability well should therefore be taken into account. J. D. Thompson (1967) suggests that one method of deciding whether "more" is "better" is to calculate what percentage of work tasks fall into each of these three categories:

1 *Independent tasks.* A task is independent if it can be performed by one person without the interaction of others.

2 *Pooled tasks.* A task is pooled if two or more people must interact in order to perform it.

3 *Sequential tasks.* A task is sequential if several people (or work units) can

only perform their respective tasks in a certain sequence in which the outputs of one task must be used as the inputs to another task.

Each of these kinds of tasks requires different types of communications support. As pointed out by Hackathorn and Keen (1981), these three types of tasks form a hierarchy of interdependency, with independent tasks obviously being the least interdependent; each type requires a different decision support system. Communication capabilities comprise one important component of a decision support system, and the designation of types of decision support are therefore relevant to communications systems as well. These support types, which correspond to the three task categories, are as follows:*

1 *Personal support.* A system which supports the individual in performing independent tasks by enabling the individual to communicate with relevant data bases and applications of software, but not with other individuals.

2 *Group support.* A system which supports pooled tasks by providing mutual two-way communication between two or more people in the group who must interact.

3 *Organizational support.* A system which supports sequential tasks by providing "nonsymmetrical" two-way communication between the individuals or work units involved. Communication can be considered nonsymmetrical in a variety of ways, including volume of messages, scope of message content, and required sequence of messages.

The user group to which the proposed system will extend new communications capabilities of a group support nature may be found to have a task-interdependency that indicates that additional group support for pooled tasks to this community of users will affect only the smallest portion of their work tasks (10 percent) and that these tasks have a relatively minor impact. This would indicate that the benefit of this extended service would be minor and therefore the organization should not be willing to pay very much for it. Although the evaluation of impact and value is subjective, the result is likely to differ from that obtained without the information provided by the task profile.

Another type of impact that is not usually easy to measure in direct monetary terms is the impact of communication medium on the effectiveness of the message. Effectiveness, in this context, can be assessed by its ability to change the recipient's perceptions and attitudes and impel the recipient toward a desired decision and action, such as agreeing to a proposal or making a purchase. Advertisers of consumer products, for example, use different types of mass media to achieve different aims.

Television lends itself to demonstration of use but must get only a single, simple proposition across in a short time span, while reinforcing the proposition through repetition of the message over relatively short intervals of time. Print

*The designation of support types are those given by Hackathorn and Keen, but the description given here is the author's and applies to communication systems rather than to the more general category of decision support systems.

media, on the other hand, can convey more information and, depending on the particular vehicle (magazine, newspaper, Sunday supplement), can provide the message with an added impact of prestige, credibility, or modishness acquired from the vehicle itself.

For the dissemination of specialized innovations, some studies have indicated that mass media can arouse interest, but interpersonal communication determines whether or not the innovation is adopted.

Some recent studies indicate that telephone communication may be more effective under some circumstances in changing people's minds and winning concessions from adversaries than face-to-face communication. The telephone may have the advantage in assessing the other parties' intentions, detecting deceptions, and pressing the stronger of two cases in a negotiation.

The effects of video displays of data and graphics are yet to be explored to reach firmer conclusions, but some evidence indicates that both video character data and graphics may lead to faster decisions, the use of less data, and possibly, to more effective decisions.

We may conclude that the communication medium is likely to have interacting effects with the messages communicated, often in subtle ways. These potential media interactions will have an impact on the effectiveness of a communication system and should therefore be assessed and evaluated at least subjectively. Such an assessment should take into account all of the available research and past observations available, along with estimates of the likely and intended uses of the system.

13.2 THE TELECOMMUNICATION MANAGEMENT PROBLEM AND DECISION ANALYSIS TECHNIQUES

The previous sections examine an approach to cost-benefit analysis of both economic and other impacts that can result from a new system. The orientation of this approach was to compare a proposed new system with an existing system. As has been pointed out, however, this is a limited way of posing the management problem.

A less constrained way of defining the problem is to consider that management would like to identify a particular system that can, within necessary parameters, best meet real and expected requirements and objectives. This formulation of the problem differs from and extends the previously considered orientation in the following ways:

1 More than two alternative systems (that is, a "singular new system" versus the "present system") should somehow be considered.

2 The problem shifts from choosing between two givens to that of designing a solution from among a large number of possibilities.

This broader outlook on the problem requires applying a range of decision analysis techniques, rather than cost-benefit analysis alone. We need to distinguish among feasibility analysis, cost-benefit analysis, and cost-effectiveness analysis. Moreover, we need to understand how these analyses can be integrated within the decision-generating processes of "satisficing," optimizing, and heuristic search.

Before we consider these analytical techniques, however, we need to provide an organizational context for defining the problem. We are concerned with selecting a design for a technical system that will be preferred by one or more persons within an organization. The human and organizational realities of the situation mean that we must define the problem as existing within a sociotechnical, rather than a merely technical, system. Every system must have a boundary and the boundary of such an organizationally embedded system is defined according to the scope of responsibility and authority of the decision makers.

This implies that the system we are considering will be different from the point of view of a telecommunication manager than from that of a general manager. We will discuss these varying viewpoints in the next sections and then consider the analytical techniques that can be brought to bear in either case. Finally, we will consider how the different points of view of general versus specialist management can be reconciled and an organizational approach can be taken to selecting a system alternative.

13.2.1 The Telecommunications Manager's Viewpoint

We can assume that the telecommunications manager has operational responsibility for the equipment, personnel, supplies, and other physical facilities directly associated with the provision of telecommunication services. The system, from this perspective, is as shown in Figure 13.1.

If we assume that the telecommunications manager is positioned in this manner in the organization, his or her managerial task is much like that of a production manager of a factory. The manager can forecast a demand but is not directly responsible for influencing it. If the goods or services are delivered when and where they are demanded, the manager's main responsibilities to customers or users are fulfilled. How well the product or service benefits the user is not essentially a production responsibility.

The production manager role, as considered here, is to hold down the cost of production while delivering what others have deemed to be required. This is one possible viewpoint or paradigm for the role of any manager seen as being responsible for fulfilling an internal service to the organization. The information system manager, the personnel manager, as well as the production manager and the telecommunications manager, might see their jobs in this way. In terms of a decision model, this viewpoint considers that:

1 Requirements are clearly given by others and provide minimum (and perhaps maximum) constraints on delivered outputs.

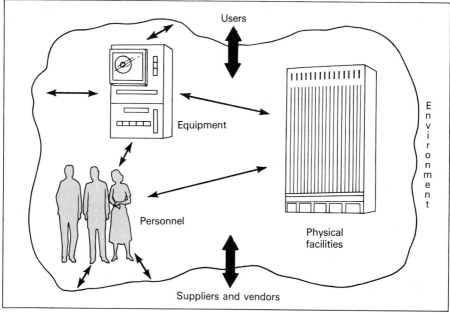

FIGURE 13.1
The telecommunication system from the telecommunication manager's viewpoint.

2 Costs resulting from the selection, allocation, and operational use of resources are to be minimized.

This model of the manager's situation, however, is seldom realistic for either the information system manager or the telecommunication manager. In most organizations, requirements are not clearly given, or if they are stated, they are neither analytically well-founded nor stable over even short intervals. Service managers must often estimate requirements and, faced with volatility and uncertainties with respect to real needs and benefits, must change their strategy and decision model to consider that:

1 Requirements are unknown and variable and therefore service capacities should be maximized.

2 Budgets are a constraint (rather than an objective to be minimized) and therefore should be made as large and unconstraining as possible.

To see more clearly how this situation may arise, we can examine the viewpoint of the general manager.

13.2.2   The General Manager's Viewpoint

The general manager sees the entire organization as a system comprised of several subsystems, as shown in Figure 13.2. The top management level is

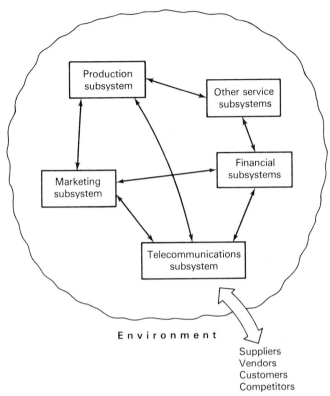

FIGURE 13.2
The telecommunication system from the general manager's viewpoint.

concerned primarily with the interaction of the organization as a system. It is also concerned with efficient, low-cost operation of the internal subsystems but cannot directly control the minutiae of operations within each organizational component. It must rely on lower-level managers to do that and can attempt to control their activities by laying down guidelines and procedures and obtaining periodic aggregate reports on activities, costs, and events.

This pattern of management division of activities and concerns usually works well but may allow certain kinds of organizational needs to fall unattended through the cracks. These gaps have most often been seen with regard to computer-based information services but are likely to apply to communications services, whether computer-related or not. The characteristics leading to organizational ineffectiveness in these service areas are:

1 The critical dependency of operational units on an internal service unit

2 The lack of sufficient common ground between operational units managers and the service unit managers and the unavailability of common language referents

3 The lack of sufficient theory or experimental wisdom to assess benefits or other impacts of new technology and system configurations

General managers who stand apart from and above both the operational units and the service units are generally in no better position to overcome these obstacles. Moreover, general managers are often unaware that the situation is as we have described it and needs any special effort. The assumption is often that the users and service providers can each express and work out their positions as to needs and capabilities. Why, they may ask, should these newer services be different from traditional services such as purchasing or building maintenance? But the combination of dynamic technological change, lack of understanding of impacts, and critical dependency makes the supply of information and communication services in a social system quite different from the supply of paper, pencils, and janitorial services.

Unaware of these differences, general managers see the telecommunications manager as fulfilling a production manager role and thereby responsible for minimizing costs of user-supplied requirements. General managers believe that they need only enter this picture as an arbiter over the demands of all user groups and over the total allowable budget.

As we have seen, however, given the gap in perceptions and realities, telecommunication managers are operating under a different model; they are likely to attempt to maximize service capabilities through the most extensive up-to-date technology available and therefore try to push the budgetary allowance as high as possible. We will examine how this gap might be closed so that the organization can aim to obtain higher net benefits after costs than it might with either of the two models previously described. But first, we must consider various decision analysis techniques that can be brought to bear on the problem.

13.2.3 Decision Analysis Techniques

We have redefined the initial cost-benefit approach discussed at the beginning of this chapter and broadened it in two ways: (1) to take into account hard-to-measure or noneconomic as well as direct economic impacts, and (2) to design and select a system alternative from among many possibilities rather than merely assessing one proposed new system, and to do so in a way that will tend to provide maximum new benefits.

Decision-Making Steps In general, the direction of our discussion leads toward describing a total process of decision making in which more than one analytical method is or can be used. The process follows the following general stages:

1 *Define the problem.* Define objectives, payoff measures to assess how well objectives are obtained, impact factors, and relationships between impact factors and objectives.

2 *Design a feasible solution.* A feasible solution to a decision problem is defined in a particular "setting" of those impact factors that are under the control of the decision maker which do not violate any existing constraints.

3 *Evaluate the solution.* Calculate or estimate the value of the payoffs that will be obtained by the currently considered possible solution.

4 *Assess the solution and accept or reject it.* If the current solution's payoffs are accepted, stop and implement the solution. If the current solution is not accepted, generate another possible solution.

Within this framework, the techniques of feasibility analysis, cost-benefit analysis, and cost-effectiveness analysis can be applied and differentiated from one another.

Feasibility Analysis   Feasibility analysis attempts to answer the question, Can it be done? This is a question that must be answered in the solution-generating stage in order to know whether or not a proposed solution violates any existing constraints.

Feasibility analysis can examine economic, technical, legal, and human behavioral or physical limits. Economic feasibility tests whether a proposed system is affordable; technical feasibility tests whether the technology exists or can be acquired; legal feasibility tests that no laws or regulations will be violated; and human feasibility analysis tries to assess whether people can actually be expected to behave in the ways the system will require.

Cost-Benefit Analysis   Cost-benefit analysis (also known as *profitability analysis*) attempts to answer the question: Is it worth doing? This is the concern of the evaluation stage. Evaluation is in terms of the new payoff values (benefits) minus the cost of the solution. If cost-benefit analysis alone were the determinant of acceptability of a solution, our acceptance-rejection stage would not be necessary, or at least it would be reduced to the trivial task of seeing if the result of the evaluation stage was greater than zero.

We prefer, however, to go beyond merely doing a cost-benefit analysis on one alternate in order to accept it if it provides any net benefit. We want to address the cost-effectiveness question: Is there another possible solution that would provide greater net benefits?

If more benefits can be delivered without incurring any higher costs, we would prefer them. Similarly, we would act in favor of attaining the same benefits for lower costs or simultaneously increasing benefits and lowering costs. This consideration of cost effectiveness can provide the assessment criterion for the acceptance decision stage. If we believe there is a more cost-effective solution we will not accept the current proposal and instead try to generate a better solution.

This description of the decision-making process still leaves considerable flexibility for specifying the precise procedures to be followed in each of the stages. The appropriate procedures to use will depend on (1) how much we know about the relationships involved in the decision problem, (2) whether or not we can measure the relationships and their impact on the objectives (that is, payoffs in terms of both benefits and costs), (3) how much time, effort, and cost we are willing to expend on the decision-making process itself (this implies, as we previously stated, that there is a meta-cost-benefit analysis that must be at least subjectively assessed on the value of a more extensive decision analysis process.

Types of Evaluation Three different major variations of the process described above that can be chosen are: optimization, heuristic search, and "satisficing."

An *optimization process* can be followed when all the relationships are expressed mathematically and have a mathematical form for which a general algorithm (iterative process) exists that guarantees finding a solution that will maximize the payoffs. Such an algorithm is the simplex method of linear programming (Charnes, Cooper, & Henderson, 1953). In this limited class of decision problem formulation, stages 2, 3, and 4 of decision analysis are repeated in a logical loop until the algorithm stops in stage 4 because the mathematical test applied finds that no solution can be better in terms of payoffs than the current solution. In this case, cost-effectiveness is guaranteed by the algorithm. Only highly structured, well-understood situations which we are willing and able to express in a precise mathematical form lend themselves to this formal optimization approach. Moreover, a mathematical model representing the situation is not sufficient to be able to optimize. An algorithm must also be known for which there is a mathematical proof of its ability to converge upon an optimal combination of the controllable impact factors (variables). It would seem that only limited aspects of telecommunication system design and evaluation would lend themselves to formal optimization. Conceptually, however, the optimal system selection problem is shown in Figure 13.3.

A *heuristic process* is similar to the optimization process just described in that the decision situation must be modeled explicitly and an algorithm can be defined to generate a solution, evaluate, and do an acceptance test. The main difference between this type of process and optimization is that the algorithm generally cannot be proven to stop at the best solution. A heuristic algorithm can be designed as useful even if it does not optimize as long as it results in a better solution than is likely to be obtained if the decision maker utilizes only unaided judgment and produces this better result within affordable time and cost constraints (again, a meta-cost-benefit test).

Both optimization and heuristic methods usually require the use of a computer and specialized software programs to make them economically feasible. Heuristic computer programs often must be written especially for the problem at hand, while optimization techniques are usually available as generalized packages which you supply with your problem definition and data.

"Satisficing" is a term first coined by Herbert Simon to describe the process of

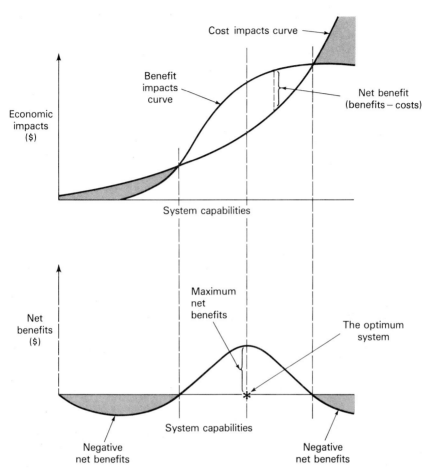

FIGURE 13.3
Cost-benefit relationships.

decision making often followed by managers. It is a process that can be followed by applying judgment to a rough concept or model of the decision problem when that is all one has and can afford. However, it can also be applied with the aid of a computer when one can more explicitly model the dependence of the payoffs on the impact factors. In either case, the algorithm or looping process through steps 2, 3, and 4 is different from both optimization and heuristic processes in the following respects:

1 No completely automatic procedure is defined with which to generate a feasible solution. The decision maker must do this.

2 Assessment and acceptance testing is done subjectively by the decision maker and not by means of a well-defined mathematical test. Moreover, the main question asked by the decision maker in this stage in a satisficing process is, Will everyone involved be satisfied with this solution (that is, find it acceptable)?

Note that stage 3 is still done and that this task can still be most efficiently done by a computer. This step is often characterized as simulation of a proposed strategy.

It can be seen that the satisficing criterion is likely to place little emphasis on cost-effectiveness unless a more cost-effective solution can be easily identified and seen to benefit one or more persons affected by the decision. At least a rough cost-benefit analysis must be done in this process to determine if the solution will have any net benefit and, therefore, an opportunity to satisfy everyone involved. This viewpoint and process assume the decision makers are rational in assessing their interests but must apply limited rationality in that they may not find it worthwhile or be able to search enough to find the optimal solution or even a better solution.

Satisficing can be seen as not necessarily a different and preferred way of thinking to that of the optimization or heuristic processes but merely a way of optimizing both the solution process and the original decision problem within available resources. It can also be seen as a process which can more easily lend itself to group decision making or to decisions that must satisfy others who have a stake in the process and who will assess benefits differently.

While judgment plays a major role in satisficing, it is important to recognize that those aspects of the problem that can be efficiently and formally assessed should be. In this manner, judgment can at least be focused where it is needed and can rest upon a better foundation. Computers can play a role in a satisficing process, probably most effectively by using the interactive, user-controlled type of approaches that have been called decision support systems (DSS). DSS utilizes either an interactive terminal or a personal computer.

In summary, we can say that optimization is the preferred process of decision making when it is both technically feasible and cost-beneficial. Heuristic search is the next best choice when it is technically feasible and cost-beneficial. When neither is cost-beneficial or feasible because of the complexity of the problem or the multiplicity of objectives and interested groups, then we resort to satisficing. In each of these processes, to one extent or another, with more or less judgmental assessments, the analytical approaches of feasibility analysis, cost-benefit analysis, and cost-effectiveness analysis are applicable.

13.2.4 Integrated Organizational Approach

We have pointed out the inadequacy of traditional organizational management approaches to the effective and efficient design and assessment of information and communication service systems. Before useful decision analysis approaches can be applied, an organizational framework is required to overcome gaps inherent in the "production manager" view of the role of the telecommunications manager.

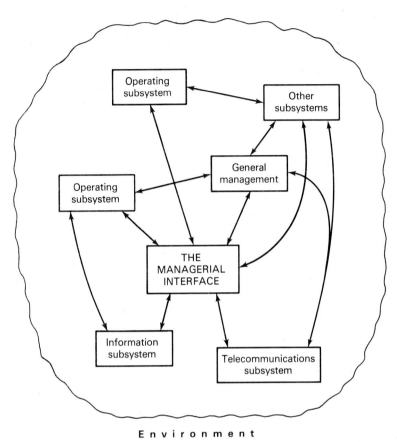

FIGURE 13.4
An integrated system view.

For the same reasons, new organizational arrangements have come into being in some organizations to better cope with information service needs. A main component of such arrangements is the introduction of a new breed of hybrid high-level manager into the organization—a manager with both technical expertise and, more importantly, an ability to speak the language and under-stand the needs of the general management community. This executive serves as a managerial interface between the user subsystems and the service subsystem (see Figure 13.4). While identifying with general management but not with any one functional area (as had been previously practiced when the computer unit managers often reported to a financial executive such as the controller), this executive has authority over the service subsystem. The "interface executive" does not, however, directly control everyday service operations. This task remains with a more specialized manager of the service unit. The interface executive is mainly oriented toward identifying and assessing user needs and potential benefits and initiating new systems approaches to delivering these benefits more efficiently. Such an executive does not have to resort to a shot-gun approach to supplying service capability because of the inability to assess real user requirements. The ability to make such assessments and to communicate with both users and technical managers is the stock in trade of this new hybrid executive.

This is the model we recommend for communication and information services. In fact, the connection between information and the means by which it is communicated is so close that the same executive should be responsible for both.

The techniques of cost-benefit analysis and other decision analysis methods discussed in this chapter would be applied by this manager (with required staff support) who would not only bring his or her own judgments to bear but also facilitate the participation of all key user managers. The old vision of the role of a telecommunications manager has been both too big and too small. No one person could be both the production manager and the executive interface. The old job needs to be separated into these two, thereby enabling those telecommunication managers who wish to remain closer to the technical management aspects to concentrate on them, while others may find a new career path toward general management.

REFERENCES

Anderson, L. G., and R. F. Settle, *Benefit-Cost Analysis: A Practical Guide,* Lexington, Mass.: Lexington Books, 1977.

Bob, Murray L., "Comment: Power of Babble," *The New York Times,* February 25, 1982.

Charnes, A., W. W. Cooper, and A. Henderson, *An Introduction to Linear Programming,* New York: Wiley, 1953.

Doren, Carl van, *Benjamin Franklin,* Garden City, N.Y.: Garden City, 1941.

Emery, James C., *Organizational Planning and Control Systems,* New York: Macmillan, 1950.

Grant, Eugene L., *Principles of Engineering Economy,* New York: Ronald Press, 1950.

Hackathorn, Richard D., and Peter G. W. Keen, "Organizational Strategy for Personal Computing in Decision Support Systems," *Management Information Systems Quarterly,* 1981, 5(3), pp. 21–27.

Thompson, J. D., *Organizations in Action,* New York: McGraw-Hill, 1967.

CHAPTER 14

REGULATION OF TELECOMMUNICATIONS IN THE UNITED STATES

Michael Botein
Communications Media Center
New York Law School
New York, NY 10013

Michael J. Sprague
Member, New York and
New Jersey Bars

14.1 PRELUDE TO REGULATION OF THE ELECTRONIC MASS MEDIA

14.1.1 Introduction

Government regulation of the electronic mass media varies in degree from one medium to another. At the very least, the federal government must be a "traffic cop" to prevent electrical interference among the many radio spectrum users. State and local authorities have elected to regulate other aspects of telecommunications. The extent to which government should regulate beyond technical standards is an area of continuing controversy.

Before discussing the regulation of telecommunications, it is important to note two characteristics inherent in the U.S. regulatory process. First, in a highly technical field like telecommunications, regulators are forever chasing innovation. Regulation is often reactionary, near-sighted, and responsive to the known impacts of a particular technological development. Second, regulators operate within the legislative process, whose policies change with the ideological climate of the day. A regulatory agency, such as the FCC, constantly receives formal and subtle pressures from numerous and diverse interest groups—from Westinghouse to the White House. The clash of these competing interests slows the administrative process and pushes regulatory proposals toward compromise positions.

It should also be noted that different types of media are regulated by different governmental bodies to different extents. For example, the FCC exercises virtually complete control over radio and television broadcast stations, but it shares authority over telephone companies with state public utilities commissions and leaves virtually all decisions about cable television to local governments.

14.1.2 Initial Radio Operations

Without glamor and fanfare, Frank Conrad, a Westinghouse engineer, helped to trigger the radio broadcasting boom in 1920 by transmitting music from a phonograph in his garage to a friend's receiver across town. Other amateur or "ham" radio operators in the suburban Pittsburgh area tuned in and liked what they heard. Soon, Conrad was playing songs requested by his "listeners."

The idea of using radio to entertain quickly attracted receiver manufacturers, such as Westinghouse, as a means of promoting sales. By the end of 1920, Westinghouse's station WFDA in Pittsburgh had become the nation's first licensed broadcaster. The station piqued the public's interest by broadcasting the Harding-Cox presidential election returns. Receiver sales boomed.

Within three years, 576 radio stations had licenses. Within a decade, Americans had purchased nearly 15 million receivers. The radio industry had arrived, but woefully inadequate regulation threatened the industry with self-destruction (Krasnow, Longley, & Terry, 1982).

14.1.3 Early Radio Regulation

The initial U.S. radio law, the Wireless Ship Act of 1910, concerned radio as a life-saving device. The act required ocean-going steamers with more than 50 persons to have a radio. The power to promulgate regulations to secure proper execution of the act was delegated to the secretary of commerce and labor.

The first comprehensive radio legislation, the Radio Act of 1912, was designed to prevent or minimize interference in the transmission and reception of distress signals from ships at sea. The act initiated government licensing of radio through the secretary of commerce and labor. As subsequently interpreted by federal courts and the Justice Department, however, the act actually gave the secretary little licensing discretion and no authority to promulgate regulations.

Then Secretary of Commerce Herbert Hoover thus could not prevent stations in the early 1920s from randomly changing frequencies and power output. Stations moved up and down the dial at will. Overlapping broadcasters and listeners looked to Congress for relief. As Hoover noted, it was the first time that business had begged for government intervention (Krasnow, Longley, & Terry, 1982).

Congress eventually responded with a compromise bill, the Radio Act of 1927, which created a temporary five-member Federal Radio Commission (FRC), with substantial regulatory authority. The act was premised on the principle that the airwaves are a public resource. Borrowing from prior public utility legislation, Congress designated the "public interest, convenience and necessity" as the FRC's licensing standard. The FRC had the power to assign frequencies, power levels, and hours of operation, as well as to adopt regulations that would insure efficient and equitable national radio service (Kahn, 1972).

14.1.4 AT&T, the Broadcaster

Although a broadcaster for only four years, the American Telephone & Telegraph Company left its lasting mark on the structure and economics of radio. AT&T joined with several other large corporations in anticipation of the mass marketing of radio. The Radio Corporation of America (RCA), originally just a patent pool, was formed in 1919 by General Electric, Westinghouse, and AT&T. Through cross-licensing agreements, GE and Westinghouse obtained the exclusive rights to sell receivers, while AT&T received the exclusive rights to manufacture and sell radio transmitters. The trio also agreed on the division of potential profits.

AT&T intended to become a major broadcaster, having already gained a near-monopoly position in the telephone industry. By 1920, AT&T's manufacturing arm, Western Electric, was operating three experimental stations. In July 1922, the first Bell-owned radio station began broadcasting from lower Manhattan. Additional Bell stations were soon in operation.

The phone giant had the manufacturing, research, and capital resources to dominate the infant radio industry. AT&T applied the economic rationale of the phone business—let the user pay—to broadcasting. Its New York station was the first station to sell time and thus an effective means of financing its programming. By 1926 U.S. broadcasting was supported by commercials (Brooks, 1972).

Utilizing its nationwide telephone system, AT&T interconnected its 17 stations to create the first radio network. By 1925, the Bell network reached 60 percent of the radio receivers in the United States. The economic advantages of a network included consolidation of program production and large audiences for advertisers.

As the dominant telephone operator, AT&T was able to stifle radio competitors by denying them access to its wire network. Some competitors were forced to use less efficient telegraph wires for networking. In 1926, Bell abandoned its dream of becoming the nation's dominant broadcaster, however; it sold its radio stations and concentrated on the telephone business.

14.1.5 The Communications Act of 1934

Radio prospered during the depression, providing "free" entertainment to millions. As the New Deal began to emerge, President Roosevelt sought to unify federal regulation of interstate communication within a single agency.

Congress responded with the Communications Act of 1934, which created the Federal Communications Commission, an independent regulatory agency headed by a seven-member board having no more than four members of the same political party. The act consolidated telegraph and telephone regulation, formerly within the jurisdiction of the Interstate Commerce Commission, with radio regulation. The act also marked the beginning of serious federal regulation and supervision of the electronic communication field. The regulatory tilt was toward the public "interest, convenience and necessity"—the licensing standard lifted from the 1927 act (Emery, 1970).

Largely staffed by reformers, the new commission immediately began an investigation of the telephone industry and undertook a congressional-ordered probe of AT&T a year later. This intense scrutiny of industry was a far cry from passive ICC oversight.

14.2 THE PARAMETERS OF FEDERAL JURISDICTION

Congress has the constitutional power to regulate all aspects of interstate electronic communication. The Constitution's commerce clause explicitly gives Congress authority to regulate all "interstate and foreign commerce." Thus, Congress has authority over communication industries as diverse as telephones, satellites, and citizens band radios.

Since the New Deal era, federal courts have upheld and expanded congressional regulatory authority under the commerce clause to a point at which any business involving more than one state may fall within the stream of "interstate commerce." For example, a cable television operator may hold the franchise of a single community in state A. Yet, because the operator obtains programming, such as Home Box Office, from corporations in other states, the cable system would fall within Congress's regulatory reach through the commerce clause.

Prior to examining the outer boundaries of Congress's communication authority, however, it may be useful to set out the parameters of constitutional guarantees.

14.2.2 Threshold Requirement of State Action

The constitutional limitations on telecommunication regulation prohibit public rather than private action—a concept normally referred to as "state action." In order to qualify for constitutional protection, not only must a person have some type of constitutional right, but he or she must also be able to show infringement of that right by a federal, state, local, or other governmental body. For example, the first amendment prohibits a governmental authority from denying use of a public meeting hall to a group with unpopular views; private owners, however, may discriminate to their heart's content in making a hall available (Gunther, 1978).

This requirement of state action may seem technical and legalistic. To a certain extent, of course, it is based upon a literal reading of the Constitution, which protects individual rights by stating that "no State" may deny certain rights. The state action requirement initially evolved out of the founding fathers' fear of undue governmental control, which they had experienced in England. To a certain extent, however, the state action requirement fulfills a very pragmatic role by restricting the courts' roles in protecting constitutional rights. Since most federal and state courts are overwhelmed by their existing caseloads, application of constitutional rights to private parties would deluge the courts with an unmanageable amount of litigation. In effect, the Constitution passes the buck to Congress, administrative agencies, state legislatures, and local governments, by allowing them to pass statutes or promulgate regulations against private infringements of individual rights. For example, the Constitution does not prohibit private discrimination in employment; but the Congress and most state legislatures have filled in this gap with equal employment opportunity statutes.

14.2.3 The First Amendment

The First Amendment to the Constitution states that no government may infringe the "freedom of the press." Consequently, this is an area in which Congress's commerce clause powers may conflict with a constitutional guarantee.

This free-speech clause has received a variety of interpretations over the years as applied to different media—newspapers, television, and cable. The Supreme Court consistently has invalidated restrictions upon the content of print media, such as newspapers and magazines. As late as 1974, the Court struck down a state statute which imposed upon newspapers basically the same equal-time requirements routinely applied to broadcasters by requiring newspapers to afford equal space to competing political candidates. In *Miami Herald v. Tornillo* (1974) the Court reasoned that the print media simply were different from and entitled to a higher degree of protection than the electronic media. This distinction between print and electronic media may make little sense in either legal or pragmatic terms; nevertheless, it remains one of the linchpins of First Amendment doctrine.

By comparison, the Court has been relatively free in allowing at least limited regulation of radio and television licensees. As early reasoning behind this doctrine was that the federal government could regulate broadcasters more extensively than newspapers because there was a "scarcity" of broadcast frequencies, thus requiring the federal government to police the practices of quasi-monopolistic broadcasters (*National Broadcasting v. United States*, 1943). This approach obviously is subject to a number of questions. Not only are there many more broadcast stations than newspapers in this country, but most communities have a number of dormant broadcast frequencies which never have been applied for because of economic reasons. Nevertheless, the scarcity doctrine still appears to be good law today.

At the other end of the spectrum, common carriers—telephone, telegraph, and satellite companies such as AT&T—have few or no First Amendment rights. The rationale is that a common carrier merely conveys a message from one place to another for any financially qualified user and has no editorial discretion. If any

First Amendment rights exist as to common carriers, they would attach to the users—that is, the actual communicators—rather than to the carriers.

Cable television's place in this First Amendment hierarchy is unclear. Cable operators exercise some editorial discretion in choosing the satellite services—as well as in producing the local origination programming—which they offer to subscribers. Aside from locally originated programs, however, cable operators generally have no significant day-to-day control over the programming which their systems carry.

Moreover, the First Amendment operates as both a sword and a shield for the media: it is a sword to the extent that it imposes affirmative obligations upon the media and a shield to the extent that it protects the media from undue governmental interference in content.

The sword, or access, aspect of the First Amendment allows a person or firm to distribute its own message over a medium, that is, a cable or broadcast channel. But it seems to have little or no application to traditional print media under the print-electronic dichotomy. Indeed, the Supreme Court has held that the First Amendment not only does not require access to newspapers but also prohibits state statutes requiring such access (*Miami Herald v. Tornillo,* 1974).

The status of the electronic media is less clear. In 1969 the Supreme Court stated that "it is the right of the viewers and listeners which is paramount" in sustaining the FCC's fairness doctrine requirements. (This rule requires broadcasters to present contrasting viewpoints on "controversial issues of public importance.") The Court also indicated that the First Amendment did not impose general access obligations on broadcasters, but that Congress could impose such requirements (*CBS v. Democratic National Committee,* 1973). Most recently, the Supreme Court invalidated the FCC's requirements for access channels on cable television systems, on the ground that the FCC lacked sufficient statutory authority under the Communications Act of 1934 to impose the requirements. But the Court also noted that the cable industry's First Amendment arguments as to the unconstitutionality of access requirements had some weight. *(Midwest)*

The Supreme Court's rather rambling discourses from 1969 to 1979 on the access to the media thus create a number of uncertainties. On the one hand, the Court has not unilaterally imposed a mandatory right of access under the First Amendment. On the other hand, the Court has held that such requirements—whether imposed by federal, state, or local governments—do not necessarily violate the First Amendment. The Court thus seems to have left a rather large gray area within which governments may operate in formulating access requirements.

The Court also has been ambiguous as to the shield, or protective side, of First Amendment doctrine. Traditionally, the Court has invalidated any type of prior restraint on dissemination of information, that is, any governmental prohibition on publishing or transmitting information. A classic example of this type of prior restraint is an injunction barring distribution of a newspaper or magazine.

These strict limitations on prior restraints, however, do not apply to subsequent punishment—criminal penalties—for obscene, indecent, or defamatory programming. Subsequent punishment by way of fines and even imprisonment in a criminal proceeding is generally permissible. The constitutional theory is that subsequent punishment may deter a programmer from transmitting certain types of material but does not prohibit it from airing a program in the first place.

In allowing the FCC to deny a license renewal because of indecent broadcasting, the Supreme Court relied primarily upon the fact that radio and television broadcasts were freely available to children—particularly at times of the day during which children might be listening or watching. This may not be the case with media such as cable television or subscription television however, for a variety of reasons. First, a cable operator needs a community's permission to wire it; a cable operator's past track record in this regard presumably forms at least part of a local government's decision about whether to allow a particular cable operator to wire its community. Second, even if a cable operator has a franchise, it must market its programming to each individual potential subscriber in a community. Any subscriber is free to refuse either cable service in general or a particular tier—perhaps with pornographic material—as he or she sees fit. Finally, precisely because of the problem of adult programming, many cable operators offer lock-out boxes or parental-guidance keys at little or no charge to allow parents to prevent their children from viewing offensive programs. In terms of obscenity, cable and some of the other new technologies thus may be far different from broadcast television and closer to the print media.

14.2.4 The Tenth Amendment

As with any constitutional provision, there very well may be some outer limits on Congress's commerce clause powers. Another provision in the Constitution, the Tenth Amendment, specifies that powers not given to Congress are retained by state—and thus local—governments. Congress presumably cannot intrude upon at least some activities of state governments or actions of local governments taken under delegated state authority.

Since the Supreme Court in recent years has decided only one major case on this point (*National League of Cities v. Usery,* 1976), it is rather difficult to predict the extent of state and local governments' powers under the Tenth Amendment. The Tenth Amendment would probably deny Congress jurisdiction only as to the internal functionings of a municipality—for example, employee safety regulations, equal employment opportunity rules, accounting procedures, and the like. Under this analysis, the Congress presumably could preempt state or local governments from most traditional types of cable regulation. It is more questionable, however, whether Congress could move into areas such as operation of a government access channel, EEO policies, and the like.

As a general rule, a state may preempt any type of municipal regulation. There has been a running and intensifying debate between cities and cable operators over state regulation of cable television. Many cable franchises prefer state to local regulation because most state authorities tend to be deregulatory in nature.

14.3   THE JURISDICTION OF THE FEDERAL COMMUNICATIONS COMMISSION

14.3.1   Types of Jurisdiction

The FCC has a variety of jurisdictional powers. First, it has jurisdiction under Title II of the Communications Act of 1934 over any "common carrier," which essentially is an entity, such as a telephone company, holding itself out to carry messages from one member of the general public to another for a set fee. Title II jurisdiction authorizes the FCC to set rates and routes and regulate other practices of common carriers. (This jurisdiction is known as Title II power, since it comes from the second part, or title, of the act.)

Many business communications services are common carriers. For example, the FCC is just now allowing the development of "cellular radio," a system which uses radio waves to provide instant telephone service from any location. Similarly, the Multipoint Distribution Service (MDS), used for high-speed data transmission, is also a common carrier.

The FCC also regulates under Title III of the act "any apparatus for the transmission of energy or communications or signals by radio." This permits FCC regulation of any user of the radio frequency spectrum for over-the-air transmissions. (This jurisdiction is known as Title III power, since it comes from the third part, or title, of the act.)

Title III authority breaks down into three distinct subcategories of jurisdiction, the most visible being regulation of radio and television stations. Title III contains special provisions applicable only to broadcasters, such as the equal-time and fairness-doctrine rules. A second type of Title III jurisdiction concerns over-the-air transmissions by a common carrier, such as a satellite. This service can be regulated under Title II as well. Third, Title III permits FCC regulation of radio spectrum users that are neither broadcasters nor common carriers, such as citizens band radio operators or a taxi radio-dispatch system. These services are generally lumped together under the generic heading of "private radio."

A number of business services are regulated as private radio users of the spectrum. Perhaps the most significant new development in this area is the FCC's recent authorization—after many years—of the Operational Fixed Service (OFS). This is basically a high-frequency, wide-bandwidth service for the high-speed transmission of data. Thus, in many ways it is similar to MDS; for largely historical reasons, however, MDS is regulated as a common carrier, and OFS as a private radio service. Another private radio service is the Digital Termination Service (DTS), which the FCC is still considering. Like MDS and OFS, DTS can provide data transmission; because its available bandwidth is more limited than that of either MDS or OFS, however, its transmission speed is somewhat lower.

Finally, the FCC wields a vaguely defined type of implied or residual jurisdiction over activities not falling squarely within either Title II or Title III. Perhaps the most striking example of this so-called reasonably ancillary jurisdiction is the FCC's limited regulation of cable television.

14.3.2 Common Carriers

The Communications Act of 1934 defines a common carrier as a "common carrier for hire in interstate or foreign communications by wire or radio or in interstate or foreign radio transmission of energy." In less circular terms, a common carrier is a firm which holds itself out by its business practice or is required by law to provide transmission services to any properly qualified customer.

A common carrier controls the transmission hardware and holds these facilities out for lease by the public on a nondiscriminatory basis, often pursuant to an FCC tariff. A common carrier does not control the content of the information transmitted over its facilities. Telephone companies, MDS, and communication satellites are common carriers.

As a result of the AT&T divestiture, the old AT&T services will end up regulated partially as common carriers and partially as private radio services. The divested Bell Operating Companies will continue to be regulated as common carriers—primarily by state agencies, and only secondarily (to the extent they cross state lines) by the FCC. Most of the remaining AT&T services will be largely unregulated, particularly activities such as provision of computer or enhanced services; Long Lines will continue to be subject to common carrier regulation by the FCC.

Telephone Regulation   Regulation of the telephone industry stems from the principle of economies of scale—the theory that certain goods or services are most inexpensively delivered by a single firm or monopoly. Interstate telephone service is regulated by the FCC, while local or intrastate service is subject to regulation by state public utilities commissions.

As regulated monopolies, telephone companies must apply continuously to the FCC and state boards for rate increases. The FCC passes upon interstate rates, state commissions on intrastate rates. Regulators must publish these applications and conduct public hearings prior to rendering a decision. In theory, tariffs are designed to permit the phone company a predetermined rate of return.

AT&T was restricted to the telephone business pursuant to a 1956 consent decree, which terminated an antitrust suit brought by the Justice Department. AT&T settled a later antitrust case by divesting itself of 22 local operating companies. In exchange, the government withdrew its antitrust case and amended the 1956 consent decree to permit the unregulated subsidiaries of AT&T to enter unregulated fields, such as the data and computer industries.

AT&T retains control of its research and development arm, Bell Labs; its manufacturing arm, Western Electric; and its regulated long-distance subsidiary, Long Lines Division. The FCC supported the settlement but urged that the local operating companies also be permitted to enter unregulated fields.

Direct Broadcast Satellites (DBS)   Satellite transmissions use a three-step process. An information provider delivers programming to an "uplink" transmitter, which sends a signal to a satellite transponder. This in turn transmits the signal to the "earth station" antennas of broadcasters, cable television operators, telephone companies, or other telecommunications businesses. Most current domestic satellites *(domsats)* operate with comparatively low power and thus require large and expensive antennas (earth stations) to be received. Hence, their use thus far has been limited mainly to large businesses.

DBS service would circumvent broadcasters and cable systems by transmitting information or programming at much higher power than domsats, directly to consumers whose homes are equipped with a meter-wide antenna receiver. A DBS subscriber would receive a device to unscramble the satellite signal.

Regulation of DBS poses a novel question for the FCC, since program delivery to the public is characteristic of a broadcaster, while satellites are regulated as common carriers. However, the FCC has decided to adopt a hands-off approach to DBS for the time being. Once the technology comes on line, some form of regulation may evolve.

Multipoint Distribution Service (MDS)   As noted before, a third type of common carrier is the multipoint distribution service, which transmits high-frequency signals from an omnidirectional antenna. MDS operates on a small portion of the electromagnetic spectrum, far above the frequencies which conventional television sets can receive. Initiated in 1962, MDS is used to transmit pay television programming, high-speed computer data, and various forms of communication suitable for radio transmission.

An MDS licensee leases its facilities on a nondiscriminatory basis in accordance with FCC tariffs. The FCC prohibits MDS operators from leasing more than half its transmission time to any one customer. Although the FCC categorizes MDS as a common carrier, it actually treats it as a hybrid of broadcasting and common carriage. In fact, most MDS stations offer much the same type of pay programming as cable systems and STV operations.

14.3.3 Broadcasters

Title III of the act gives the FCC jurisdiction over the use of any "apparatus for the transmission of energy communications or signals by radio in interstate or foreign commerce." This subjects all users of the radio spectrum for over-the-air transmission to FCC licensing.

Licenses are awarded and renewed based on the "public interest, convenience and necessity." In theory, the FCC considers an applicant's character and legal and financial qualifications as well as proposed programming format. Broadcast licenses confer exclusive use of the assigned frequencies within a specific area, with the corresponding protection against interference from other channels.

The current Washington craze is deregulation, or decreasing government interference in the marketplace. To this end, the FCC has eased license renewal standards and eliminated many reporting and record-keeping rules.

Although it is a formal administrative procedure, the broadcast license renewal process essentially has been ritualistic, with licenses denied only to a handful of stations found guilty of gross misconduct—generally offenses such as lying to the FCC or rigging promotional contests. A fully evidentiary hearing upon notice is necessary before refusing to renew a license. Even when a denial is voted, the broadcaster may continue to operate for years while the decision is appealed. The FCC can also impose milder sanctions, such as fines and short-term renewals. Quite naturally, these are much more common than denial of license renewals.

The trend is toward more permanency in broadcast licensing. In 1981, Congress extended broadcasters' license terms from three to five years for television, and from three to seven years for radio. And the FCC wants to make it harder for a competitor to vie for a license at renewal times, when requesting the FCC to give them an incumbent broadcaster's license. Challengers would have no right to a "comparative hearing," unless a preliminary review determined that a renewal applicant did not provide responsive service to its community or was guilty of a serious broadcast-related dereliction.

Networks Broadcasting's major economic programming and opinion-shaping power is the television network triumvirate: ABC, CBS, and NBC. The trio compete fiercely for rating shares but work hand-in-hand on most regulatory matters. Recently all three have faced increased competition from satellite-cable networks as well as public broadcasting. The networks link their "flagship" or owned-and-operated (O&O) stations by satellite to scores of affiliated, independently owned stations, thereby creating a nationwide program distribution system, which commands the premium advertising rates.

The FCC has no direct jurisdiction over the networks, except for license renewals of flagship of affiliated stations. However, it has found indirect ways to regulate the networks, generally by forbidding affiliates from engaging in particular business practices with the networks—for example, taking more than a certain amount of network programming.

Noncommercial Broadcasters In 1967, Congress laid the cornerstone for the present system on public broadcasting with the passage of the Public Broadcasting Act. The act created a nonprofit Corporation for Public Broadcasting (CPB) the production of national programming, and channel federal funds to local facilities. Under the act, CPB is prohibited from owning or operating any broadcast station, cable television system, or production facility. Management was vested in a CPB board of fifteen presidential appointees, balanced by political affiliation.

To achieve its mandate of establishing a national system, CPB joined with industry representatives in 1970 to create the Public Broadcasting System (PBS) and National Public Radio (NPR). Both PBS and NPR are governed by representatives of member broadcast facilities. NPR produces programming for national distribution, however, using CPB-allocated funds, while PBS obtains its programs from its member stations and does not produce programs itself.

In terms of audience size, public television plays a very small role in broadcasting in the United States, although its television network encompasses 295 stations. PBS has nationwide satellite interconnection system for its member stations, which reach approximately 87 percent of the nation's households. By contrast, in most other countries broadcasting is predominantly a state-owned enterprise (Sprague, 1980).

Subscription Television (STV) A subscription television licensee delivers pay programming on VHF or UHF frequencies already allocated for conventional television. STV is the only type of broadcast station—as opposed to cable, MDS, or DBS—authorized to deliver pay programming.

Since STV operators broadcast over conventional television channels, their signals can be picked up by any receiver. An STV transmission thus must be scrambled or coded in order to exclude free riders. Each subscriber has a terminal unit to unscramble or decode an STV signal for viewing.

Cable Television Unlike most other electronic media, there is virtually no federal regulation of cable television. As noted below, the FCC's jurisdiction over cable is unclear and arguably quite limited. Moreover, the FCC has deregulated cable almost entirely. Although 11 states currently regulate cable to some extent, most impose only minimal requirements. As a result, most cable regulation tends to focus—almost by default—on local franchising processes.

A cable operator needs a franchise from the community to be served. A franchise is basically just permission to use a city's streets and other public property, although it may also contain a wide variety of regulatory provisions, such as fees to be paid to the city, subscriber complaint procedures, service standards, or requirements of access channels for public use. In what is usually a fierce bidding war for the right to wire a community, an applicant tries to present a diversified package of programming at the lowest possible price to potential subscribers. The community governing body, the city council, board, and the like, usually awards a cable franchise in return for a percentage of the operator's gross revenues and a package of regulatory requirements.

The cable franchising process is an important time for local business interests to be heard. To an increasing extent, local governments are sensitive to the business communities' need for low-cost, high-speed, reliable data transmission services. Cable naturally is an ideal medium for this type of application, since its high bandwidth allows it to carry huge amounts of data. For example, a single cable can carry far more data than an MDS, OFS, and DTS station operating simultaneously. Many franchises today thus require a cable operator to provide all or part of a cable as a separate institutional loop for data transmission.

In a regulatory sense, a cable operator is neither a broadcaster nor a common carrier. It is thus not surprising then that the FCC's jurisdiction over cable is still somewhat unclear. The FCC initially premised its authority over cable on the theory that cable had an adverse economic impact upon conventional television broadcasting and that regulation thus was necessary to protect the public's ability to receive "free" television. In *United States v. Southwestern Cable Co.* (1968) the Supreme Court basically endorsed this theory, stating that the FCC's authority over cable was limited to protecting "free" broadcast television. In a 1972 case, the Court indicated that the FCC could regulate cable for a variety of public interest purposes (*United States v. Midwest Video Corp.,* 1972). But in 1979, the Court once again gave the Commission's jurisdiction a very restrictive interpretation (*United States v. Midwest Video Corp.,* 1979). At the present time, it is difficult to predict the extent of the FCC's jurisdiction over cable.

14.4 PLAYERS IN THE COMMUNICATIONS POLICY GAME

14.4.1 The Lineup

Although an independent regulatory agency such as the FCC is characterized as an arm of Congress, the Senate and House of Representatives are only two of the many players in the FCC's policy game. While Congress is certainly the most prominent influence on FCC action (or inaction), the executive branch, the courts, industry, and the public routinely affect FCC decision making.

The roles of the three governmental branches are defined by separation-of-powers principles, whose purpose is the dispersal of government authority in order to prevent absolutism, as well as the allocation of functions to expert agencies. The separation-of-powers doctrine has been interpreted broadly enough, however, not to impede effective government operations.

14.4.2 Congress

Congress, of course, has the central role in receiving the powers it delegates to the FCC. In creating the FCC, Congress broadly defined the substantive and procedural parameters within which the agency would operate.

In the communications field, the Senate has the constitutional power of advice and consent on presidential nominations of FCC commissioners. A lot of behind-the-scenes bargaining goes on, however, which gives Congress a strong voice in the selection of commissioners. Another effective congressional control is appropriations power. Annual budget hearings give both houses of Congress a chance to review FCC action and tell agency officials what is expected of them.

Congressional committees also have oversight responsibilities. Although a typical oversight hearing before a congressional committee has no direct legal impact, it gives members of Congress an opportunity to give low-visibility instructions to the FCC on a particular regulatory issue.

The burgeoning federal bureaucracy has come under attack in recent years. The Communications Act of 1934 granted a broad mandate to the FCC because Congress has neither the desire nor the expertise to grapple with the complex and time-consuming process of telecommunications regulation. But many observers on Capitol Hill feel that regulation has gone too far.

As a result, there have been several recent legislative proposals designed to check administrative discretion. These proposals include a regulatory reform act, which would be the first major overhaul of administrative procedure since 1946. Generally, the reform act would make adoption of regulations more difficult, while giving Congress, the courts, and even the White House greater powers in dealing with independent agencies like the FCC. Other pending bills would require a cost-benefit analysis of the economic impact on business of any major regulation and mandate agency review of every regulation now on the books.

Finally, Congress can keep a tight rein on agencies like the FCC with a legislative veto, which permits both the House and the Senate to reject any agency-adopted regulation upon a majority vote. To date, however, there is no statute applying the legislative-veto concept to the FCC.

14.4.3 The Executive Branch

Like most congressional agencies, the FCC does not deal with the White House except on matters of great national or international significance. But the executive branch can impose a general regulatory philosophy on the FCC.

The president can influence FCC policy most directly through the nomination of commissioners. Since few FCC commissioners serve out their full seven-year terms, every president has the opportunity to fill several seats—and often enough to create a majority on the commission. For example, President Reagan filled four seats in his first six months in office. An FCC nominee must obtain approval of the Senate, of course, which is subject to influence from industry lobbyists. Nominees thus rarely exhibit an anti-industry outlook.

The White House also influences FCC policy indirectly through its appointments to the federal bench and to quasi-public corporations such as CPB and the Communications Satellite Corporation (Comsat).

Executive branch agencies, such as the Justice and Commerce departments, interact with the FCC. For example, the Justice Department regularly files comments in FCC proceedings and sometimes challenges its actions in court when antitrust issues arise. Moreover, the Justice Department is technically the FCC's lawyer on most appeals and thus can shape both FCC litigation positions and decisions to appeal particular cases.

During the Carter administration, the executive branch National Telecommunications and Information Administration (NTIA) was quite active in recommending communications policy to the president and the FCC. Under the Reagan administration, however, NTIA lost much of its funding and independence.

14.4.4 The Judiciary

Courts can review and revise the FCC's actions for violations of the Constitution, the Communications Act, and the Administrative Procedure Act. In constitutional terms, judicial review acts as a restraint on administrative, legislative, and executive branch action. The lower federal courts, and ultimately the Supreme Court, are the final arbiters of constitutional questions—such as whether an FCC rule infringes upon free-speech rights.

The Communications Act provides that appeals from FCC licensing decisions be filed in the United States Court of Appeals for the District of Columbia Circuit. But appeals of FCC rules may be filed in any of the 11 circuit courts of appeals in which an appealing party does business. Court of appeals decisions are final, subject to Supreme Court review by a writ of certiorari, a discretionary decision allowing the Court to pick and choose which cases it will hear. Since all licensing appeals must be heard by the D.C. circuit, this court has developed its own expertise. Its numerous communications opinions have shaped licensing policy.

14.4.5 The Industries

Telecommunications companies spend millions of dollars annually to influence FCC action to gain or maintain competitive advantage. Financially powerful communications entities, such as AT&T or the television networks, employ full-time lobbyists who present their employers' case directly to congressional and commission personnel.

In addition, all industries are represented before the FCC and Congress by a variety of trade associations. For example, in the broadcasting field, the National Association of Broadcasters is the leading industry voice. The NAB represents an economically diverse membership of more than 5000 radio and television station licensees. This diverse membership often prevents the NAB from providing a unified front. Moreover, a potent and separate lobby among the NAB's membership is the networks.

But the image of industry lobbyists wining and dining FCC staff members is largely inaccurate. FCC procedures prohibit unreported communications with persons having a direct or indirect interest in the outcome of an FCC proceeding. These ex parte rules require that an interested party be made aware of a communication between an interested party and commissioner or FCC staff member.

14.4.6 The Public

Although a single user's complaint in theory can bring the FCC's wrath down upon any regulated business, the public is generally the least influential player in the communication policy game.

Public-interest groups were given the ability—or, in legal terms, *standing*—to intervene in licensing procedures in a 1966 D.C. circuit decision written by Judge Warren Burger. In *Office of Communication of United Church of Christ v. FCC* (1966) Judge Burger wrote that citizen input was essential in order that holders of broadcasting licenses be responsible to the needs of their communities.

The heyday of the citizens group movement at the FCC parallels the civil rights movement of the late 1960s and early 1970s. Even the FCC got caught up in the spirit and created a Consumer Assistance Office in 1976. But the overall impact of citizen groups has begun to wane; funding for liberal-based activists has dried up considerably. Some liberal groups have been replaced by conservative cousins, whose aim is to rid television of "sex and violence."

14.5 CONCLUSION

Managers must be aware of this frustratingly complex and rapidly changing regulatory environment. Although many of the principles discussed above may seem highly technical, they have a significant impact on the type and availability of telecommunications services. To take a low-visibility example, the FCC's delay in authorizing OFS and increasing the number of MDS channels created headaches for managers for years. Understanding the legal, regulatory, and often political dimensions of telecommunications policy makes it possible for managers to deal with present problems and plan for future developments.

BIBLIOGRAPHY

Brooks, J., *Telephone: The First Hundred Years,* New York: Harper and Row, 1976.

CBS v. Democratic National Committee, 412 U.S. 94 (1973).

Emery, W. *Broadcasting and Government,* East Lansing, MI: Michigan State University Press, 1971.

FCC v. Pacifica Foundation, 438 U.S. 726 (1978).

Gunther, G., *Cases and Materials on Constitutional Law* (9th ed.), Mineola, N.Y.: Foundation Press, 1978.

Kahn, F., *Documents of American Broadcasting*, Englewood Cliffs, N.J.: Prentice-Hall, 1973.

Krasnow, E., Longley, L., and Terry, H., *The Politics of Broadcast Regulation*, New York: St. Martin's Press, 1982.

Miami Herald Pub. Co. v. Tornillo, 418 U.S. 241 (1974).

National Broadcasting Co. v. United States, 319 U.S. 190, 213 (1943).

National League of Cities v. Usery, 426 U.S. 833 (1976).

Office of Communication of United Church of Christ v. FCC, 359 F.2d 994 (D.C. Cir. 1966).

Sprague, M., *New Communications Media and Public Broadcasting: Impacts and Opportunities*, New York: New York Law School, 1980.

United States v. Midwest Video Corp., 406 U.S. 649 (1972).

United States v. Midwest Video Corp., 440 U.S. 689 (1979).

United States v. Southwestern Cable Co., 392 U.S. 157 (1968).

CHAPTER 15

INTERNATIONAL TELECOMMUNICATIONS

Alan E. Negus
Consultant in Information Systems and Services
Biggleswade, Bedfordshire, U.K. SG18 8DU

15.1 INTRODUCTION

The provision and use of international telecommunications facilities is a far more complex matter than is the case for purely national services, for both technical and regulatory reasons. It has been said that the international telephone network, especially with the widespread introduction of international subscriber dialing, is the most complex technological system developed by humanity.

In one sense, international telecommunications are no different from national services, as they encompass the same techniques and methods and the same political and commercial considerations. Inevitably, however, the international situation is far more complicated, not just because of the increase in scale, but because different standards and conventions have been adopted and different attitudes and points of view prevail.

By and large, the technical aspects are covered elsewhere in this book, where the different methods of transmission, some of the difficulties of transferring from one medium to another, and the different requirements of alternate routing systems are raised. On an international scale the problems become more apparent, and ways must be found to ensure smooth interconnection, for example, coping with different signaling methods where direct dialing is to be provided, or allowing for the connection of leased circuits with slightly differing characteristics. Obviously, different techniques are more or less favored depending on circumstances. Satellite transmission provides the most outstanding example; it is particularly attractive for international transmission, not only for its ability to nullify the effects of distance and hostile terrain but also for the degree of independence it gives from changing political attitudes, where routes relying on cable or line-of-sight microwave links are clearly vulnerable.

Here, we are concerned with the organization of international telecommunications and regulatory issues and how they affect the user; technical matters are discussed only with reference to the need for international agreement on standards.

Naturally, quite involved administrative and organizational arrangements are necessary to ensure an equitable division of traffic and revenues, in addition to both national and international regulation of traffic. In a work of this nature it is therefore quite impossible to cover organizational and regulatory issues in great detail, as the amount of variation between one route and another, and between one type of traffic and another, is too great. Moreover, changes are constantly occurring, particularly in the area of tariffs, where the relative costs of dialed voice circuits, leased circuits, and special data networks demand constant reassessment. Consequently, it is always advisable for the user to seek the advice of the local service provider for the most recent information pertaining to any desired communication channel.

In most countries, and for most users, access to international telecommunications facilities is provided by the same organization that provides national services. This chapter, therefore, starts with a short section to illustrate the different arrangements that may apply. It is followed by a section describing the arrangements for the provision of international services in terms of the organizations providing those services. There are many issues which affect regulation of international traffic. The more important of these, which include technical, commercial, and political aspects, are discussed separately, without reference to specific instances, because of the impossibility of giving a comprehensive treatment that could remain accurate in a rapidly developing situation. The final section covers the international organizations that deal with regulation and cooperation between service providers.

It should be noted that some organizations have multiple responsibilities, and the divisions are not always clear. There are the bodies that provide domestic or internal services. Others provide only—or mainly—international links, and still others are concerned with the arrangements for cooperation between various service providers. Although this breakdown is followed in this chapter, it should be stressed that some organizations fall into more than one of these categories.

15.2 PROVISION OF DOMESTIC SERVICES

As noted earlier, access to international telecommunications facilities is almost invariably via the same organization as provides domestic services, even though other organizations may be involved in providing the service. There are some exceptions to this rule—in the case of large users or highly specialized services, for example—but even in those cases, some of the facilities may be provided by the domestic service provider.

The situation in the United States, as described in Chapter 14, is far from typical. Indeed, in most other countries there is a state monopoly, where services are provided either by a state-owned corporation or, more usually, by a government department, which is often responsible for both telecommunications and postal services. The organizations go under a variety of names but are often referred to as PTTs. Naturally, the detailed arrangements differ from country to country, and in some cases there has been a move to relax the state monopoly.

In the United Kingdom there has been a gradual tendency to relax the monopoly. For many years, both post and telecommunications were provided by the General Post Office, or GPO as it was known, with its own minister, the Postmaster General. (That is with the exception of telephone service in the city of Hull, which was, and is, operated by the local municipal authority—the only remaining example of a pattern that was common in Britain before the GPO took over the service from many different franchise holders.) Following the Post Office Act of 1970 there was a change whereby the GPO became a public corporation, rather like other state enterprises such as the Gas Board, instead of being a separate government department. This had some implications for the staff involved and for the chain of command to the government; no longer was there a minister solely responsible for the British Post Office Corporation, as the new organization was known. On the other hand, most users would distinguish little change. More recently the BPO has been split into two separate public corporations—the Post Office and British Telecom (BT), which is responsible for telecommunications services. These changes brought about changes in attitude, of course, but the state monopoly remains. However, at about the time of the split there was a liberalization of British Telecom's monopoly; other suppliers were able to offer, subject to government regulation, both communication channels and equipment to attach to the BT network, as well as other services such as electronic mail, using the BT network. At the time of writing a proposal is being seriously considered by the government to further relax the state monopoly by selling 51 percent of BT to private investors, although a major motivation for this proposed change is to give BT the ability to raise private finance for capital projects.

What the effect of these changes will be remains to be seen: the first competing carrier, project Mercury, owned jointly by Cable and Wireless, British Petroleum, and Barclay's Bank, has yet to offer services, and few items of equipment have yet received approval for connection to the network. It is also too early to say whether other countries will follow this example.

It is also important to stress that the government, as in the United States, will remain as the overall authority responsible for the regulation of telecommunication services.

For the most part, then, the organizations involved with telecommunications are state-owned bodies, and in all countries the state regulates telecommunication services. The main examples of private involvement occur in the United

States and Canada. Hong Kong and Bahrain are also exceptions; services are operated by Cable and Wireless, which has often been regarded as a private company, although it was, until recently, wholly owned by the British government. At present, the private Cable and Wireless holds 40 percent of the shares of the Bahrain PTT, Batelco.

15.3 INTERNATIONAL TELECOMMUNICATIONS

International telecommunications were originally the subject of bilateral arrangements between two adjoining countries. The first arrangements were, naturally, for telegraph and came not long after the introduction of the telegraph in 1838. The first undersea cable, linking England and France, came into use as long ago as 1851, and the first transatlantic cable, linking Britain and the United States, was inaugurated in 1866—just three years after the founding of what is now the International Telecommunication Union (ITU). However, before examining the role of the ITU and other bodies involved in regulation and coordination, it is necessary to note some other organizations involved in international telecommunications, primarily as providers of transmission facilities.

For most international traffic, the mechanism was, until recently, a direct physical connection between the domestic networks of adjoining countries, made by the administrations in those countries, with long-distance traffic carried over a number of such links and traversing one or more intervening countries en route. There are two exceptions to this general rule, one being traffic to and from the United States, which is handled by a number of independent companies, often called IRCs (international record carriers), the other being satellite links, which carry a growing proportion of all traffic.

In terms of business volume, the major IRCs are RCA Global Communications and ITT World Communications, which between them handle about three-quarters of the external traffic to and from the United States. Other IRCs are Western Union International, TRT Telecommunications Corporation, and the French Telegraph Cable Company, a subsidiary of the French PTT. Canadian international traffic is handled by Teleglobe Canada, a Crown corporation, although internal traffic is handled by private companies.

Satellites are operated by consortia set up for the purpose, with circuits then being leased to IRCs or other carriers. The longest established of these are Amsat, the American Satellite Corporation, Comsat, the Communication Satellite Corporation, and Intelsat, the International Telecommunications Satellite Consortium, which was set up in 1964 and now has over 100 members, although over one-third of the investment is still held in the United States. Comsat designs the satellite systems for Intelsat, which in turn leases circuits to other carriers. In 1982 about two-thirds of the transoceanic international communications, including television, was handled by Intelsat satellites.

There are several other organizations operating or planning to operate satellites, including Eutelsat, which will operate mainly within Europe. Another organization with satellite facilities is Intersputnik, which has 14 member states, including the Soviet Union, although services are also used by a number of other countries.

An example of the complexity of international arrangements, particularly when satellite transmission is involved, is given by the case of Satellite Business Systems. SBS is a U.S. company set up by IBM, Comsat, and Aetna Insurance to provide high-speed digital communications. It has been granted permission by the FCC to operate as an IRC and is therefore in a position to make arrangements with administrations in other countries. In September 1982 an agreement was announced between British Telecom and SBS for a link between Britain and the United States, using Intelsat V. Access in Britain will be via the public telephone network, but in the United States there will be no connection to the telephone network; access will be via dish antennae.

15.4 TECHNICAL ISSUES

Whenever access is via the domestic network the carrier must take care of any incompatibilities between terminal equipment or communication channels insofar as voice traffic is concerned, so differences here are of no concern to the user, except for trivial matters such as recognizing different ringing or busy tones.

However, if other devices are to be connected, the sending and receiving equipment must be compatible. Therefore, the user must be fully aware of all requirements, although it is usually possible to get some sort of advice and assistance from the local carrier. Moreover, for computer-to-computer communications, it is necessary to be aware of any technical complications introduced by the communications network itself. For example, on a packet-switched network it may not be possible to send codes which have meaning to all PADs on the network (although this is a limitation of domestic networks as well as international).

Some other characteristics of international links become more noticeable with data traffic, particularly in the case of online terminal access to remote machines. One such phenomenon is the propagation delay inherent in satellite links and the effect this has on full-duplex working. The orbital height of geostationary satellites is such that a signal takes approximately 0.25 seconds to reach the satellite and return to a ground station. For voice traffic or for half-duplex operation of a terminal, the use of one or even two satellite links will not be noticeable to the user, but in the case of full-duplex operation, when two satellite hops may be involved, the delay between striking a key and seeing the echoed character appear on the screen can be a full second. This delay can be even more restricting (its effect is more annoying than anything else in the case quoted above) when relatively large amounts of data are to be transmitted over a dialed connection, or even a leased circuit. Here the delay in receiving a "buffers-full" signal from the receiving device can result in quite significant losses of data; it can either reduce considerably the effective data transfer rates that can be employed to far below the theoretical capacity of the link or demand the introduction of complex error-checking procedures. In this context, it should be noted that even quite short terrestrial calls may involve two satellite hops, particularly when no direct land-line connection is available, either because of hostile terrain, or because the territory of an unfriendly country intervenes. While a call may be perfectly possible using just one satellite link, the volume of traffic between a given pair of countries may be such that it is impracticable to dedicate satellite channels to that link. The chosen method in these circumstances is often to route calls via a ground station in a third country with which both countries have a number of channels. This situation should not occur with leased circuits, of course.

15.4.1 Standards

Standards are important for all forms of telecommunications, merely to ensure that equipment will perform satisfactorily.

Coverage of all the standards applicable to international communications is outside the scope of this work, whole volumes being devoted to this topic. Fortunately, as far as the user of international telecommunications is concerned, it is generally not necessary to know the requirements of more than a small number of these standards—most of which are equally applicable to national networks—although it is necessary to be aware of any differences between national and international standards, as some can cause difficulties.

The majority of relevant standards are issued by the CCITT, although certain ISO standards may also be applicable. For the most part, those that do affect the user deal with the specification of equipment, such as modems, or with the representation of data in terms of character sets, packet sizes, etc. In many cases it is sufficient to know that the equipment conforms to the appropriate standard, detailed knowledge being unnecessary for the typical user. Some of the relevant standards are listed in Table 15.1.

15.5 INTERNATIONAL REGULATORY ISSUES

As mentioned earlier, the complexity of international telecommunications arises from a number of reasons, one of which is the variety of technical systems and standards employed. However, with the exceptions noted earlier, this aspect concerns only the providers of services, and it may be the regulatory aspects which are of more concern to the user, influencing, as they do, what services are available, what may be done with those services, and what those services will cost. The range of topics which could be considered under this heading is tremendous, and the differences that exist from one country to another, or from one service to another, magnify this diversity. Moreover, there are constant changes, often quite small but sometimes more significant, which mean that it is impossible to provide complete and detailed analysis of all eventualities. Quite

TABLE 15.1
SOME CCITT RECOMMENDATIONS

V 21 200 baud asynchronous modem. Similar to Bell 103.

V 22 1200 bps full-duplex synchronous modem (with asynchronous terminal interface). Similar to Bell 212.

V 23 600/1200 bps asynchronous modem operating at half-duplex on dial network or full-duplex on a leased four-wire circuit. Similar to Bell 202.

V 24 Interchange circuits between data circuit-terminating equipment and data terminal equipment. Similar to, and operationally compatible with, EIA RS-232-C.

V 25 Automatic calling and/or answering equipment.

V 50 Standard limits for transmission quality of data transmission.

X 2 International user facilities in public data networks.

X 20bis Use on public data networks of data terminal equipment designed for interfacing with asynchronous V-Series modems.

X 25 Interface between data terminal equipment and data circuit-terminating equipment for terminals operating in the packet mode on public data networks.

---

drastic changes can occur with a change of government. In this section, therefore, we concentrate on introducing some of the issues that affect regulation of international telecommunications services and on showing just some of the ways in which these regulations impinge on the user.

Many of the regulations are made at the national level, as, indeed, are tariffs. Hence, the political views of a government clearly have an important bearing. How these views are manifested is, nevertheless, conditioned by international agreements which are made in a number of different forums, as discussed in the next section.

One of the most important considerations is the provision of domestic services—who provides what, under what conditions—as this inevitably reflects national attitudes to international communications. Some of the variety in national provision has been indicated earlier.

Generally, what is available for international communications is no different in type from what is available within a country. Of course, the complete range of services that is available nationally may not be provided, there being less choice of speeds for leased circuits and less choice of special services. For example, reverse charging may not be possible. This relationship to national services arises naturally, since access is, in the vast majority of cases, via the national network.

However, there are some aspects that are more noticeable in the case of international telecommunications services, as differences in national policies as well as technical differences can introduce a number of difficulties and complexities.

Restrictions on what can and cannot be attached to a network can result from commercial or political as well as technical reasons. For example, one nation might simply refuse to handle traffic from another, including transit traffic, or there may be a desire to protect the service supplier's revenues. Such restrictions may be justified on technical grounds, since, incontrovertibly, any device which might physically damage some part of the network must be prohibited.

15.5.1 Customs and Excise Taxes on Information

Taxes in most countries follow the line taken with other products or services, there being no special recognition of information services as such. (This is not surprising, as no one within the information industry, let alone outside, really defines it well!) Therefore there is tremendous variation from country to country and from service to service. It is, in fact, complicated by the charging policies adopted by PTTs and carriers and the arrangements made between them. Thus, tax on an overseas telephone call is usually made at the rate pertaining in the caller's country (except for reverse charging). The fact that part of the revenue may go to the called country, or transit countries, where different rates of tax may be in force makes no difference to the user.

The situation regarding data communications is equally confused and is the subject of considerable debate in many countries. For example, books and other printed publications are often free of tax, while precisely the same information attracts taxes of one sort or another when transmitted digitally. In many cases, exports are free of tax; it therefore becomes attractive in some circumstances to obtain information from a foreign source, rather than a domestic one, other things being equal, depending, of course, on the tax status of the user and the use that is to be made of the information. No doubt there will be some rationalization as telecommunications and information services become more widespread: certainly, some clarification is needed.

One other aspect that should be mentioned is the hidden-tax element noted by some observers in the charging policies of those PTTs required to make contributions to government funds.

15.5.2 Privacy and Rights to Information

With the increase in international data traffic, whether for access to overseas information services or for the transfer of information between branches of the same organization, the implications of national legislation and attitudes to matters such as privacy and access to information have become more apparent.

A number of countries, including Austria, Canada, Denmark, France, Germany, Iceland, Israel, Luxembourg, Norway, and Sweden, have adopted data protection laws which protect the rights of individuals; a number of other countries are intending to introduce such laws. The aims of the laws are summarized by a resolution adopted by the data protection commissioners from those countries at their fourth annual conference held in 1982. The resolution reads:

The conference recognizes the need in all countries for a mechanism independent of government and other authorities that has power to investigate non-compliance with an individual's legal right:

1 to know, subject to protection of the general public interest and the privacy rights of third parties, what records are maintained about the individual concerned;

2 to know the purpose for which personal information is collected;

3 to ensure that such records are relevant, accurate, complete and up-to-date, and to make annotations if corrections are not made or accepted by the collector or storer of the records;

4 to know the uses (including transfer to other countries) made of such records and to be protected from uses not connected to the purpose for which the data were originally collected.

This is not the place to discuss the content and the effect of data protection laws, which naturally vary somewhat from country to country. However, the implications for international communications cannot be ignored, as it seems likely that there may be barriers put up to prevent access or transfer across national boundaries to countries where no equivalent legislation has been enacted. Any such restrictions might, of course, limit access to any information, even if no personal data were involved in a particular search.

Access to information in the broader sense is rarely the subject of legislation as it is in the United States, although there are political pressures in a number of countries to introduce such provisions.

Another possible barrier to access to information across international frontiers comes in the form of restrictive marketing agreements. Often arrangements are made whereby one organization is given exclusive rights to market a product produced in another country. This is quite a normal trading arrangement. In many areas of commerce it works without disadvantage and is often of benefit to the consumer, who can have some confidence in the supplier's standing and commitment to the product. However, the effects of similar arrangements in the world of information services does not always work to the advantage of users. There are instances where marketing arrangements made initially for a printed service inhibit or even prevent access to the same information from a computer-based information service, even though the agent in that country does not provide an equivalent service. It is worth commenting that such restrictions do not exist only in the world of commercial information services, some of the worst offenders being services originating from national governments or international intergovernmental agencies.

15.5.3 Access to Communication Media

As mentioned earlier, access to communication media is ultimately controlled by government, although the way in which control is manifested varies from country to country. Control really falls into two areas: first is control of devices and equipment that can be attached to networks, and second is control of the services that can be provided over those networks. Clearly, any equipment connected to a network must be electrically safe, capable of working with that network, and unlikely to cause any danger to the network. It would be a foolish provider of services that did not take steps to ensure compliance with any appropriate standards. Such compliance can be sought in different ways—by requiring "type approval" for all devices, for example.

In many countries compliance is guaranteed by the simple expedient of demanding, with effective legislation, that all equipment to be connected to the network be supplied by the PTT. While this is certainly a valid solution to the technical problem, it does restrict the choice of the user and may mean that some uses are not possible. The situation varies from country to country and from time to time. Thus, in the 1980s users in Holland are allowed great freedom in what may be attached to the network, while the user in West Germany finds that almost all equipment must be provided by the Bundespost. In the United Kingdom, the range of devices that may be provided by the user is being steadily expanded, although some restrictions remain. British law requires that equipment attached directly to the network operated by British Telecom must be approved by the British Approvals Board for Telecommunications, an independent organization appointed by the government. One of the great concerns expressed by users is that restrictions on what may be attached to the network often appear to be adopted solely to increase the revenue-earning capacity of the PTT, and complaints about prices and quality of service, for example, delays in delivery and installation, are often more common than complaints about any limitation in technical performance or capability.

Provision of services will also be subject to controls, not usually in terms of the content of those services—although normal laws concerning public morals, libel, and the like apply—but more in terms of how services may be provided. In most countries legislation lags considerably behind the technology, and matters are further complicated by the sheer impracticability of policing the use of telecommunications networks in any effective manner. Thus the growth of answering services and electronic mail services is sporadic and operates in an uncertain climate. The very power and complexity of international telecommunications services makes regulation extremely difficult and often allows a user to find ways around restrictions placed by a domestic carrier, or even a way to gain access to international circuits at a lower price.

Two examples will illustrate this. In the mid-1970s a number of American information retrieval systems became technically available in Europe through the Tymnet communications network. Nodes of the network were operational in a number of European cities, as such a service was permitted to give access to Tymnet time-sharing computers. The information retrieval services were connected to the Tymnet network to provide cheaper and more reliable access to users in the United States—a valid use under U.S. legislation at the time. However, in many European countries such use of a private network for third-party traffic was specifically prohibited, with the result that some PTTs, while allowing the node to remain for access to Tymnet's own computing services, made it a condition that access to the information retrieval services operated by third parties should be barred. Other countries did not do this, with the consequence that some users found that an international call to a node in another European country provided access, via Tymnet, at a far lower cost than calling direct to America. The situation has now changed, of course, with the introduction of international packet-switched data services in most European countries.

A similar situation arose in the early 1980s as a result of great differences in telex tariffs, which made it attractive for companies in the United Kingdom to offer a service to users in other European countries whereby messages could be forwarded to the United States at considerable cost savings. Such services caused great concern to some European PTTs, but under current laws and the provisions of the Treaty of Rome, they could not be prohibited.

Both these examples indicate how national regulations or tariff policies can be made ineffective or bypassed by the more perceptive users, with the spread of easy international communications. Such effects will, no doubt, become more apparent as services continue to grow.

The long-term trend must surely be toward the adoption of less restrictive regulations and more competitive tariffs; without these the use of communications services provided within a country—and hence the revenues earned for international traffic—will inevitably be limited. Some of the less-developed countries are well placed in developing their communications services to learn from the lessons that are apparent in other countries.

15.6 AGENCIES DEALING WITH REGULATION

Regulation within countries is carried out by governments or their agencies. Often the regulatory authority is the PTT, or Administration as it is sometimes called, while in other cases a separate body is set up. In the United States this is the Federal Communications Commission, whose activities and responsibilities are covered in Chapter 14, although individual states also regulate certain aspects within their jurisdiction.

At the international level these national bodies come together at the International Telecommunications Union (ITU), which was founded in 1863 and was a founding agency of the United Nations. ITU members now number over 150.

The ITU, based in Geneva, has four branches—CCIR, CCITT, IFRB, and the General Secretariat. CCIR, the International Radio Consultative Committee, and IFRB, the International Frequency Registration Board, do deal with telecommunications—in the allocation of frequencies for microwave links and satellite transmission, for example—but the most important agency in the context of international telecommunications is CCITT, the International Telegraph and Telephone Consultative Committee. (The initials come from the French.) CCITT dates from 1956 when it was formed by the merger of two separate bodies formed in 1925 that dealt with telegraph and telephone.

CCITT holds a plenary assembly every four years to discuss the findings of working groups and ratify those findings as agreed. The recommendations of each plenary session, which include all unaltered matters agreed upon at previous sessions, are published in ten volumes, numbered with roman numerals. Most of the volumes are further divided into two or more fascicles, identified by an arabic number. Each fascicle is issued as a separate physical volume. Each issue of the CCITT book is assigned a color for binding and is known by that color. Thus the seventh plenary assembly, held in Geneva on November 10–21, 1980, resulted in the Yellow Book.

CCITT deals with a wide range of topics as can be seen from the table of contents of the Yellow Book, which is shown in the Appendix at the end of this chapter.

Although CCITT membership is made up of administrations, a recently formed body, INTUG, now has observer status at plenary assemblies and is permitted to make submissions. INTUG, the International Telecommunications User Group, represents users in all countries. Membership of INTUG, an association registered in the Netherlands, is open to all interested parties, corporate and individual, and includes user organizations in Australia, Belgium, France, Germany, Japan, Switzerland, and the United Kingdom, as well as a number of international companies. The secretary is C. L. Metcalfe, Beechy Lees Lodge, Pilgrims' Way, Otford, Kent TN14 5SA, England.

European PTTs and administrations are members of another body, CEPT (Conférence Européene des Postes et Télécommunications), which was formed in 1959, largely at the instigation of the Commission of the European Communities, although membership is not, nor was it from the beginning, restricted to Community countries. CEPT, which holds plenary sessions every two years, does not have the same standing as CCITT, as resolutions only apply to its members. However, decisions taken by CEPT do have a significant influence on CCITT work, owing to the strength of the members of CEPT within CCITT.

An organization with a similar role to that of CEPT is the Arab Telecommunication Union (ATU), based in Baghdad. The ATU is related to the Arab League, in rather the same way as the ITU is related to the United Nations. The ATU deals specifically with matters related to the use of Arabic—for example, in developing a code for the digital transmission of Arabic characters—as well as relations and agreements between the national PTTs.

Other international organizations deal with broadcasting. (ITU obviously has authority for allocation of frequencies through IFRB and CCIR.) The European Broadcasting Union/Union Européenne de Radiodiffusion (EBU/UER), often known as Eurovision, was founded on February 12, 1950, and is a system of international broadcasting cooperation including news and program exchanges. There are over 100 member organizations in about 75 countries. The activities are channeled through the Television Programme Committee, the Radio Programme Committee, the Legal Committee, and the Technical Committee. The active members are national broadcasting organizations in Europe, together with some in the Middle East and North Africa.

The International Radio and Television Organization (OIRT), based in Prague, Czechoslovakia, has as members the broadcasting companies of the socialist countries. Other regional organizations are the Asian-Pacific Broadcasting Union, the Union of National Radio and Television Organizations of Africa (URTNA), the Arab States Broadcasting Union (ASBU), the Caribbean Broadcasting Union (CBU), and the Association Inter-America de Radiodiffusion (AIR).

RECOMMENDED READING

Papers on different aspects of international telecommunications services are spread through a wide range of journals. For example, many computer journals devote occasional issues to communications, some of the material dealing with international services. Much of the precise information needed is available only in the form of publications from local service providers, such as the PTTs, or from equipment vendors.

Cawkell, Anthony E., "Privacy, Security, and Freedom in the Information Society," *Journal of Information Science,* 1982, 4(1), pp. 3–8.
International Telecommunications Union, *CCITT Yellow Book,* Geneva: Author, 1981.
Martin, James, *Future Developments in Telecommunications* (2d ed.), Englewood Cliffs, N.J.: Prentice-Hall, 1977.
Schiller, Herbert I., *Who Knows: Information in the Age of the Fortune 500,* Norwood, N.J.: Ablex, 1981.
Turn, Rein, *Transborder Data Flows: Concerns in Privacy Protection and Free Flow of Information,* Arlington, Va.: American Federation of Information Processing Societies, 1979.

In addition, the following serial publications are recommended:

• *Transnational Data Report.* Published eight times a year by North-Holland, it contains many articles and notes on the different aspects of international communications—particularly regulatory issues.

• Various publications sponsored by the International Institute of Communications are published by Routledge and Keegan Paul, with titles of the form *Broadcasting in* (name of country).

• A number of Unesco publications are entitled *Communications Policies in* (name of country).

• Brief details on broadcasting systems around the world are given in the *Europa Yearbook.*

APPENDIX: CCITT YELLOW BOOK (APPLICABLE AFTER THE SEVENTH PLENARY ASSEMBLY, 1980)

Volume I

Minutes and reports of the Plenary Assembly; Opinions and Resolutions; Recommendations on:

- The organisation and working procedures of the CCITT (Series A)
- Means of expression (Series B)
- General telecommunications statistics (Series C)

and list of study groups and questions under study.

Volume II

- FASCICLE II.1—General tariff principles—charging and accounting in international telecommunications services. Series D Recommendations (Study Group III).
- FASCICLE II.2—International telephone service—operation. Recommendations E.100–E.323 (Study Group II).
- FASCICLE II.3—International telephone service—network management; traffic engineering. Recommendations E.401–E.543 (Study Group II).
- FASCICLE II.4—Telegraph and "telematic services" operations and tariffs. Series F Recommendations (Study Group I).

Volume III

- FASCICLE III.1—General characteristics of international telephone connections and circuits. Recommendations G.101–G.171.
- FASCICLE III.2—International analog carrier systems. Transmission media—characteristics. Recommendations G.211–G.651 (Study Group XV, CMBD).
- FASCICLE III.3—Digital networks—transmission systems and multiplexing equipments. Recommendations G.701–G.941 (Study Group XVIII).
- FASCICLE III.4—Line transmission of non telephone signals. Transmission of sound program and television signals. Series H, J recommendations (Study Group XV).

Volume IV

- FASCICLE IV.1—Maintenance; general principles, international carrier systems, international telephone circuits. Recommendations M.10–M.761 (Study Group IV).
- FASCICLE IV.2—Maintenance; international voice frequency telegraphy

and facsimile, international leased circuits. Recommendations M.800–M.1235 (Study Group IV).

FASCICLE IV.3—Maintenance; international sound program and television transmission circuits. Series N recommendations (Study Group IV).

FASCICLE IV.4—Specifications of measuring equipment. Series O recommendations (Study Group IV).

Volume V

Telephone transmission quality. Series P recommendations (Study Group XII).

Volume VI

FASCICLE VI.1—General recommendations on telephone switching and signaling. Interface with the maritime service. Recommendations Q.1–Q.118 bis (Study Group XI).

FASCICLE VI.2—Specifications of signalling systems Nos. 4 and 5. Recommendations Q.120–Q180 (Study Group XI).

FASCICLE VI.3—Specifications of signalling systems No. 6. Recommendations Q.251–Q.300 (Study Group XI).

FASCICLE VI.4—Specifications of signalling systems R1 and R2. Recommendations Q.310–Q.490 (Study Group XI).

FASCICLE VI.5—Digital transit exchanges for national and international applications. Interworking of signalling systems. Recommendations Q.501–Q.685 (Study Group XI).

FASCICLE VI.6—Specifications of signalling system No. 7. Recommendations Q.701–Q.741 (Study Group XI).

FASCICLE VI.7—Functional specification and description language (SDL). Man-machine language (MML). Recommendations Z.101–Z.104 and Z3.11–Z3.41 (Study Group XI).

FASCICLE VI.8—CCITT high-level language (CHILL). Recommendation Z.200 (Study Group XI).

Volume VII

FASCICLE VII.1—Telegraph transmission and switching. Series R, U Recommendations (Study Group IX).

FASCICLE VII.2—Telegraph and "telematic services" terminal equipment. Series S, T Recommendations (Study Group VIII).

Volume VIII

FASCICLE VIII.1—Data communication over the telephone network. Series V Recommendations (Study Group XVII).

FASCICLE VIII.2—Data communication networks; services and facilities, terminal equipment and interfaces. Recommendations X.1–X.29 (Study Group VII).

FASCICLE VIII.3—Data communication networks; transmission signalling and switching, network aspects, maintenance, administrative arrangements. Recommendations X.40–X.180 (Study Group NII).

Volume IX

Protection against interference. Series K recommendations (Study Group V). Protection of cable sheaths and poles. Series L Recommendations (Study Group VI).

Volume X

FASCICLE X.1—Terms and definitions.
FASCICLE X.2—Index of the Yellow Book.

CHAPTER 16

MANAGING A TELECOMMUNICATIONS FACILITY

Charles J. Schweis
CIBA-GEIGY Corporation
Ardsley, NY 10502

16.1 ORGANIZATION OF THE TELECOMMUNICATIONS FACILITY

Organization of the telecommunications facility depends largely on the makeup of the corporate structure. Some corporations are centralized while others are decentralized, and often within these structures facilities can be set up on a national or regional basis. Also within these various organizational structures telecommunications can be found under many different department headings.

Before we get too deep into organization it might be beneficial to highlight the nature and scope of what a telecommunications facility may encompass. Telecommunications include the systems and equipment involved in the transmission and reception of voice and data information—telephones and associated switching equipment, data communications, data phone service, facsimile, message switching systems, radio systems, telex, tie lines, WATS lines, TWX, microwave, satellite, answering services, telecommunication interfaces, video and audio teleconferencing, etc. The telecommunications function is influenced by the complexity and changes in equipment and regulations, the size and geographic logistics of the company, and the magnitude of company expenditures.

Under a centralized concept, one might find a corporate department located at the headquarters facility that would control all telecommunications activity. This department could consist of a director or manager, who would be supervising an operational staff with direct line responsibility, and also a staff of professional analysts. These staff analysts would be responsible for the evaluation, recommendation, and implementation of new voice, data, and video telecommunications services to all operating units of the corporation.

Within a decentralized environment the activities mentioned above are generally performed by local site personnel associated with some general-services area or maybe even handled by two different sections. Some sites may have a general-services group that would handle voice telephone station moves, installations, and repairs and possibly even the total evaluation process of a new PBX, while all data communication activities might be handled by an individual within the data processing section.

The organizational concepts used within most medium-to-large corporations today call for a national coverage structure. Some large-to-very-large concerns have a regional structure in place reporting back to the corporate headquarters. The corporate staff is usually under the direction of a vice president or director of telecommunications. Reporting to this position would be a regional manager with a staff of professionals, who would help with the evaluations and implementation of any systems that the corporate group recommended.

In organizing a telecommunications department, a manager might ask a number of questions: Just where do I start? What are my responsibilities? Where should the department report in the organization? How many people do I need? What specific talents should they possess? How do I justify the required personnel? How do I train personnel? What type of records do I maintain? What should I know about data transmission? What knowledge should I have about computers? How can I use a computer? How far into the future should I plan—one, three, five, or more years ahead? How do I acquire long-range strategic planning information? What type of leased facilities do I require? What carrier can best serve my needs? How do I keep abreast of technological changes? How do I handle rate increases? This list of questions is by no means complete, nor have we covered areas that are not dealt with on a continuing basis.

The purpose of a telecommunications department within a corporation is to render service. The department itself does not create the demand for telecommunications equipment, service, or facilities. Neither does it create, manufacture, or sell a commodity which results in customer sales and direct profits. Thus, the department is, by definition, service-oriented. If the need for telecommunications were not being generated internally by other operating units, the telecommunications department would dissolve.

Along with the telecommunications department there exists a strong need for a corporate policy, usually approved at the managing committee or board of directors level, and ensuring that all telecommunications are coordinated from a corporate viewpoint. This policy would be in place in order to achieve an orderly and economic growth of telecommunications companywide. It would require that the corporate staff coordinate the planning, evaluating, recommending, and eventual implementation of all telecommunications within the corporation.

This policy should define the scope of the area known as telecommunications. A definitive definition might be

Telecommunications includes all of the electromechanical and electronic devices and hardware systems necessary for the transmission and reception of information by such modes as voice, printed message, graphic displays, pictorial impressions, tone signaling, digital and analog coding, and other impulse variations from one location to another by such media as cable, wire, radio, satellite, or any other media or mode available now or in the future.

Telecommunications managers should be sensitive to their company's policies and knowledgeable about its current and long-range objectives. They must constantly be alert to changes and make necessary adjustments in plans, facilities, and operating practices. The telecommunications manager's basic responsibility is to plan, implement, and supervise the telecommunications activity within his or her company.

Figure 16.1 depicts a telecommunications department organization that might typically exist today.

The following descriptions explain the areas defined within the organization chart. They are not all-inclusive but are representative of areas most telecommunications departments cover.

16.2 TELECOMMUNICATIONS STRATEGIC PLANNING

16.2.1 Short-Range Planning

Short-range planning deals with today's world, one- or two-year cycles, which calls for awareness of users' immediate needs. For example, this area reacts to that new sales office or warehouse one of the operating units has been planning for a while but forgot to bring into the early planning sessions that have been going on for months. Now they realize that without telecommunications services it's not going to happen. When this happens the telecommunications facility

FIGURE 16.1
Typical telecommunications organization. This chart is not intended to imply a final reporting structure, but to show the sections that should be maintained and duties performed.

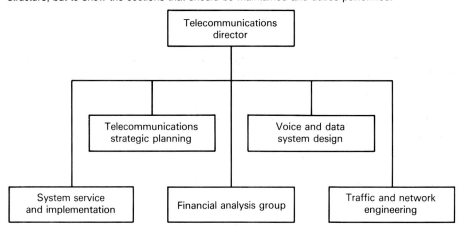

must not only react to the immediate problem at hand but know how to merge it into the long-range plan.

16.2.2 Long-Range Planning

Because technology is increasing at a greater rate than ever before, managers must be in tune with the direction of the company and its operating units. Although there are numerous vendors vying for the company's business, they too must plan production to meet their users' needs. Whether it be a computerized telephone system, message switcher, or computer mainframe, telecommunications managers will find themselves tied into a long-range plan, encompassing a three- or five-year cycle or even longer.

16.2.3 Project Planning

It sounds easy, but the many parts to a project and the number of people involved will soon have you talking to yourself. Whether you use the PERT or Gantt chart or any other method, the most important ingredient is communications, verbal communications with not only the project team but, most importantly, the user. By defining the phases and activities to be accomplished and the documentation required for proper project planning, managers can provide a basis for performing realistic audits during and after the development phase.

16.2.4 Network Systems Planning

The problems involved in creating a single integrated system whereby hardware and software from numerous diverse vendors can interface effectively is one of the telecommunications department's most difficult tasks. The network planner must be able to identify the most logical design solution and optimize the solution in order to achieve cost and performance objectives.

16.2.5 Tariff Analysis Impact

Tariffs play an important part in the overall contribution to the planning cycle. With proper analysis the future impact of tariff changes can be planned for. Tariffs tend to develop a ripple effect on all regulatory agencies. Once the FCC makes a ruling at the federal level, the same type of ruling tends to occur at the state and sometimes even the local level.

16.3 VOICE AND DATA SYSTEM DESIGN

16.3.1 Private Branch Exchange (PBX)

Generally any sizable company has many more sites than it does staff personnel to evaluate them. Because PBXs, automatic call distributors and sequences, and other ancillary equipment are constantly being evaluated, request-for-proposal (RFP) specifications must be consistently developed. An RFP is a formal document prepared by potential users to define the specifications for the system that they want and request proposals from qualified bidders to deliver that system. This area plays an important part in the liaison with strategic planning. A PBX telephone system, as noted in Chapter 5, is a switching system which provides internal telephone communications between extensions or stations within a specific office, plant, or other facility as well as between these stations and the long-distance toll network or an existing private tie-line network.

16.3.2 Cable Facilities for New Buildings

An area that is consistently overlooked and often ignored in planning systems for new buildings is the need for proper planning for cable facilities. This is an area that few department managers ever get the chance to participate in. Telecommunications department managers must educate higher management to the need for their input early in the planning, since cabling a new building properly will allow the company to move forward as the state of the art progresses. Generally the layout for cable runs and cross-connect closets of new buildings are handled by the building architect.

16.3.3 Foreign Exchange (FX) Services

Often overlooked as a viable alternative to transmissions services, an FX line is a private line which permits users at one location to call any other user (customer, vendor, etc.) for telephone or data transmission. A foreign exchange line is intended for high-volume calling and is used in place of long-distance toll calling, primarily to reduce costs. Cost for this type of service is based on distance plus terminal charges and local message units.

16.3.4 Facsimile Networks

With effective analysis of needs and proper marketing, facsimile can be a viable solution to specific telecommunications problems. With the maturation of the facsimile industry throughout the 1970s it is only reasonable that the 1980s will provide important business opportunities for the proper use of facsimile networks.

16.3.5 Microwave Networks

Many telecommunications managers will be surprised to learn that they can develop their own microwave networks. Microwave is not limited to large systems, but now many companies can justify their own systems for short-haul communications, not only gaining economic benefits but also further enchancing their networks.

16.3.6 Message-Switching Systems

Message switching is the technique of receiving a message, storing it until the proper outgoing circuit and station are available, and then retransmitting it to its destination. Usually this type of service operates in what is generally known as a stand-alone system, where the computer used is dedicated solely to the communications task. Its software is developed and specialized only for that function. TWX, Telex, and Dial-up are the common forms of this service.

16.3.7 Modem Evaluations

The term *dataset* is a synonym for modem. All data communication systems use some type of modem, whether it be stand-alone, rack-mounted, or integrated into the terminal. Modems translate the digital signal from the terminal to analog and from analog back to digital for receipt at the terminal or computer. Prior to the Caterfone decision in 1968 (Chapter 14) the majority of modems in use were manufactured by the Bell System. Since that decision numerous vendors participate in this market.

16.3.8 Radio-Paging Systems

Radio-paging systems are ideal for large plants; they are also used extensively within security and maintenance groups of most corporations. Most vendors will aid in the design of a proper system, but radio paging is one of the most visible of telecommunications services. If base stations are licensed but improperly designed the FCC may order a change.

16.3.9 Wide-Area Telecommunications Service (WATS)

WATS is a special billing arrangement for customers who make or receive many long-distance calls in certain patterns and volumes. When there is a pattern of many calls from a single point to many points in a given geographic area, the situation may exist for the use of out-WATS service. Conversely, when there is a pattern of many calls from many points in a restricted geographic area to a distant single point, generally an in-WATS arrangement might be appropriate. Each of these services provides for originating calls in both directions, a combination of separate out-WATS and in-WATS lines must be installed, each at a prescribed monthly rate. Each WATS line, whether in or out, can accommodate only one call or transmission at a time.

16.3.10 Front-End Controllers

A front-end controller consists of a data processing device used to condition communications signals and convert them for introduction into a host processing system. These controllers usually provide the control functions necessary to handle multiple simultaneous data paths, and the associated computer systems provide the memory, processing capability, and input-output facilities.

16.3.11 Environment Preparation

Environment preparation refers to design layout and construction preparation of the particular area that is intended for the PABX message switcher, front-end controller, or other planned projects. The list of various needs—air conditioning, power requirements, raised floors, and so forth—is endless and changes with each project.

16.3.12 Transmission Facilities Planning

Facilities planning is an area that is one of the most important aspects of developing a network. With the great variety of services available, many items must be taken into consideration—volume of traffic, holding times, or direction and scope of traffic. Will direct distance dialing suffice, or is WATS needed? Should FX be considered for high-volume bedroom communities? If plant facilities are to be far removed from the residence of most of the company's employees, FX service rather than direct distance dialing might be cheaper and more practical.

16.3.13 Contract Negotiations

Here is an area best left to the experts. Most sizable concerns today have a legal department that handles the various needs of the corporation, but some telecommunications managers tend to shy away from it. When you are entering into a major project, even in the conception stage it is wise to have the vendor pass on blank copies of all contract documents so that members of the legal department can peruse the documents without being under pressure and possibly help you avoid any pitfalls along the way in developing your project.

16.3.14 Financial Project Approvals

Developing capital appropriation requests and operating budgets for large projects probably represents about 20 percent of your effort. Here again, the telecommunications department tend to rely on figures submitted by the vendor. Use your company's financial people whenever possible; only they know what the corporate return on investment percentage or what the cost of money is.

16.4 TRAFFIC AND NETWORK ENGINEERING

16.4.1 Network Configuration

Network configuration relates to how your network is put together. Is it, for example, a two-node network? What node will be the master? Which locations wlll be the satellite operations? Which will be tributary? Many considerations go into network design. Bringing about the intergration of switched data with a batched-data network and supporting these networks with the public- or private-line multipoint type of facilities is just one consideration. The use of concentrators or multiplexers is another.

16.4.2 Network Optimizing

This goes hand in hand with configuration. Is your network an intelligent or passive network? When PBX users in Texas go off hook will their call switch through Chicago or New York? When data users sign on, do they have access to the proper node? Can the user access the proper data base?

16.4.3 Network Enhancements

Should you have centralized or decentralized data collection for call accounting? Are station rearrangements going to be performed from the main node in the network, or is each location going to be responsible for its own. Basically, these are known as system features which will enhance your network.

16.4.4 Facilities Planning

Being cognizant of your company's direction and growth patterns will aid you in planning for the proper facilities for your network. The telecommunications manager must be aware of what is offered not only by the Bell System but also by the other common carriers. If FX service is justified, a satellite vendor can provide enormous savings. Typically, satellite costs can save you as much as 60 percent of terrestrial facilities.

16.4.5 Traffic Software

The need for traffic software to analyze data collected from your various systems is overwhelming. Traffic must be constantly analyzed to determine the need for alternative services and reconfiguration of your networks.

16.4.6 Automatic Route Selection

This feature provides for the automatic routing of outgoing calls over various alternative customer facilities based on the direct distance dialing number. The

PBX routes the call over the first available facility such as WATS or FX. This feature is both economic and efficient, maximizing the use of lines.

16.4.7 Station Message Detail Recording

This feature provides a record of the PBX station identity, starting time, duration, and trunk group used for outgoing and incoming calls. It enhances internal chargeback and budgeting of telephone expenses.

16.4.8 Customer Administration Panel Operations

This is an interface that works in conjunction with your telephone system. Most PBXs, be it Bell System or interconnect, have the ability to operate with a CAP arrangement. This generally allows the user to make station rearrangements and changes, for example, to move station numbers or change the features and restrictions assigned to a station. Features might include automatic callback, call forwarding, and call pickup, with restrictions covering denial to either toll facilities or tie-line services.

16.4.9 Customer Administration Center Operations

This interface can handle everything that a CAP does and more. With this type of operation the user can not only make station moves and feature changes but collect traffic data and rearrange trunk configurations with the various facilities management software of the system.

16.5 FINANCIAL ANALYSIS GROUP

16.5.1 Budgeting Development

It helps operating budgets if they are maintained with as many definitive descriptions as possible. By this we mean they should be developed with separate itemized budgets for each service, such as WATS, FX, tie-line networks, equipment rental, terminals, CRTs, etc. Don't mix apples and oranges by budgeting all toll expenses or equipment in one line item. It makes evaluation of new services very difficult.

16.5.2 Voice and Data Cost Allocation

Management of today's systems is becoming more and more complex. As systems become more user friendly, your networks will grow, and as they grow, so will the need for cost allocation. Telecommunications departments now have the ability to operate with zero budgets or become profit centers if so desired by management.

16.5.3 Network Inventory Control

One of the primary objectives of the telecommunications manager should be knowing what hardware, software, and facilities the company has. This will help you not only in future evaluations of new services or projects but also in developing national account status with certain vendors—which in turn equates to dollar savings through discounts.

16.5.4 Data-Base Management

It is not surprising to discover the same data exists in two, three, or more files serving multiple needs within the same department. With the tools available today savings can be achieved by consolidating this information into one data base to serve your various needs.

16.5.5 Network Systems Marketing

This is a new area to telecommunications departments. As systems and networks grow and become more user friendly, there will be a continual need to educate users about your service offerings. Just as vendors have salespeople and marketers to educate you, you must educate the employees of the company about the tools available to them so that they may achieve greater productivity. This in turn aids in the growth of your company.

16.6 SYSTEM SERVICE AND IMPLEMENTATION

16.6.1 Switchboard Service Operations

With the many services switchboards perform, functional layout design supported by properly trained personnel is a must. Many switchboard operations handle functions additional to their normal call-handling routines.

16.6.2 Network Operations

Another name for network management centers, an area whose main functions are to monitor the network's operation, permit routine maintenance, and effect rapid restoration of service when a failure occurs. Service failures can occur in either the local loop, the long-haul circuit itself, or hardware at either end. With the proper tools at their command, network operations personnel can usually isolate the trouble quickly. If the circuit involved is a data circuit, network operations can revert to dial backup facilities until the primary is restored. When a voice circuit is affected operations can usually remove it from the trunk group so users do not go high and dry. Network management centers are costly for companies to maintain and depend largely on how much higher management values good service.

16.6.3 Network Fault Isolation and Trouble Reporting

Within the network operations fault isolation and trouble-shooting equipment are primary tools, along with well-trained personnel.

16.6.4 System Maintenance and Training

Because every operations center is different, training of personnel to perform proper system maintenance is difficult. This is an area that does not lend itself to promotion of existing employees and generally requires hiring from outside the company.

16.6.5 Network Systems Quality Assurance

As systems become more and more complex and your user base grows, so will the need to monitor the network and supply your users with good quality.

16.6.6 Job Descriptions

The next things needed to support everything mentioned heretofore are job descriptions and the people to fill them: job descriptions for the various managers, supervisors, analysts, and operational personnel. The extent to which job descriptions are written is dependent upon the size and scope of the telecommunications department being organized.

Job descriptions are quite important. They should not be left to the personnel department or shoved off as being incidental. Job descriptions will make or break your organization. Do not be locked into one description, say, for a switchboard operator. Today, there is no such job description. The levels or grades set up initially will determine budget considerations. Generally, today one might find a family of job descriptions such as: EPBX (Electronic Private Branch Exchange) operator II; EPBX operator I; senior EPBX operator; chief EPBX operator; unit head, switchboard operations; supervisor, switchboard services; and manager, voice systems support—all in one telecommunications department. Each job description has its own level of experience and expertise. We are not saying that titles alone will bring about financial rewards, but preplanning will help you move your organization forward. This type of hierarchy is relevant to all areas within a telecommunications facility.

16.7 EQUIPMENT: ITS USE, PROCUREMENT, AND MAINTENANCE

The nerve center of any corporation today is generally the corporate telecommunications center. It is known by many different names throughout the industry—

central telecommunications, teletype center, TWX center, to name a few. Owing to the increasing technology within the industry the makeup of these centers has changed drastically over the years.

As mentioned earlier, the effect on equipment and services provided within the corporate communications center would depend upon the size and scope of the organization it serves. Most communications centers today have the basic services needed to support their users. Typically, this consists of TWX, telex, and facsimile type services.

TWX (teletypewriter exchange) is a service provided by Western Union Telegraph Company. It is a basic plain-language type of system which provides dial point-to-point connections with a transmission speed operating at 10 CPS (characters per second) or 110 Baud. The direct distance dialing facilities of AT&T are used to supplement their own facilities.

The Western Union Telegraph Company generally will supply a model 33 teletypewriter (generic term referring to the registered trademark of Teletype Corporation and to teleprinter type equipment). The units can be either supplied in a keyboard send-receive (KSR) or an automatic send-receive (ASR) version. The KSR unit uses the keyboard for input and the printer for everything that is transmitted and received. All data is transmitted while the unit is online with the called party. This type of unit is very rarely used nowadays; line charges can be costly because it is almost impossible to type at the rated speed of the service, which is 100 wpm. The units most commonly used are the ASR models, which have the capability of preparing data for transmission on a medium such as paper tape, cassette, magnetic tape, or buffer storage. It is then possible to transmit at the rated transmission speed of the service you are using.

Telex, another service of Western Union, is similar to TWX in that it also is a plain-language service. The popularity of telex is based upon its lower cost and simplified use in international message transmission. Telex is also a time, and distance-sensitive service, being billed in increments of one-tenth of a minute.

Types of equipment vary within the communications centers of different corporations. As mentioned, the general types of equipment used over the years for both TWX and telex have been teleprinter models supplied by the vendor, in this case Western Union, which have been manufactured by Teletype Corporation. As technology has progressed so has the number of vendors that have entered the marketplace. Many vendors now supply terminal unit along with a dial-up DDD port. Also the units are provided in different media configurations. Some units have buffer memory, while others have floppy diskettes as the storage medium. Also many vendors now incorporate a CRT into their terminal configuration.

Another piece of equipment that has become quite prevalent in the communications center of today is the store-and-forward message switcher. With today's computerized systems the store-and-forward message switcher has replaced many of the mundane operations of "torn-tape" systems. Many of the systems make it possible to incorporate word processing, electronic mail, and world-wide administrative message networks into a single telecommunications network.

The communications center of today is the nucleus of the office of the future. Centers are interfacing not only with mainframe computers but with word processors of all makes and models. Many departments can now dial up an intelligent terminal or a store-and-forward message system.

Many systems will provide interfaces to the TWX, telex, and DDD networks and act as a front end to mainframe computer systems. Traffic is usually routed from station to station throughout the network via three or four character mnemonics. An example of mnemonics would be "LPCC," which would equate to a terminal in the corporate legal and patent department. Mnemonics could be made up of just alpha or alphanumeric characters that would be somewhat synonymous with the identification of the terminal. The use of such systems allows a corporation to serve all users regardless of time zones because they usually operate 24 hours a day, 7 days a week. This allows companies to expand their New York business day, for example, to coincide with their Los Angeles business day. An international concern also gains in dealing with its overseas subsidiaries. Important information can be exchanged within the same business day, thus eliminating delays in corporate decision making.

Until recent years the corporate communications center was a facility that handled only certain types of administrative message traffic. It was used primarily for telegrams, mailgrams, administrative traffic to outside vendors, and some internal information transfer. But with the growth of technology, there has been a concommitant explosion in information and information transfer as well. Today these centers interface with mainframe computer centers and are involved with applications such as inventory control, order entry, order processing, and various data dissemination and collection.

Facsimile is not new; it has been around for approximately 140 years, but it is only within the last decade that it has flourished. It is used for the transmission of pictures, maps, diagrams, etc. The image is scanned at the transmitter, reconstructed at the receiving station, and duplicated on some form of paper. This type of service generally uses voice band facilities as a transmission medium.

Vendors abound in today's marketplace. There seem to be as many vendors as there are terminals to serve our needs. There are several hundred different models of teleprinters, CRTs, and other assorted terminals.

The acquisition of equipment for various systems depends largely on the organizational structure of the corporation. Once the telecommunications group has evaluated and recommended a piece of equipment or a system to the operating unit, it generally becomes the responsibility of that unit to complete the purchasing cycle. This process would change only if the system being implemented was to be shared by many operating units and controlled by corporate. If a system is implemented and purchased by corporate they usually create an internal chargeback to the users.

16.8 MANAGING AND MEASURING PERFORMANCE

Measuring performance of a network and of personnel is another major area of concern for all telecommunications department heads. As shown in the organizational chart of Figure 16.1, System Service and Implementation would be responsible for network performance. The tools used for network fault isolation, trouble reporting, and quality assurance are many. Whether you are concerned with voice, video, or data networks there are various pieces of equipment that allow you to test and monitor quality assurance.

Because of the ever-increasing number of networks within any given corporation, be they voice or data, users have become more reliant on their reliability. Increased reliability, faster trouble isolation, detection, and correction, and reduced downtime are essential for user satisfaction. The cost of achieving this depends largely on the grade of service you wish to provide your users.

As systems increase in their complexity, documentation, procedures and statistical data collection and analysis must be constantly updated. Successful telecommunications management depends largely on utilization of the proper resources in both hardware and personnel. How personnel is measured will vary from organization to organization. Measuring performance is difficult and depends largely on the policies set down by the department head. Many of these precepts are mentioned again in the context of a business management case history in Chapter 17.

RECOMMENDED READING

Asten, K. J., *Data Communications for Business Information Systems*, New York: Macmillan, 1973.

Held, Gilbert, *Data Communications Procurements Manual*, New York: McGraw-Hill,

Kuehn, Richard A., *Cost-Effective Telecommunications*, New York: AMACON, 1975.

Martin, James, *Telecommunications and the Computer*, Englewood Cliffs, N.J.: Prentice-Hall, 1969.

——*Teleprocessing Network Organization*, Englewood Cliffs, N.J.: Prentice-Hall, 1970.

——*Systems Analysis for Data Transmission*, Englewood Cliffs, N.J.: Prentice-Hall, 1973.

Chapter 17: A Management Information System

Chapter 18: Telecommunications and the News

PART **FIVE**

CASE HISTORIES

The stories of the telecommunication systems in use in two quite different major companies in the United States are presented here. Chapter 17 is about the Insurance Company of North America, now merged with Connecticut General to form the new CIGNA Corporation. It stresses the technological, especially data processing aspects. Chapter 18 is about the Washington Post, which, although published in Washington, D.C., is a worldwide news gathering and disseminating company. In both cases, the key point is that these companies could no longer operate without the most modern telecommunications systems.

CHAPTER **17**

A MANAGEMENT INFORMATION SYSTEM

Roger L. Schelm
CIGNA Corporation
Philadelphia, PA 19101

17.1 BACKGROUND OF THE INA CORPORATION

This chapter describes the evolutionary development of data processing and data communications within INA Corporation for the period 1977 through 1981. While this was being written in 1982, INA and Connecticut General merged to form CIGNA Corporation.

In 1981, INA Corporation was one of the nation's largest financial services organizations, offering products and services in property-casualty insurance, life and health insurance, health care, and investment management. Headquartered in Philadelphia, INA operated in approximately 145 countries and employed more than 25,000 people worldwide. The corporation ranked seventh in *Fortune* magazine's listing of diversified financial companies in the United States, based on assets of over $10 billion. Property-casualty insurance was INA's first business and in 1981 was its largest activity. This business was conducted primarily through Insurance Company of North America, founded in 1792 as America's first stock insurance company, and other subsidiaries and affiliates that were major factors in the worldwide commercial insurance market.

INA's property-casualty operations handled the full scope of risks for corporations and institutions, regardless of size or complexity. The company also provided risk management services for self-insureds, including claims management, statistical reporting, and loss control services. While commercial insurance business accounted for 80 percent of INA's property-casualty written premiums, the company also offered a wide range of personal insurance products and services.

INA's life and health insurance business began in 1957. This business was conducted principally by Life Insurance Company of North America, INA Life

Insurance Company, Investors Life Insurance Company of North America, and the Horace Mann Companies. These operations offered coverage to businesses, professional and trade associations, other groups, and individuals. These included group life insurance, accident and health coverages, pension plans, reinsurance, individual life insurance, and annuities.

INA entered the health care field in 1969. Its operations in this area included prepaid health care (HMOs) through INA Healthplan, Inc., and rehabilitation services through International Rehabilitation Associates, Inc. Both were the leading investor-owned organizations in their respective fields.

INA's investment group was formed in early 1980. It was responsible for management of INA's insurance portfolios, outside portfolio management, real estate development and holdings, equity participations, and special investments.

17.2 DATA COMMUNICATIONS

The history of INA's data communications in the late 1970s is a history of the computer-based business applications systems.

In 1977, the corporate processing center (CPC), located in southern New Jersey, was the central computer and data communications facility for INA Corporation. Originating from the CPC, the communications network consisted of four data networks: two for insurance operations, one for the operating systems, and one for computer program development. The latter utilized IBM's Time-Sharing Option (TSO), a full-function time-sharing system for interactive computing. The two principal operational networks for insurance processing were the online electronic insurance system (EIS) and the batch-oriented remote job entry (RJE) system. The RJE system handled batch processing and the major printing support for the business applications.

17.3 ELECTRONIC INSURANCE SYSTEM

17.3.1 Business Requirements

In the early 1970s, INA's premium and transaction volumes were increasing dramatically; for example, it was predicted that some insurance transaction volumes would more than double within four years. Processing and managing the vastly expanded workload associated with this growth required more time and staff.

The managers of the marketing service and claims offices, located throughout the United States, needed a system that would evaluate insurance risks against previously defined criteria; calculate premiums and commissions; maintain an integrated policy, premium, and claims data base; issue the insurance policy and renewal documents; bill producers (agents and brokers) and insureds; register data concerning policies in force; record and process claims and their payment; and produce management reports for INA's property and casualty insurance business.

Recognizing this need, senior corporate management placed significant emphasis on data processing studies and planning projects which led to the development of INA's EIS. Its phased-implementation schedule, which provided benefits in the early phases, eased its acceptance by skeptical office managers. By the mid-1970s EIS and its use of data communications were recognized as essential elements of doing business at INA. The growth of insurance business data and its handling requirements required the leapfrog in technology support that EIS provided.

17.3.2 Description

The EIS (pronounced "ice") network electronically connected INA's offices for policy and claims processing, data inquiry, and insurance policy production. EIS employed state-of-the-art equipment and techniques in electronic data processing to handle the various areas of insurance data activities, ranging from initial entry of a policy through policy updating and claims processing to reinsurance and management reporting.

This was one of the first insurance processing systems, if not *the* first. Designed to process all transactions for INA's insurance business, it addressed the operational processing of a policy and a claim and, secondarily, addressed the statistical, communication, MIS, and administrative aspects of the business.

The EIS name was designed to reflect incorporation of the following concepts:

• *Electronic.* Use of state-of-the-art equipment and techniques in the electronic data processing field
• *Insurance.* Coverage of major types and functions of risk-handling activities engaged in by INA and its associated companies
• *System.* Integrated handling of areas and activities of insurance processing, including initial entry of policy data, policy updating and renewal, claims processing, and reinsurance and reporting.

The Electronic Insurance Systems Division (EISD) had immediate responsibility for all EIS effort, including development of major system concepts; system design, implementation, and testing; and installation. Each major action of EISD occurred only with the participation and advice of INA's insurance organizations and with corporate approval.

The EIS information processing equipment was located within the CPC in New Jersey, approximately 10 miles from INA headquarters in Philadelphia. Input devices in INA field locations throughout North America directly connected to the CPC over the EIS network of communications lines.

17.3.3 Scope of EIS

EIS was designed to provide the full spectrum of processing activities for INA's extensive and diversified insurance business. General goals included:

- Reducing time lag in recording data for policy issuance and claim payment for the insured and agent
- Increasing accuracy
- Reducing time lag in responding to inquiries from the insured and agent regarding policy coverage and claim processing
- Reduced costs
- Providing a central, integrated data base of corporate insurance data for management information reports

The introduction of EIS was handled by personnel trained in human relations to ensure that the use of technology was not intimidating. Unlike today, when technology is embraced by large numbers of people, in the 1970s most people had not come into contact with computers or terminals. Acceptance was accomplished through a human-relations-oriented education and training process. Video training tapes were utilized extensively throughout the introduction of EIS. It was a unique learning experience for the participants and did much to win their support for the system.

17.3.4 Modular Design

A basic feature of EIS was the use of a modular, or building block, design. The modular design allowed for a phased-implementation schedule with controlled investment. Insurance or data processing activities were differentiated into self-contained units called *modules* so as to achieve optimum independence from each other. Thus, as a given activity changed, only the related module was affected, not the whole system. Its modular design enabled EIS to provide the capability of growth to meet increased business volumes and changing requirements. This has allowed EIS to accommodate changes throughout its existence.

In EIS, a software module was a set of related functions that were complete and consistent, could be precisely specified, and had a well-defined interface with other functions or modules. Modules were divided into insurance-oriented and computer-oriented groups. These two main groups were defined as follows:

1 Computer-oriented modules, which provided such capabilities as transmission, reception, and validation of data entries; maintenance, updating, and extraction of data in the various files of the data base; and scheduling and control of the actual processing activities of insurance-oriented application modules.

2 Insurance-oriented applications modules, comprising
    a Common-insurance-function modules, which could be generalized for all insurance business and which covered such functions as premium receivables and claims processing.
    b Policy-handling modules, distinguishable by, and hence implemented by, line of business. This was the largest group of modules, and included such insurance fields as personal residential, workers' compensation, personal auto, and commercial multiple risk.

17.3.5 New and Improved Services Provided

EIS offered many new services and greatly improved response time over currently available services. An example of a new service was the system that evaluated an insurance risk against previously defined criteria and calculated the probability of loss. An example of improved service was the automatic generation of renewal and payment notices by the computer. EIS also reduced the office's workload, since many transactions that formerly required extensive handling and time-consuming tracking were automated.

17.3.6 Key Operating Features

EIS provided a rapid and comprehensive data handling system that included entry, validation, error correction, storage, update, retrieval, and document issuance elements. Key operating features of the system are summarized as follows:

• Expedited data entry and minimized transcription errors through use of self-coding worksheets and CRT terminals that provided a picture of data being entered or corrected

• Provided for online data entry from marketing support and claims office locations, including an immediate transaction-level edit for format and completeness

• Provided response within seconds to inquiries on policy status, coverage, etc.

• Completed processing overnight, including detailed edits for content, relationship, and consistency

• Distributed notices of errors detected in overnight processing by the following morning

• Printed and mailed policy documents within 24 hours of transmission of correct data

17.4 GROWTH

In 1977, the nationwide, online EIS network consisted of approximately 30 communications lines serving slightly less than 100 locations to support over 400 CRTs and more than 150 printers. The batch-oriented RJE network provided 20 remote job entry stations in key locations in the United States, with the principal concentrations at the CPC in New Jersey and INA's headquarters facility in Philadelphia. In addition, the system for operating the computers utilized approximately 40 CRTs and printers. The fourth network for program development with TSO supported less than 20 terminals. Its principal usage was by the systems software specialists. Business applications computer programmers principally centered their development around batch entry utilizing RJE and were just starting to use online program editing with TSO.

In order to assure a high level of network availability, a plan was developed by the technical management to staff a network technical control organization. A commitment was made to obtain and retain a cadre of communication specialists with management and planning orientation. This was an early recognition that in order for a company to be in control of its communication future, it must have a staff to plan, monitor, and control it.

During the late 1970s, in order to ensure optimum network configuration and low cost, numerous trips were made to IBM's network architecture facility in North Carolina to perform network modeling and run snapshot simulations. The information obtained from these simulations allowed multiple alternatives to be considered and assisted the development of the network design and the related conversion phasing. The pressure to achieve an optimal solution and to do it in a cost-effective way was the driving force for the usage of these simulation services. Because of today's interwoven integration of computers and communications, network modeling and simulation have become critical planning functions for the managers of large computer-communication facilities.

17.5 1978

17.5.1 Centralization Impact

In 1978, the number of communications lines in the EIS network showed modest growth. However, the RJE network had large growth because of senior management's decision to move to centralization of computer capabilities in order to take advantage of the economies of scale. This central data center concept was implemented, and the work on the computers in remote offices and subsidiaries, ranging from IBM 370/20s to IBM 360/158s, was transferred to the central mainframes located in the CPC, and the data was transmitted utilizing the RJE network. Some temporary lines were added during the larger conversions in order to minimize any interruption to business. The operating system network grew to keep pace with this increased workload. TSO showed dramatic growth as the online computer program development system provided increased productivity for the programming staff.

17.5.2 Quest

Also in 1978, INA's in-house time-sharing facility, Quest, was introduced to provide the capabilities of time-sharing computing and decision support for INA professionals. The impetus for the introduction of the Quest system originated with the professional managerial staff who utilized such products in college or were starting to use similar products from commercial time-sharing services. The Quest system was based on the IBM virtual storage personal computing (VSPC) program product. It supported the IBM 3270 CRT and a wide range of typewriter-type terminals. Software availability ranged from programming languages—APL, BASIC and FORTRAN—to preprogrammed user-friendly business application packages for financial planning and information storage and retrieval. Two of these IBM-produced packages included ADRS, a department reporting system, and APLDI, an information retrieval system. The INA professional could direct the charts, graphs, and textual output from these applications to special graphics devices for multicolor charts, transparencies, or 35-mm slides. One communication line and four special graphics devices were connected. A public packet-switched common carrier was contracted and installed for connection to the VSPC software. This provided a reasonable cost dial-up facility for use of the Quest system.

17.5.3 Systems Network Architecture

The rules by which terminals and computers talk to each other are called network protocol. Before 1978 the various data networks serving the corporate processing sites did not all use the same protocol. To make communication possible among all sites and to reduce the redundancy of network equipment, all networks had to be upgraded to a compatible protocol.

To accomplish this INA chose IBM's systems network architecture (SNA), a communications package consisting of both hardware and software components. A major feature of SNA is the use of a standard network protocol to resolve the incompatibilities in the transfer of information among different application systems, computers, and terminals.

During 1978, planning, development, and testing was accomplished for IBM's SNA. Changes made in anticipation of the SNA implementation included changing all EIS network equipment to SNA-compatible equipment. SNA single-system support provided the following benefits:

1 A single-system resource-sharing facility whereby a terminal operator could access several application programs on the same computer from a single terminal

2 Support of a distributed processing terminal

3 Support of efficient line control

On the other hand, the network control operator for the EIS network required the installation of additional support programs to assist in the monitoring and control of the network. This reflects the fact that greater flexibility and ease-of-use in one area often must be balanced against increasing complexity in another.

17.6 1979

In 1979, the EIS network experienced modest growth as the number of CRTs and printers increased to just short of 500 and 190, respectively. The RJE network continued its rapid growth as the centralization of computer capabilities continued. The operating system network had only limited growth. However, during the year, INA introduced a new network for computer program development. This was the Applied Data Research, Inc., ROSCOE system. ROSCOE (Remote Operating System Conversational Operating Environment), an online conversational system designed primarily for use in the development and implementation of computer-programmed application systems, was installed to replace the TSO facility for the business applications computer programmers. Approximately 50 CRTs were provided for program development this first year—double those previously provided using TSO. The time-sharing system, Quest, experienced major controlled growth as it was offered throughout the corporation.

The EIS network conversion to SNA's common-line control protocol was initiated during this year and completed in 1980. This was accompanied by a conversion from a half-duplex-line protocol to a full-duplex-line protocol. Also, in order to extend the EIS network to Alaska, it was necessary to install a satellite link through a vendor, RCA Satcom.

During 1979, INA also began to upgrade the EIS network from 4800 to 9600 bps dataphone services and AT&T's dataphone digital service (DDS). DDS was an all-digital, highly reliable communications service which replaced INA's analog modems and lines in the 1979–1980 time frame. These upgrades were initiated to provide the performance benefits of improved response time and increased availability. One-quarter of the 4800-to-9600-bps upgrades were handled in order of heaviest-to-lightest communication load to obtain the greatest advantage early in the project.

During the same year, an in-house coaxial cable program within the CPC was gaining a foothold, reducing the number of remote lines needed for the computer systems. Usage of coaxial cable was practical for the operating system network, the TSO network, and, because the programmers were resident in a connecting building, the ROSCOE network. As a result of the increased use of the ROSCOE system by applications programmers the remote lines for TSO were removed. The ROSCOE network had rapid growth from 50 to over 75 CRTs for programmer access. Online program development had definitely been accepted by the programmers!

The operating system increased by one communication line and four devices. The RJE network growth slowed to modest proportions to handle small increases in demand. The EIS network showed small growth. However, a large growth occurred in CRTs: from almost 500 to over 650. Printers on the EIS network increased to 195.

17.7 1980 AND 1981

17.7.1 General Growth

In 1980, the multiple system network facility, MSNF, which provided a capability for traffic to flow between terminals and programs distributed across multiple computers and networks, was installed across the computer systems at the CPC. An additional IBM 3705 communication controller was obtained to improve availability. In order to reduce costs a private multiplexor circuit was installed for Philadelphia-based professionals using the dial-up facility of the Quest and ROSCOE networks.

Additional IBM network-control software tools were installed to assist in the operation of the networks. These tools were very important to the running of the network because of its increased complexity and importance. The communications networks had become the nerve system of the corporation's businesses. In addition, distributed processing was supported with the installation of SNA.

17.7.2 CPC II

Major plans were underway for use of satellite transmission systems with the approval of plans for a second corporate processing center (CPC II) to be located in the Denver, Colorado, area. The recognition of the dependency on data processing by the corporation initiated disaster contingency planning in the late 1970s. A portion of the work led to the decision to develop the CPC II and equally split the computer workload between the two CPCs, with each to provide backup for the critical computer workload of the corporation. The extensive amount of communications planning necessary to accomplish this split cannot be overstated. As part of these plans, INA developed a satellite network to connect CPC I to CPC II, as well as to the Horace Mann subsidiary in Springfield, Illinois.

During the period in which the CPC II was brought online, many types of network support were required to make it a successful installation. Active data networks were transferred without measurable impact by using AT&T "twin-tailing" techniques, thereby permitting the relocation of application processing without network outage. Intersite high-speed trunk lines between CPC I and II were provided by AT&T (56,000 bps terrestrial) and RCA (56,000 bps satellite). Ten-meter dish-satellite antennas were installed at both CPC I and CPC II, and a 5-meter antenna was installed at Horace Mann.

By 1981 the EIS network had experienced growth to the point where it utilized and supported over 1300 CRTs and printers in the field. In the future, growth in the EIS network will be driven by the changes brought by the implementation of distributed processing systems. Quest grew to over 75 lines with over 150 devices and dial-up. Quest is expected to continue to grow at the rate of 20 to 30 terminals per year for 1982 and the foreseeable future.

17.8 PLANNING FOR THE FUTURE

Looking back, it is doubtful that INA could have survived in the 1970s without its commitment to data processing and data communications. Up to this point only minor change has occurred in the way people work as a result of data processing and communications, but in the future these changes can be expected to be significant. Work will be restructured, functions combined, new jobs created, and new management techniques introduced. It will be essential for human-resource management planning to be integrated into the strategic, tactical, and operational technology planning.

Also, it will be necessary to place greater emphasis on long-range data (and voice) communications planning owing to the complicated rate tariffs, constant changes in rates, increased competition in the field, and restructuring of AT&T. Guidelines and standards must be developed to assist and direct managers in the development of the long-range data communications plans. The impetus for dramatic uses of technology should be forthcoming from the planners and managers who understand the technology. They should be encouraged to bring forth proposals to utilize technology to decrease expenses, increase marketing, improve distribution methods, and favorably affect other facets of the business. Today, as expense control and reduction can be characterized as the "vehicle of change," technology can be characterized as the vehicle's "engine."

Changes in the communications environment are expected to come faster, be more complex, and be more far-reaching in the future. The last five years are only an introduction to the changes in communications that will need to be handled in the future. Successful communications plans are necessary for company survival and prosperity in the marketplace of the 1980s and 1990s.

CHAPTER 18

TELECOMMUNICATIONS AND THE NEWS

Elizabeth Loker
Donald Till
The Washington Post
Washington, DC 20071

18.1 BACKGROUND

In 1877 the first primitive telephone switchboards were being installed, the French telegraph service officially adopted the Baudot code as the standard for transmitting text over telephone lines, and Stilson Hutchins founded *The Washington Post*. Since that time, the telecommunications and newspaper industries have matured together, with newspapers always in the forefront of users seeking faster and more reliable ways to gather and distribute its news. Even earlier in the 19th century, news wire services, the wholesalers of the news-gathering business, seized upon the telegraph as a means of getting their dispatches to individual newspapers as quickly as possible. In many respects, the rise of the modern newspaper paralleled, and was made possible by, the rise of speedy, efficient communications technology.

Julius Reuter (1816–1899), founder of Reuter's News Agency, was among the earliest and most imaginative users of the new technology. There was a time in 1850 when there was a 90-mile gap between the Paris–Brussels telegraph lines and the Berlin–Arkin lines. Reuter bridged the gap by pigeon post until just after Christmas 1850, when the Berlin-to-Paris link was made, and the pigeons were retired.

In these early days, telegraph circuits provided a means of transferring information quickly over a long distance, albeit with manual operating procedures and cumbersome physical-document delivery at each end. Telegraph networks expanded rapidly; continents were linked by undersea cable; mechanical innovations improved the speed of transmission. The next major breakthrough, in the 1920s, came with the development of the page teleprinter. Wire services moved quickly to establish private teletypewriter networks, and newspapers installed teleprinters to receive news from all parts of the world. The clack of the teletype machine was quickly absorbed as part of the background noise of the modern newsroom.

As the worldwide telephone system expanded through the decades of the 20th century, newspapers and wire services came to depend heavily on the network, both for voice services, dictating stories by phone, and for facsimile and newsphoto transmission.

The old telegraph speed of 60 words per minute—the maximum speed an operator could handle—faded long ago. News dispatches are now transmitted by satellite around the world. Transmission of full newspaper pages to widely separated printing plants is common practice.

The modern newsroom is a very different place today than it was even 10 years ago. Gone is the noise of the teleprinters and typewriters. News dispatches are sent directly from computer to computer, news photos appear on fully automatic receivers, the video display terminal has replaced the typewriter, and the phototypesetter has replaced the linotype machine with its pots of molten lead. These advances in production technology, along with the evolution of modern telecommunications facilities, make possible much-expanded news coverage and increasing levels of integration within newspaper systems.

As the next major steps in modern telecommunications unfold, the newspaper industry is examining new ways to apply it to printing and, ultimately, to the distribution of its product to its readers.

18.2 OVERVIEW OF NEWSPAPER PRODUCTION

While the demands are different, the basic tasks in assembling a newspaper are the same for both large and small publications. News reports must be written or assembled from wire service transmissions, the copy must be edited and composed to fit the space available, and the news text must be integrated with advertisements, photographs, and drawings to create newspaper pages. Next, the page must be converted into printing plates for attachment to cylinders on high-speed rotary presses. Naturally this oversimplification leaves out many steps in the process of creating, selling, and producing material for use in the paper. But these basic steps highlight the areas where automation and communication technologies play an important role.

18.3 TELECOMMUNICATIONS AND NEWSGATHERING

Let us first clarify that *tele*communications in a newspaper environment does not necessarily imply communication over vast distance. The circuits used may indeed connect the newsroom, or, more accurately, the news-editing systems, to a correspondent writing on another continent, but such circuits also connect reporters in the local courthouse, the state assembly chambers, or the city police department's offices to the news system. To *The Washington Post*'s Raytheon

News Editing system these lines serve as inputs, just as VDTs in the newsroom do. These "inputs" come in all shapes and sizes. Local reporters may simply phone in and dictate their on-the-spot report to a person who enters it on VDT. Reporters may carry along a portable terminal to the Washington Redskins' football game, typing in the story as the game progresses and filing over a dial-in line minutes after the game is over. Foreign correspondents typically use telex to file their reports, though portable terminals compatible with overseas telephone equipment are becoming more common.

Wire service stories and supplemental news services arrive on a wide variety of input lines ranging in speed from 60 to 1200 words per minute and in widely varying formats, from uppercase text only to completely encoded "typesetter-ready" material such as stock tables and sports scores.

Telecommunications, then, allows the original author wherever he or she may be, to file the story quickly and easily into the newspaper's computer system. Within the office, communication technology facilitates the flow of news stories from writer to editor to composition and final typesetting. Increasingly, the movement does not stop here. The story may also be made available to other newspapers and then filed in a near or distant "archival data base" as part of the newspaper's library.

Once all the stories for an edition of the paper have been assembled on their pages with the appropriate photos and advertisements, *The Washington Post,* like many other newspapers, must make those pages available to remote platemaking and printing facilities. In the case of *The Washington Post,* this is done by scanning the pages in a laser-driven reading device, called an Eocom Laserite, and transmitting the pages by microwave radio to the production plants in Springfield, Virginia, and the southeast section of Washington, D.C., where they are received by Laserite "page writers" that take the first step in the platemaking process.

18.4 CONSTRUCTING THE APPROPRIATE COMMUNICATIONS COMPLEX

A newspaper is an extremely perishable commodity. A news story that fails to reach the paper in time for that day's edition may be useless the following day. If the newspaper is not ready to be printed on time, and the paper cannot be delivered, important railway or airplane connections for out-of-town sales will be missed. It is extremely important, therefore, that the communications facilities used in the newspaper's operations be available when needed and have adequate backup should they fail.

Given unlimited financial resources, it would be possible for the paper to establish local, national, and international telecommunication networks that were virtually failsafe and available 24 hours per day. Such networks are expensive and resources are limited; thus, the challenge is to find a balance that provides sufficient reliability at the proper level of investment.

The newspaper has a need for two different kinds of incoming telecommunication facilities. News reports from the wire services are delivered on dedicated circuits 24 hours a day, 7 days a week. In addition, the paper needs temporary facilities on short notice at any time of the day or night to receive incoming copy. Dedicated services are provided either by lines leased from telecommunications carriers, or, increasingly, by satellite channels. Telex, TWX, telephone, packet-switching services, and other volume-sensitive facilities where connection is made by dial-up are used to serve the second need. Backup of these usual communication lines is normally either the public telex or telephone network.

The collection of news copy from the paper's own reporting sources constitute only a small fraction of the content received. In addition to the standard news wire services, photos, weather maps, stock tables, television program listings, and supplemental feature stories must all be accommodated by the telecommunications system.

The two major U.S. wire services, the Associated Press and United Press International, provide communication facilities to deliver their own reporting and make capacity available to other information providers. These services range from the provision of a low-speed dedicated channel to high-speed delivery at 1200 words per minute via the AP Datafeature and UPI Datanews circuits. Both provide the computer resources to manage this traffic and use standardized protocols agreed upon under the auspices of the American Newspaper Publishers Association.

The collection of material from the newspapers' own reporters and stringers from national and international sources poses other kinds of problems, particularly in the international arena. Almost without exception, telecommunication facilities outside the United States are provided through government-owned monopolies. The quality and scope of these services range from excellent and instantaneous to almost nonexistent. Political problems can totally disrupt telecommunications from a nation, as was the case when martial law was declared in the Polish crisis of 1982–1983. At the time, not a single telephone or telegraph line into or out of the country was available. Time differences between parts of the world often mean that correspondents filing their stories have a difficult time maintaining their contact with the newsroom staff, further complicating things when something goes wrong.

In general, international facilities are provided under recommendations established by the international telecommunications union in Geneva. Newspapers are users of these facilities, as are airlines, banks, and other institutions. Over the years, however, some consideration has been given to the unique requirements of the press.

For many years, a special "press telegram" rate permitted the transmission of news intended for publication at a fraction of the standard rate. During World War II the British government established a Commonwealth press rate which allowed the transmission of press cables between the United Kingdom and any part of the British Commonwealth for a penny a word. Many foreign newspaper organizations quickly established London offices to take advantage of this. Today London remains a major hub of international press communications, even though the press rate is no longer offered.

For many years, short-wave radio facilities have been offered to the press at special rates. These are used less today than they were in the past but still provide the only means of delivery to some areas of the world. In the late 1960s, the U.S. international record carriers—ITT, RCA, and Western Union—began to offer a press bulletin service (PBS) to newspapers. The service provides dedicated low-speed teleprinter channels (60 to 100 words per minute), one way or bidirectional, at very low rates. Much of the world's international news traffic is now carried by the PBS, which is accepted by about 50 countries.

18.5 MANAGING THE COMMUNICATIONS COMPLEX

In its three separate roles—as a newspaper, joint owner of a supplemental news service, and member of an international consortium—*The Washington Post* uses different services to meet specific requirements.

As a newspaper, *The Washington Post* newsroom is equipped with a large computer system for writing and editing news stories prepared by the staff and received from other information suppliers.

As a partner in the *Los Angeles Times–Washington Post* news service, it transmits stories from its editorial computer to the news services' computer. Editors at the news service then select, edit, and incorporate this copy into the file, along with copy from *The Los Angeles Times* and other sources.

As a member of the consortium, *The Washington Post* shares costs and communication facilities with other consortium members, providing an international network which carries the bulk of foreign-correspondent traffic into its computer system.

All of the telecommunications services are merged, coordinated, and supervised in a communication center (ComCen) in Washington. This center is one node in a triangular network linking computers in Los Angeles, Washington, and London.

The ComCen is staffed by professional operations personnel and serves as a funnel for incoming and outgoing traffic for the paper, the news service, and the consortium. This kind of arrangement offers all users of the ComCen a more sophisticated and reliable system than any individual member could reasonably afford.

18.6 PRODUCTION AND DISTRIBUTION OF THE NEWSPAPER

Several years ago, *The Washington Post* needed to expand its capacity to print copies of the newspaper for distribution in its circulation area. At the time, the decision was made to build a new printing plant in the northern Virginia suburbs, where real estate and building costs were lower than they would be in downtown Washington. As many other newspapers have found, it is also advantageous to print and distribute at least a portion of the press run at a remote plant, since the area served by the distributors and carriers has expanded as the suburbs have spread farther from the city. Today *The Washington Post* is printed in three locations: at the main offices in downtown Washington, at a plant in Springfield, Virginia (12 miles distant), and in southeast Washington (about 3 miles from the main offices). Approximately 30 percent of the papers are printed downtown, 40 percent at Springfield, and 30 percent at the southeast plant.

All prepress functions, including the composition of pages, are done in the downtown plant. Pages are composed and then scanned by a page-reading device and sent over the communications network to laser-page writers that expose a negative to be used in the platemaking process.

At the time the Springfield plant was constructed, *The Washington Post* purchased and installed a private microwave system to link the plants. The Rockwell 12-GHz digital microwave system provides a wide-band 44-megabit transmission path which can be multiplexed into seven channels of 6.312 megabits each. This permits transmission of a full page of the newspaper via each of these channels in about 1 minute. Of the available channels, *The Washington Post* uses two primary and two spare for page transmission. Another channel is further subdivided to provide up to 72 channels of digital-pulse-code-modulated telephone and data transmission capacity of varying speeds, the lowest speed being 300 baud.

The system is two-way between the composing room in the downtown plant and Springfield. The composing room's page reader is also hard-wired to its local platemaking equipment. The service to the southeast plant is one-way only.

All aspects of the system contain redundant components to provide backup. A spare channel is switched in automatically, without loss of signal if any of the primary or spare channels fail in operation.

A repeater station is located atop an apartment building roughly halfway between downtown Washington and Springfield. This provides two independent hops of approximately 6 miles each, giving protection against signal fading. (Signal fading occurs in a 12-GHz signal during heavy rainfall.) The repeater station is also used to transmit the signal back to the plant in southeast Washington because of line-of-sight obstructions between downtown and southeast Washington.

All sites in the network area are equipped with remote-alarm systems so that a technician can be advised of local or remote faults as they occur. The transmitters, receivers, and multiplexing equipment are powered by 48-volt batteries continuously charged from the AC power network via high-quality, regulated charging equipment. The batteries will support the operation of the microwave systems for 8 hours in the event of a power failure at any site. (One power outage of 5 hours at the repeater station went unnoticed by operations personnel at the plants, since all equipment continued to function normally.)

Alternatives to a private microwave system for applications like this one were explored before *The Washington Post* purchased this system. Terrestrial communications provided by the telephone company were ruled out, since the fastest line available was 1.544 megabits, only about one-quarter the speed of the microwave system. With the number of pages that must be transmitted on deadline each night, a maximum of a minute per page was considered mandatory. Satellite transmission is an alternative; however, it is far too expensive for the distances involved. Other newspapers, like *The Wall Street Journal,* whose printing plants are located all over the country, rely on satellites. As the future develops, optical fiber may become an economical alternative for short-distance applications. These transmission lines have many of the advantages of microwave without the problems of FCC frequency coordination and licensing, and the signal does not fade as atmospheric conditions worsen. Optical-fiber technology is still out of reach for private users in most cases because of the expense of laying cable runs between the sites.

18.7   DISTRIBUTION OF THE NEWS SERVICE

As mentioned earlier, *The Washington Post* acts as the communication systems manager for the *Los Angeles Times–Washington Post* news service. The news service editorial operation in Washington selects and distributes stories from the two newspapers to 220 U.S. and 229 foreign newspaper clients each day. Several other services are also integrated into the service, with LAT-WP serving as distribution agent for Agence France Presse and Deutsche Presse Agentur, and for stories from other Times-Mirror-owned newspapers.

Material for the news service is distributed over many channels to better serve its worldwide subscriber base. In the United States, subscribers may receive the transmission in one of several forms: computer to computer at 1200 words per minute via either the AP or UPI networks; at 88 words per minute in 6-level typesetter-coded format or by airmail-printed delivery if necessary. The transmission to overseas clients varies by country. To Asia and Australia, communications are at 60 wpm in 5-level Baudot code; to Europe, the Middle East, and Africa at 100 wpm in 5-level code; and to South America, Central America, the Caribbean, and some European countries the service is distributed by the Deutsche Presse Agentur.

In addition, the news service has developed a system called DataCall, principally for use by foreign clients. This service provides a convenient way of handling the 60,000 words per day of English language copy provided by the news service. Instead of receiving the entire feed, DataCall users are equiped with a teleprinter and dial-up modem operating at either 300 or 1200 baud. Using the telephone network or international packet-switching services, subscribers call the LAT-WP computer in Washington and obtain a list of the news items available for release at the time. Each list includes a description of the story and an identification code. Subscribers can select only the items they wish to translate and use.

18.8 THE ELECTRONIC LIBRARY

After publication of each final edition of the newspaper, *The Washington Post*'s library staff selects stories for inclusion in an electronic library. This archive of *Post* stories is made available to the public through Mead Data Central's Nexis service, and indexes to the *Post* are available through other online information retrieval services. Stories are transmitted daily from the editorial system to Mead's computers in Dayton, Ohio. The transmissions are made using a modified version of the ANPA standard protocol.

18.9 EMERGING ISSUES

New applications of telecommunications are beginning to be investigated in two important areas. Much work remains to be done in both areas before they become economically feasible, even though the technology seems relatively simple. The first area has to do with the receipt of national advertising materials. Many large national advertisers, through their advertising agencies, prepare for publication identical advertisements for insertion in papers all over the country. At present, all these ads are mailed or delivered by special courier services to the papers. Since both the AP and UPI have moved toward satellite distribution of their services, satellite receiver dishes have become commonplace at the newspaper plant. The ANPA's technical committees have been investigating the possibility of using these facilities for transmission of advertising materials in addition to news. Currently, there remain several logistical problems to solve. It is also not clear as yet whether satellite distribution can compete economically at the volumes anticipated.

The other major application that appears to be technically, if not economically, viable at present is the delivery of news and advertising to the newspaper's traditional subscribers using a videotex or teletext system. Several experiments are underway throughout the industry to test product concepts and consumer reactions to electronic delivery.

Perhaps the most important point to be made about the *Post*'s telecommunications system is that there is no longer a question of whether or not to have such a system. A modern news gathering and publishing organization such as *The Washington Post* can no longer operate without it.

RECOMMENDED READING

Bagdikian, Ben H., *The Information Machine,* New York: Harper & Row, 1971.

Compaine, Benjamin H., *The Newspaper Industry in the 1980's: An Assessment of Economics and Technology,* White Plains, N.Y.: Knowledge Industry Publications, 1980.

Francis-Williams, Edmund, *Transmitting World News,* New York: Arno, 1972.

Smith, Anthony, *Goodbye Guttenberg: The Newspaper Revolution of the 1980s,* New York: Oxford University Press, 1980.

Chapter 19: Management and Telecommunications in the Future

PART **SIX**

THE FUTURE

The book concludes with an overview of what we have covered so far and a look into the future. This is not a technology forecast but a view of how changing telecommunication technology has and will continue to change the practice of management and the very nature of work.

MANAGEMENT AND TELECOMMUNICATIONS IN THE FUTURE

Charles T. Meadow
DIALOG Information Services, Inc.
Palo Alto, CA 94304
Albert S. Tedesco
WWSG-TV
Philadelphia, PA 19128

19.1 INTRODUCTION

In many ways, it would be fitting to end this book with a prediction of the management-related telecommunications technology of the future. However, such predictions have a distressing habit of not working out or, almost as embarrassing, of coming to pass before the book in which they were written is published. One reason for the hazardous nature of prediction, which we hope by now we have conveyed to you, is that the technology that survives is as much dependent on the behavior of users as on the inventions of the engineers. Microfilm did not revolutionize the world. Television did. Electronic games played a large role in creating the personal computer industry. Who would have predicted that, say, 10 years ago? The telephone, 100 years ago, had a spectacular rise, which no one could have predicted. In fact, Pierce (1977) noted, "In 1876, when Bell invented the telephone, there was no need for it." It was the right invention at the right time, but recognized as such only in retrospect. It dramatically and permanently changed the behavior of its users and this, more than its technological cleverness, made it what it has become, the central telecommunications system of the modern world.

We intend, then, in this final chapter, to review some of the salient points that were made in earlier chapters with regard to the role of telecommunications in management. Then we will consider their impact on management of the future.

19.2 SOME TRENDS AND OBSERVATIONS ON MANAGEMENT AND TELECOMMUNICATIONS

"The nature of the business enterprise and the nature of communications will be so interrelated that they will be largely the same subject." (Freeman, 1981). This quotation appeared in Chapter 1 and is the theme of this book. More succinctly, *management is communication.*

Communication is at least a two-party process. One person, one computer, even one company does not communicate. Communication, as Shannon (1949) pointed out, requires both an origin and a destination, a transmitter and a receiver, someone talking and someone listening. In human terms, meaningful communication also involves acting upon a message received. This may mean carrying out the orders of headquarters, or becoming convinced to buy a product, or correctly operating a machine. The point here is that mere possession or operation of the technology of communication is not enough. Communication, in human terms, must get the recipient to do the right thing. This calls for skill on the part of a communicator and responsibility as well.

A corollary of the previous point is that the perceptions of an organization on the part of an employee, customer, regulator, competitor, or supplier will often be formed solely as a result of a brief encounter through an electronic medium of communication. This may be a computer terminal (as a bank teller machine), a television advertisement, an information retrieval service, or a telephone conversation. Other than in the routine provisioning of an office with telephones and computer terminals, how to form that perception of the company may be the first and most important of a typical manager's considerations relative to telecommunication.

New technology brings with it new behavior. If managers *can* communicate with their subordinates in the field, they *will;* and if they do, the relationship of the field and headquarters is forever changed. If television news reporters *can* broadcast news while it is happening, they *will,* and this may forever change the viewers' perceptions, as in the U.S. Democratic Party political convention in Chicago in 1968, the war scenes from Vietnam in the 1970s, or even live sports broadcasts brought vividly into the home. (One of the editors, on the night this paragraph was written, sent the other a message, via electronic mail, over 3000 miles, to the effect that he had watched the basketball championship, seen "their team" win, and felt he knew the players personally, never having met one of them.)

The installation of a new computer system in an office changes the office. Information, once difficult to get, is now readily available, not only to a few managers, but to much of the office staff. Attention shifts to what to do with it, how to keep it accurate, what, given the new information, is *now* the information most wanted.

Information and communication systems, once users become dependent upon them, create their own scarce resources, and therefore the need for regulation and the excuse to squabble over them. Conflicts over control of radio frequencies arise at the extreme local level, when a personal computer interferes with television reception. Computer manufacturers are unwilling to provide shielding, at extra cost, hence they encroach on someone else's frequency. At the international level, these conflicts arise when scarce radio frequencies become as much the object of international bargaining as does ownership of land. In an office, "combat" may occur over rights to use the computer, who may have a password, who does and does not use a terminal, who may have access to long-distance telephone lines or the facsimile machine.

Whether or not one subscribes to the idea of Marshall McLuhan's global village, the world is growing more and more interconnected, in the telecommunications sense. We have seen that once telephone networks connected only affinity groups, such as all a town's doctors or pharmacists, but now the telephone network is a global affair. The simple electronic "beeper" or the more complex radiotelephone do, in fact, constitute a form of electronic tether between a person and the home base, which may itself be a transitory thing. In the United States, there is the tendency to refer to the place where a president is vacationing as "the vacation White House," meaning that the White House, the seat of the U.S. Government, is wherever the president is, that the building in Washington is merely a symbol. The information and communications machines, brought in to enhance management, become one of the most precious resources of management and must be protected at all costs.

Where once great value was imputed to stores of human knowledge, now much of that knowledge can be put into computers or can be gotten from a human being located in some other place. More and more, what is valued in human beings is skill and finding, evaluating, and using information. The world grows less and less tolerant of failure to find information if it is known to exist somewhere in the world.

19.3 MANAGEMENT IN THE TELECOMMUNICATIONS WORLD

The major changes that are forecast for management all relate to communications. The computer, which we have tended to regard as a communication tool, is one agent of this change. It brings to modern, and even more to future, managers more information about operations, markets, world economic trends, and technological developments than their predecessors of a generation ago ever conceived of. The computer, coupled with other communications media, reduces the time scale in which decisions are made and thereby creates more demand for information to be produced and for faster delivery. It also increases the amount of work expected to be done, and the amount and type of information generated, to support a decision-making effort.

Physical decentralization is another trend. Whether manifested as a move of production facilities relentlessly toward lower-priced labor markets, or headquarters to suburbs or sunbelt locations, or individuals to their home offices, telecommunications enables these trends to exist and is further spurred by them to continue to develop new products that still further accelerate these trends.

Corporate structural changes are another trend: mergers, acquisitions, and divestitures, all place upon management a requirement to be ready and able to communicate with new, possibly distant, people on short notice.

Workflow patterns are changing. There are more typing pools, more "matrix" organizations, more contracting out of certain tasks (for example, operating the computers), more work shifted to the secretary, no longer burdened with so much typing, copying, and filing. The secretary is now a more important person than before the day of word processing and photocopiers.

Leadership style is moving toward more and more participatory management. Although this does not necessarily require technological aid to communication, it does make managers and employees more conscious of communication in all its manifestations. The growth of WATS telephone services to enable companies to provide direct, person-to-person communication about problems with the company's products or services is a manifestation of this trend.

This is what Freeman meant by saying that management and communications will be largely the same subject. It will shortly be no longer a bonus to the firm if a manager knows how to understand telephone traffic models: he or she will be expected to. Similarly, as AT&T loses no opportunity to inform us in television advertising, the sales manager who discovers that the telephone is less expensive than air travel will be the rule, not the exception. A dogged insistence on having messages to the field typed and posted may cost a company its competitive edge.

Successively, the telephone, television, and videotex have broken down traditional (and often artificial) barriers to communication between people. Modern management's tendency to move people and organizations, to buy and sell subsidiaries, and to operate the company more openly mean that new communications technologies will break down more barriers. Which ones? That, manager of the future, will be your job to determine, implement, and learn to adapt to.

19.4 IS IT UTOPIA?

The forward progress of technology seems always to bring with it some negative effects. These are not limited to communications technology, nor to the 20th century. The telephone was denounced as an instrument of the devil when first introduced, and the famous—or infamous—Luddites of the early 19th century attacked factory machinery to protect their jobs. Medical advances have often been seen as thwarting the will of God, and even today fluoridating water is seen as a political issue in some places.

A favorite theme of fiction is the dehumanizing effect of technology, especially information technology. Orwell's *1984* and Huxley's *Brave New World* emphasized the dangers that technology brings, as it allows for excessive control by those in power. Vonnegut, in *Player Piano,* also brought out the degradation of people put out of work by what we now call intelligent machinery, and in an earlier day we had the folksong *John Henry* lamenting the degradation of men put out of work by machinery able to outperform them physically. Yet, Saint Exupéry, quoted several times earlier, and other writers, became poetic about the wonders of one machine or the other—an airplane, a sword, or a pen.

Is technology a liberator or an enslaver? The answer, not surprisingly, depends on the people who use and control it. While many decry the poverty and alienation of today's industrial society and yearn for a more bucolic life, it is almost certain that their idea of country life includes farming with a tractor and fishing with rods and reels. Certainly, most people in the industrialized countries are better off today, and fewer are worse off, than were their ancestors of 200–300 years ago in such categories as material possessions, health, education, and political and religious freedom—hardly an inconsiderable benefit of the industrial revolution.

Yet, the negative side is or can be there. Some critics feel that *1984* was written about conditions in the then-current United Kingdom (immediate post-World War II era), with the date set fictionally into what seemed then the remote future.

What is the essence of the Orwellian prediction? It is that an excess of control will inhibit, or even eliminate, free choice. Or, we may say it eliminates uncertainty and hence a role for chance in human affairs. *Information,* in the engineering sense, is the dispelling of uncertainty, some amount of choice about the meaning of symbols or events, and information resolves that uncertainty. *If there is no uncertainty, then there also is no information.*

The total removal of uncertainty is also the removal of the challenge, worry, and agony in human affairs, and also the pride, fun, and sense of accomplishment of having done the "right" thing, scaled the mountain, or won a contract against all odds. A world without uncertainty as to what is going to happen, or is going to be allowed to happen, or what the consequences of some action might be is a world without challenge, and so without accomplishment.

As a simple example, we all like and respect reliable employees—those, for example, who are present and ready when a job has to be done, especially those who sense the need and appear without being coerced. But what is reliability when the employee is tethered to an electronic beeper? Where is the pride in reliability and dedication when there is no choice? Similarly, there is pride in being a branch manager, but what happens to that pride when the home office makes all the decisions? How can a middle manager prove his or her trustworthiness when there is no occasion for trust because no uncertainty is allowed to exist?

For each negative, there seems to be a positive outcome of technology, a sort of Newton's third law of the sociology of science. While much of modern managerial control systems dehumanize, teleconferencing and electronic mail can—they have the potential to—put some humanity back into the process. In this present world, we pay a premium for people who are "good with people," who can negotiate, sell, convince, in face-to-face encounters. Articulation, tone of voice, and body language are all important parts of person-to-person communication. Much electronic and paper mail transmission systems do away with these subtle communication forms.

There is a story, perhaps apocryphal, that John L. Lewis, late leader of the United Mine Workers of America, when in a formal negotiating session and ready to get really serious, would excuse himself to the men's room. It was understood that his opposite number was to appear at the next urinal and there get down to business. Such a technique has no place in computer conferencing systems. The most modern electronic forms are bringing back person-to-person communication, albeit over long-distance, and not quite in the John L. Lewis style. These systems, which are on the brink of becoming ubiquitous office tools, could either humanize or dehumanize our organizations. We do not yet know which way it will work out.

Our final challenge to our readers is that it is up to you to see to it that technology is properly used, that it be a benefit, not a cost, to humanity. In the words of Hippocrates, quoted earlier by one of our authors, "Make a habit of two things—to help, or at least do no harm."

REFERENCES

Freeman, Harry L., "The Long-Term Outlook in Communications," in Robert W. Haigh, George Gerbner, and Richard B. Byrne (eds.), *Communications in the Twenty-First Century*, New York: Wiley-Interscience, 1981.

Pierce, John R., "The Telephone and Society in the Past 100 Years," in Ithiel de Sola Pool (ed.), *The Social Impact of the Telephone*, Cambridge: MIT Press, 1977.

RECOMMENDED READING

Naisbitt, John. *Megatrends: Ten New Directions Transforming Our Lives*, New York: Warner Books, 1982.

Cetron, Marvin, and Thomas O'Toole, *Encounters with the Future*, New York: McGraw-Hill, 1982.

Drucker, Peter F., *The Changing World of the Executive*, New York: Times Books, 1982.

Oettinger, Anthony G., "Information Resources: Knowledge and Power in the 21st Century," *Science*, 1980, *209*, 191–198.

Paisley, William, "Information and Work," in Brenda Dervin and Melvin J. Voight (eds.), *Progress in Communication Sciences* (vol. 2), Norwood, N.J.: Ablex, 1980.

Sheppard, C. Stewart, and Donald C. Carroll (eds.), *Working in the Twenty-First Century*, New York: Wiley, 1979.

Weizenbaum, Joseph, *Computer Power and Human Reason*, San Francisco: W. F. Freeman, 1976 (a computer scientist rebutting the reasoning power of computers).

INDEX

INDEX

371